GOD THE FATHER, GOD THE SON

By the same author:

I Am Not Ashamed
Preaching and Preachers

GREAT DOCTRINES SERIES
Volume 1

God the Father, God the Son

Dr Martyn Lloyd-Jones

Hodder & Stoughton
LONDON SYDNEY AUCKLAND

British Library Cataloguing in Publication Data
A record for this book is available from the British Library

ISBN 0 340 65165 2

Typeset by Watermark, Cromer, Norfolk
Printed and bound in Great Britain by
Clays Ltd, St Ives plc

Hodder and Stoughton Ltd
A Division of Hodder Headline PLC
338 Euston Road
London NW1 3BH

Contents

Preface

On Friday evenings after the war, Dr Lloyd-Jones held discussion meetings in one of the halls in Westminster Chapel in London. The subjects of these discussions were practical issues in the Christian life and the meetings were attended by many people. The questions which arose demanded a knowledge of biblical teaching of all kinds; often, too, a matter of doctrine would arise which the Doctor would deal with, usually in his summing up at the end of the discussion. It was partly as a result of this, partly, too, because the numbers were becoming too large for the hall, and, perhaps even more, because so many people were asking him about the biblical doctrines, that he felt it right to move the 'Friday night meeting' into the Chapel itself and to give a series of lectures on those great subjects. He did this from 1952 to 1955 and after that he began his magisterial series on the epistle to the Romans which continued until his retirement in 1968. The doctrine lectures were very much appreciated by the large congregations who heard them and, over the years, many have borne testimony to the way in which their Christian lives have been strengthened by them.

Later, the Doctor himself felt happier about preaching doctrines as a part of regular exposition – 'If people want to know about a particular doctrine, they can find it in the doctrine text books,' he once said. But the great strength of his doctrinal studies is that they are not arid text-book lectures. He was, above all, a preacher and this shines through in all of them. He was also a pastor and wanted men and women to share his sense of wonder and his gratitude to God for the mighty facts of the gospel; so his language is clear and not encumbered by complex academic phraseology. Like Tyndale, he wanted the truth to be in words 'understanded of the people'. Also he did not want the teaching to remain in the head only, so there is an application in each lecture to make sure that the heart and will are touched also. The glory of God was his greatest motive in giving these lectures.

Those who know the preaching and the books of Dr Lloyd-Jones will realise, on reading the lectures, that his views on a few subjects developed over the years and that his emphases may not always have been the same. But this is all part of the richness of his ministry as it has been of the ministry of many of the great preachers of the past. However on the essential, fundamental truths of the Word of God, there is no change and his trumpet does not give an uncertain sound.

We have had one difficulty in preparing these lectures for publication. They were delivered in the early days of tape recording so that in a few places the words have been difficult to decipher and a few tapes are missing. Also, only a very few of the lectures were taken down in shorthand so in one or two cases we have neither a tape nor a manuscript. Fortunately, however, the Doctor kept his very full notes on all the lectures so we have used them, though, of course, it means that these chapters are not as full as the others.

The Doctor's tapes are distributed by the Martyn Lloyd-Jones Recordings Trust and, of all his tapes, by far the largest number of requests is for these doctrine lectures. The lack of knowledge of the vital truths of the Christian faith is greater now than ever before – certainly greater than it was in the 1950s – so it is our prayer that God would use and bless these lectures again to our strengthening and to His glory.

The Editors

1

My Purpose and Method

It is always good for us to start with a text. Not that I am going to preach, but I do want us to begin with some words which will give the background of all I propose to say now, and which will explain what I am proposing to do in this series of studies on biblical doctrines. I refer to Deuteronomy 29:29: 'The secret things belong unto the Lord our God: but those things which are revealed belong unto us and to our children for ever, that we may do all the words of this law.'

Now, inevitably, we shall have to begin with introductions; that is necessary, I think, for several reasons. One is that some people may question the rightness of what we propose to do. We live in an age in which we do not hear very much about doctrines, and there are some people who are even foolish enough to say that they do not like them, which seems to me to be a very pathetic and regrettable attitude. Lectures or sermons on biblical doctrines were once very common but they have become comparatively uncommon, especially during this century. However, though we shall not deal with that criticism directly, it makes a good starting point, and it leads me to say that there are certain things which we must have quite clear in our minds. We shall consider three things: *what* we are going to do in these studies; *how* we are going to do it, and *why* we are going to do it.

What, then, are we going to do? This is to be a series of studies on biblical doctrines. What do we mean when we talk about a biblical doctrine? The answer is that the Bible is particularly concerned about teaching certain truths, and nothing is more important than that we should grasp that and that we should start with it. The Bible is a book which has a very definite objective. All its teaching is designed to a certain end; it is concerned with putting before us its doctrines, the

1

particular truths which it wants to emphasise and to impress upon the minds of all of us.

Let me put that more clearly in the form of a negative. The Bible is not, for instance, a general history of the world. We do not always remember that, but notice how it crowds two thousand years into just eleven chapters in Genesis. The Bible is not primarily interested in world history; it has another object.

Or let me put another negative. The Bible is not even concerned to give us a complete history of everything that God has ever done – He has done many things which are not referred to in the Bible – but it selects certain things which help to bring into focus its own purpose and plan. The four Gospels, for instance, do not pretend to be a complete biography of the Son of God, our Lord and Saviour Jesus Christ. No; they are concerned about presenting certain truths about Him, for instance, they only deal with about three years of His life – there is very little apart from that. They tell us about His birth – yes; but the main emphasis in the Gospels is His public ministry; what happened to Him after the age of thirty.

John in his Gospel puts this very clearly to us. He tells us, 'Many other signs truly did Jesus in the presence of his disciples, which are not written in this book.' Then, 'But these are written, that ye might believe that Jesus is the Christ, the Son of God; and that believing ye might have life through his name' (John 20:30–1). John did not set out to give us an exact, detailed account of our Lord's life. No; he had an object in view, and the last verse in his Gospel says, 'And there are also many other things which Jesus did, the which, if they should be written every one, I suppose that even the world itself could not contain the books that should be written' (John 21:25).

'What, then, is the Bible about?' asks someone. Surely there can be no hesitation about answering that question; the Bible, in its essence, is the grand story of redemption. It is the history of what God has done about men and women as the result of their sin, and everything else that we find in the Bible is, in reality, incidental to that. The Bible is concerned with presenting to us the message of redemption by God and from God, in a way that we can understand and see and believe. So when we talk about biblical doctrines we mean these aspects of redemption which are unfolded to us in the Bible. They are the various truths that we find in the Bible about this great question.

Now there are many classifications, but let me suggest to you some of the doctrines which we are, therefore, of necessity bound to consider. One is, of course, the book itself. Why do we pay attention to this book? Why do we confine ourselves to it? What does the Bible teach us about itself? Clearly we must start with that. We cannot go on to consider the doctrines of the Bible unless we have a clear idea as to what the Bible itself is, and what it claims to be.

Then, of course, having accepted our authority, our standard, we start with the great doctrine which always must come before every other doctrine, and that is the doctrine of God. 'In the beginning *God*' (Gen. 1:1). We meet God here. It is His revelation. So as we come to the Bible we learn the truth about Him and, strictly speaking, that is what is meant by the term *theology*.

Next, obviously, is the doctrine of man. I have said that the business of the Bible is to teach us about redemption and redemption is what God is doing about man. That is what is called *anthropology*.

Then we come to the doctrine of our Lord and Saviour Jesus Christ – *Christology*, because, after all, all redemption is in Him and in Him alone. Everything that happens in the Old Testament looks forward to Him, He is the climax, and the Bible has a great deal to tell us about Him.

But having found how redemption has been provided, the next matter that occurs to us is: How is this doctrine applied to us? The Bible has great teaching about this, the doctrine of applied salvation or *soteriology*.

Then, what happens to us when we are redeemed? Well, we are brought into the Church and are made members of the mystical body of Christ. So, clearly, you would expect the Bible to tell us something about the Church, and it does. This is called *ecclesiology* – the doctrine of the *ecclesia*, the Church.

And then, naturally, we ask this question: Here we are, the redeemed, members of Christ, of His body, the Church. What for? What is going to happen to us? What will it lead to? The Bible meets us again at this point, because it has its doctrine of the last things, which is called *eschatology*. Biblical teaching is all leading up to something, to a grand climax and consummation. There remain certain ultimate, last things, and you find a great deal about that in the Bible.

Now those are some of the truths that, God willing, we hope to consider together, and that is all I am proposing to do. So let nobody think that we are concerned here with giving a general survey or synopsis of the Bible and its contents. That is a perfectly good thing to do, but that is not what we shall be doing. I have given you the general outline of these doctrines, and we shall address ourselves to that. We shall find the doctrines in the text, in the word, and our business is to extract them and study them.

But let us now look at our second question: How are we going to do this? And here, again, we must be careful to have a good definition, and to be clear in our minds as to what it is we are really attempting, because there is often a good deal of misunderstanding at this point. Let me again put it as a negative. I am not going to give a series of lectures on theology. I wonder whether that comes as a surprise to anybody? I wonder whether anybody thought, 'Well, surely, you cannot lecture on biblical doctrines without giving lectures on theology!' I suggest to you that the two things are not the same, and it is important that we should know the difference as we contemplate this series of addresses. We must of necessity confine ourselves to what the Bible says and to what the Bible alone says.

Now theology does not do that; it takes them in a wider field. Theology starts by saying that God has not only revealed Himself in the Bible, but in history. He reveals Himself experimentally in experience, and theology says that before it gives you biblical doctrine, biblical dogma, it must take into consideration these other aspects of revelation. Of course, theology includes that as well, but theology includes more than the Bible. In other words, the theologian does something like this: he goes to the Bible; he studies it; he traces and extracts its doctrines or he considers what somebody else has already done. He then proceeds to reflect upon these doctrines; he thinks about them and analyses them. He tries to bring them into a scheme. He brings in philosophy, which means human thought and thinking, and he takes all these things together and reflects upon them, and the end of that process is what is called theology.

So I trust that I am making it clear that that is not what I propose to do. It is not that I do not believe in theology – I do. But when I say I am going to give a series of addresses on biblical doctrines, I do not mean that I am going to give lectures on theology.

Let me give you an example to explain precisely what I mean by this. There was a famous Bible lecturer and expositor in America at the end of the nineteenth and the beginning of the twentieth century who published a booklet called *The great doctrines of the Bible*. Now I was very interested when I turned to that book to see what this author had to say, for instance, on the doctrine of God. To my amazement I saw that his first heading was this: 'Proofs of the existence of God'. The moment I saw that I said to myself, 'He should not have put that title to his book; he should have said that it was a book on Christian theology, because you do not find the proofs of the existence of God in the Bible.'

What I mean by these proofs is this. People argue that you can arrive at a belief in God by just looking into your own conscience. You say to yourself, 'I think, so there must be . . .' I think of God, but the idea must have come from somewhere, there must be something corresponding to my thought. Therefore there should and there must be God,' and so on. Then they take the argument from nature. They say that you look at nature and, as you do so, you see the order and design, and you say that it all must have come from somewhere – there must be a creator. A very good argument.

Again, there is the moral argument. I recognise that there is good and better in this world, and that suggests to me that there must be a best somewhere, there must be an absolute perfection, and that is what is called the moral argument for the existence of God. Now this writer to whom I referred goes through all that in his book, and many other arguments; but that is something which the Bible never does. Here is a man who tells us that he has written a book about the great doctrines of the Bible, but who is behaving as a theologian!

I am not saying that there is no value in those arguments for proving the existence of God, but I do want to emphasise that you do not find them in the Bible. And it is interesting to observe how this man, who gives a text for everything he says, suddenly has no text whatsoever in this particular section. So he has gone beyond what he had said he was going to do.

But we shall deal with biblical doctrines. The Bible does not give us proofs of the existence of God, it proclaims Him; it just tells us about Him. Also, though, as I have said, it is not that I do not believe in theology, yet I do want to say, in passing, that we must remember that there is a danger in connection with theology. The moment you bring in philosophy and speculation, and your own thoughts and human reason, you are beginning to do something that may be dangerous, not of necessity, but it may be. Now, we shall avoid all that.

We shall also avoid something else. We shall not attempt to defend these doctrines. That, again, is a perfectly good thing to do – it is called *apologetics*. But we are not concerned to defend the doctrines and I say this because some of you, when we go on to particular doctrines, may be disappointed that I am not doing so. For instance, when we come to the doctrine of creation, the whole question of evolution arises but it will not be my primary purpose to deal exhaustively with it. Biblical doctrine does not make you do that. Of course, we shall have to refer to evolution, but primarily we shall be expounding positively what the Bible itself has to say.

So the position we occupy is that, again, of Deuteronomy 29:29: 'The secret [the ultimate explanation of] things belong unto the Lord our God.' Again, we shall be dealing with the doctrine of sin and somebody will want to know, 'Where does evil come from?' I cannot tell you. The Bible does not tell us. You can speculate; you can reason but that is not biblical doctrine. We must confine ourselves to the things that have been revealed, not to the secret things that are ultimately in the mind of God.

That, then, is more or less a definition of the way in which we are proposing to consider these doctrines. And that brings us to the last point. *Why* do we believe that this should be done? Now these are some of the answers I would suggest to that question. The first is that the Bible itself does it and therefore we are bound to do it. I told you at the beginning that the Bible is not merely a general history. It is a book which is concerned to bring certain particular truths clearly before us and those truths are doctrines. So to read my Bible properly means that I must consider doctrine. The Bible wants me to grasp its doctrine. In other words, I may know my Bible very well, but unless I realise the importance of grasping its doctrines, my knowledge of the Bible may be quite useless to me.

Let me put it to you like this. Is that not exactly what the prophets did? You read about them in the Old Testament – what were those men doing? Well, they were taking hold of those doctrines – the doctrine of the law in particular – and they were enforcing them. They were applying the law. They went to the nation and they said, 'You people think that because you have the law, you know it, but you don't!' They said, 'The law is bringing this before you, and this is what you have to grasp and to understand.' They preached doctrine to the people.

Is this not also exactly what our Lord Himself did? What was He really doing in the Sermon on the Mount except this very thing? He said, 'Ye have heard . . . But I say unto you . . .' (see Matt. 5:27–8). He took the law and expounded it in the form of doctrine. He explained it. He said that a mere general acquaintance with the law was of no value; you must know exactly what it says. He extracted the principles, and He applied them and enforced them.

It is also, obviously, the very thing that was done by the apostles. Read the book of Acts and observe the preaching of those first Christian preachers. What did they do? Well, you do not find that they took a text and then gave its exact meaning in the Greek and the Hebrew, and then analysed it, and so on. No, no! Their way of preaching was to proclaim doctrines. They had a message, and they presented that to the people; they used their Scriptures to show that this was the doctrine.

And, of course, that is what is meant by preaching; that is the purpose and function of preaching. It is not merely an opportunity for a man to express his own thoughts. It is not merely, I repeat, to give an alternative translation of the Scriptures. No, its purpose is to bring truth to the congregation. The apostles did that, as preaching in its essence always does.

Or take the epistles of the New Testament. What are they? Well, in these epistles certain great doctrines are taken and are underlined and enforced. There was a particular need of that in particular churches. So the writer of the epistle brings his doctrine, and applies it in a practical manner. All along you see that they are concerned with the expression and elucidation of doctrine. That is my first reason, therefore, for doing this; I argue that the Bible demands it. It does it itself and it exhorts us to do so.

Another reason is that it is dangerous for us to study the Bible without doing this. We talk, do we not, about missing the wood because of the trees, and what a terrible danger that is! The real trouble with the Jews at the time of our Lord was that they stopped at the letter and never arrived at the spirit. In other words, they never got at the doctrine. They were content with a general familiarity with the words but they did not get the Word. And it is something that we all have to realise as a terribly dangerous possibility for us, for if we stop at the letter only it profits us nothing; it even misleads us. It may be the cause of the damnation of our souls. Not to arrive at your doctrine after you have studied your Scriptures means that your study is thoroughly unprofitable. It may be very intellectual. It may be a good way of spending your time. I have known people who have used the Bible as others have used crossword puzzles, or even jigsaw puzzles, for fitting things together, but they have never arrived at doctrine. Their study is of no value. It is profitless.

But another reason for studying biblical doctrine is that the Church throughout the centuries has always found that it is essential to emphasise the doctrines of the Bible. In the very first days of the Church no one was received into church membership without making the confession, at all costs, that Jesus is Lord. But the moment you say, 'Jesus is Lord,' you are making a doctrinal statement. Then, after a while, the early Christians found that it was not enough merely to say, 'Jesus is Lord,' they found it necessary to introduce what was called a baptismal formula. Candidates for baptism were catechised; they were asked certain questions, and they had to be able to answer them.

But you remember what happened? Very soon heresies began to arise; people within the Church began to say things that were not correct. They were quite genuine and sincere, but many were saying things which were wrong and which were harmful. And these heretical and false teachers, of course, not only caused confusion within the Church, they were also misleading to people outside the Church. The rise of heresy within the Church, led the early Church to draw up what we commonly call the creeds, for example, the Apostles' Creed, the Nicene Creed and the Athanasian Creed.

Now those creeds became essential because there was so much error and heresy in the Church, and the Church, under the guidance of the Holy Spirit, said, 'We must make it quite clear as to what we do believe and what we do not believe. It is not enough merely to give people an open Bible. Perfectly sincere and genuine and able men and women may read this book and say things that are quite wrong. We must define our doctrines,' and the definitions of doctrines are what we call the creeds.

Then, of course, after a while, the Church, which, in a sense, had been one, was divided into two – into the Eastern and the Western Church; but, more or less, the doctrine was the same. The Church was dead, I know, but it was governed by these three great creeds.

Then came the Protestant Reformation. New life, new vigour, new understanding came in, and again the Church found it was absolutely essential to extract its doctrines, and to state them in a perfectly clear and definite manner. So you had what is commonly called among Protestants, the great Confessions. These are nothing but a listing together and an exposition of the doctrines of the Bible. The leaders, again, said, 'It is not enough to give people an open Bible. We must guide them. We must help them. They are liable to go astray. So we must tell them that we believe this about God and that we do not believe that. We must tell them about Christ and about the Church and so on. The Church of England had its Confession which is called the *Thirty Nine Articles*. There were also many famous Confessions on the Continent, those, for example, of the Moravian Church and the Reformed Church. And then there was the great Confession that was drawn up in Westminster Abbey in the seventeenth century and is therefore known as *The Westminster Confession*. It is the Confession of the Church of Scotland and of all Presbyterian churches everywhere throughout the world.

Now all these Confessions, and the catechisms which go with them, are nothing but a statement of biblical doctrines, so that people within the Church might know exactly what to believe and what not to believe and the reasons for this belief. They were all designed to build us up in the faith, and to enable us to know exactly where we stand.

Now if all that was necessary in the early days of the Church, if it was necessary at the time of the Reformation and in the seventeenth century, surely it is something which is urgently needed at this present hour? Today the Church is surrounded by cults; these people come to your doors speaking, as they say, 'from the Scriptures'. They say that they believe the Bible which we teach. The moment they make a statement you feel instinctively that there is something wrong with it, but you cannot answer them. Now one of the purposes of studying biblical doctrines is to enable us to discover together the error in such teachings. Not that I am going to lecture on the cults; what I shall do is this: I shall remind you of what the Bible does teach. Then, having a firm grasp and knowledge of that, we can test every other teaching presented to us.

But not only are there all these errors and cults around the Church, even in the Church herself there is terrible confusion. There is an absence of doctrine, there is a lack of clear definition and a readiness to allow anybody to say anything they like. And this means that there was never a time when it was more urgently necessary that Christian people should consider together the doctrines of the Bible. We must know the ground on which we stand, and be able to withstand every enemy that comes to attack us, every subtle foe, every ploy used by the devil who comes disguised as an 'angel of light' to ruin our souls.

But I have a higher reason for considering these doctrines with you. Ultimately it is the only way truly to know God, to come into His glorious presence and to learn something of the wonders of His ways with respect to us. Yes, let us go on reading our Bibles and studying them, but let us not get lost in the detail. Let us pick out these great, mighty, mountain-peaks of doctrine, and realise there who God is, and what He has done for us in the person of His dear Son, and in spite of our sin.

That, at any rate, is the object which I have in my mind. I am not doing this in order to give you some intellectual knowledge or information that you did not have before. God forbid that I should attempt to do that, or that anybody should think of what we are doing in that way. 'Knowledge,' says Paul, 'puffeth up, but charity edifieth [builds up]' (1 Cor. 8:1). So the atmosphere of this series of discourses or discussions on biblical doctrines will not be that of the classroom. There will be no examinations at the end to determine how much you have learned, and no diplomas given to you! No, no. We are concerned with God – to know Him. It is worship. Any consideration of the Bible is worship and to me there is nothing so dangerous as to approach the Bible and its teaching as you approach any other text book.

People often say to me, 'What is wrong with these theological colleges? I have known many a good man who has gone in all right, but look at him when he comes out!' Now, that may not always be true – people often say things like that – but if it is true sometimes, I think I can tell you why it is. It is that in such places they far too often approach the Bible as if it were a text book. They far too often approach these great doctrines as if they were human thoughts and ideas. They do not come to them always in the atmosphere of worship and of awe. They are interested in translation and in intellectual knowledge. That is essential, but we must not stop at that.

The doctrines of the Bible are not a subject to be studied; rather we should desire to know them in order that, having known them, we may not be 'puffed up' with knowledge, and excited about our information, but may draw nearer to God in worship, praise, and adoration, because we have seen, in a fuller way that we have ever seen before, the glory of our wondrous God. May He give us cause to do this, and grant that as a result of these doctrines, we may all come to know Him, the only true and living God, and Jesus Christ whom He has sent – and as a result may all be revived. And so I express the hope that through us, and others like us, the whole Church may be revived, and that we may witness again in our midst the manifestation of God's glorious power.

2
Revelation

It would be well for us, perhaps, to bear in mind the words which are to be found in Acts 14:15–17:

> Sirs, why do ye these things? We also are men of like passions with you, and preach unto you that ye should turn from these vanities unto the living God, which made heaven and earth, and the sea, and all things that are therein: who in times past suffered all nations to walk in their own ways. Nevertheless, he left not himself without witness, in that he did good, and gave us rain from heaven, and fruitful seasons, filling our hearts with food and gladness.

Now, any consideration of the biblical doctrines, and of Christian doctrine in general, is obviously concerned ultimately with this great question: How is God to be known? The cry is there in the human heart, as expressed so perfectly by Job: 'Oh that I knew where I might find him!' (Job 23:3). We take for granted what has often been pointed out – that there is in the entire human race what you may describe as 'a sense of God'. Many say that they do not believe in God, but, in saying that, they have to fight against something fundamental and innate within themselves which tells them that God is, that they have dealings with Him and that somehow or another they have to come to terms with Him, even though those terms may for them be a complete denial of Him. Here, then, I say, is something that is basic to human nature, and fundamental in the whole of human-kind. And this sense of God, this feeling of God, is something that either blesses men and women or else torments them. And everybody has to face it.

Those who are concerned about this, and who are anxious to find

God and to know Him, are confronted by two possible ways of doing so. The first way, and the one that comes instinctively to us because of our fallen condition, is to believe that we, by our own efforts and seeking, can find God; and from the very beginning of history men and women have been engaged in this quest. They have done so by two main methods. One is to follow this kind of instinctive, intuitive feeling that we have, and that is put in various forms. People sometimes talk about an 'inner light', and say that all you have to do is to follow that light and its leading.

This is the way of the mystics and others. They say, 'If you want to know God, then the best thing to do is to sink into yourself; within everyone there is an inner light which will ultimately lead to God. You do not need knowledge,' they say. 'You do not need anything but a resignation of yourself and your powers to this light and its leading.' Now that intuitive method is something with which we are all familiar. It takes numerous forms, and is present in many of the cults in the modern world.

The other method that has been adopted has been the one that is based upon reason and wisdom and understanding. People may start, perhaps, with nature and creation, and they reason on from that. They maintain that as a result of that process they can arrive at a knowledge of God. Others say that by looking at history, and by reasoning on the course of history, they can arrive at a belief in God. Yet others say that the way to arrive at God is to indulge in a process of pure reasoning. They say that if you sit down and reason truly and properly you must arrive at a belief in God. It is illustrated, you remember, by the moral argument: that because I am aware in this world of moral good and better, then that implies that there must be a best somewhere. But where is it? I do not find it in this world, it must therefore be outside the world, and the belief is that that is God.

Now again, I do not want to go into these things. I am simply reminding you that those are the ways in which many people think that they can find God, and arrive at a knowledge of Him. But the Christian answer is that that method is inevitably doomed to failure. The apostle Paul puts it in those memorable words: 'The world by wisdom knew not God' (1 Cor. 1:21); and it is significant that he said that to the Corinthians, who were Greeks, and who were therefore familiar with philosophical teaching. But in spite of Paul having said that, people still rely on human ideas and reasoning to find God.

It seems to me that this is not a matter to argue about, because it is just a question of fact; and the fact is, that one cannot arrive at a knowledge of God along those lines, for two very obvious reasons. The first is (as we hope to see later as we consider these particular doctrines) the nature of God Himself: His infinity, His absolute character and qualities, and His utter holiness. All that in and of itself makes it impossible to have any knowledge of God by means of reason or intuition.

But when you add to that the second reason, which is the character and the nature of men and women as they are in a state of sin, the thing becomes doubly impossible. The human mind is too small to span or grasp God and to realise Him. And when you understand that because of the fall all human faculties and powers are affected by sin and by natural enmity, then, again, a knowledge of God by human endeavour becomes a complete impossibility.

Now the Bible has always started by saying that, and yet people in their foolishness still try these outworn methods which have already proved to be failures. So we must start by laying down this postulate: our only hope of knowing God truly is that He should be graciously pleased to reveal Himself to us, and the Christian teaching is that God has done that. So clearly the first doctrine which we have to consider together is the biblical doctrine of revelation. I cannot arrive at God by my own unaided efforts. I am dependent upon God revealing Himself. The question is: 'Has He done so?' The answer is: 'Yes, He has,' and the Bible tells us about this.

So, before we come to consider these various doctrines and truths concerning God and our relationship to Him – which is the ultimate quest upon which we are all engaged – we must be perfectly clear about the question of revelation. What is revelation? Well, I think that this is as good a definition as you can get: Revelation is the act by which God communicates to human beings the truth concerning Himself, His nature, works, will or purposes, and it also includes the unveiling of all this – the drawing back of the veil that conceals this, in order that we may see it.

Now, according to the Bible, God has revealed Himself in two main ways. The first is what we call *general revelation*; the other, obviously, is *special revelation*. So, first, let us look at general revelation. What is this? Now I have already referred to the fact that certain people by observing nature think that they can arrive at God by a process of reasoning and the Bible agrees to this extent: it tells us that

God has revealed Himself, in general, and first, through creation and nature. Paul made a most important declaration on this subject to the people of Lystra. He said, '[God] left not himself without witness, in that he did good, and gave us rain from heaven, and fruitful seasons, filling our hearts with food and gladness.' Immediately before that, Paul had said, 'He made heaven, and earth, and the sea, and all things that are therein' (Acts 14:17, 15).

The other classic statement on that same point is to be found in Acts 17:24; again, you find the same thing stated in Romans 1:19–20: 'Because that which may be known of God is manifest in them for God hath shewed it unto them. For the invisible things of him from the creation of the world are clearly seen, being understood by the things that are made, even his eternal power and Godhead; so that they are without excuse' – another momentous passage. All those statements remind us that God, after all, has left His marks, His imprints, in nature and creation; they are 'the works of His hands'. And, of course, running as a theme through the Bible is the message: 'The heavens declare the glory of God' (Ps. 19:1) and so on. Everything that has been made is in itself a revelation of God. That is the first definition of general revelation.

But, of course, you get the same type of revelation in what is commonly called *providence*: the ordering of things in this world, their maintenance, their sustenance, and the fact that everything keeps on going and continues in life. How is it all to be explained? Well, ultimately it is a question of providence. I do not want to go into this now, because when we deal with the doctrine of the providence of God we shall look at the whole question in greater detail. But let us just remember in passing that, through the ordering of providence, the seasons, the rain and the snow and the fructification of crops are all manifestations of God.

The third aspect of general revelation is history. The whole history of the world, if we could but see it, is a revelation of God.

But now we have to say that in and of itself general revelation is not sufficient. It ought to be sufficient, but it is not. And that, it seems to me, is Paul's argument in that first chapter of Romans, where he says, 'They are without excuse' (v. 20). The evidence is there, but that has not been enough. Why? Because of sin. If men and women had not been sinners, by looking at the miracles and the works of God in creation, in providence and in history, they would have been able to arrive, by a process of reasoning, at God. But because of their sin, they do not; they deliberately turn their backs upon doing so. That is the great argument in the remainder of Romans 1, which I trust you will read carefully for yourselves. Paul says, 'Because that, when they knew God they glorified him not as God, neither were thankful; but became vain in their imaginations, and their foolish heart was darkened. Professing themselves to be wise, they became fools' (vv. 21–2). And he goes on to say that they began to worship the creature rather than the creator.

So we can sum that up like this: the evidence that is provided in creation and so on is enough to render men and women inexcusable when they stand before God and do wrong. But it is not enough to bring them, as they are in sin, to a knowledge of God. So the question is: Is there any hope? This rational way of looking for God, even at its best and highest, would only, as Paul argues, bring us to a knowledge of God as creator. His power, says Paul, is manifest in this way, but that is not the knowledge of God for which we long and which we covet. Men and women cry out for a more intimate knowledge. We want to know God in a more personal sense. We want to be related to Him. When we are awakened, that is the knowledge that we want, and such knowledge, creation and providence and history at their best cannot provide: they can simply teach us that God is all-powerful and that He is the creator.

Well, then, we ask again: Is there any hope for us? And the answer is to be found in the second type of revelation of which the Bible speaks, and that is what we call *special revelation*. And the special revelation which we find in the Bible has a very distinct and definite object, which is to reveal to us the character of God, the nature of God, and especially the character and nature of God as they are revealed in His saving grace. That is the thing about which we are concerned: how to know God and to be loved by Him and to be blessed by Him.

Now the Bible makes a unique claim at this point; it claims that it and it alone gives us this special knowledge of God. The Bible claims for itself that it is the record of God's special revelation of Himself and of all His gracious and saving purposes with respect to men and women. The Bible claims more than that for itself, but we shall only deal with this first claim now. And, of course, it has a great deal to say about this subject. In a sense, that is the great message of this book from beginning to end: it is God revealing Himself. It is not the great religious quest of mankind. No; it is the great eternal God drawing back the veil and giving an insight into and a knowledge of Himself and of His great and gracious purposes. That is the subject matter of the Bible.

Let me interject a remark at this point. When we study the Bible it is of vital importance that we should always keep this idea, this concept of revelation, clearly before our minds. It is the only way to understand the message of the Bible; we become lost in it if we do not do that. We must realise that the one great object and intention throughout is God revealing Himself; and you and I must discover the ways in which He has been pleased to do this.

Let me summarise them. Many classifications are possible, but it seems to me that this is the one that follows most closely the Bible's own order. First and foremost, the Bible tells us that God has been pleased to reveal Himself to men and women through what are called theophanies – manifestations of God, the various appearances of God.

Take, for instance, Exodus 33, which is a most important passage when considering this doctrine of revelation. God told Moses that He was going to accede to Moses' request, and that He would manifest His glory to him. Moses had uttered that great desire: 'Show me thy glory.' 'You are giving me,' he said in effect, 'this great task of leading these people. Who am I, and who are the people who are going to do it with me? Before I can do this great work,' said Moses, 'I want to know that your presence will accompany us.' Then God said, 'My presence shall go with thee,' but Moses became bold, and said: May I go further – 'Show me thy glory.' Let me see it.

And then God told Moses: You cannot see Me face to face, for no man can see Me in that sense and live. Nevertheless, I will reveal My glory to you.

So God took Moses and placed him in the cleft of a rock, and then He covered him with His hand. I am bound to introduce the term, am I not? That was a marvellous piece of *anthropomorphism*: that God, the eternal Spirit, should condescend to speak of Himself in human terms, and to act in a human manner. He covered Moses with His hand, and then He passed by, and Moses, we are told, was only allowed to see the back parts of God. He was not allowed to see His face. He saw God, in a sense; he saw the glory of God; he saw the back parts of God passing by. This is a staggering statement. You see how vital it is to this whole question of revelation – that the great, eternal God thus granted this glimpse of Himself to a human being so that men and women might know something about Him.

Then you also have very frequent references to the *Angel of the Covenant*. I have no doubt but that they are right who say that every reference to the Angel of the Covenant is a reference to the Lord Jesus Christ. He appeared in this world before the incarnation. He was not incarnate, but He appeared. He took on Himself certain forms, in order to give a revelation. Gideon was granted such a revelation – study it for yourself in Judges 6. And then the father and mother of Samson were also privileged to see one of these theophanies, in order to strengthen their faith. God has been pleased to give many of these appearances of Himself.

Then the next manner in which God has been graciously pleased to reveal Himself has been by means of *direct speech*. We are handling immensities and profundities here. But the Bible tells us that the voice of God has been heard in this world. Adam and Eve heard it in the Garden of Eden. God uttered words. And you get the same thing, of course, in connection with the giving of the law to Moses. The voice of God was again heard, and this is something with which we have to deal, and upon which we must meditate and ponder deeply and seriously as we are thinking of this whole question of revelation. Think and find out for yourself other examples of this direct speech and voice of God.

My next heading is that God has been pleased to reveal Himself by means of *miracles and signs and wonders*. Now you get this in the Old Testament and New Testament alike. There are miracles recorded in the Old Testament: think of the miracles worked through Moses in the presence of Pharaoh, for instance, think of the dividing of the Red Sea, and the miracles that certain of God's servants, such as Elijah and Elisha, were able to perform, and so on. These were miracles, and miracles are always manifestations of God's power, and therefore of God Himself. God caused thunder and lightning to appear at very special times, such as the phenomena in connection with the giving of the law, and the mount that was on fire; all these were revelations and manifestations of God. He has done certain extraordinary things in nature and creation.

Then when you come to the New Testament, you find the miracles of our Lord, and their main function was revelation. You find, too, the miracles which were worked by the first apostles and by the first preachers; and we have the authority of Hebrews 2:4 for saying that these were done by the apostles because God was thus attesting their gospel. The writer says that they preached the gospel, 'God also bearing them witness, both with signs and wonders, and with divers miracles, and gifts of the Holy Ghost.' In that way God affirmed that they were His servants, and that the gospel was true. And, of course, towering above every other miracle was the great and grand miracle of the resurrection.

We shall have occasion, later, to look at some of these things in detail, but here I am concerned to emphasise that these 'signs and wonders and divers miracles' show the obvious intention of God to tell men and women that He was revealing Himself – and they looked at these things. How often are we told in connection with these miracles that the people 'glorified God'. They feared; they were filled with a sense of awe; and they glorified Him. Why? Because they knew that the miracle was a manifestation of the power of God, and therefore they had had a glimpse into the character and the being of God Himself.

But let us go on to some further ways in which this special revelation has come to men and women. The next is that God has been pleased to reveal Himself at times by means of *visions and dreams*. The classic passage about this is Job 33:15–16, where we read this: 'In a dream, in a vision of the night, when deep sleep falleth upon men, in slumberings upon the bed; then he openeth the ears of men, and sealeth their instructions.' And how often God spoke through dreams and visions! You remember the dreams that were given to Joseph, the husband of Mary, the mother of our Lord. And as you go back through the Old Testament you find that God constantly spoke like this. Through these visions and dreams God told people to do certain things, or warned them of things which He was going to do, and the result was that they realised that God *is*. It was God who gave them the vision or the dream or the warning or the prophecy, or whatever it was, and therefore they were revelations, they were proofs of the being of God.

Then I must put in a category on its own – *inspiration*. This is a most important question. We will have to touch on it again, later, but we must put it in at this point. We are told in the Bible that God can inspire people: inspire them to write His word; inspire them to understand; give them a message in that particular way. That is the whole basis, ultimately, of prophecy. So in doing that God was again revealing Himself, revealing the truth concerning Himself, the fact that He is, and what He is going to do.

But, after all, when we are dealing with this question of special revelation, the great and mighty thing is what we may describe as the biblical account of God's redemptive acts. Nothing is so momentous a revelation of God as this. What am I speaking about? Well, I am thinking of Noah and the flood. God manifested Himself to Noah; gave him a revelation; gave him to understand what He was going to do; and then proceeded to do it in the waters of the flood and the judgment upon the earth and the marvellous saving of Noah and his family, the eight people in the ark. This was a tremendous act, not only of revelation, but of redemption. All the ancient world was condemned and destroyed but this family. So it was a part of salvation and redemption. The separation of these people was essentially a part of the act that culminated in the coming of the Son of God into this world.

And you have the same revelation, of course, in an almost equally striking manner, in the call of Abraham and the events of his life. God took that man, when he dwelt among the pagans; He singled him out and drew him out. Abraham did not know where he was going, but God led him. God was again bringing to pass this great plan and purpose of redemption. It had started away back with Noah, now it was becoming still more special in Abraham. And everything that God said and did to Abraham was a marvellous piece of revelation.

Then there was another manifestation of this in the call of Moses. We have already referred to one appearance of God to Moses. But what about the burning bush (Exod. 3)? What about that bush, all aflame and afire and yet not consumed? What was it? It was God, God revealing Himself. Not only God revealing Himself, and the fact that He is, to Moses, but God taking another momentous step in this great question of redemption. It is part of the great redemptive plan – a great redemptive act.

And it leads on to the Red Sea (Exod. 14), to that event which is so frequently referred to in the Scriptures. You find that the psalmists, every time they give a list of what God has done for Israel, always emphasise what God has done at the crossing of the Red Sea. You will find it occurring as a kind of theme in many of the psalms (e.g. Ps. 106). Why? Well, because it is momentous. It is central. God was saying to the people that He had separated them unto Himself from the captivity of Egypt, and led them out. It is all a part of the process of redemption, and you get it again in the captivity of Babylon, and the return of the remnant to the land.

Of course, all this is vital and important, though it seems to pale into insignificance when we come to the fact of facts, the focal point of all history, the central point of the whole course of humanity: 'When the fulness of the time was come, God sent forth his Son . . . To redeem them that were under the law' (Gal. 4:4–5) – the revelation of God in Jesus Christ. This, of course, is going to occupy us at great length, but it is essential that I should, at this preliminary stage even, mention the name that is above every other name. For in times past, says the writer of Hebrews, God spoke in thoughts or visions, here a little and there a little, but now He has spoken in His Son, the effulgence and the holiness, the ultimate revelation, the essence of the great act of redemption; and, in particular, in connection with our Lord, we must emphasise the resurrection as another great redemptive act, which proclaims the sufficiency of His work and announces and reveals that God is satisfied and that mankind can be saved.

Likewise, we must include the day of Pentecost, and we must never stop short of that, for what happened, when the tongues as of fire descended upon those people, was all a part of the great redemptive action of God. It was a vital act, in which the Holy Spirit came upon the Church to do His great and glorious work; to apply the redemption that had already been worked out.

But, in addition to all that I have mentioned, God has spoken to men and women and has instructed them concerning Himself and His purposes. He did not only reveal Himself through His actions and the appearances and the dreams and the visions – God taught about Himself directly, literally. He spoke to Adam. He spoke to Cain and to Noah. He spoke in a special way to Abraham, the friend of God, as he is called. God told Abraham His secrets because he was His friend. He gave the great promise to him, the promise in that sense starts with Abraham, and that is why you find so many references to it throughout the Scriptures. God told him the secret and what He was going to do. 'Abraham,' says our Lord, 'rejoiced to see my day: and he saw it, and was glad' (John 8:56). God taught him about it.

Now I want to emphasise this for those of you who are interested in modern theology and in the difference between the so-called Barthian and evangelical theology. So I am underlining the difference at this point. The Barthian theologians deny the fact that God has revealed what they call 'propositional truth'. Propositional truth means that there are statements of truth, of doctrine, in the Bible which I can accept and believe. We contend that God has done that, that here there are propositions of truth revealed by God.

He did so, of course, in a very striking way in the giving of the law to Moses; the purpose of that was that the children of Israel should live in a given way. The primary function of the law was to give expression to the holiness and the character of God, and the people were to live in that way because God is God, because He is like that. So God was teaching about Himself in giving the law. Furthermore, 2 Samuel 7, in which His promise is given specifically to David, is one of the most important chapters of the Old Testament. Then the prophets – the foretelling, the teaching given to them about God and His holiness and His law – all that was part of the revelation of future events: truth communicated.

But, of course, in the New Testament we find the basis of our belief in the authority of the New Testament Scriptures. The truth was given by God through the Holy Spirit to the apostles, even as the Lord Himself in John 16 had promised it would be.

Thus in the Bible we have the record of God's greatest redemptive acts. But we have also God's comment upon those acts; God's exposition of them; God's explanation of the way of salvation as well as the unfolding of the way itself. And the Bible claims that it and it alone has this revelation – there is no other. If God does not reveal Himself, I cannot know Him; but He has revealed Himself, and that revelation is to be found in this book. Whether I see it or not, it is here. It has been given, and the question that arises is: Can I trust this book? Is it reliable in what it says, and what it claims? Am I entitled to believe its claims and to submit myself to its authority? We must, therefore, continue by discussing the authority and the reliability of the Scriptures.

3
The Authority of the Bible

We come now to consider the whole question of what the Bible has to say about itself. This is inevitable if we follow the biblical sequence in our consideration of the doctrines, but we also arrive at it in this way. As we have seen, the ultimate end and object of all who are concerned about the Christian faith is to know God. We have also seen that if we are to know God, then God must be pleased to reveal Himself. And He has revealed Himself, not only in creation, history and providence, but more. He has revealed Himself in the way recorded in this book, the Bible, which is the record of God's revelation of Himself. So we have considered the various ways in which, according to the Bible, God has done that.

But obviously, therefore, the questions that at once arise are: Can we accept the Bible's testimony? Can we regard it as authoritative? How do we justify our claim as evangelical Protestant Christians that it is here, and here alone, that we have an authoritative statement with respect to God's revelation to men and women? Why do we look to this book rather than to the Church, to some tradition, to some 'inner light' or to our own reason and understanding? That is our position, and that is our claim. And it is, therefore, necessary that we should justify that, and the way to do so is to consider what the Bible itself has to say about this matter.

Now you notice that I emphasise that, because in dealing with biblical doctrines we must keep ourselves to that. There are other things that could be said. There are other arguments that could be adduced and it is the province of theology to do that. But we are trying to keep ourselves to a positive exposition of biblical doctrines. I shall not, therefore, conceive it to be a part of my business to consider the so-called 'higher criticism' movement. Theology and apologetics both do that. But here we are trying to be more positive, so let us bear in mind our definite and limited objective.

Now the Bible claims that it is not only the record of divine revelation; it goes beyond that. It claims that it is God's Word. It claims to be divinely inspired, and its authority is based upon that. Now it is important that we should be clear in our minds as to the difference between revelation and inspiration, because the two things are not the same. Everything that is in the Bible is not revelation, but everything in the Bible is inspired.

Let me explain what that means. Revelation means God's unfolding of Himself. You will see at once that there are many things in the Bible which are not revelation. Take, for instance, the book of Ecclesiastes, or the statements recorded in the Bible which were uttered by sinful, ungodly people. There is no revelation in such statements; nevertheless, the Bible says that all these statements, as they are recorded, are done so in an inspired manner. The statements do not help us to know more about God. They do not in any way at all help us to gain a knowledge of God. There is no revelation, no self-disclosure on the part of God. But what the Bible claims is, that all it contains is an inspired record and therefore an infallible and an inerrant record.

Obviously, then, the first question which we must consider is: What is meant by inspiration? When we say that the Bible is divinely inspired, what exactly do we mean? Let us start again with a negative. We do not mean that certain portions of the Bible are inspired and that others are not. There are some people who think that. There are, they say, portions and particular statements and teachings, especially those concerned with the Lord Jesus Christ, that are inspired. But, they say, those historical books and various other sections are not inspired. Now that is not what we mean when we say the Bible is divinely inspired.

Neither do we mean simply that the men who wrote were writing in an exalted or creative way. When a poet has produced a masterpiece, you have often heard people say that the poet was 'inspired'. But we do not mean that the writers of the books of the Bible were inspired in that way when they came to write these books. Others say they regard inspiration as just meaning that the ideas which were given to the writers were inspired. That is true, of course, but we mean much more than that. Neither does it mean that the books – the writings as such –

are the product of human origin on to which the divine breath or *afflatus* has come.

So, what do we mean? We mean that the Scriptures are a divine product breathed out by God. Inspired really means 'God-breathed'. We mean that God breathed these messages into men and through them, and these Scriptures are the result of that divine action. We believe that they were produced by the creative breath of the almighty God. Put in a simpler form, we mean that everything we have here has been given by God to man. And, of course, this obviously carries with it the idea that this is true of the particular words. So I shall try to demonstrate to you that the Bible claims for itself what is called *verbal inspiration*. It is not merely that the thoughts are inspired, not merely the ideas, but the actual record, down to the particular words. It is not merely that the statements are correct, but that every word is divinely inspired.

Now again we could spend time in discussing the various theories about inspiration, but I am concerned rather to expound what the Scripture itself says – and it claims this verbal inspiration. Yet we must make it clear that when we say that the Bible is verbally inspired by God in this way, we are not teaching some sort of mechanical dictation. We do not mean that the writers sat down, as it were, as a shorthand-writer does, and that God dictated all the words to them. The difference of style between the writers is evidence that that is not the case. You notice that each one seems to have his own idiosyncrasies and habits, his own individual style. You can tell at once that something has been written by Paul rather than by Peter or John.

Moreover, if you read the introduction to the Gospel of Luke, you will find that Luke says that he himself had read various other records in order to examine certain reports. And you often find the same thing in the Old Testament. So our whole conception of inspiration must allow not only for the individual writer and his characteristics, but also for his research and for his consulting of other authorities. What, then, does inspiration mean? It means that the writer has been controlled by the Holy Spirit of God in such a way that he cannot be guilty of error in what he writes.

There have been many illustrations of this. To me the best is the one that thinks of it in terms of a man on horseback riding from one place to another. Today he rides one horse, then tomorrow he takes the same journey but on a different horse. The horse he rides today is high-spirited, full of verve and of power. The horse he will ride tomorrow is rather older and has become tired and lethargic. Now in both instances the man riding the horse goes to and from the same places, but the particular way in which the two horses carry him may be altogether different. One may prance about a good deal, but he is kept on the route until he reaches the destination. The mannerisms – the style, as it were – vary tremendously, but both horses are guided and controlled by the same rider, and the result is the same.

Verbal inspiration means that the Holy Spirit has thus overruled and controlled and guided these men, even in the choice of particular words, in such a way as to prevent any error, and above all to produce the result that was originally intended by God.

How, then, does the Bible claim this? I suggest to you that the following headings will be of some help. Incidentally, I am attempting the impossible in trying to cover it all so briefly; it is a subject upon which great books have been written. I am simply trying to give you a scheme whereby you can work this out for yourselves in your study of the Scriptures. If you want a very great and learned book on the subject, it is called *The Inspiration and Authority of the Bible*, by Dr B. B. Warfield. Those of you who like studying a masterpiece on any subject will be well advised to get a copy of that book. And there are many other books on this subject which you can consult for yourselves.

My first heading is this: the Bible makes specific claims in this matter of inspiration. Take, for instance, certain terms which the Bible uses of itself, such as the term *Scripture*. That designates 'holy writings'; not ordinary writings; special – holy writings.

Then take the description it gives of itself as the *Word of God*. How often you find the Bible using that term about itself! Now here is a striking and interesting fact – and someone has taken the trouble to count all this – the words, 'The Lord said', 'The Lord spake', 'The word of the Lord came', and cognate expressions are actually used 3,808 times in the Old Testament alone!

But let us come to some more specific claims. Take again that great prophecy, which is very crucial in this matter, spoken by Moses and recorded in Deuteronomy 18:18. These are the words: 'I will raise them up a Prophet from among their brethren, like unto thee, and will put my words in his mouth; and he shall speak unto them all that I shall command him.' Not only is that a prophecy of the coming of our Lord, it also tells us much about Moses himself and his own ministry. Then, of course, all the prophets of the Old Testament make this claim. They do not say that they suddenly decided to write; they say, 'The word of the Lord came . . .' (see, for example, Ezek. 1:3; Hos. 1:1; Jonah 1:1), and they tell you exactly when it came. They were called, they were commissioned, and the word was given to them. So they are constantly saying something like this: 'Thus saith the Lord'. That is their claim.

Another interesting fact, and a very valuable argument, is that some of these prophets tell us quite honestly that at times they were reluctant to speak. Jeremiah often did not want to speak but he was compelled (Jer. 1:6–7). The very reluctance is seen in the way in which he disclaims his own authorship, but the 'burden' came. It was placed upon him by God, and he simply delivered what God had given him.

Still another important fact is that you will find the prophet saying that he does not understand even what he himself is writing. Take the statement in Daniel 12:8 where Daniel says, 'I heard, but I understood not.' You find Peter saying the same thing:

> Of which salvation the prophets have inquired and searched diligently, who prophesied of the grace that should come unto you: searching what, or what manner of time the Spirit of Christ which was in them did signify, when it testified beforehand the sufferings of Christ, and the glory that should follow. Unto whom it was revealed, that not unto themselves, but unto us they did minister the things, which are now reported unto you by them that have preached the gospel unto you with the Holy Ghost sent down from heaven; which things the angels desire to look into.
>
> 1 Pet. 1:10–12

Then the apostle Paul makes a crucial statement. He says, 'Which things also we speak, not in the words which man's wisdom teacheth . . .' He is referring, you see, not only to the subject matter, not only to the doctrine, but to the way in which he speaks it. The words with which he speaks, he says, are not after man 'but which the Holy Ghost teacheth; comparing spiritual things with spiritual' (1 Cor. 2:13). The whole of that chapter is very important in this connection.

Then there is that interesting and to me always very fascinating statement which you will find in 2 Peter 3:15–16, where Peter, referring to 'our beloved brother Paul' says this: '. . . even as our beloved brother Paul also according to the wisdom given unto him, hath written unto you; as also in all his epistles, speaking in them of these things; in which are some things hard to be understood, which they that are unlearned and unstable wrest' – notice – 'as they do also the other scriptures, unto their own destruction.' By using that phrase, 'the other scriptures', the apostle Peter there equates the epistles of Paul with the Old Testament Scriptures and puts them on the same basis.

Then there is that important statement in Ephesians 2 where Paul says that Christians 'are built upon the foundation of the apostles and prophets' (v. 20). Now you and I are built upon that foundation. We do not regard as authoritative anything that has been said subsequent to the New Testament canon. Here is our foundation and we do not accept any teaching of any church or of any tradition as being divinely inspired. This is the basis, and the Church is to be built upon this teaching because of its unique authority.

Now this brings me to what I would call the crucial passages. The first is in the second epistle to Timothy. 'All scripture is given by inspiration of God, and is profitable for doctrine, for reproof, for correction, for instruction in righteousness: that the man of God may be perfect, throughly furnished unto all good works' (2 Tim. 3:16). So runs the *Authorised Version* but the *Revised Version* is different; it reads, 'Every scripture inspired of God is also profitable for teaching . . .' This is a very serious matter because there is no question at all that at this point the *Revised Version* is not only wrong but is tragically and lamentably wrong. It suggests at once that there are scriptures that are not divinely inspired. The *Authorised Version*, however, is quite clear about it: 'All scripture is given by inspiration of God.'

So what can be said at this point? Well, the *Revised Version* makes the apostle Paul guilty of what is called tautology, saying the same thing twice over, expatiating upon the obvious. To render it 'All scripture [every scripture] inspired of God is also profitable' makes the thing ridiculous because every scripture inspired of God is of necessity profitable, and there is no need to say so. But the *Authorised Version*, you notice, does not say that. It says, 'All scripture is given by inspiration of God, and is profitable . . .' which is a very different way of putting it.

Again, the *Revised Version*, of course, simply contradicts what the Scripture says about itself. The Bible does not differentiate between parts and portions; it does not say that certain Scriptures are divinely inspired but others are not. All Scripture is given by inspiration of God. Furthermore, the *Revised Version*, when it introduces that word 'also', is doing something that it does not do elsewhere. The authorities are very easily able to convict these translators of being inconsistent with themselves. For instance, in Hebrews 4:13 you find this statement: '. . . all things are naked and opened unto the eyes of him with whom we have to do.' Now to be consistent with themselves, the *Revised Version* translators should have translated that like this: 'All naked things are also opened unto the eyes of him . . .' But they did not do it there, and thus they have not carried out their own principle, because they saw it was obviously ridiculous; if everything is 'naked' it must be 'open'.

There are various other examples which could be given of the same thing, but we must move on. However, we need to remember that certain important members of the committee that produced the *Revised Version*, such as Archbishop Trench and Bishop Wordsworth and others, strongly protested at the time. Dr Tregelles, who was one of the greatest Bible students of the last century, made a similar protest, as other authorities have done. Let us therefore always remember when we are dealing with that verse that we must adhere resolutely to the *Authorised Version* and the statement there is as definite as this: 'All Scripture is given by inspiration of God.'[1] There is no exception.

The second crucial passage is 2 Peter 1:20–1: 'Knowing this first, that no prophecy of the scripture is of any private interpretation. For the prophecy came not in old time by the will of man: but holy men of God spake as they were moved by the Holy Ghost.' A most vital statement. Now the interpretation of this is, of course, important. What does Peter mean by saying that 'no prophecy of the scripture is of any private interpretation'? Well, he is not simply saying that no one has a right to his or her own particular interpretation of the Scriptures. No, Peter is concerned here about the origin of prophecy, the origin of Scripture, and what he means is that no prophecy of the Scripture gives any individual's private understanding or interpretation of things. In other words, he does not mean that prophecy arose in the way that some of the so-called higher critics have been teaching during the past century. They have said something like this: 'Now these prophets were very great and able men. They were profound thinkers. They looked out upon life and upon history, and then they meditated and ruminated upon it, and as a result of this, they evolved a theory, elaborated an idea, and then they wrote it.'

---

1. Compare also the *New International Version* which reads, 'All Scripture is God-breathed . . .' (Ed.)

But here Peter is telling us that prophecy does not come like that. It is not anyone's private interpretation of life and of people and of God and of history, because prophecy 'came not in old time by the will of man'. It was not man at all, he says, who produced it.

What is it, then? 'Holy men of God spake as they were moved by the Holy Ghost.' There are various translations of this word 'moved'. Some say that it should be 'carried along'; others would say that it means 'borne along'; some would even say 'driven along'. Probably all are right; the word can carry all those various meanings. What is important for us is that they all agree in this – that when these prophecies were written, it was not a case of a man in control of himself, using his natural powers and propensities and abilities, thinking things out and then writing as best he could. Not at all! The whole time he was controlled by this gale of the Spirit, by this wind of God, this divine energy. This divine afflatus came upon him, and it held him and carried him, and he was borne along by the Spirit. And it was as a result of that process that these prophecies and these Scriptures came into being.

There, then, are what I call the great specific claims which are made by the Bible for itself in this matter of verbal inspiration. They put it at that, and nothing less than that. That is the origin of the Scriptures; they say, 'All scripture is given by inspiration of God.'

But now let me give you a second heading. It is always fascinating to me to notice the things that the Bible assumes about itself and its own statements. I put first the statement which was made by our Lord Himself. When He was facing certain dissenters and quoting Scripture to them, He said, 'Is it not written in your law, I said, Ye are gods? If he called them gods, unto whom the word of God came, and the scripture cannot be broken; say ye of him, whom the Father hath sanctified, and sent into the world, Thou blasphemest; because I said, I am the Son of God?' (John 10:34–6). The crucial statement is, 'The scripture cannot be broken', which means it cannot be annulled or withstood; it cannot be denied.

Then consider also Galatians 3:16, which is again a vital statement in this whole question. It says, 'Now to Abraham and his seed were the promises made. He saith not, And to seeds, as of many; but as of one, And to thy seed, which is Christ.' You see the importance of that? The apostle there attaches significance just to one single letter – 'Now to Abraham and his *seed* were the promises made.' With regard to this whole question of verbal inspiration, this is one of the most important statements of all. The whole argument of the apostle depends upon the fact that the Scripture says 'seed' and not 'seeds'. If it had said 'seeds', then this particular argument would have been irrelevant, but because it uses the singular and not the plural, it is a reference to the Lord Jesus Christ. You cannot possibly attach too much importance and too much weight to that particular argument.

Then sometimes you will find that the Bible combines a statement from the New Testament with one from the Old Testament, and refers to the two together as 'Scriptures'. Take, for instance, 1 Timothy 5:18: 'For the scripture saith, Thou shalt not muzzle the ox that treadeth out the corn. And, The labourer is worthy of his reward.' Now two Scriptures are there – the first is from Deuteronomy 25:4, and the second is a statement by our Lord that is recorded in Luke 10:7. Yet you notice the way in which Paul puts it – 'For the scripture saith'. That, again, is significant because it shows that the Bible regards both the New and the Old Testaments as holy writings – the Scriptures.

Then another important piece of evidence is the way in which the New Testament quotes the Old Testament. It is very difficult to know which are the best passages to choose, but here is one out of the book of Acts: 'And when they heard that, they lifted up their voice to God with one accord, and said, Lord, thou art God, which hast made heaven, and earth, and the sea, and all that in them is: who by the mouth of thy servant David hast said . . .' (Acts 4:24–5), and then there is a quotation from Psalm 2. What they are saying is that it is God who said this by the mouth of His servant David. Or take another example from Acts: 'Wherefore he saith also in another psalm . . .' (Acts 13:35) – a reference again to God, showing that He, as it were, is the author of the psalms. The psalms of David are the psalms of God; it is God who worded them.

But perhaps there is nothing more interesting than the way in which you find this in the epistle to the Hebrews. Here is one example: 'Wherefore (as the Holy Ghost saith, To day if ye will hear his voice' (Heb. 3:7), which is a quotation from Psalm 95. Work through your New Testament and observe the way in which it quotes from the Old Testament and attributes the words to God and the Holy Spirit or uses the expression, 'It saith' – which always means the same thing.

My final general heading is that as we read the Bible we can make certain other obvious deductions which clearly prove this doctrine of inspiration. Sixty-six books were written over a period of at least sixteen hundred years, by over forty authors, and yet there is only one type of doctrine in the whole Bible and only one type of morality in the whole range of the Scriptures. Can you explain it in any other way?

Take the Old Testament. Look at the one spirit that pervades it – the hope of the Messiah. Over all the centuries, with these differing men, there is one messianic hope. And in the New Testament there is only one great theme – Jesus Christ and Him crucified. It all points to Him – focuses upon Him. The variation between the writers makes no difference; there is still this one great theme.

But the most vital testimony which we must adduce is the testimony of the Lord Jesus Christ Himself. Read your Gospels and notice the way in which He constantly quotes the Old Testament. Notice the way in which He assumed that it is authoritative, that it puts a matter beyond argument and beyond any dispute whatsoever. He just said, 'It is written,' and that is final (see, for example, Luke 19:46; John 6:45). He obviously accepted the Old Testament *in toto* as authoritative, final and supreme.

There are certain specific statements which He made: 'Think not that I am come to destroy the law, or the prophets: I am not come to destroy, but to fulfil. For verily I say unto you, Till heaven and earth pass, one jot or one tittle shall in no wise pass from the law, till all be fulfilled' (Matt. 5:17–18). And in a sense that is the whole of the Old Testament – Moses and the prophets – 'I am not come to destroy, but to fulfil.' Then you will find Him, for example, saying this: 'And he answered and said unto them, Have ye not read, that he which made them at the beginning made them male and female' (Matt. 19:4). We will have to come back to this, but let us remember that that quotation alone is sufficient to show that our Lord regarded what we read in the early chapters of Genesis as being authoritative for the whole question of man and woman and their appearance in the world. So if you begin to play fast and loose with the authority of the Scriptures, and with the verbal inspiration of the Scriptures, you are of necessity involved in difficulties about the person of the Lord Himself.

Then you will find many other statements. Let me ask you to read for yourselves Mark 12:26–7, and then consider also Luke 24:44: 'And he said unto them, These are the words which I spake unto you, while I was yet with you, that all things must be fulfilled, which were written in the law of Moses, and in the prophets, and in the psalms, concerning me.' It is the whole of the Old Testament again. The law of Moses is not merely the Ten Commandments and the moral law; it is the five books of Moses. Moses, the Prophets, and the Psalms, He accepted it all and asked the disciples to consider its teaching concerning Him. And He expounded it to them.

And again I refer to John 10:35, where He tells us, 'If he called them gods, unto whom the word of God came, and the scripture cannot be broken.' So, in the last analysis, our authority for our understanding of inspiration is to be found in the Lord Jesus Christ Himself. That was His view of the Scriptures.

Now I know that there are many who want to ask a question at this point. What about the various differences? What about certain discrepancies, and so on? Well, there is a very comforting answer to all that. There are, as we have them in our versions, certain things which we simply cannot explain, and it is our business to say that quite readily and frankly. But let me hasten to add that most of these so-called difficulties and discrepancies which the critics bring forward can be explained; indeed, most of them have been explained. Many of them have been explained in the last few years as a result of archaeology, and of further linguistic understanding of the Scriptures.

Still, there are a certain few differences that remain, but it is significant that they are never with respect to doctrine or historical facts. It is a matter of figures or something which is comparatively unimportant and which can be explained quite readily – the mistake, perhaps, of a copyist, or of some translator. There is nothing which in any way interferes with vital, essential doctrine. So what we affirm and state is this: the original documents, as originally written, are inerrant and infallible. We say even of this *Authorised Version* that apart from a mere handful of minor discrepancies, which hitherto have not been explained and which are completely unimportant, this is the word of God and the only infallible rule for faith and conduct.

There are other arguments also that one can produce, but they do not arise from biblical statements – the style, the elevation of thought, what the reading of the Bible has done for people throughout the centuries, the testimony of the saints to the Bible. But finally you cannot prove to anybody that the Bible is uniquely and divinely inspired. Ultimately, people have to be enlightened by the Holy Spirit. So let me finish by quoting a passage from the *Westminster Confession of Faith*, which states it all perfectly:

We may be moved and induced by the testimony of the Church to an high and reverend esteem of the holy Scripture, and the heavenliness of the matter, the efficacy of the doctrine, the majesty of the style, the consent of all the parts, the scope of the whole, (which is to give all glory to God,) the full discovery it makes of the only way of man's salvation, the many other incomparable excellencies, and the entire perfection thereof, are arguments whereby it doth abundantly evidence itself to be the word of God; yet, notwithstanding, our full persuasion and assurance of the infallible truth, and divine authority thereof, is from the inward work of the Holy Spirit, bearing witness by and with the word in our hearts.

Chapter I:V

4

How We Find the Doctrines

As we approach our third study, it would be well for us to keep in the forefront of our minds verses 18–21 in the second chapter of the first epistle of John:

> Little children, it is the last time: and as ye have heard that antichrist shall come, even now are there many antichrists; whereby we know that it is the last time. They went out from us, but they were not of us; for if they had been of us, they would no doubt have continued with us: but they went out, that they might be made manifest that they were not all of us. But ye have an unction from the Holy One, and ye know all things. I have not written unto you because ye know not the truth, but because ye know it, and that no lie is of the truth.

I call your attention to that particular statement because it does present us with the exact context in which we must consider another general point before we come to deal with the particular doctrines which are taught in the Bible. We can summarise the position we have arrived at like this: the ultimate goal of our quest is a knowledge of God. We are not interested in doctrines merely as doctrines, but simply as they bring us to know God. The supreme 'end of man is to glorify God and to enjoy Him for ever' (*The Shorter Catechism*).

The problem, therefore, is: How are we to know God? By our own efforts we cannot arrive at God. God must reveal Himself, and in His infinite grace and kindness He has done so, not only in creation and in history and in providence, but supremely in this book which we call the Bible. And then we went on to consider some aspects of inspiration. We took a very general view of it, and saw that it could be divided up quite naturally into certain groupings.

Then that in turn led us to the question: Can we rely upon this book and its proffered revelation? We considered that, and came to the conclusion that the Bible is a divinely inspired book. We saw that the Bible itself teaches what is known as the doctrine of verbal inspiration. We therefore accept it as full and final and infallible in all matters of faith and practice.

'Very well,' says someone, 'having done all that, why don't you start by immediately taking the first great central doctrine – the doctrine of God?'

But I cannot do that, and I will tell you why. The problem that arises at the moment is this. 'Now,' you say, 'here is a book that contains these doctrines that are essential to a knowledge of God.' Very well, I take my Bible and I open it, but I do not find that the Bible is just a collection of stated doctrines. There is a lot of history here, a great deal about kings, princes, births, deaths, and accounts of marriages, and so on. If the Bible were just a collection of doctrines plainly stated, there would be no difficulty at all, and all that we would have to do would be to find page one, then look at the first doctrine, expound it and consider it together.

But the Bible is not like that – merely literature. We do not go to the Bible in that way. The question, therefore, arises: How are these doctrines to be found in the Bible? How is one to discover them? Now that is no idle question, as I think I can show you very easily. But it is never enough to say, 'I am not interested in doctrines. I'm a Bible person. Let these clever people argue about doctrines if they like; you give me the Bible and I am satisfied.' That is a very foolish, indeed, a ridiculous, statement to make, because people who come to the Bible must believe something as the result of reading it. The question is: Are they believing what they ought to believe?

Most of the cults which are so prominent in the world today claim that they are based upon the Bible. 'Of course,' they say, 'we believe everything that the Bible says; our teaching is based upon it.' Indeed, you will find that some of these people appear to know their Bibles very well. So it is no use just saying to them that you do not believe as they do because you believe the Bible. We must know how doctrine is to be found in the Bible if we hope to deliver these people in any way at all, if we are anxious to make them true Christians and to bring them to a real knowledge of God. We must be in a position to explain to them where they go wrong and where they are not biblical, and to help them to understand the source of their error.

Now you notice that in the early Church that very position obtained. There were a number of people in the Christian Church all claiming to believe the truth, but some, says John, had left them: 'They went out from us, but they were not of us; for if they had been of us, they would no doubt have continued with us: but they went out, that they might be made manifest that they were not all of us' (1 John 2:19). They were guilty of error and of heresy somewhere or another.

As it was in the days of the early Church, so it is still, and there never has been a time when it has so behoved God's people to know what they believe, and why they believe it, as at this present hour. So how do we arrive at a knowledge of these doctrines? What are we to do? Given that we have the book which we now believe is authoritative and divinely inspired – God's oracles, God's word, God's truth, revealed in a unique way – how do we find the doctrine that is in it? Now it seems to me that the best thing we can do is to consider the three main propositions which will guide and help us in this matter.

The first we will have to deal with, whether we want to or not, is the place that reason, understanding and intellect have in these matters. I admit that this is a very difficult subject. But it is vitally important and we must have some clear ideas in our minds as to what our position ought to be with respect to this. We already touched upon it in a very general way in our introduction. The point we then established was that by means of reason alone no one can arrive at God. The intellect is insufficient. 'The world by wisdom knew not God' (1 Cor. 1:21). That is a fact which can be proved. And you notice, incidentally, how all these clever people in the world today are, one after another, now becoming ready to admit that people, who were so highly regarded during the post-war period, are confessing the utter inadequacy of the human mind and reason, and confess the need for something beyond it. But now I am rather anxious to emphasise this same general concept in a slightly different manner. So I put it to you in the form of a number of propositions.

The first thing we must do, in view of all that we have seen together, is agree to grasp the Bible as our full and final authority in all matters of revelation. Having seen that we cannot get anywhere without the Bible, then the obvious thing to do is to say, 'Very well, I accept the Bible. I don't know anything apart from it. I have no knowledge of God apart from what the Bible tells me. I may theorise, and other people may do the same thing, but I really do not know anything apart from what I find in this book.' So the first decision we must make is that we are going to be, as John Wesley put it, men and women 'of one book'. Here is my only source, my only authority.

But I want to underline this and even to emphasise it still further. I must submit myself *entirely* to the Bible, and that will mean certain things. First, I start by telling myself that when I come to read the Bible and its doctrines, I am entering into a realm that is beyond the reach of my understanding. By definition, I shall be dealing with things that are beyond my power to grasp. The very idea of revelation, in and of itself, I suggest to you, must carry that implication. We are going to try to know God, and to study the doctrine concerning Him, and it must be the case that these truths are beyond our understanding. If I could understand God, I would be equal with Him. If my mind were able to apprehend and to span the truth about God, then it would mean that my mind is equal to the mind of God, and that, of course, is altogether wrong.

For instance, in our next lecture we hope to be dealing with the doctrine of the Trinity. Now there by definition is a doctrine that no one can possibly understand, but let us agree to say that before we come to the doctrine. Let nobody think, however, that this means committing intellectual suicide when we take up the Bible. It simply means that we recognise that there is a limit to reason. We agree with the great French mathematician and philosopher, Pascal, that the supreme achievement of reason is to teach that there is an end and a limit to reason. Our reason takes us so far and then we enter into the realm of revelation, where God is graciously pleased to manifest Himself to us.

But now I am anxious to emphasise the second point. It means that we must accept truths where we cannot understand them and fully explain them. Not only must we agree that we cannot, of necessity, understand everything, but also, when we come up against particular doctrines and truths, we must accept them if they are in the Bible, irrespective of the fact that we can or cannot understand them. Now I rather like to think of faith in that way. I am not sure but that the best definition of faith we can ever arrive at is this: faith means that men and women decide quite deliberately to be content only with what they have in the Bible, and that they stop asking questions.

You can tell very soon if a man is a true man of faith or not. Just listen to him. Some people are always asking questions: 'But I do not see this, and I cannot understand that.' But faith means that we are content to be shut up to this book, and that we say quite readily, 'God has revealed everything He wants to reveal, and everything that is good for me to know is in the Bible. If it is not in the Bible, I am content not to know it.' Bear that in mind, for instance, when you are discussing the problem of evil – how it entered into this world. The Bible does not tell us why God ever allowed it, and therefore if you take the faith position, you will not even ask questions about it. You are just content to say, 'I do not know; the Bible doesn't tell me, and I know nothing beyond what the Bible does tell me.' This is a most important principle.

But let me go on to elaborate it a little more by putting it in this way: there is nothing that we must avoid so strenuously as the constant temptation to mix philosophy with revelation. Now you may think, some of you, that this does not apply to you. 'I am not interested in philosophy, I have never read a book on philosophy in my life,' you say. But, my dear friend, that does not mean that you are not a philosopher! We are all philosophers. You should not confine the term philosopher to people who make it their business or their duty in life to study or to teach it. Everyone who has an opinion about anything is automatically a philosopher. And I think I can show you in a minute that every one of us is not only a philosopher, but that we are always getting into trouble because we philosophise too much. So I am warning everybody against this danger of mixing philosophy with revelation.

Now this is the way in which we do it. We are ready at all times to reject certain doctrines, or, perhaps, if we do not actually reject them, we hesitate to believe them, though they are clearly taught in the Bible. We do this because we cannot understand them, or because we cannot explain them, or because they do not seem to fit into our scheme of things. Quite often when you confront people with a specific statement from the Bible, instead of saying, 'Well, I am prepared to believe that though I do not understand it,' they say, 'But, if that is right, then how can God be a God of love?' or something like that. The moment they speak like that they are speaking as philosophers, and I think that if you examine yourselves you will find it is something that you do quite frequently.

Indeed, I am afraid that those of us who are evangelical are very often guilty of being most inconsistent at this point. We argue with a so-called modernist and we say, 'Fancy! He doesn't believe in miracles, and he doesn't believe in the supernatural, because he says he cannot understand a miracle' – and we denounce that. Yes; but sometimes when we come up against some of these great terms, which you will find in the first chapter of Ephesians, like *predestined* and *elect according to the foreknowledge of God*, we evangelicals begin to say, 'Well, if that is right I don't see how God is fair,' and so on.

But that is exactly the same thing as your modernist friend was doing with regard to miracles. We see it very clearly in his case because we happen to be all right on the question of miracles. But when it is a doctrine we do not take to so readily, we use exactly the same argument as the modernist who brings out his philosophy. So this is something that must apply to all of us. I must not hesitate to believe a doctrine because I cannot fit it in; neither must I reject a doctrine because I cannot understand it. If this is the truth of God, and the thing is clearly taught, then I am to accept it whether I understand it or not.

Then one final point I would put under this heading is this: we must never allow ourselves to be governed by our own logic or by our own desire to have a perfect system. It is a danger to which we are all exposed. We instinctively like to have a complete system; we do not like gaps or ragged edges. It is again because we are all philosophers. It is because the philosopher always wants a complete whole, wants to be able to understand everything, wants to be able to state everything, and we are all like that. The danger is, you see, that we press our own logic and our own schemes to a point which goes beyond the teaching of the Scripture. At that point we are again guilty of sin and of error. We must give full weight to every statement of Scripture. We must never minimise one or ignore it in order that our scheme may be complete.

I could give you many illustrations of that. There are people, for instance, who have always been described as hyper-Calvinists, and that is their trouble. They go beyond the Scripture and are driven by their own logic and by their own arguments, and they claim things which cannot be demonstrated from the Scriptures. They are so anxious to have a perfect scheme that they fall into that very subtle and dangerous trap.

So, then, the ultimate thing which we would say under this heading would be this: we must submit ourselves not only to the authority of the book, but also to the guidance, the inspiration and the illumination of the Holy Spirit. I should never read the Bible in exactly the same way that I read any other book. If all I have said about it is true, then I must come to it realising my inability, realising that any natural capacity I may have is not enough here. I must see that spiritual things must be understood in a spiritual way, and therefore I should start always by asking God by the Holy Spirit to enlighten me, to illumine me, to keep me from error and subtle dangers and to lead me into all truth. Then, having done that, I come to my Bible; and, with a mind which already knows its limits, and which is thus enlightened by the Holy Spirit, I begin to discover the doctrines of the Bible.

Very well, then, that brings me to my second main heading, which is the method by which one arrives at the doctrine. Again, I would remind you that the Bible is not a mere collection of doctrines, and as we now come to seek our doctrines in the Bible, it is not going to be a mere matter of stringing a number of texts together. Some people seem to think that this is the way. Having discovered a number of statements about a given matter in every part of the Bible, they give you a string of texts and leave you at that. Now that is not the way to arrive at the doctrine, because patently that is not going far enough.

Rather, I suggest we should do this: we do collect our texts; we discover every statement that we can find in the Bible on a particular subject. Then, having gathered them together, and having collated them, we proceed to discover the doctrine which lies at the foundation. That is what we are concerned about. Here are these various statements. What is the doctrine they are propounding? What are they telling us? What is this basic something that is common to all these statements? That is our doctrine.

Now as we do that, there are certain rules which must be observed most carefully. First of all, let us look at a number of general rules. Here is the first. Any doctrine that we claim to believe from the Bible must always be clearly found in the Bible. It must be capable of demonstration from the Bible. If I cannot prove to you that the doctrine which I hold is found in the Bible, or that the Bible proves it or demonstrates it, then I must reject it.

Let me give you some illustrations of what I mean. You will find, as we have seen, that people come to you saying that they believe the Bible. Then they propound their doctrines to you, and you ask: 'But where did that doctrine come from?'

'Ah,' they will tell you, 'someone once had a vision or a message.' You are familiar with such statements. But what I would emphasise here is that we must say that we are not prepared to accept any such statement. We do not care who says it, nor what marvellous experiences that person may have had. It is quite immaterial to us if it cannot be proved and established in and from the Scripture.

But wait a minute – I am not only referring to the cults. This is our evangelical reply, for instance, to the Roman Catholics. You see, they come and tell you certain things. 'But,' you say, 'I don't find that in the Scriptures.'

'Of course not,' they reply, 'but we have our tradition; revelation did not stop at the end of the New Testament canon – the truth has been received directly from God since then. The Apostolate and the apostolic understanding have continued, and we therefore argue that the Church and her tradition and her teaching are of equal authority and value with the Scriptures.'

And again we say a firm and resolute, No! We do not care what authority a teaching may claim for itself. If it cannot be proved from Scripture, we reject it.

And we say exactly the same thing, of course, to any claim for any doctrine which may originate from human ability or understanding. Take, for instance, the Roman Catholic doctrine about transubstantiation. Roman Catholics teach that as the result of the action of the priest, the very bread at the Communion Table has been turned into the literal body of the Lord Jesus Christ. 'But,' you say, 'it still looks like bread!'

So they reply, 'Of course it does,' and then they bring in their philosophy, by which they tell you that there is a difference between the *substance* of a thing and the *accidents*. What they mean by 'accidents' are qualities like colour and texture. And they say that the substance has been changed but the accidents remain the same. A marvellous bit of philosophy! But we do not accept any doctrine, however subtle and clever the explanation may be, if we cannot find it in the Scripture itself, or prove it from the Scripture.

But let me go on to a second point. Our doctrine must be *exclusively* scriptural. Not only must we reject all doctrine that has patently come from outside the Scriptures, but we must not even accept a doctrine that is partly scriptural and partly something else. It must be pure, unadulterated Scripture. This is another most important point in view of the constant tendency of philosophy to creep in by the back door.

Then the third point I would make under this heading is that the doctrine must be plain and clear in the Scriptures. May I introduce you to a technical term. I am trying not to do this, but this is a great term – one that was used by our Protestant fathers. They talked about the *perspicuity* of the scriptural doctrine, by which they meant that true scriptural doctrine is always plain and clear. Scripture itself emphasises that everywhere. It presumes it.

We often make a great mistake when we come to study the Scriptures because we do not stop to remind ourselves of the type of people for whom they were written. It would have saved a lot of ink and a lot of trouble if everybody who became an expositor of St Paul's epistles had reminded himself, before he started expounding, that the epistles were not written to students or to professors of doctrine at Oxford and Cambridge, but to slaves, and to common, ordinary people! 'Not many wise men . . . not many noble, are called,' said Paul (1 Cor. 1:26). It was to such people that the epistles to the Ephesians and to the Colossians and so on were written; and it is because we forget this that we get into difficulties. When St Paul wrote these epistles he took it for granted that the people to whom he was writing would understand them. They did not have these learned professors to expound them. No, no. He was writing to them that he might teach them, and he knew that they would understand. This is what the fathers meant by the perspicuity of the Scriptures.

Now that is why I am afraid that sometimes I express a certain amount of impatience with people who always seem to base their doctrine on the meaning of a Greek or Hebrew word. In the light of what we have just said, that, of necessity, must be wrong. We should be able to arrive at the meaning of the doctrine from the text of the passage. So I would put it like this: we need no special authority to guide us in these matters. The apostle John says that we have no need of teaching in that sense because of this anointing. 'Ye need not that any man teach you: but as the same anointing teacheth you of all things, and is truth, and is no lie . . .' (1 John 2:27). So we reject the Roman Catholic suggestion that ordinary people are not fit to be reading their Bibles and that only the Church can truly expound it. No, we say that these documents were written to people like ourselves, and we and they were meant to understand them.

In the same way, we disclaim altogether the idea that there is any absolute need of some special philosophy or linguistic understanding, or knowledge of any other language in order to understand these matters, as long as we are given a plain and accurate translation. So I say again that we reject the Roman Catholic teaching.

We also reject much of the theology of the last one hundred years because it has been mostly philosophical theology. And we reject many types of theology that are very popular at this present time, because before you can understand them you have got to understand the special meanings given to the words 'history', 'time' and 'myth'. You have to be clever and philosophical, and by definition this must be wrong. We can trust to the plain teaching, we believe in the perspicuity of scriptural doctrine.

Those, then, are my general rules, so now we turn to the particular. Now that we have collected our texts together, what do we do about them? Well, you will find that there are two main things we have to do. Sometimes it is quite a simple matter to deduce the doctrine from the statements. You just look at the statements, and you say, 'That quite inevitably means so and so.' That is deduction – you draw out the meaning.

But there is another method, and that is called 'induction'. Take for an example of induction the doctrine of the Trinity. You will not find the doctrine of the Trinity stated either implicitly or explicitly any-where in the Bible. But you will find that there are references to 'God the Father', – 'God the Son', and 'God the Holy Spirit' – and, having come across these statements, you say to yourself, 'Now I adduce the doctrine of the Trinity, that God is one and three Persons. That is not deduction, it is induction. You are building up the doctrine from cer-tain statements. So you arrive at your doctrine by the two processes of deduction and induction.

Let me give you some simple, practical points. We must never found our doctrine on just one statement in the Bible, still less on part of a statement. There are people who have gone wrong because they have done this, sometimes even relying on half a verse. They forget the other half because this is the one that suits them. That is some-thing we must never do.

And the other rule is that we must never arrive at any conclusion from Scripture which makes us contradict something which is stated in Scripture. We must always compare Scripture with Scripture. We must be 'workmen' who are 'rightly dividing the word of truth' (2 Tim. 2:15). That is a scriptural exhortation. So if I have arrived at a doctrine, and then find that something else clearly stated in the Bible is contradicted, then I know that my doctrine must be wrong. You see the importance of doing what we did in the last lecture, the import-ance of establishing the doctrine of verbal inspiration, of saying that *all* this book is God's book? The Bible is one great message. It always forms a complete whole, so that never must one point contradict another. It is amazing to notice in the history of the Church how some of the chief heresies have arisen because great men have forgotten that simple rule.

But now I have to deal with one final question. 'In view of all that you have been saying,' you say, 'surely every Christian should be able to agree with every other Christian about every single biblical doctrine? And yet,' you add, 'there is nothing so plain and clear as the fact that there are differences among Christians. What have you to say about that?'

Well, I just want to make a number of comments. Why are there these differences of opinion? The first reason is that people will persist in falling into the various errors that we have already enumerated. They drag in their philosophy, or they base their doctrine on one text or on half a text, or on something like that. If people will do these things, there must be differences of opinion, because some of us will refuse to do that, and therefore you have two schools of thought without going any further.

But then there is another cause for such differences. There is always this tendency on our part to start with a theory, and, having started, we try to force Scripture into our theory. I have already referred several times to the teaching of the Roman Catholic Church. That is surely the essence of the Roman Catholic errors. Having postulated a given Church and a given order, everything has to be forced to fit into that scheme. They do not base all their doctrine upon the Bible. They claim that some doctrine has come to them from outside the Bible, and that what is given is equal to what is found in the Bible.

This, again, is not something that applies to Roman Catholics only. It is just as applicable to many Protestants. If you start out with a particular theory about free will, or something like that, then I assure you that you will get into difficulties about certain biblical doctrines. We must be careful that we do not come with preconceived ideas and prejudices and philosophical theories. This is a very prolific cause of trouble and disputation.

Another way in which people arrive at these differences is that very often they elaborate their theory on details about which we cannot be certain. Now if you want an illustration of that, let me mention the word 'prophecy'. Perhaps this is the greatest danger where this subject is concerned. When we study prophecy we tend to elaborate on details about which no one can be absolutely certain. People say, 'I am certain,' and then out comes the theory. But if we cannot demonstrate the points from the Bible, we have no right to elaborate a theory.

Another cause of trouble is that people will persist in taking as literal that which is obviously meant to be symbolical. For example, some time ago, I was travelling in a train and after a while I found myself involved in a discussion with a Roman Catholic. Of course, he inevitably brought me to this point: he said that surely the Bible says, 'This is my body.'

I said, 'But our Lord was there at the time; He obviously could not mean that the bread was His actual body when He was speaking in the body. It must be symbolical.'

'Ah,' he replied, 'that is the trouble with you Protestants – you always say things like that. But you must take it literally.'

'Very well,' I said, 'if you say that, this is what I say to you. Our Lord said, "This is my body which is given for you".'

'Yes,' said the Roman Catholic.

'Yes, but then,' I said, 'He went on to say, "This cup is the new testament in my blood." He did not say the wine in the cup. He said, "This cup". Are you telling me that He was referring to the cup in a literal sense?'

And, of course, he had to admit that he could not say that. 'So,' I said, 'why not be honest enough to say that it is all symbolical? The cup stands for the wine, and the wine is the symbolic representation of the blood.' If we once take as literal what is meant to be symbolic, we are bound to be in trouble.

But again let me remind you that this is not only true of Roman Catholics. Have not we known people who do this with a book like the book of Revelation, which tells us that all is symbolical? And has not there often been grievous trouble because people will take the symbols and deal with them literally? It is exactly the same procedure. So we must beware of this in every area.

Our Lord Jesus Himself had to tell some of His own disciples, 'It is the spirit that quickeneth; the flesh profiteth nothing: the words that I speak unto you, they are spirit, and they are life' (John 6:63). He had been telling them that unless they ate the flesh of the Son of Man and drank His blood, they had no life in them. And they said, 'How can we do this?' They were materialising it, literalising it. He said, 'My words are spirit; the flesh profiteth nothing.'

And lastly, of course, the thing to avoid above everything else is the party spirit. It is the greatest curse of denominationalism that we start with certain prejudices because we were brought up with them, and our fathers believed in them, and we say they must be defended at all costs. That is a terrible way to approach God's truth. So let us pray to be delivered from the party spirit and the prejudices that are always characteristic of such a spirit.

So then, my next point is that there are certain matters in the Scriptures about which we cannot speak with finality. There are certain things about which equally good and capable men and women are not agreed and cannot agree. When we come to such matters, surely it is our business to say that we do not know. We cannot prove them, and we are content to wait until we arrive in glory and all things are made plain and clear to us. At the moment we see and understand in part, only 'through a glass, darkly' (1 Cor. 13:12). Our knowledge is not full. It is not final. Let us be content with the revelation that is given.

But there are certain doctrines about which we are and must be absolutely final, and they are the doctrines that are essential to the way of salvation. I am not referring to the mechanism of salvation. When you come to that you find good people often differing. I accept that. I am prepared to say, 'I believe this and I am not prepared to believe that.' And another man says, 'All right – as long as we both agree about the way of salvation.' When we come to this doctrine I shall emphasise these points further. But there must be no disputing about the person of Christ, about the miraculous and the supernatural, about the substitutionary death upon the cross and about the literal, physical resurrection. There is no argument there. This is final; this is absolute.

But with regard to all other matters, where we cannot be final and absolute, let us be sympathetic. Let us be tolerant. Let us admit our inability to prove, and let us together enjoy the great salvation in which we all participate, and look forward to the day when the hidden things shall be made plain, and we shall know even as we are already known.

5

The Existence and Being of God

'O the depth of the riches both of the wisdom and knowledge of God!' (Rom. 11:33). That is how the apostle Paul ends the eleventh chapter of Romans, and we can do nothing better, as we study these biblical doctrines, than to hold those eloquent words in our minds. For having completed the general introduction to the whole subject, we can now proceed to the particular doctrines. A great deal more could be said by way of introduction, but we must move on, and the first doctrine to which we must pay attention, a doctrine that is placed first in the Bible itself, is the doctrine of God.

Now that is not quite as obvious as it sounds, because if you consider the typical approach to theology and to biblical matters over the past hundred years or so, you will find that almost invariably the starting point is with man. Everything associated with what is sometimes called modernism is always characterised by that; the theology is always subjective; it always starts with man himself. Because modernism is interested in itself, and in its so-called psychological ideas of origin, inevitably it starts either with man or with the world, and from that goes on to study the doctrine of God.

But that is not what the Bible says. The Bible starts with God; you remember its great opening statement which really tells us everything: 'In the beginning God . . .' It is very important that we should emphasise this and grasp it clearly. The knowledge of God is ultimately the sum of all other doctrines; there is no sense, there is no meaning or purpose, in any other doctrine apart from this great central, all-inclusive, doctrine of God Himself. There is no point in considering the doctrine of salvation, nor the doctrine of sin, unless we have started with the doctrine of God. But quite apart from such, more or less logical, considerations, we start with the doctrine of God because God is God, and because if we put anything or anybody before Him we are thereby dishonouring Him. We are failing to worship Him as we should and failing to conduct ourselves in His presence as the Bible teaches us to do.

So we inevitably start with this tremendous statement with which the Bible opens: 'In the beginning God.' Now, obviously, as this doctrine is all-inclusive, we are face to face with an endless theme, a theme which cannot possibly be exhausted. And as I understand the teaching of the Bible, and as seems quite inevitable from the nature and being of God, it is a theme which will occupy God's people throughout the endless ages of eternity. But, even so, it is vital that we should try to classify our knowledge as far as we can go; we must try to have our thoughts concerning God arranged in an orderly fashion. This will help us in every part of our Christian life and especially in our worship. There can be very little doubt, it seems to me, but that God Himself has given us His book, the Bible, with its revelation, in order that we may do that very thing. But, as we have already agreed, it is not enough merely to take the Bible in a general kind of way. We must underline the great outstanding principles and, knowing these, we can then proceed to worship God.

Clearly, the first matter with which we must start is this: the *existence of God*. We say we want to worship God and to know Him, so the first thought that comes to our minds is the existence of God, because, as we all know full well, there are many people who tell us that they do not believe in it. It is not so much that we are concerned with them and their arguments, as that, from our own standpoint, it is essential that we should be clear in our thinking about this subject.

Now the only point I want to make under this heading can be put like this: the Bible does not argue about the existence of God, it declares it. The Bible does not give us any proofs of the existence of God, it assumes it. Take that opening phrase; Genesis does not start by saying, 'Well, by the following proofs we establish the existence of God, and because He was existent, we establish that at the beginning He created . . .' – not at all! 'In the beginning God created . . .'; it just states His existence and His being. Of course, in Acts 14 and 17, and in Romans 1, the Bible does teach us that, because of the goodness of God, disbelief in God is entirely without excuse. But it only puts it like that, negatively; it does not say, positively, that by reference to nature, and so on, the existence of God can be proved. It says that if someone does not believe in God, there is evidence that can be brought against him, because God has left His marks in nature. Therefore, as Paul argues, man in unbelief is inexcusable. In Romans 1:20 he writes, 'For the invisible things of him from the creation of the world are clearly seen, being understood by the things that are made, even his eternal power and Godhead; so that they are without excuse.'

I do not want to stay here with the question of proofs, but I am anxious to be practical, and I have no doubt that many of you have read about the 'proofs' of the being and existence of God, and feel that they have some value, so it does behove us to say a little about our attitude towards them. There are a number of arguments, and you will find that most text books on biblical doctrines and theology go into them in great detail. There is the so-called *cosmological argument* which is an argument from nature: that every effect has a cause. Then there is the argument from order and design called the *teleological* argument, which says that everything leads up to something – that is clearly evident. Then there is the *moral* argument, which concludes that our awareness of good and bad, our sense of right and wrong point to the existence of a moral God. Next there is the so-called argument that people everywhere, even in the most primitive races, *think and feel* there is a God. It is suggested that there must be some ground for thinking so, and that that is a proof of the existence of God.

Now what the Bible teaches about such arguments is that they can never create faith. They are useful in a negative sense but they will never lead to faith and, according to the Scriptures, no one can believe in God without faith, without the inward work of the Holy Spirit that leads to faith. You remember the way it is put in Hebrews 11:6 where we are told that someone coming to God 'must believe that he is, and that he is a rewarder of them that diligently seek him,' so that, ultimately, no one will believe in God without the gift of faith, which is the gift of God Himself.

When men and women believe in God by faith, the proofs are of value in supporting their faith, so they are of some help, but I doubt if they have any further value. If you are interested in them, you can make use of them in that way, to strengthen and support your faith and to show to people with whom you are discussing these matters that these things render them inexcusable.

Then the next matter that must come before us is *the possibility of knowing God*. There is God from eternity to eternity, and the Bible obviously starts there. But God having made the world, and having put us in the world, the question for us is: Is it possible to know this God who is held before us in the Bible, the God whose existence the Bible asserts? This is a very important aspect of the whole subject. This question of knowing God is the end, the supreme end, of all religion; it is the great thing that should be in the forefront of the mind and heart of every one of us. What is your need, what is your object, why are you studying these doctrines?

Well, according to the biblical teaching, our supreme need should always be to know God, so the question is: Can He be known? For there are people who believe in the existence of God, but who suggest to us that He cannot be known. Such teaching was very popular some two hundred years ago. It is known under the name of *deism*, and there are quite a number who believe that teaching today. They believe that God made the world as a watchmaker makes a clock. Then He wound it up and, having wound it up, He put it down, and had no more interest in it and nothing further to do with it. According to that theory, obviously God cannot be known.

Now we see many reasons for saying that these ideas are totally wrong, but the aspect of the matter I am anxious to emphasise is this – and it is one that needs to be stressed most of all to those of us who are evangelical Christians – we must always be careful to emphasise that the knowledge of God comes before any particular blessing that we may desire from Him. The goal of all our seeking and all our worship and all our endeavour should not be to have a particular experience; it should not be to petition certain blessings; it should be to know God Himself – the Giver not the gift, the source and the fount of every blessing, not the blessing itself.

I think you will agree with me that we always need that reminder. We are all of us so prone to start with ourselves and our problems. Sometimes I am almost filled with alarm as I get the impression from certain people and books that really they are not interested in God at all except as an agency who can give them blessings, for that is surely wrong and utterly unbiblical. Listen to our Lord Himself saying it: 'Blessed are the pure in heart: for they shall see God' – that is the *summum bonum*; that is our end and object and goal. That statement in Matthew 5:8 is one of the great beatitudes, the one that sums them all up. There is nothing beyond that; it should be the thing above everything else which we covet, and all our efforts should be because of that.

Or take again our Lord's definition of eternal life. What is eternal life? I wonder what our answer would be if we were faced with that question. Our tendency would be to describe it in some sort of subjective manner, something we have received, an experience we have had, and so on, and it does include that. But our Lord's definition is: 'And this is life eternal, that they might know thee the only true God, and Jesus Christ, whom thou hast sent' (John 17:3).

So let us keep this in its right position. Oh yes, it is right to feel we should like to know we are forgiven; it is right to feel we should like to be delivered from that sin – all that is perfectly legitimate – but if those things come before desiring to know God, then our whole attitude is very wrong and faulty. Could it be that most of our particular problems arise from the fact that we do not start with this desire to know God and put this before everything else?

So, then, the question is: Is it possible? And here I have to introduce a term, a big and yet vital word. The Bible teaches what is called the *incomprehensibility of God*. It means that God cannot finally be comprehended or understood by human beings; it means that we can read around the doctrine of God and try to grasp it with our minds, but, by definition, God is incomprehensible, we can never know Him in the ultimate, final and complete sense. Read it as it is stated in 1 Timothy 6:16, or again in Romans 11:33, or in Isaiah 55:8–9. God dwells in that light which no one can approach. God in His eternal and absolute being is incomprehensible.

Yet we see that though God is finally incomprehensible, He is nevertheless knowable; He cannot be comprehended, but, thank God, He can be known. Let us be clear about this. There are those who would have us believe that God cannot be known in His real being, that He can only be known in His dealings with men and women. But that is a position that is quite wrong when you put it into the light of biblical teaching. God, of course, is known most easily in His dealings with men and women, but, as we have seen, the Bible does teach that God can be known, even in His essential being.

Now I am not denying the doctrine of incomprehensibility when I say that – let me show you how I reconcile it. The knowledge that we have of God's being will never be anything but a partial knowledge, but though it is partial, it is nevertheless real; though it is not complete, it is a true knowledge, enough to lead us to glorify Him. And we have this knowledge of God because it has pleased God Himself to give it to us. Surely that is the point and purpose of all the teaching we have in the Bible. Here we find the revelation that God has given of Himself in the light of various statements He has made; surely these are meant to teach us about the being of God as well as His dealings with mankind.

Then, too, there is another term, *anthropomorphisms*: those statements in biblical teaching where God is spoken of as if He were man. They refer to God saying this and feeling that and, surely, they, too, are designed to lead us to know something about the being of God Himself.

A further argument which I would adduce is the various visions which are recorded in the Scriptures as having been seen by some of God's prophets and other servants, like, for example, that which happened to Moses when he was placed in the cleft of the rock – the vision of God (Exod. 33:18–23). What were these? Well, surely, they were but examples and illustrations of God manifesting something of His own glorious being. These were not His dealings with men and women in salvation and so on, but God was granting to His servants just a glimpse of His transcendent glory, and they never forgot it. So we argue that although God is incomprehensible, He, by His infinite grace and kindness and condescension, can be known. He is known.

If, then, that is so, the next question is: What do we know about God? What can we know about Him? And here I think it is right to start with what the Bible teaches us about God in His own essential nature and being. Now at this point I must pause for a moment. I said when we began these studies, and I want to go on repeating it constantly, that we are studying these things together not simply to entertain one another intellectually. If I thought that anybody had that motive – I say this quite seriously and solemnly – then I would not go on with these studies. Our object is to know God, and to know God is to worship Him, and here am I, a little pygmy man, a preacher in time, talking about the essential nature and being of God!

No, at this point there is only one thing to do, we must do what Moses did when he saw the burning bush. At first he said, 'I will now turn aside, and see this great sight' (Exod. 3:3), and he was going to investigate this remarkable phenomenon, this bush that was burning and not consumed. But the word came to him, 'Draw not nigh hither: put off thy shoes from off thy feet, for the place whereon thou standest is holy ground' (v. 5). More and more, as I consider these things, and spend ever-increasing time in reading my Bible, I understand why the ancient Jews never mentioned the name Jehovah. They were filled with such a sense of awe and reverence, they had such a conception of the majesty of God, that in a sense they dared not even utter the name. I much prefer that, to hearing people saying, 'Dear God'. I do not find such an expression in the Bible. I do find 'Holy Father', but never 'Dear God'. We must approach Him 'with reverence and godly fear: for our God is a consuming fire' (Heb. 12:28–9).

So then, bearing all that in mind, let us approach this subject in that spirit, and let me remind you of some of the things that the Bible tells us about the essential nature of God's being. Here it is very interesting to observe that we can, in a sense, only deal with negatives; because of our finite condition and God's transcendent greatness and glory, even our positive statements are in and of themselves negative. Take, for instance, the first statement. The Bible teaches us about the *infinity* of God – God's nature is infinite. Now that really means not finite; you cannot put it positively. It means He is an absolute being; He is not derived from something else nor conditioned by anything else – 'I am that I am' (Exod. 3:14). 'Who shall I say,' said Moses to God, 'is sending me to do this work?' and God told him to say, 'I am hath sent me unto you.' What a staggering thought; an ultimate, absolute being!

In other words, God's infinity suggests to us that He is the cause of everything else; all existence, all being, derives from Him. His infinity also reminds us that He is free from all restrictions and all bounds; there is no limitation whatsoever where God is concerned, He is everything, everywhere, unlimited. Or perhaps the best way of thinking of it is this: the exaltedness of God, the sublimity of God, the ineffable majesty of God, or the transcendence of God, above and beyond everything: 'I am that I am.' We read in Revelation 4:8, 'Holy, holy, holy, Lord God Almighty, which was, and is, and is to come' – the infinity of God is emphasised everywhere in the Bible, from beginning to end, and we should never pray without reminding ourselves of that. So often we are misled by the very anthropomorphisms for which we thank God, but let us try to remember that the being whom we approach in prayer is this infinite, absolute being.

Then the next quality which is always emphasised in the Scripture about God's essential being is His spirituality. This was stated once and for ever by our Lord Himself. 'God is a Spirit,' He said, and strangely enough this tremendous statement was made not to someone like Nicodemus, but to the woman of Samaria. Of course, our Lord said that to her partly because she had obviously got a false conception of God – 'Should we worship,' she asked, 'in this mountain, or in Jerusalem?' 'No,' said our Lord, 'God is a Spirit ...' (John 4:24). Stephen said the same thing in his famous address in the seventh chapter of Acts, 'Howbeit the most High,' he said, 'dwelleth not in temples made with hands' (Acts 7:48). And Paul preaching to the people of Athens used exactly the same words: 'God that made the world and all things therein, seeing that he is Lord of heaven and earth, dwelleth not in temples made with hands' (Acts 17:24). What do we mean when we say that God is a Spirit? Well, so far as our language can express it, it excludes the whole idea that God is corporeal, that He is confined to a form or to a body. In His essential being God has none of the properties that belong to matter. And that leads us to say – and this is most important from a practical point of view – that He can, therefore, never be discerned by the bodily senses. People who seem to think they have visions will always do well to bear that in mind – 'No man hath seen God at any time,' writes John (John 1:18). 'Now unto the King, eternal, immortal, invisible . . .', says Paul writing to Timothy (1 Tim. 1:17), and it is because of the spirituality of God's being that the Old Testament frequently forbade the making of images and likenesses. You find this in the first two of the Ten Commandments and it is repeated elsewhere.

Why is this? It is because the moment you begin to do that you are obviously forgetting the spirituality of God – the essential spiritual nature of His being. But perhaps the most striking proof of the spirituality of God is another truth concerning Him which we shall be considering later, namely His omnipresence, the truth that God is everywhere, and that He is everywhere at one and the same time.

I anticipate a question at this point. Someone may say, 'All that is right, but what about the incident where God put Moses in the cleft of the rock, and then told him he should see His back parts (Exod. 33:23)? And what did our Lord mean when He said, 'Ye have neither heard his voice at any time, nor seen his shape' (John 5:37)? There are two simple answers to that question. The first is that though God is spiritual in His essential being, when He so chooses, He may also give appearances of Himself. We are told how our Lord before His incarnation appeared as the Angel of the Covenant, so, when He chooses to teach something about Himself, He can give appearances of Himself and yet it is not His true self.

Second, let me put it like this: God, in order to tell us about Himself has spoken a language that you and I can understand. It is almost impossible for us to grasp the idea of infinity and spirituality, so God

speaks as if He were man. He is only doing it that we might understand; so that we may know and trust Him, He speaks as if He were
a man – that is the whole idea of anthropomorphism. And so let us
sum up. God is invisible, without parts, without body, free from any
and every limitation.

That, then, brings us to the last characteristic of God's essential
being and that is *personality*. The actual term is not used in the Bible
but it is implied throughout, and thank God that it is. What does personality mean? Personality exists where there is mind, intelligence,
will, reason, individuality, self-consciousness and self-determination.
Where you have these things, there you have personality, and the
Bible asserts that God is a person. How vitally important this is. It
was important when our Lord was here in this world, because of the
problem of pantheism, which is still popular in various forms. Believers in pantheism say that everything that is, is God, and God is everything that is. They say that we must not talk about the person of God,
because He is not a person. The pantheist worships nature for that
reason; he finds God in nature.

Now people do not talk so much about pantheism today. They say
they believe that God is a great Mind or a great Force or a great
Energy. Mind with a capital 'M'. But He is not a mind, He is a person.
Neither is He a Force with a capital 'F', nor Energy with a capital 'E',
because all these conceptions deny consciousness. To say He is just
energy, unconscious energy, unconscious might, force and dynamism
is not biblical. The Bible says that God is a person and this is absolutely vital to any true sense of worship, and to our having a feeling
of confidence about ourselves and about the world.

How, then, does the Bible teach us that God is a person? It does so
directly and indirectly. Indirectly, it tells us that God has left marks of
Himself and of His mind and sensibility in creation. You see there the
evidence of His mind and His will and His ordering. What about the
laws of nature? Where do all our wonderful inventions come from?
They have simply been discovered because we have found out that
there are such things as 'laws of nature'. And the answer is that they
originate from God; in the laws of nature, from design and order, we
see the work of God, as Paul argues in Romans 1. They are all an
indication of the mind and the will of God in operation.

But there is a great deal of direct evidence for saying that God is a
person. Have you not noticed how the presence of God is always
described in a personal way? Take the name of God that we have

considered: 'I am', that is a personal statement, it is a person who can say, 'I am', and God says that He speaks of Himself in this manner. Every single representative of God has declared that God is a person and not simply an unconscious force. Then take the way in which the Scriptures contrast God with the idols. Read it in Psalm 115 – you notice the contrast? These idols, says the psalmist, have eyes, yes, but they cannot see, they are not persons; mouths they have, but they cannot speak; they have hands but they cannot handle; and God is contrasted with all these dumb idols. Paul says of the Thessalonians that they turned from idols to serve the living and true God (1 Thess. 1:9). Not only that, the Bible teaches us that people converse with God and that He is able to have specific dealings with men and women, He chooses particular people and He blesses particular people – again, all that is personal.

But, of course, the final proof is the Lord Jesus Christ Himself. In the incarnation, in the person of His Son, God has declared that He is personal. Our Lord said, 'He that hath seen me hath seen the Father' (John 14:9), and, 'I and my Father are one' (John 10:30); therefore God must be personal, because it was a person who was speaking. Furthermore, our Lord's teaching of God was always in terms of this personal quality. He spoke of Him as 'the Father' and you see this in its most glorious form when you take a look at the Lord Jesus Christ praying. In John 17, for example, what is He doing? He is praying, not to 'whatever gods may be', but to 'Holy Father', the person. And thus in every way, everywhere, the Bible asserts that God is a personal being.

And finally the Bible teaches also that God is *one unity*: 'Hear, O Israel: the Lord our God is one Lord' (Deut. 6:4), and when we come to the doctrine of the Trinity, we shall deal with that. We refer to it now, to make our consideration of this doctrine, as taught in the Bible, complete – 'There is *one God*, and one mediator between God and men, the man Christ Jesus' (1 Tim. 2:5).

And so we see that the glorious truth we have been trying to look at together is just this, that this infinite, absolute, sublime, transcendent, glorious, majestic, mighty, everlasting being who is Spirit, who is truth, who dwells in light no one can approach, this God has been graciously pleased that you and I should know Him, that we should talk to Him and that we should worship Him. And He is prepared to listen to us, to meet with us, and receive our unworthy and poor worship, and our praise and adoration. Blessed be the name of God!

6

The Attributes of
God's Absolute Personality

As we resume our consideration of the great and central doctrine of
God, let me remind you that we have seen that the existence of God is
not argued in the Scriptures. It is assumed. Furthermore, we saw that
we can deduce from the Scriptures that God is knowable but incomprehensible. We can know Him but that does not mean that we can
understand God fully or exhaustively. And then we went on to consider something about the essential being and nature of God. We
mentioned His infinity, His spirituality, His personality, and the
essential unity of the Godhead.

But fortunately for us, the Bible does not stop at that; it goes
further. Having revealed that God, in His ultimate being and essence, is
quite incomprehensible, for the very reason that He is characterised by
those qualities which I have just enumerated, the Bible goes on to tell us
more about Him, and obviously its object is that we may know God
and worship Him more truly. And that is really our reason for considering this great doctrine of God, because unless we do understand
what the Bible tells us about God, our worship can never be real.

Our Lord said to the woman of Samaria, 'Ye worship ye know not
what . . .' (John 4:22). They thought they knew God. And in the same
way, the apostle Paul said to the Athenians, 'Whom therefore ye
ignorantly worship, him declare I unto you' (Acts 17:23). They were
worshipping an unknown God. And this is vital – though we may say
that we believe in God and believe that we are worshipping Him, we
are not of necessity doing so. And we can never worship truly until we
worship in the way in which our Lord taught the woman of Samaria.

He said, 'God is a Spirit: and they that worship him must worship him in spirit and in truth' (John 4:24); and He also said, 'For the Father seeketh such to worship him' (John 4:23).

So this is not some mere theological discussion that we are engaged upon. I would go on reminding you that our intention is essentially practical. The whole object of these considerations is that we may learn how to worship God, and how truly to be God's people. God has stooped and condescended to meet us, and He has been pleased to grant us further and more detailed revelations concerning Himself.

Now these further revelations are customarily divided into two main sections. The Bible tells us something of what are called the *attributes* of God and it also gives us certain *names* by which God has revealed Himself. The great theologians and Bible students of the past, especially in the Middle Ages, at the time of the Reformation and in the seventeenth century, spent a great deal of their time in discussing which of these should be taken first. This is a very interesting discussion which cannot finally be settled; it ultimately becomes a matter of one's own choice and predilection. For myself, I feel that we are more or less bound to take first the attributes and then the names.

My reasons are these. It seems to me that our approach to God should be something like this. The Bible reveals to us that God is in a glory that no man or woman can ever approach, in a light that is utterly inaccessible, that is, God in His ultimate nature and being – and we tried to look at this in the last lecture. The next thing to say, obviously, is that there are certain things that characterise God, which He has been pleased to reveal to us, and those are His attributes. But God has even come nearer to us than that. He has given certain names to Himself, and the object of these names is, as it were, to bring God still closer to us, that we may not be left baffled and bewildered, but may know that at any rate God has told us this and that about Himself.

Now that is my personal reason for looking at the attributes before we come to a consideration of the names of God. And again I would remind you that we are entirely dependent upon the biblical revelation for our knowledge of both. But, you see, already we are beginning to find that the Bible is nothing but a great book in which God has been pleased to reveal Himself. You cannot get away from revelation. It is God showing Himself, manifesting Himself, in order that we may know Him, in order that we may worship Him, in order that we may have fellowship with Him.

So, then, once more we bear in mind the injunction to take our shoes from off our feet because the ground whereon we are standing is holy ground; once more we remind ourselves that God is not a phenomenon which we are to investigate, and that when we approach the attributes of God's great and eternal personality we are as far removed as can be imagined from the scientific procedure of dissection. No, no; we simply take what God has been pleased to tell us about Himself. We note it. We try to bear it in mind. And humbly, and full of worship and praise, we thank Him for His condescension.

Let us, therefore, realise that analysis, which is indeed absolutely essential if we are to know what we are doing, must nevertheless not be the ordinary kind of scientific or logical analysis. I am so afraid of going astray at this point. I am so afraid of myself, apart from any of you, because the mind, though it is a gift from God, can, because of the fall, be very dangerous to us. I want to make this abundantly clear, and let me put it, therefore, in this particular way. We normally think of analysis, do we not, as something like this: you analyse a flower. You pull off the petals and stamens, and you count them and check them off, and at the end you have nothing left. That is our usual conception of analysis. But we are going to do nothing at all like that now. God has been pleased to give this revelation in order that we may have some concept of Him. So these are not separate parts which go to make up a whole. They are aspects of God, particular views of God, and if I may use such a term, even portraits of God. But there is no division in the personality. So, while we are compelled by the inadequacy of language to talk about analysis, let us remember what we are doing.

So, we start by considering some of the attributes of God and by attributes I mean some of the perfections of God or, to put it another way, some of the virtues of God. Peter says in his first epistle, '. . . that ye should shew forth the praises of him who hath called you out of darkness into his marvellous light' (1 Pet. 2:9). That is it. The Christian is meant to show forth the attributes of God – these perfections, these excellencies of God.

Or, if you like, here is another definition of God's attributes: they are things about God, certain aspects of His great and glorious eternal nature, which He has been pleased to reveal to us, and which, in a measure, we can lay hold of. Now here again, the authorities have been very busy trying to classify these attributes, trying for their own sakes and for the sake of others to put them into certain categories. But once more I would suggest to you that it is something which is finally impossible. All sorts of classifications have been suggested. Some have said that the division should be into the natural attributes of God and the moral attributes of God, that is, into attributes which belong to God in and of Himself, and those which have a kind of moral implication.

Well, it does not matter very much what we may call them. I would suggest some classification like this: first, the attributes of absolute personality which belong to God, and second, the moral attributes of God.

In the last lecture we said that God is a person; He is a personality in an absolute sense. Now what are the attributes that belong to His personality? They are, of course, expressive of His eternal being, and the first one, therefore, which we have to note, is the *eternity* of God, and with it the *immutability* of God. God is without beginning and without ending; He is everlasting. You will find a great statement of that in Psalm 90: 'Before the mountains were brought forth, or ever thou hadst formed the earth and the world, even from everlasting to everlasting, thou art God' (v. 2). You will find it in the same way in Psalm 102. His eternity is something which we just assert and wonder at.

But we must look a little more at the immutability of God. This means that God is absolutely unchangeable. He can never be different in essence. God is always everlastingly the same. It is never possible that God should differ in any respect from what He always is and always has been. One of His great names suggests that: the name of Jehovah[1] – I am that I am – which means, I am always the same; I am the unchangeable One. It is not possible, in other words, that God should possess one attribute at one time, and another attribute at another time. Now I think you will see at once the importance of emphasising that, because we ourselves are very changeable; we are one thing one day and something else another day, though we are still the same person. We are not immutable – we are mutable. But that is something that is inconceivable in God. God in His absolute perfection is always the same.

James makes a great statement of this when he talks about '. . . the Father of lights, with whom is no variableness, neither shadow of turning' – or – 'that is cast by turning' (Jas. 1:17). That is God in His nature and in His character, He is not only without change but utterly without even the possibility of change.

---

1. Jehovah is the AV translation of the Hebrew *Yahweh*.

At this point somebody probably wants to ask this question: 'Does not the Bible tell us that God repented of certain things? Do we not read in Genesis 6, 'And it repented the Lord that he had made man on the earth'? Do we not also get the idea of God repenting in the book of Jonah, when He did not destroy the city of Nineveh? How can you at one and the same time say that God is immutable and unchangeable, and still tell us that the Bible talks about God repenting, because repentance means to change one's mind?'

And clearly the answer is this: God's character never changes, but His dealings with people change. What we are asserting, and what the Bible asserts everywhere, is that God, in His character, in His being, is always eternally the same, but, obviously, in His dealings with human beings, God varies His procedure according to whether they repent or not. In other words, when we use a term like 'immutability' we must be very careful that we do not deny the idea of the personality of God. As someone once put it, I think very well, 'The immutability of God is not the immutability of a stone.' A stone is immutable; it never changes at all. A stone is always a stone and never will be anything else. But that is not the immutability of God. His is not the immutability of lifelessness or a machine. His is the immutability of absolute perfection. Because God is personal in His dealings with men and women, He varies His actions.

Now this is, I think you will agree with me, one of the most profound and glorious doctrines of all. I know nothing, in a sense, in my Christian life and experience which is so comforting as the doctrine of the eternity and immutability of God. Of course, to the sinner it is one of the most terrifying of all the doctrines. In other words, God is eternally righteous. God is eternally holy. Is there anything more wonderful, especially in the modern world as it is?

> Change and decay in all around I see,
> Oh Thou who changest not, abide with me.
>   H. F. Lyte

Is it not a wonderful and a glorious thing to know that God never changes? We are so changeable; other people are so changeable; everything is changeable. But you can be absolutely certain that the everlasting God is always the same. High doctrine, yes, but a most practical and comforting doctrine. I would like to stay with it, but we must go on.

The next attribute of God (and let me remind you that we are still dealing with attributes that belong to His essential, eternal being) is His *omnipresence*. This means that God is present everywhere. Now you remember that we have already agreed that God is Spirit, so when we say that God is everywhere we are not speaking in a bodily sense. It is almost impossible to grasp these ideas, is it not? Yet they are taught us so plainly in the Bible that it is our duty to face them and to take hold of them and to possess them with our minds and our understanding.

We must say also that He is not of necessity present in the same way everywhere, because the Bible tells us that heaven is His dwelling-place (1 Kgs. 8:30). (You remember that great term I have already had to introduce – the term *anthropomorphism*. These terms are absolutely essential in order to give us some understanding.) So we have to say that God is present everywhere, and yet there are certain places – almost that word is inadequate – where God is specially present. We have to say that in order to safeguard ourselves against pantheism, which, as we saw in our last lecture, says that God is a kind of permanent captive in everything, but which denies His personality.

Now this is how the Bible tells us about the omnipresence of God: take, for instance, Jeremiah 23:23–4: 'Am I a God at hand, saith the Lord, and not a God afar off? Can any hide himself in secret places that I shall not see him? saith the Lord. Do not I fill heaven and earth? saith the Lord.' He fills the heavens. He fills the earth. He is everywhere. Then in particular on this point take Psalm 139: 'Whither shall I go from thy spirit? or whither shall I flee from thy presence? If I ascend up into heaven, thou art there: if I make my bed in hell, behold, thou art there. If I take the wings of the morning, and dwell in the uttermost parts of the sea; even there shall thy hand lead me, and thy right hand shall hold me' (vv. 7–10). It does not matter where I go, God is there. And Paul makes the same point in preaching to those learned Athenians: 'For in him we live, and move, and have our being . . .' (Acts 17:28). You cannot get out of the presence or the sight of God – the omnipresence of God.

Here again, I suggest to you, is a great and comforting doctrine. The psalmist in Psalm 139 looks on it, of course, as a warning; and he is right. All these great questions which we are considering are warnings. These attributes of God, they are at one and the same time warnings and comforts. If you have sinned against God, you will find it impossible to get away from Him. Read again Francis Thompson's poem, 'The Hound of Heaven': 'I fled him down the nights and down the days . . .' You cannot get away wherever you are, down 'the labyrinthine ways' of your mind or anywhere else. Yes, but is it not a wonderfully comforting thing to think and to realise that it does not matter where your circumstances may put you, God is still with you. There is no place anywhere in which you may ever find yourself but that God will be there.

And that in turn brings me to His next great attribute: the *omniscience* of God. God knows all things, and His knowledge is always absolute knowledge. It is perfect knowledge, a complete knowledge of everything.

There are very many statements of this, of course, in the Scriptures. Take, for instance, Psalm 147:5: '. . . his understanding is infinite.' Then in Proverbs 15:3 we read, 'The eyes of the Lord are in every place, beholding the evil and the good.'

So then, let us divide it up like this. The Bible tells us quite a lot in detail about this knowledge, this omniscience of God. For instance, it tells us about God's knowledge of nature: 'He telleth the number of the stars; he calleth them all by their names' (Ps. 147:4). But let me give you another example. Do you remember those tender words of our Lord in which He tells us that not a single sparrow falls to the ground without our Father (Matt. 10:29)? Everything in the realm of nature is known to God. It is quite inconceivable to us, but the Bible asserts that it is true of God. Look up into the heavens on a starry night and see all that multiplicity of stars. He knows them, every one, and He has a name for every one. There is nothing in creation but that God knows it in that intimate and personal sense.

But we are obviously more interested in God's knowledge of us and of our human experience, and here again Psalm 139 is very eloquent. Incidentally, in this particular psalm you get a perfect exposition of the attributes of God; they all seem to have been grouped together. The psalmist says, 'Thou knowest my downsitting and mine uprising, thou understandest my thought afar off' (v. 2). My very thought! He knows all about me. 'Thou compassest my path . . . and art acquainted with all my ways' (v. 3). Indeed, he goes further in verse 4 and says this: 'For there is not a word in my tongue, but, lo, O Lord, thou knowest it altogether.' What an exact and detailed knowledge God has of us! We read of how He said to Moses, 'I have surely seen the affliction of my people' (Exod. 3:7). He knew what His people were suffering there in Egypt, He knew of the hardships.

Now God's people, alas, in their lack of faith and of knowledge, are often tempted to think that God does not know. You will find that in many a psalm. Does God not know? asks the psalmist: 'Has God forgotten to be gracious?' (Ps. 77:9). Does He not realise what is happening to us? But we must never think that. It is our ignorance that makes us speak like that. God knows all about us. Let me again quote our blessed Lord; He says, 'But even the very hairs of your head are all numbered' (Luke 12:7). Can you think of a more detailed knowledge than that? God knows us in detail to that extent.

Then there is that mighty statement in Hebrews 4:13: 'Neither is there any creature that is not manifest in his sight: but all things are naked and opened unto the eyes of him with whom we have to do.' There is not a more grand and more eloquent statement of the omniscience of God than that. It sums it up perfectly. That is God's knowledge of us and of our human experiences.

But, further, of course, the Bible everywhere tells us that God has a perfect knowledge of all human history past and future. Take the prophets, for instance, and the prophecies; take the second chapter of the book of Daniel, with its foretelling of the kingdoms that were to come. There God reveals His complete and perfect foreknowledge. The eighth chapter of Daniel does exactly the same thing; and there are many other examples of this same principle. In Acts 15:18 you find this stated explicitly in these words: 'Known unto God are all his works from the beginning of the world.' God sees the end from the beginning; He knows everything from eternity to eternity.

Now we have to use terms like foreknowledge, and so on. In a sense they are quite meaningless when you are speaking about God, for with God there is no time; there is no past, present and future where He is concerned, all is one great, living, eternal present. We cannot grasp that, but the Bible teaches it. We are living in time and we think in such terms. But God is above time. He is in eternity, and He sees everything in one, as it were. Thus there is no difficulty about speaking of the foreknowledge of God. He sees the whole of history as He looks at it. He is in it always. So we are not surprised that Paul cries out saying, 'O the depth of the riches both of the wisdom and knowledge of God!' (Rom. 11:33).

The mention of the word *wisdom* brings me to another subsection of this same heading of omniscience, because we read a great deal in the Bible about the wisdom of God; and the wisdom of God is a part, an aspect, of His perfect knowledge. So bear that in mind while I draw a few distinctions between knowledge and wisdom. I think it is essential to do this because you find the two things mentioned so often in the Bible.

What, then, is the difference between knowledge and wisdom? I feel that this is one of the most urgently needed distinctions at this present time. If I understand anything at all about the modern world and its educational systems, I would say that we have gone wrong because we have failed to draw the vital distinction between knowledge and wisdom. We today go in for knowledge. We are growing encyclopaedias. It is the age, is it not, of digests – collections of knowledge – and we are a most knowledgeable people. I suppose that modern men and women know far more than any of their predecessors have ever known. Yes; but what is so obviously lacking in the modern world?

Let me suggest a few things for you to reflect upon. First, the source of knowledge is study; the source of wisdom is discernment. You get your knowledge by studying, but you do not get wisdom that way. People can study a great deal but not get wisdom, because they lack discernment, because they lack the ability to see.

Second, knowledge is what is commonly called discursive in its character, whereas wisdom is more intuitive. Knowledge is something that you can arrive at by conversation and talk and consideration. Whereas wisdom is, in a sense, almost something that someone is born with as a gift. We all realise that, do we not? There are some people who seem to be born naturally wise people. They may not have very great knowledge, but if you want advice you go to them. There are other people who have a great deal of knowledge, but you would never dream of taking their opinion, because you feel they are lacking in wisdom. You will often find, for example, that many a member of the legal profession may make a good advocate but a very poor judge, though he may have a great knowledge of law. The two things are very different.

Then there are further differences between knowledge and wisdom. Knowledge is generally theoretical; wisdom is always practical. Knowledge, as such, is not really concerned about life and living; it is simply interested in the knowledge of things for the sake of knowing them. But wisdom always has a practical objective. It is the capacity to make use of the knowledge you have; to apply it; to bring it down to the practical level. It wants to live. It wants to do something.

And my last distinction is that in knowledge you have the mind acting apart from the will, whereas where wisdom is concerned you have the mind acting in subservience to the will. In other words, wisdom is the right kind of knowledge. And I think you will agree with me that this kind of knowledge is seriously needed in the modern world. You have great numbers of clever people, but, oh, what a tragic lack of wisdom!

Well, the Bible emphasises the wisdom of God. God applies His knowledge; He brings it to bear. And you will see it, supremely, in three main respects. You see the wisdom of God in creation. I hope to discuss this when we come to the doctrine of creation. But there are many people who are troubled about the hypothesis and theory of evolution, and what troubles them, they say, is that they see a kind of similarity of pattern all along. Yes, I agree, I see the same thing, but what I see there is not evolution, but the wisdom of God in creation, in the design and perfect arrangement, and in all the harmony, all the co-operation. Look into the book of nature, and if you have eyes which are at all Christian, you will see everywhere the marvellous wisdom of God. The multiplicity is a manifestation of wisdom; the way He repeats Himself – spring, summer, autumn, winter – and always does things in the same way.

But if you want to see the wisdom of God you must come and look at it as it is manifested in redemption. That is the great argument, is it not, in 1 Corinthians 1: 'The Greeks seek after wisdom' (v. 22). Why, says Paul, if you want wisdom look at the Lord Jesus Christ, who is 'the power of God, and the wisdom of God' (v. 24). 'But of him are ye in Christ Jesus, who of God is made unto us wisdom, and righteousness, and sanctification, and redemption' (v. 30).

Then you also see God's wisdom in His providential arrangements – the providence of God. Again, I hope to deal with that separately; I merely mention it at this point. But as you consider what the Bible has to tell about the great providence of God, you will see this extraordinary display of His perfect wisdom.

I must come next to the *omnipotence* of God: God is all-powerful. The omnipotence of God is that by which He brings to pass everything He wills. So when you are considering this, you must sub-divide it into two main sections: first, the will of God, and second, the power of God.

The omnipotence is the will of God being put into operation. How often we read in the Bible about the will of God – for example, Paul writes of 'him who worketh all things after the counsel of his own will' (Eph. 1:11). What is the will of God? It is the final ground of everything, of all existence. It is the final explanation of everything that has ever happened or everything that will happen. And the Bible teaches that the will of God is sovereign; in other words, it is not determined by anything but by God Himself. It is the expression of His Lordship, His absolute being.

But remember, His will is never arbitrary. It is never exercised except in perfect harmony with all the other attributes of God's great and glorious being. It is the same God who is omniscient, who is omnipresent. It is the same God who is glorious and wonderful. It is the same God who is love and compassion and mercy. We must not divide these things, though we distinguish them for the purposes of thought and understanding.

Furthermore, you will find that the will of God expresses itself in two main ways. He declares certain things which He Himself is going to do: that is called the *decretive will* of God. He also prescribes certain things for us to do: that is the *prescriptive will* of God. The terms are not of great importance, but constantly in the Bible you see these two aspects of God's will: God tells us what He Himself is going to do and He gives commands to us about what we are to do.

As for His power, it is endless. He is omnipotent. 'Is any thing too hard for the Lord?' God asked Abraham (Gen. 18:14), and the angel Gabriel said to Mary, 'For with God nothing shall be impossible' (Luke 1:37). His might, His power, His strength are endless. The Bible is full of this! He made everything out of nothing – He spoke and it happened. He said, 'Let there be light: and there was light' (Gen. 1:3). He sends His frosts and His snow. Read the psalms and you will find that they glory in the endless power of God.

This sovereign will and power of God have been manifested most of all, and most clearly, in three ways: in creation, in salvation and in providence. And I suppose there is no greater manifestation of the power of God than the one to which Paul refers in the first chapter of Ephesians: '. . . his mighty power, which he wrought in Christ, when he raised him from the dead' (vv. 19–20). This idea of omnipotence is staggering! There are many things we do not understand about the will of God. But we are not meant to understand them; we are meant to look at them with reverence and with awe and worship. We are meant to realise that there would be no hope for us at all were it not for the omnipotence of God. I say it with reverence, nothing less than the omnipotence of God could save a single soul. But, thank God, He is omnipotent, and we are saved by the power of God in and through the Lord Jesus Christ.

Then, finally, the Bible also tells us about the *absolute blessedness* of God. It speaks about His utter, absolute perfection. God is the sum total of all excellency. There is nothing higher or greater or better than God. Every conceivable perfection is in God in an absolute manner, and He is exalted above all shortcomings and all limitations. The Bible therefore speaks of the perfection of God and it also speaks of the blessedness of God. Take those many expressions in Paul's epistles – for example, Paul's words, 'the glorious gospel of the blessed God' (1 Tim. 1:11). What does Paul mean when he refers to God as 'blessed'? Well, he means that God's own perfection is the object of God's own knowledge and of His own love. He rejoices in Himself. He delights in Himself and is perfectly and absolutely self-sufficient. God is, according to the Scriptures, well-pleased within Himself and His glorious being: the blessedness of God.

The last thing is the *glory* of God and this is the biblical way of describing His greatness, His splendour, His majesty. We read of the glory of God filling the house – the Temple (1 Kgs. 8:11), and of the glory of God being manifested in dimmed vision to certain people. This means they had some conception of the greatness, the splendour, the majesty, the might of His being.

So we have looked together at some of the attributes of God. We have not started considering the so-called moral attributes of God. We have dealt only with the attributes of God that belong to His essential being and personality. And unless we are at this moment more anxious than ever before to fall at His feet, to yield ourselves utterly and unreservedly to Him, realising that the greatest privilege that has ever come to us is to worship Him and to commune with Him, then we have spent our time in vain. We have been looking at the blessed God who dwells in that light that is unapproachable (1 Tim. 6:16), whom no one has seen nor ever can see, and who has been graciously pleased to tell us about Himself. So let us thank Him and worship Him.

7

The Moral Attributes of God

We are dealing, let me remind you, with the attributes of God. We have considered those which belong to His absolute personality and we come now to consider what are commonly called the moral attributes of God, sometimes described as the *communicable* attributes of God. Those attributes which we have just dealt with belong only to God; they are incommunicable and, I say with reverence, even God cannot convey them to His people. The attributes that we shall now consider – the moral attributes – are, in a sense, communicable. Something corresponding to them is to be found in men and women.

What are these? Well, first we must place the *holiness* of God. What is holiness? I think we almost inevitably tend to deal with it in negative terms, and we define it as meaning that God is entirely separate from and apart from sin. Holiness primarily means separation – separation from evil.

But, of course, holiness is also something positive. It is essential, absolute purity. The Bible teaches us everywhere that God is holy, and a part of the manifestation of this holiness is His hatred of sin and His separation from sin, from the sinner and from all that is evil.

Let me give you certain outstanding examples and illustrations of the Bible's teaching on this. God has revealed His holiness by granting visions of Himself to certain people. There is the great case of Moses, in Exodus 34 and in other places, where God appeared, as it were, to Moses, and Moses was overwhelmed by the sense of His holiness. The same thing happened to Job, to Isaiah and to Ezekiel. Anyone who has ever come anywhere near to God has always been impressed by His absolute holiness. The Bible teaches this in certain terms that it uses; it refers to God as 'the Holy One' (Isa. 40:25), and we have

God's injunction: 'Be ye holy; for I am holy' (1 Pet. 1:16), which is a specific, explicit statement of God's holiness.

Now we often forget, I fear, that in a sense, the great business of the Old Testament is to reveal the holiness of God. We have been far too influenced, many of us, by the false teaching of the past century, which would have us believe that Old Testament history is just the history of man's search for God. It is not. The Old Testament is primarily a revelation of the holiness of God, and of what God has done as a result of that, and, therefore, you find this teaching everywhere. What was the purpose of the giving of the law if not to reveal and to teach the children of Israel about the holiness of God? There He separated a people unto Himself, and He wanted them to know what sort of people they were. They could only know that as they realised and appreciated His holiness: so the giving of the law was primarily to that end.

Then take all the various instructions about the making of the tabernacle – the division into the outer court and the holy place, and the holiest of all, into which the high priest alone was allowed to enter once a year, and that not without blood. The tabernacle was simply designed to represent, as it were in actual practice, this great teaching about the holiness of God. Then, take all that you read about the ceremonial law and about the clean and unclean animals. Why all this? Well, the reason given is: you are a holy people and I am a holy God; you are not to eat what everybody else eats. There was to be this division, this separation, between clean and unclean. All that long list of rules and regulations is also a part of the teaching of the holiness of God.

Then, of course, the prophets constantly taught about God's holiness. This was their great burden and message. It is summed up perfectly in the book of Habakkuk, where we are told, 'Thou art of purer eyes than to behold evil, and canst not look on iniquity' (Hab. 1:13).

And, again, you get the same emphasis in the New Testament. Our Lord, for instance, addressed God as 'Holy Father' (John 17:11). That is the supreme teaching about the holiness of God. Even He, who was equal with God, and had come out of the eternal bosom, even He addressed Him as 'Holy Father'. And there is a definition of this in 1 John: 'God is light, and in him is no darkness at all' (1 John 1:5). So the Bible is full of this teaching. It refers to God the Father as the 'Holy One of Israel' (Ps. 71:22; etc.). The Lord Jesus Christ is referred to as 'thy holy child Jesus' (Acts 4:27), and the 'Holy One' (Acts 3:14). Then we speak of the 'Holy Spirit', thus the three Persons in the glorious Trinity are constantly referred to and described in terms of this quality of holiness.

But I suppose if you were to be asked to say where the Bible teaches the holiness of God most powerfully of all you have to go to Calvary. God is so holy, so utterly holy, that nothing but that awful death could make it possible for Him to forgive us. The cross is the supreme and the sublimest declaration and revelation of the holiness of God.

I should like to tarry with this great theme, but I cannot; we must move on. Let us just remind ourselves that surely the purpose of the biblical revelation of God's holiness is to teach us how to approach Him. It is not mere theoretical knowledge that we are asked to try to grasp with our understandings. Its purpose is very practical. In the words of the author of the epistle to the Hebrews, we are to approach God 'with reverence and godly fear' (Heb. 12:28). He is always to be approached in that way, wherever you are; when you are alone in a room, or when you are meeting as a family to pray, or when you are in a public service, God is always God and He is always to be approached 'with reverence and godly fear'. No such expression as 'Dear God', for example, is to be found in the Scriptures.

There are many illustrations of this. Think again of Moses at the burning bush (Exod. 3); then there is the terrible case of that man Uzzah who put out his hand to steady the Ark as it was being carried on a cart (2 Sam. 6). That is a terrible declaration about how we are to approach God and worship Him. Read the account of how the law was given; how the mount was burning with fire, and nothing was allowed to approach it (Exod. 19:16–25): the holiness of God.

This doctrine also teaches us, of course, the terrible nature of sin. You will never have a knowledge of sin unless you have a true conception of the holiness of God. And that is perhaps why the modern conception of sin is so inadequate. We do not spend sufficient time with the doctrine of God, and with the holiness of God. That is the way to see sin – not primarily by self-examination but by going into the presence of God. People sometimes say, 'But you don't expect all of us to feel that we are miserable sinners, do you? You don't want all of us to say with Charles Wesley, "Vile and full of sin I am"? That may be all right for drunkards and people like that, but it's not true of us!'

Some people are troubled by this. They say, 'I have never really felt I am a sinner. How can I, when I have been brought up in a Christian home, and have always gone to a place of worship? Surely I'm not expected to have that awful sense of sin?' But the answer to all that is this: If you really came into the presence of God and had some conception of His holiness, you would soon know yourself as a vile, terrible sinner. You would say with Paul that there is no good thing in you (Rom. 7:18). The way to appreciate your own sinfulness is not to look at your actions, nor your life, but to come into the presence of God.

And finally, of course, God's holiness shows us the absolute necessity of the atonement. That is the reverse of what I was saying just now about the cross as the manifestation of the holiness of God. Yes, but as it manifests that, it also shows us that without shedding of blood there is no remission of sin, that God's holiness insists upon it, demands an atonement for sin.

The next moral attribute of God that the Bible emphasises is the *righteousness* or the *justice* of God. Now this follows, of course, inescapably, from the holiness of God. What is righteousness? Well, it is holiness manifested in God's dealings with us. I think that is as good a definition as you can get. Or, you can look at it like this: it is that quality in God which always reveals God as doing that which is right. It is that in God which makes Him incapable of doing anything which is wrong. Righteousness and justice are the carrying out of God's holiness and the expression of it in the government of the world.

There are many ways in which this conception can be analysed and a good one is this: righteousness is the demonstration of God's *legislative holiness*. God gives His laws in order to impose upon us His righteous demands. He legislates for us. Justice, on the other hand, is God's *judicial holiness*, by which, of course, He exacts penalties from those who have been guilty of breaking His law, those who have been guilty of sin.

A further definition still is that the righteousness of God is God's love of holiness, and the justice of God is God's abomination of sin. And I think that that is the definition that most commends itself.

Now the righteousness and the justice of God, of course, are revealed almost everywhere in the Scriptures. The wrath of God is taught in both the Old and New Testaments. Our Lord Himself taught it; one of the cardinal doctrines of the whole Bible is that God has a hatred of sin which He expresses in His wrath. If anyone does not believe, says John, then 'the wrath of God abideth on him' (John 3:36). We are all by nature, says Paul, 'the children of wrath' (Eph. 2:3).

But God's righteousness and justice are not only manifested in His wrath. He reveals these same qualities in forgiving us our sins: 'If we confess our sins, he is faithful and just to forgive us our sins, and to cleanse us from all unrighteousness' (1 John 1:9). Having prepared the way of forgiveness, if we conform to it, the justice of God comes in, and by His justice God forgives us. And God prepared the way of forgiveness by providing propitiation for our sins – and this is the most remarkable thing of all. The classic statement of that is in the epistle to the Romans: 'Whom God hath set forth to be a propitiation through faith in his blood, to declare his righteousness for the remission of sins that are past, through the forbearance of God' (Rom. 3:25). It was God's justice, coupled with His love, His mercy and His compassion, that provided the offering and the sacrifice – the propitiation – that was necessary.

Another way in which God manifests His justice and His righteousness is that He always keeps His word. What He has promised He always fulfils. I shall come back to that again later on. But He always shows us that He is the vindicator of His people. Now that is the whole message of the prophet Habakkuk. You remember his problem: 'How,' says Habakkuk to himself, 'can God possibly allow His own people to suffer in this way, and those heathen, those sinful Chaldeans, to be the very people who are going to punish them and to destroy them? How can God do this kind of thing?' And his answer to the problem is this: 'It is all right,' he says. 'Don't only look at the immediate and the present; take the long view and you will find that God will manifest His righteousness and His justice. The children of Israel deserve punishment at the moment, and He is using these Chaldeans temporarily; later on, they will be routed, and destroyed. God is absolutely just, and if you take the long view you will see it.'

He also rewards the righteous. Listen to Paul putting it at the end of his life, in 2 Timothy 4:8: 'Henceforth,' he says, 'there is laid up for me a crown of righteousness, which the Lord, the righteous judge, shall give me at that day: and not to me only, but unto all them also that love his appearing.' I am not worrying about that, says Paul. He is a righteous judge, and the crown He has promised, He will certainly give. Henceforth this wonderful grace is given in Christ. God in the cross, then, is doing that.

Next, we read in Romans 3:25 that God *declares* His own righteousness and absolute justice. He is justifying His own forgiveness of the sins of those who repent. This is a very great and exalted conception. We see it finally, in this respect: God not only forgives the sins

of the sinner in salvation, He goes beyond that. He declares sinners to
be righteous; He makes them righteous. That is a very vital truth. If
we are not clear about this question of the righteousness of God and
the justice of God we might think that all that God does to us is to forgive us our sins. Not at all! Because God is righteous, we must be
made righteous also; and He *declares* us to be righteous in a legal or
forensic sense. That is justification by faith. But He also *makes* us
righteous. That is our sanctification. This will continue until ultimately we shall be without spot and blameless, without rebuke, righteous and holy, even as He is Himself.

But let me come now to the third great attribute of God under this
section of moral attributes, and here we come to the *goodness* or the
love of God. You notice the order in which we are taking them – holiness, righteousness and justice, goodness and love. It is a dangerous
and terrible thing not to put these attributes in the right order. People
have often been guilty of that, and the result is that they have made
shipwreck of their faith.

So we come now to the goodness and the love of God. In the Scriptures these two words are more or less interchangeable; sometimes
the truth is put in terms of the goodness of God, sometimes in terms
of the love of God; and the same points are covered by both these
terms.

Yet there is a kind of distinction between them, and I suggest it is
something like this: the goodness of God is that perfection of God
which prompts Him to deal bounteously and in a kindly way with all
His creatures. 'Behold therefore the goodness and severity of God,'
says Paul (Rom. 11:22). 'The Lord is good to all: and his tender
mercies are over all his works' (Ps. 145:9). Watch the terms 'good'
and 'goodness' as you read your Scriptures, and you will find they
generally cover that conception of God's bounty.

God's love is that attribute in God by which He is eternally moved
to communicate Himself to others. The Scriptures make it quite clear
that the love of God is something that communicates itself; God is
eternal, and God is eternal love. That, incidentally, will be our introduction to the doctrine of the Trinity. The very fact that God is love
is proof, in a sense, of the Trinity. Because God is eternal and eternal
love, there must have been someone whom He always loved. That
makes the doctrine of the Trinity an absolute necessity. However, for
now, we are trying to define the difference between goodness and love.

How, then, do these glorious qualities in God reveal and manifest themselves? For convenience, I have tried to put them under certain headings. First, God manifests His goodness and His love towards His creatures in general. You find this, for instance, in Matthew 5:45: 'For he maketh his sun to rise on the evil and on the good, and sendeth rain on the just and on the unjust.' That is the goodness of God to all His creatures, indiscriminately. Then we are told in Matthew 6:26 that He feeds 'the fowls of the air'. In Acts 14:17 you will find Paul arguing at Lystra that God 'left not himself without witness' in this respect, 'that he did good, and gave us rain from heaven, and fruitful seasons, filling our hearts with food and gladness'. All this is a manifestation of the goodness of God. Even when men and women have forgotten Him, and have lost their knowledge of Him, God continues to be good to them in that way.

But having said that, let us come to something more particular and still more glorious. The second way in which the goodness and the love of God manifest themselves is by means of what the Bible calls the *grace* of God. I am not surprised that the great Philip Doddridge, when he thought of this word, burst out saying, 'Grace – it is a charming sound, harmonious to mine ear!' There is no more glorious word than the word 'grace'. Grace, this great word that you find so constantly in the Scriptures, is the goodness or the love of God towards those who do not in any way deserve it. It is the unmerited goodness or love of God towards those who have forfeited every claim upon Him and His love, and who deserve judgment and condemnation.

The Bible teaches that the grace of God is the source of every blessing that is ever bestowed upon us. Everything comes out of the fountain of eternal and everlasting grace. I do commend to you a close and careful study of this word in the first two chapters of the epistle to the Ephesians. Oh, it is all goodness, all of His grace, this amazing grace of God! 'The grace of God,' says Paul to Titus, 'that bringeth salvation hath appeared to all men' (Titus 2:11). And then read Titus 3 as well; it is again a most magnificent statement about the grace of God. So read these chapters and rejoice and abandon yourself in worship as you begin to understand the wonderful love and goodness of God which He has revealed in the Lord Jesus Christ.

And the next thing in the manifestation of the goodness and the love of God is the *mercy* of God. If you like alternative terms, it is the *loving-kindness* of God, the *tender compassion* of God. All these words have their special meaning. Have you noticed how, in the salutations in many of the epistles, you have, 'Grace, mercy and peace'?

So mercy and grace are not the same thing. What, then, is mercy? It can be defined as the goodness or the love of God towards those who are in misery or distress as the result of their sin, and irrespective of their deserts. Be alert to that word 'mercy', and you will find that it means that. Psalm 103 has some glorious statements about the mercy of God. And in the introduction to Luke's Gospel, you find these words: 'He hath holpen his servant Israel, in remembrance of his mercy' (Luke 1:54). Then verses 77 and 78 read like this: He is sent, 'To give knowledge of salvation unto his people by the remission of their sins, through the tender mercy of our God.' And you find God's mercy constantly stated in the New Testament epistles. Paul says, 'Therefore hath he mercy on whom he will have mercy, and whom he will he hardeneth' (Rom. 9:18). But you will find it most of all in the salutations in the introductions to the epistles.

One other subdivision of this goodness and love of God – and what a glorious one this is again! – is the patience and longsuffering of God. Not one of us would be here tonight were it not for this! If God were not longsuffering we should all have been blotted out. But God is longsuffering. What does it mean? It means that He bears with the froward and the evil; He shows forbearance towards sinners who, in spite of all His benefits and mercies, still sin against Him. Paul puts it like this: 'Or despisest thou the riches of his goodness and forbearance and longsuffering; not knowing that the goodness of God leadeth thee to repentance?' (Rom. 2:4). He says again, 'What if God, willing to shew his wrath, and to make his power known, endured with much longsuffering the vessels of wrath fitted to destruction' (Rom. 9:22). Peter puts it clearly when he tells us that God has been patient with those spirits and beings, 'Which sometime were disobedient, when once the longsuffering of God waited in the days of Noah' (1 Pet. 3:20). And there is that famous statement in his second epistle where he says that we must 'account that the longsuffering of our Lord is salvation' (2 Pet. 3:15).

Now that brings me to the fourth moral attribute of God, and that is God's *faithfulness*. This, in a sense, is included in His righteousness and justice, and also in the idea of the immutability of God. Yet I feel, with many others, constrained to put it as a separate heading because of the emphasis which is so frequently placed upon it in the Scriptures. What does it mean? Well, I have never met with a better definition of the faithfulness of God than this: when you say that God is faithful you mean that He is one upon whom you can safely lean. It means one on whom you can absolutely rely; one upon whom you can depend; one upon whom you can stay yourself, without ever being in any doubt that He will suddenly let go and let you go.

The Bible has some glorious statements about this. It tells us that the faithfulness of God reaches unto the clouds (Ps. 36:5). It tells us endlessly that God always keeps His promises, and never breaks His covenants. It tells us that God will always fulfil every word that has ever gone out of His mouth (Isa. 55:11). It tells us that God will always faithfully and certainly defend and deliver His servants at all times of trial, testing and conflict. It tells us that God can be relied upon to confirm and to establish all whom He has called, guarding them from the evil one, and keeping them and guiding them until His purposes are fulfilled in them.

Listen to one great statement of all that: 'God is faithful, by whom ye were called unto the fellowship of his Son Jesus Christ our Lord' (1 Cor. 1:9). Whatever else may happen, whatever may be going wrong, Paul tells those people to be sure of this – God is faithful. Or, again, he says, 'And the very God of peace sanctify you wholly; and I pray God your whole spirit and soul and body be preserved blameless unto the coming of our Lord Jesus Christ' (1 Thess. 5:23). Then notice, 'Faithful is he that calleth you, who also will do it' (1 Thess. 5:24). It is absolutely certain: nothing can frustrate Him; nothing can make Him forego what He has promised; nothing can cause Him to change what He has purposed with respect to you. If you are a child of God, your ultimate destiny is absolutely sure.

Then there is another statement of this and what a comfort it is! We have sinned against Him; we cannot forgive ourselves and we do not know what to do. But this is our hope: 'If we confess our sins, he is faithful and just to forgive us our sins . . .' (1 John 1:9). He has said He will do it, and because He has said it, He will do it. He is faithful. You need not worry, therefore; cast yourself on the faithfulness of God, and tell the devil that you have been forgiven, that you have confessed your sins, and that the faithfulness of God guarantees your forgiveness.

So I would sum up this section on the faithfulness of God in this way: our Lord once turned to His followers and said, 'Have faith in God' (Mark 11:22) – that is the *Authorised (King James) Version*. But the great and saintly Hudson Taylor[1] always said that that should be

---

1. The nineteenth century founder of the China Inland Mission, now the Overseas Missionary Fellowship.

translated not so much, 'Have faith in God,' as, 'Hold on to the faith-fulness of God.' It became the motto of his life and work. Of course, that is to have faith in God, but, you see, if you put it in that way – 'Have faith in God' – the emphasis seems to be on your faith. 'It is not that,' said Hudson Taylor, 'it is the faithfulness of God that matters. When you have no faith in yourself, hold on to His faithfulness.' God is immutable. God is faithful. He will never change. That is what faith in God really means. Whatever may be happening to you, wherever you are, hold on to the faithfulness of God.

So then, far too hurriedly, I am afraid, we have dealt with the attri-butes of God. Before I leave them, let me again stress this: though for the sake of clarity, and for intellectual comprehension, we have to take them one by one, we must be very careful never to isolate any one of them in our thinking about God. God is altogether in every one of His attributes at the same time; so that we must never put up one of the attributes against another. We must never contrast the holiness of God and the mercy of God. God is holy, God is mercy – altogether, always, at the same time.

I must emphasise this because, owing to our limited minds and our limited comprehension, we have to make these distinctions. But God forbid that we should divide anything in God Himself! We cannot actually do it, of course, but we can do it falsely to our own destruc-tion. So remember at all times that the whole of God is in every attri-bute, and that God is all of these things at the same time. His love is a holy love. The tragedy of forgetting that, and of pitting His love against His justice! No, no! Everything in God is loving. Everything in God is just and righteous altogether, always. We must always pre-serve in our thinking the perfection of balance that is in God Himself.

8

The Names of God and the Holy Trinity

We have just been considering the so-called moral or communicable attributes of God, and as we did this we reminded ourselves that we are not merely concerned with some intellectual or theoretical pursuit. All this is necessary in order that we may know God, in order that we may worship Him truly, in order that we may have communion with Him, and be blessed by Him. So while we are concerned with very high doctrine, it all has a very practical purpose. The history of the Church throughout the centuries shows us very clearly that it is because people have ignored some part of the biblical teaching or revelation concerning these great doctrines, that errors and heresies and calamities have come into individual lives and into the life of the Church as a whole. So that all along we are carrying these two great thoughts together. We desire to know God – yes; but not merely that we may have knowledge, it is also that we may come into conformity with Him and with His plan for our lives. We also remind ourselves that in order to know God, we are entirely dependent upon God's revelation of Himself.

So the next thing we have to say is this: God has given us the truth about Himself and His attributes in a very special way, by applying special names to Himself; and so we come to the great subject of the names of God. You cannot read the Scriptures without noticing that certain names are given by God to Himself and the purpose of these names is again to focus attention upon some aspect or another of the being of God, the character of God. So we can regard these names of God as defining the attributes of God still more specifically.

The name always stands for the character. We often say about a man that he has 'a very good name'. We may be speaking about a doctor or a lawyer, and when we say that about him we mean that he has a good character in that respect. He has certain qualities and abilities that we like. A name, therefore, stands for who the person really is; his character, his propensities, and perfections. And whenever you find these names used of God in the Bible, you will always find that that is exactly what they do; and so you find that there are certain people in the Bible who ask God His name.

The famous incident concerning this is that of Jacob at Peniel, that fateful night when he was going back to his own country. He had become a wealthy man, everything seemed to be perfect. Yes; but there was one great difficulty. He knew that his brother Esau was coming to meet him, and he remembered his sin against him, and he was afraid. So he sent his wives and his goods – everything – across the river and remained behind alone on the other side. Then a man began to struggle with him and Jacob realised that this was something very unusual. He was conscious that there was something divine in this, so he said to the person with whom he was struggling, 'Tell me, I pray thee, thy name' (Gen. 32:29), by which he meant: Who are you? Tell me the truth about yourself. 'I have a feeling,' he said in effect, 'that you are somebody unusual. I want to know exactly.

That the name of God stands for the character of God is seen again in Psalm 22:22, 'I will declare thy name unto my brethren . . .' And, in the New Testament, you will find that our Lord's great claim just before His death upon the cross was, 'I have manifested thy name unto the men which thou gavest me' (John 17:6). Later He said, 'I have declared unto them thy name' (v. 26). To declare the name of God is to tell the truth about God. It is to put this great truth about God's being in a form that men and women can grasp and apprehend.

So then, let us note some of the names which are ascribed to God in the Scriptures, and the meaning which they carry. First of all is the name *El*. This means being first, being supreme. It carries the idea of strength and of power – mightiness. Then the next name is *Elohim*, which is plural in form. This again carries the idea that God is someone who is to be feared as well as someone who is powerful, and this is the name that God generally uses when He is speaking of Himself in terms of creation. Then the next name is *Elyon*, which means the high and exalted One. You see, each one of these names tells us something in particular about God and as it is used in the narrative, it is meant to convey a particular impression with regard to God's person and personality.

Then there is the great name *Adonai*, meaning the Almighty Lord, the Ruler to whom everything is subject and to whom people are related as servants. It is the name that was, therefore, frequently used by God when addressing the children of Israel. Now all these names describe God as a transcendent God, great and high and mighty and uplifted in His glory.

But then, again, we thank God that He has not stopped at that, because God has given Himself certain other names which are designed to show the relationship of that exalted, eternal, almighty being to His creatures and His creation. For instance, there is the term *Shaddai*. Now this describes God as possessing all power in heaven and in earth, but especially God as subjecting all these and making them subservient to the work of His grace. Now you see the importance of that. This name describes God in His power over the elements, in His power over nature and creation. Yes, but not merely His power, it particularly emphasises God's control of all these things for the purpose of His grace and of His mercy, and of His dealings with men and women. For example, He controls the wind, the rain and the snow in order that we may have food to eat. That is the meaning of *Shaddai*.

But, after all, the most important and the most significant name for us is the great name *Yahweh* (translated *Jehovah* in the AV). This, the Bible itself tells us, is the best name of all. It means that God describes Himself as *I am that I am*. Or you could translate it as *I shall be what I shall be*. And both are true. The name describes, therefore, His unchangeableness, and especially His unchangeableness in His relationship to His people. Perhaps the best way to think of it is this: the name carries the meaning that God is the self-existent One – I am who I am; I shall be whom I shall be – who nevertheless does reveal Himself to His people. It carries both the ideas together.

Thus you can describe this name *Jehovah* as the great covenant name of God. You find the Bible saying that God has entered into covenants with His people. He made a covenant with Adam. He made a covenant with Noah. He made a covenant with His own Son. God is a God who makes covenants – He promises, he covenants, to do certain things. Now when He does that you generally find that He describes Himself by that great name *Jehovah*. And what a wonderful conception it is! This almighty being, whom we worship, who is self-existent in Himself, nevertheless chooses to reveal and manifestly to bind Himself to mere creatures of time like ourselves; to those whom He has brought into being.

But you will find in the Scriptures that certain qualifying terms are very often added to this great name of Jehovah. Take, for instance, the name *Jehovah-sabaoth* – 'the Lord of hosts' (1 Sam. 1:3). Now there has been a great deal of discussion as to the meaning of the term *sabaoth*. Some say it means the stars in the heavens; others say that it means the armies of Israel. But I think we are probably safer in thinking that the 'hosts' – Jehovah of hosts, Jehovah of *sabaoth* – refer to the angels. He is the Almighy self-existent One, who is the Lord of all the angelic hosts.

Then there is the great name *Jehovah-jireh*, the name which God gave to Abraham when he was about to offer his son Isaac. The provision for the sacrifice – the ram – was found in the thicket, and Abraham spoke this name *Jehovah-jireh* – 'The Lord will provide' (Gen. 22:14).

Then, also, a name was given by God to Moses just after the Exodus: *Jehovah-ropheh* – the Lord that heals. God said to the people after He had sweetened the bitter waters of Marah for them, 'If thou wilt diligently hearken to the voice of the Lord thy God, and wilt do that which is right in his sight, and wilt give ear to his commandments, and keep all his statutes, I will put none of these diseases upon thee, which I have brought upon the Egyptians, for I am the Lord that healeth thee' (Exod. 15:26).

The next name is *Jehovah-nissi*: the Lord my banner. The children of Israel had been fighting the enemy, and God reminded them that He was with them, and that He would be with them. He would be their banner under which they would conquer and prevail (Exod. 17:15).

Then *Jehovah-shalom* was the name by which God revealed Himself to Gideon. You will find it in Judges 6:24: it means, the Lord sends peace; the Lord our peace. He is indeed the God of peace. It was as the God of peace that He brought again from the dead our Lord Jesus, that great shepherd of the sheep (Heb. 13:20) and He had revealed Himself as the Lord of peace way back in the lawless time of the Judges.

Then there is the very beautiful name in Psalm 23: the Lord my Shepherd – *Jehovah-ro'eh*. 'The Lord is my shepherd; I shall not want.' And in Jeremiah 23:6 you will find *Jehovah-tsidkenu*: the Lord our Righteousness. You will find it in capital letters in many Bibles – THE LORD OUR RIGHTEOUSNESS. And then, *Jehovah-shammah*: the Lord is present. That is in Ezekiel 48:35: 'The Lord is there.' So you see that every one of these names carries with it a very great and wonderful meaning, full of comfort and consolation. And the purpose, in a sense, of preaching the Scriptures and expounding them is that these names of God, and their meaning and significance, should be brought home to us.

As our blessed Lord Himself said, 'I have manifested thy name unto the men which thou gavest me out of the world' (John 17:6) – He had been revealing God in all these characteristics. He had been teaching His followers how to think of God, and how to know Him. He had shown them that God must not be thought of as some vague Energy. No, no. God is personal and as a person He acts and reveals Himself. It is through the names that God gives to Himself that He tells us this wonderful truth about Himself. And it is as we come to know God in terms of these names that we will find peace and comfort and joy in believing.

Our trouble is that we will believe that preaching God is sufficient, without really troubling to find out all that He has told us about Himself. But God has given us all this revelation about Himself, and finally He has revealed Himself in the person of His Son, the greatest name of all, the Lord Himself. He is Emmanuel – God with us, the mighty ruler, the eternal God, who has come down among us and into time.

Well, I am afraid I shall have to leave this question of the names of God. But as we read our Scriptures and as we meditate upon these names, we shall find that they have a great wealth of teaching. Sometimes we realise very little of this and thereby impoverish our experience.

But now, having said that, let me go on to what many would say is the greatest, the most vital and the most important aspect of this exalted doctrine of God, and that is, of course, the doctrine of the blessed *Holy Trinity*. Even in considering the names of God and His various attributes, we have, in a sense, been preparing ourselves for this great doctrine. But whether you recognise that or not, no one can read the Bible without, of necessity, coming face to face with this doctrine of the Trinity. Now I have said more than once during the course of these lectures that I have felt very much like Moses at the burning bush, and I have heard a voice saying to me, 'Be careful; take your shoes from off your feet because the ground whereon you are standing is holy ground.'

Well, if we have felt that hitherto, how much more must we feel it as we consider this exalted doctrine of the Holy Trinity. For it is beyond any question the most mysterious and the most difficult of all biblical doctrines. There is no doctrine which shows so clearly what we agreed about at the very beginning – our absolute dependence upon the revelation that we have in the Scriptures. No human being would have thought of the doctrine of the Trinity. It comes directly from the Bible and from nowhere else at all. Men and women have thought of God; they have their gods; but no one has ever thought of the Trinity.

Another comment I would make, as we approach this doctrine, is that there is no question at all but that the doctrine of the Trinity is the most distinctive doctrine of the Christian faith. This may come as a surprise to some of you, but I hope to establish it as we go along. Does it not occur to you, therefore, in the light of this, that it is rather a curious thing that we hear so little about this doctrine? I speak in particular to those who are evangelical Christians: Why is it that we have emphasised this doctrine so little?

I have no doubt that the answer is because of its difficulty, because of its mystery. But that is no excuse. Indeed, every doctrine which we find in the Scriptures we must regard as from God, and there is none more important than this. I fear it is another example of the laziness that has come upon us – the desire for comfort, and the tendency to rest upon experiences, and to avoid anything that demands intellectual effort. But if we have neglected the doctrine of the Trinity, shame on us! It is, in a sense, the most exalted and the most glorious of all doctrines; the most amazing and astonishing thing that God has been pleased to reveal to us concerning Himself.

How, then, do we approach this doctrine? I start at once by saying that we must not attempt to do so in terms of philosophy. I put it like that because many people think they can explain the doctrine of the Trinity in those terms. They have used illustrations like this: they have said that the doctrine of the Trinity is comparable to the sun and the rays coming out of the sun; others have compared it to the seed and the soil and the flower, you see the unity and yet the division, the three in one and the one in three, they say.

But I feel that all these attempts to understand the doctrine of the Trinity philosophically not only do not help us, but are probably very dangerous to us. It seems to me that there is only one thing to do, and that is to acknowledge that we stand before the mystery which is revealed in the Bible. We cannot hope to understand it. We cannot hope to grasp it with our minds; it is entirely beyond us and above us. We are simply meant to look at it with wonder, with awe and with worship, and be amazed at it.

If I would venture to say even half a word philosophically, I would say that, as we have said in passing, the doctrine of God as love, or emphasising that one of God's attributes is love, does seem to me in and of itself to imply a plurality of Persons in the Godhead. If the eternal God is love, then He has always loved, before creation, before time. But who has He loved? Does this not almost of necessity insist upon the Trinity? And that is really what the Bible teaches, that the three blessed Persons in the Trinity have loved one another perfectly from all eternity. But you need not even accept that. I simply put it to you as a suggestion in passing.

No, let us come back and look at the word, and discover what the Bible itself has to tell us. Now you will notice as you go right through it that no single explicit statement of this doctrine is made. Nowhere in the Bible will you find a statement that God is three Persons – Father, Son and Holy Spirit. But by implication the doctrine of the Trinity, as we shall come to see, is to be found in the Old Testament and in the New. It is suggested everywhere and in the most unlikely and unexpected places.

But before I give you that evidence, let me lay down certain points which are of vital importance in this connection. The doctrine of the Trinity does not mean that there are three Gods – what is called *tritheism*. We have to make this negative statement, because the Unitarians are always ready to charge Christians with believing in three Gods. They say, 'You call us Unitarians; we call you Tritheists, with your doctrine of Father, Son, and Spirit. You are really talking about three Gods.'

Now we reject tritheism completely. The particular emphasis throughout the Old Testament is that there is only one true and living God. We read, 'Hear, O Israel: The Lord our God is one Lord' (Deut. 6:4). That was the message that was repeated constantly to the children of Israel, and it was absolutely essential, of course, because the children of Israel were the one nation in the world who had been given this information and this knowledge. They were surrounded by nations who believed in a variety of gods. The problem in the time of the Old Testament was the problem of polytheism; people believed in the various gods of war and peace, and so on – Baal, Asherah, Jupiter, Mars, Mercury – all these various gods – and above everything else the children of Israel were called to proclaim the unity of God and the fact that there is only one God.

Our Lord, in effect, said the same thing when He used the words, 'I and my Father are one' (John 10:30). Not two. Then you will find that James also makes this point. He says, 'Thou believest that there is one God . . .' (Jas. 2:19). So, then, as we consider this great and blessed doctrine of the Holy Trinity, whether we finally understand what we are saying or not, we must keep on saying that we do not believe in three Gods. There is only one God.

But, second, I lay down this postulate: while God in His innermost nature is one, He nevertheless exists as three Persons. Now we are already in trouble, are we not? Do you not want to ask me at this point: Are you saying that there are three Persons, different in essence? If you are – then there must be three Gods? To which my reply is this: 'Hear, O Israel: Jehovah, our God, is one Jehovah.' I must say that.

What is the trouble, therefore? Well, the trouble, once more, is due to the inadequacy of language. We have to talk about 'persons' because we cannot think of a higher category than persons, and as we think of persons we think of individuals, and we are separating them. But as the Bible uses these expressions, they obviously mean something different. Now I do not pretend to understand. Nobody understands. The greatest minds in the Church throughout the centuries have been grappling with this and trying to explain it, and they cannot understand it. So they can do nothing beyond what we are doing now. They say that God is one, but nevertheless that God, who is one, in His ultimate innermost nature exists as three Persons.

Let me give you the statement of the famous *Westminster Confession of Faith* with regard to this doctrine: 'There are three Persons within the Godhead – the Father, the Son, and the Holy Spirit; and these three are one God, the same in substance, equal in power and glory.' I would strongly recommend that you buy a copy of the Westminster Confession . You will find some of these great definitions there in their most convenient form. That is what it says about this great doctrine of the Trinity, which I can put like this: the Father is God, the Son is also God, not two Gods, but the same God in essence. The same eternal being is Father and Son.

We must say this; the first verse in the first chapter of the Gospel of John makes us do so: 'In the beginning was the Word, and the Word was with God, and the Word was God.' It seems to be contradictory, but it is true. That is what I am trying to say. The Word is God as the Father is God, and yet there are not two Gods – there is only one Godhead. Again, I remind you that our Lord said, 'I and My Father are One.'

You will also find the apostle Paul saying, 'Christ . . . who is over all, God blessed for ever' (Rom. 9:5). In Colossians 2:9, Paul says, 'For in him dwelleth all the fulness of the Godhead bodily.' Then in Titus 2:13 we are told to look for 'that blessed hope, and the glorious appearing of the great God and our Saviour Jesus Christ.' Jesus Christ is God. Not only is the Father God but the Son is God. There are explicit statements of that.

But not only that; you cannot read your Gospels without finding that attributes are ascribed to the Lord Jesus Christ which can only be ascribed to God, His eternity, for instance: 'Before Abraham was, I am' (John 8:58); He does not hesitate to say it. Then there is His holiness; also His life. Our Lord says, 'For as the Father hath life in himself: so hath he given to the Son to have life in himself' (John 5:26). And He also says, 'As thou hast given him power over all flesh, that he should give eternal life to as many as thou hast given him' (John 17:2). That is only true of God. Then there is His immutability: 'Jesus Christ the same yesterday, and to day, and for ever' (Heb. 13:8). You may remember that we considered that in considering the attributes of God.

Next His omnipotence: 'All power is given unto me in heaven and in earth' (Matt. 28:18). Nothing is impossible to Him. Then His omnipresence: 'Lo,' he says, 'I am with you alway, even unto the end of the world' (Matt. 28:20). His omniscience: Jesus knew everything; nothing was hidden from Him. He knew what was in a person, and He did not need anybody to tell Him (see John 2:25). He knew people's thoughts. He could say to Nathanael: 'When thou wast under the fig tree, I saw thee' (John 1:48). He could read the innermost thoughts and imaginations of men and women. It was through Him that all things were created. It is by Him that all things subsist. He has a right, He tells us, to judge (John 5:27), and He will be the Judge. Thus you see that attributes of deity and of the Godhead are freely ascribed to Him. So we say that the Father is God and we say that the Son is God.

Yes, but we must also say that the Holy Spirit is God. Do you remember the terrible words that were spoken by Peter to Ananias and Sapphira? He said, 'Ananias, why hath Satan filled thine heart to lie to the Holy Ghost . . . thou hast not lied unto men, but unto God' (Acts 5:34). You have been lying, he said, to the Holy Spirit, and because you have been lying to the Holy Spirit you have been lying to God.

Then we are told in the New Testament about the blasphemy against the Holy Spirit: our Lord said, 'All manner of sin and blasphemy shall be forgiven unto men: but the blasphemy against the Holy Ghost shall not be forgiven unto men' (Matt. 12:31) and you will find the same in the parallel passages.

There is also the baptismal formula found at the end of Matthew's Gospel: '. . . baptizing them in the name of the Father, and of the Son, and of the Holy Ghost' (Matt. 28:19). And the ápostolic benediction says, 'The grace of the Lord Jesus Christ, and the love of God, and the communion of the Holy Ghost, be with you all' (2 Cor. 13:14). So, you see, the Bible asserts that the Holy Spirit, in the same way as the Father and the Son, is also God. There are also many other examples in the Scriptures where the three Persons refer to one another. You find our Lord referring to 'another Comforter' (John 14:16), whom He and the Father are going to send; and so on.

There are those who have tried to deny the doctrine of the Holy Trinity in this way: they say, 'There are not three Persons, there is only one Person, there is only one God; but that one God can reveal Himself in different ways. He once revealed Himself as the Father; then at other times He reveals Himself as the Son; and again at other times He reveals Himself as the Holy Spirit.' And they try to use human analogies to help us to understand: they say, for example, that the same man can be a husband and a father and a preacher – one person in three relationships.

But the Bible rejects all that. Father, Son, and Spirit are not merely modes in which God appears. No, no. There are three Persons in the Godhead. The Persons refer to each other; Christ spoke about the others and referred to the others, not meaning Himself but the other Persons in the Holy Trinity. So we reject any teaching that there is only one God who shows Himself in these different forms. Furthermore, this can be proved quite conclusively, since we find the Scriptures naming the three Persons together. For instance, when the annunciation was made to the virgin Mary about the birth of her Son, the three Persons were mentioned: the power of God, the power of the Spirit, and the power of the Son who would be born (Luke 1:26–38).

You see this again at the baptism. There was the Son in the river; the Holy Spirit descended upon Him in the form of a dove; and the voice of God the Father was heard saying, 'This is my beloved Son, in whom I am well pleased' (Matt. 3:13–17). Then in this connection, study very carefully chapters 14, 15 and 16 of John's Gospel. In John 15:26 you will find that put perfectly in this way: 'But when the Comforter is come, whom I will send unto you from the Father, even the Spirit of truth, which proceedeth from the Father, he shall testify of me.' Here the Son is speaking about the Comforter, whom the Father is going to send. And again I would remind you of the baptismal formula and the apostolic benediction.

Even in the Old Testament there is much teaching about the Holy Spirit and about the Son. Now you would not expect to find the doctrine of the Trinity expounded as clearly in the Old Testament as in the New, for the reason that I have given – the constant threat of polytheism. But, in addition to that, you obviously could not have had a complete or explicit doctrine of the Trinity until the Son had appeared incarnate, and until He had sent the Holy Spirit. It was only then that men and women could possibly receive the doctrine, and even now, as we have found, it is a holy and a mysterious doctrine, and difficult to grasp.

But it is there in the Old Testament. In the very first chapter of Genesis you will find the doctrine of the Trinity quite plainly, if you will look for it. Take that name of God – *Elohim*. It is a plural term. God speaks of Himself in the plural. Do you remember what He says about the creation of man in Genesis 1:26: 'Let *us* make man in *our* image.' Why is that? There is only one adequate explanation; it is because of the blessed Holy Trinity. Then when man had sinned, it is stated of him in Genesis 3:22: '. . . Behold, the man is become as one of *us* . . .' And then in connection with the Tower of Babel, in Genesis 11:7, we read: 'Let *us* go down, and there confound their language . . .' And then you find it in Isaiah chapter 6:8: 'Also I heard the voice of the Lord, saying, Whom shall I send, and who will go for *us*?' You see, these very terms suggest the Trinity.

Then you remember that in one of the earlier lectures we referred to the Angel of the Covenant, to whom so many references are made in the Old Testament, and we were driven to the only possible conclusion – that the Angel of the Covenant is none other than the Lord Jesus Christ Himself. Yes; in that form He revealed Himself. It was not His incarnation; it was a theophany, an appearance of the Son as the Angel of the Covenant.

And you remember, too, the references to the Holy Spirit away back at the beginning of Genesis. We are told that the Spirit 'brooded' upon the waste. It was the Spirit who enabled the prophets to speak. It was the Spirit who came upon Bezaleel and enabled him to do skilled work in the building of the tabernacle (Exod. 31:2–5). Thus you see that there is a wealth of teaching in the Old as well as the New Testament with regard to this great doctrine of the Holy Trinity.

Let me ask a final question: What is the relationship between the three Persons? The answer in the Scriptures everywhere is that they are co-eternal; there is no subordination as such. When the Son is called the Son, it does not mean that He is subordinate or any less than His Father. The fact that He is the Son means that He is equal to the Father. He is 'the express image of his person' (Heb. 1:3) – not subordinated to Him or different from Him. He is the same as and equal to the Father of whom He is the Son.

Very well, I can sum it up like this: the Trinity has existed in the Godhead from all eternity. A statement of the *Athanasian Creed* with regard to this gives a perfect definition: 'The Father is God, the Son is God, and the Holy Ghost is God; and yet there are not three Gods but one God. The Father is Lord, the Son is Lord, the Holy Ghost is Lord, and yet there are not three Lords but one Lord. For as we are compelled by Christian truth to acknowledge each Person by Himself to be God and Lord, so we are forbidden by the same truth to say that there are three Gods or three Lords.' And in reality you can never get beyond that. The scriptural truth, the Christian truth, insists upon our saying that there are three Persons, and yet we must not say that there are three Gods. This is a great and eternal mystery.

But – and in many ways this is the most glorious aspect of this doctrine – though the three Persons in the Trinity are co-equal and co-eternal, for the purposes of our salvation you have what has sometimes been called the *economic Trinity*. A division is made among the three Persons, and, for the purposes of this work and of this salvation, there is a kind of subjugation of the three Persons. The Father creates; the Father elects; the Father planned salvation. The Son was sent by the Father to work out this salvation. The Holy Spirit was sent by the Father and the Son to apply the salvation.

Now that is a staggering thought. That these three blessed Persons in the blessed Holy Trinity for my salvation have thus divided up the work. The Son has put Himself at the disposal of the Father, and the Spirit has put Himself at the disposal of the Father and the Son. The Spirit does not speak of Himself, but testifies to the Son. The Son did not speak of Himself, but received His words and His works from the Father, though He was equal and eternal – the economic Trinity. So that while, in a sense, we can say that it was the Father who sent the Son, and the Son who came and did the work, and the Spirit applied it, we must at the same time say this: God was in it all. 'God was in Christ' reconciling the world unto himself, not imputing their trespasses unto them' (2 Cor. 5:19). There was a kind of division of labour and yet a unity in purpose and a unity in doing it all.

Well, I told you when I began that we were approaching the greatest mystery in the Bible and in the Christian faith – the most exalted and the most sublime truth. May I beg of you, do not try to understand all this with your minds. It is for us humbly and as little children to receive the truth as it is revealed; to stand in worship, in adoration and amazement. It is beyond us, but it is true. And it is all true in a special way for us and for our salvation.

9

The Eternal Decrees of God

In our consideration of these biblical doctrines we come now to a new section of the particular doctrine with which we have been dealing, namely the doctrine of God. You will recall that we have considered what the Bible tells us about the being, the nature, and the character of God as He has been pleased to reveal that to us in the Scriptures. We have also considered the names which God has applied to Himself as a part of this revelation of His essential being, and His relationship with creation. And that, in turn, brought us to the consideration of the great, mighty and inscrutable doctrine of the blessed Holy Trinity.

Now, still considering the doctrine of God, we come on to the next section, which is obviously this: the works of God; the activity of God; what it is that God has done. This is a kind of subsection or branch of this general doctrine concerning God Himself. And the question is: What comes next? What do we proceed to consider? We are about to consider the works of God, so if you were asked the question: 'What do you think comes next in the biblical sequence and in the logical order?' I wonder what your answer would be. I may be wrong, but I think if I were to put the question many would be likely to say that obviously we come on immediately to the doctrine of creation.

Now, of course, there is one sense in which that would be the correct answer, but actually it seems to me that it is not, although you will find, if you look up certain books which deal with these matters, that that is precisely what they do. You could quote quite a number of authorities who do go directly from the doctrine of God's nature and character to the question of creation. But that seems to me to be quite wrong. It is unscriptural, and therefore it is not the right and true thing to do.

Before we come to consider the doctrine of creation, there is something that we must consider first, and we do so because the Bible tells us about it. It is this: the Bible, before it tells us what God has done, leads us to the character of all God's activities. There is a great deal in the Bible, as I want to try to show you, about the way in which God does things, and it is important that we should consider that before we consider exactly what He has done.

There are certain great principles which underlie and characterise all God's works. In other words, before God proceeded to create the world and man, God had thought, God had willed and had determined on certain things. So this consideration must come in at this point. Certain things were decided in the eternal mind and counsel of God before He did anything at all in the matter of actual creation, and it does seem to me therefore that this is the obvious chronological (if one may use such a term), certainly the obvious logical sequence which should be followed.

Now the description which is given in the Bible of God's manner or method of working, is what is commonly called the doctrine of the *eternal decrees of God*. These are things which God determined and ordained before He had done anything at all. Now I want to admit very frankly that I am again calling your attention to an extremely difficult subject. I do not apologise for that because, as I shall show you, this is not a question of choice. The business of someone expounding the Bible is to expound the whole Bible. But I do admit that it is a very difficult subject, and I imagine that that is why many of the books do not include it. But it is so scriptural that it must be faced. It is like the doctrine of the Holy Trinity – beyond our minds, in a sense. But as we saw with that doctrine, we must not avoid it just because it is difficult.

For your encouragement, however, I think I can promise you that some of these primary, preliminary doctrines are the most difficult because we are dealing with the mind of the Eternal, and are therefore considering something which is beyond our finite understanding and the grasp of our puny and pygmy intellects. From one standpoint the doctrines of man and of creation and salvation, are of necessity very much easier.

'But,' somebody may say, 'in view of its difficulty and inscrutability, why consider it at all? Why not take us straight on to the doctrines of creation and of man and of the fall? That is what we are really interested in; that is what we want to know.' Well, certain answers must be given to such an objection. My first reason for calling your attention to this doctrine, as I have said, is that it is revealed in the Bible, and because of that, it is obviously meant for our consideration and study.

May I put it like this: Is it not rather surprising to notice and to consider how prone we are to read only parts of the Bible? I wonder whether you read the ninth chapter of the epistle to the Romans as often as you read the eighth? If you are a haphazard Bible reader you probably do not. Now we have no right to pick and choose with the Bible. We have already agreed that it is the inspired Word of God. If I believe that about the Bible from cover to cover, I must take my *whole* Bible. The fact that there are parts which baffle me must not keep me from it. I must read the whole and must grapple with it all; I must try to understand it all. And as this great doctrine of the decrees of God is in the Bible, then it is my business to study it.

Another reason is this – and I think you will agree with me when we have finished with it – that it will reveal to us fresh aspects of the glory of God Himself. It will give us, as it were, a greater and a grander conception of God, and that in turn will promote our worship of God. I am never tired of saying that the real difficulty of evangelism today is that we do not spend sufficient time with the doctrine of God. We are so interested in a subjective experience and subjective salvation that we forget this great doctrine of God Himself; and it accounts for many of our troubles and problems. The more we know about God in His infinity, the more we shall worship Him.

So another reason for considering this doctrine is that it will save us from many errors. Most of the errors into which men and women have fallen throughout the centuries, and many other questions which have arisen, have been due to the fact that they have never quite realised as they should the Bible's teaching with regard to the eternal decrees of God.

And my last reason for calling your attention to it is that, speaking for myself, I know of nothing that gives me greater consolation than this particular doctrine. I do not hesitate to say that nothing gives me greater comfort than to know that behind me, little creature as I am passing through this world of time, there is this doctrine of the eternal decrees of God Himself.

Very well, then, if that is why we are considering it, let me say just a word on how we are going to consider it, and this is most important. The first thing you always have to do when you are considering this doctrine is to get rid of your prejudices and any kind of party spirit. By 'party spirit' I mean that we all tend to take up certain positions and, without knowing it, we are sometimes much more concerned to defend what we think we have always believed, than to find out the truth.

The other negative is that we must not approach this subject philosophically. I know I keep on talking about this! Philosophy is a great curse in the realm of the Christian faith, because philosophy by definition is always something that tries to understand everything as a whole. That is the quest of philosophy – to span everything with the human mind. But we are now dealing with something for which the mind is utterly inadequate. So we must realise that as we approach this subject there are aspects of it which, by definition, we are not going to understand.

Therefore, positively, we must approach the subject with humility; we must approach it with reverence; we must approach it by faith, and with a ready admission of our own limits. We must approach it with an open mind, seeking and searching for the teaching of the Scriptures. We must come in a childlike spirit, ready to receive what is revealed to us, and ready, may I add, not to ask questions beyond the revelation of the Scriptures.

Indeed, I am increasingly coming to think of faith in this way: faith is a readiness to submit oneself to the biblical limits. It is a readiness not to ask questions about things which are not revealed in the Scriptures. Faith is saying, 'Very well; I will take all that is given, and I do not want to know more than that; I am content with the revelation.' We must approach this great doctrine in this way.

Above all, we shall have to realise that there are certain things which we, with our finite minds, will not be able to reconcile with one another. Now I am trying to avoid the use of technical terms as far as I can, but here I must introduce the word *antinomy* – not antimony. What is an antinomy? It is a position in which you are given two truths which you yourself cannot reconcile. There are certain final antinomies in the Bible, and as people of faith we must be ready to accept that. When somebody says, 'Oh, but you cannot reconcile those two,' you must be ready to say, 'I cannot. I do not pretend to be able to. I do not know. I believe what I am told in the Scriptures.'

So, then, we approach this great doctrine like this: in the light of the things we have already considered about the being, the nature, and the character of God, this doctrine of the eternal decrees must follow as an utter, absolute necessity. Because God is who and what He is, He must work in the way in which He does work. As we have seen, all the doctrines in the Bible are consistent with one another, and when we are considering any particular doctrine we must remember that it must always be consistent with everything else. So as we come to study what the Bible tells us about the way in which God works, we must be very careful not to say anything that contradicts what we have already said about His omniscience, His omnipotence, and all the other things that we have agreed together are to be found in the Scriptures.

Now, having said all that, let me come to a positive statement of the doctrine, and in order to make it clear I shall put it in the form of a number of principles. The first is that *from eternity God has had an unchangeable plan with reference to His creatures*. The Bible is constantly using a phrase like this – 'before the foundation of the world' (see Eph. 1:4). As the apostle Paul said about our Lord's birth, 'When the fulness of the time was come . . .' (Gal. 4:4).

We can put this negatively: God never does anything half-heartedly. There is never anything uncertain about His activities. If I may put it in still another form, God never has an afterthought. Remember that we have agreed that He is omniscient and omnipresent, that He knows everything from the beginning to the end, so He cannot have an afterthought. Nothing is accidental, haphazard, uncertain or fortuitous. God has a definite plan and purpose about creation, about men and women, about salvation, about the whole of life in this world, about the end of it all, about the ultimate destiny. Everything that God has done and has brought to pass is according to His own eternal plan, and it is fixed, certain, unchangeable, and absolute. That is the first statement.

The second is that *the plan of God comprehends and determines all things and events of every kind that come to pass*. If you believe that God has determined certain ends, then you must believe that He determines everything that leads to those ends. If you believe that God decided to create at a given point, that He decided that the end of the world, according to time, is to take place at a given point, surely, if the end is determined, everything that leads to that end must also be determined; and you realise that there is also a kind of interrelationship between all events and things that happen, and that all are leading to that end. So the doctrine of the eternal decrees of God says that all things are ultimately determined and decreed by Him.

Therefore, if everything is determined by God it must include, of necessity, the free actions, the voluntary actions of free and voluntary agents. Now that is a fundamental statement; let me break it up a little and give you the scriptural evidence. With regard to the whole system, this is put very plainly by the apostle Paul. He says, 'That in the dispensation of the fulness of times he might gather together in one all things in Christ, both which are in heaven, and which are on earth; even in him: in whom also we have obtained an inheritance, being predestinated according to the purpose of him who worketh all things after the counsel of his own will' (Eph. 1:10–11). Now that applies to everything. Paul is speaking there of the whole cosmos being united in Christ, and he says that God is going to bring this to pass in that way.

Then there is further scriptural evidence to show that God, in this way, governs and controls and determines events that appear to us to be quite fortuitous. In the book of Proverbs we read, 'The lot is cast into the lap; but the whole disposing thereof is of the Lord' (Prov. 16:33). We call a 'lot' a matter of chance and of accident, do we not? You 'cast' a lot. Yes, says this passage in Scripture, 'but the whole disposing thereof is of the Lord'. Or in the New Testament we read that our Lord says, 'Are not two sparrows sold for a farthing? and one of them shall not fall on the ground without your Father' (Matt. 10:29). A little sparrow drops dead and falls on to the ground. Accident, you say. Chance. Not at all! 'Not one of them shall fall on the ground without your Father.' The life of a little sparrow is in the hands of God. But, He continues, 'The very hairs of your head are all numbered' (v. 30). There are events which appear to be quite accidental, but they are controlled by God.

Then take our free actions. Read Proverbs 21:1: 'The king's heart is in the hand of the Lord, as the rivers of water: he turneth it whithersoever he will.' The king appears to be free, but God is controlling him as He controls the very rivers. Ephesians 2:10 tells us, 'For we are his workmanship, created in Christ Jesus unto good works, which God hath before ordained that we should walk in them.' And in Philippians 2:13 we are told, 'For it is God which worketh in you both to will and to do of his good pleasure.'

But come to something more extraordinary and striking: the Scripture teaches us that *even sinful actions are in the hands of God*. Listen to Peter preaching on the Day of Pentecost at Jerusalem: 'Him, being delivered by the determinate counsel and foreknowledge of God, ye have taken, and by wicked hands have crucified and slain' (Acts 2:23). Then Peter puts it like this in Acts 4:27–8: 'For of a truth against thy holy child Jesus, whom thou hast anointed, both Herod, and Pontius Pilate, with the Gentiles, and the people of Israel, were gathered together' – notice – 'for to do whatsoever thy hand and thy counsel determined before to be done.' The terrible sin of those men was determined beforehand by the counsel of God.

And then you have a striking example of the same thing in the book of Genesis, the famous statement of Joseph to his brethren. Joseph, retailing the facts of his story, turned to his brothers and said, 'So now it was not you that sent me hither, but God . . .' (Gen. 45:8). From our standpoint it was they who had done it. They had done a dastardly thing, a very wicked thing, for mercenary motives and as the result of their own jealousy. 'But,' said Joseph, 'it was not you that sent me hither, but God.' These sinful actions came under this great eternal decree of God.

Now let us be clear about this. In view of what we have already agreed about the holiness of God, we must at once say this: God does not cause evil in any sense or in any degree. He does not approve of evil. But·He permits the wicked agents to perform it and then He overrules it for His own wise and holy ends.

Or take it like this if you prefer: the same decree of God which ordains the moral law that prohibits and punishes sin, also permits its occurrence. But it limits it and determines the precise channel to which it shall be confined, and the precise end to which it shall be directed, and overrules its consequences for good. The Bible clearly teaches us that. Listen again to this account of Joseph and his brethren in Genesis 50:20: 'But as for you,' said Joseph, 'ye thought evil against me; but God meant it unto good, to bring to pass, as it is this day, to save much people alive.' And I suppose in many ways the most striking example of all is to be found in the betrayal of Jesus by Judas: a free and voluntary action, and yet a part of God's great eternal purpose and plan.

Now that brings me to my third general proposition, which is that *all the decrees of God are unconditional and sovereign.* They are not dependent in any sense on human actions. They are not determined by anything that people may or may not do. God's decrees are not even determined in the light of what He knows people are going to do. They are absolutely unconditional. They do not depend upon anything except God's own will and God's own holiness.

But – and I want to make this quite clear – that does not mean that there is no such thing as cause and effect in life. That does not mean that there are no such things as conditional actions. There is such a thing in nature and in life as cause and effect – yes. But what this doctrine says is that every cause and effect, and free actions, are part of the decree of God Himself. He has determined to work in that particular way. God has decreed that the end which He has in view shall certainly and inevitably be brought to pass, and that nothing can hinder or frustrate it.

Now let me give you my evidence for all this. Take the prophecy of Daniel: 'And all the inhabitants of the earth are reputed as nothing: and he doeth according to his will in the army of heaven, and among the inhabitants of the earth: and none can stay his hand, or say unto him, What doest thou?' (Dan. 4:35). Nothing can stay the hand of God or even question it. Or listen to our Lord stating this very thing in Matthew 11:25–6: 'I thank thee, O Father, Lord of heaven and earth, because thou hast hid these things from the wise and prudent, and hast revealed them unto babes. Even so, Father: for so it seemed good in thy sight.' Why has God withheld these things from the 'wise and prudent', and 'revealed them unto babes'? There is only one answer – it is that 'even so' it seemed good in His sight.

Paul also says the same thing: 'Having predestinated us unto the adoption of children by Jesus Christ to himself, according to the good pleasure of his will' (Eph. 1:5). I do commend to you a careful study of the first half of that first chapter of the epistle to the Ephesians. Observe all it says, and you will know that everything that God has done is always 'according to the good pleasure of his will'. Nothing else at all. It is entirely of grace.

But, of course, you find this doctrine stated most clearly of all in that great and mighty ninth chapter of the epistle to the Romans. I want at this point especially to emphasise verse 11. You will find that it is a verse in brackets; but what a verse! What a statement! '(For the children being not yet born, neither having done any good or evil, that the purpose of God according to election might stand, not of works, but of him that calleth.)' Paul's argument is that God had decreed that the elder should serve the younger because before either of them were ever born he had said, 'Jacob have I loved, but Esau have I hated' (v. 13).

'Why,' you ask, 'did God love Jacob and hate Esau? Was it because of what they did?' No. Before they were ever born, before they were ever conceived, God had chosen Jacob and not Esau. It had nothing to do with their works in any respect.

God's purpose is unconditional and absolutely sovereign. Listen to Paul again: 'What shall we say then? Is there unrighteousness with God? God forbid' (Rom. 9:14). God forbid that you should even think it! It is impossible:

> For he saith to Moses, I will have mercy on whom I will have mercy, and I will have compassion on whom I will have compassion. So then it is not of him that willeth, nor of him that runneth, but of God that sheweth mercy. For the scripture saith unto Pharaoh, Even for this same purpose have I raised thee up, that I might shew my power in thee, and that my name might be declared throughout all the earth. Therefore hath he mercy on whom he will have mercy, and whom he will he hardeneth.
>
> Rom. 9:15–18

Let me come on to the fourth principle, which is that *the decrees of God* are *efficacious*. Now this, of course, follows of necessity. Because God is a sovereign Lord, because of His omnipotence and His almightiness, His purposes can never fail. What God determines and decrees must infallibly be brought to pass. Nothing can prevent it. Nothing can frustrate it.

And that brings me to the fifth: *the decrees of God are in all things perfectly consistent with His own most wise, benevolent and holy nature*. I think I need not argue that. In other words, there is no contradiction in God. There cannot be. God is perfect, as we have seen, and He is absolute, and all that I am saying now fits in perfectly with all that we have previously considered. As I warned you in the introduction, you and I here upon the earth, with our finite and sinful minds, are confronted with a problem. It is this: Why did God decree to permit sin? And there is only one answer to that question: We do not know. We know that He did decree to permit sin, or sin would never have taken place. Why, we do not know. It is an insoluble problem. But we shall see it all clearly when we are in glory and face to face with God.

Two things we can be certain of and must always assert: first, God is never the cause of sin. In Habakkuk 1:13 you will find it said, 'Thou art of purer eyes than to behold evil.' James says, 'God cannot be tempted with evil, neither tempteth he any man' (Jas. 1:13). Second, the purpose of God is, in all things, perfectly consistent with the nature and the mode of action of His creatures. In other words, though we cannot reconcile it, there is an ultimate reconciliation. The decrees of God do not deny the existence of free agents and free actions. All we say is this: though God has granted this freedom, He nevertheless overrules it all in order that His ultimate ends may come to pass.

How can God decree everything and yet hold us responsible for what we do? Here is the answer:

> Nay but, O man, who art thou that repliest against God? Shall the thing formed say to him that formed it, Why hast thou made me thus? Hath not the potter power over the clay, of the same lump to make one vessel unto honour, and another unto dishonour? What if God, willing to shew his wrath, and to make his power known, endured with much longsuffering the vessels of wrath fitted to destruction: and that he might make known the riches of his glory on the vessels of mercy, which he had afore prepared unto glory.
>
> Rom. 9:20–3

'But,' you may ask, 'how do you reconcile those two?'

I answer, I cannot. I know the Bible tells me the two things: that man, in a sense, is a free agent, and on the other hand, that God's eternal decrees govern everything.

Now I must come to my last proposition, which is that *the salvation of men and women and of angels, and of certain of them in particular, was determined by God before the foundation of the world*. He does this entirely of His own good will and His grace. I would again refer you to Matthew 11:25–6. And in John 6:37 we read, 'All that the Father giveth me shall come to me.' In verse 44 our Lord says, 'No man can come to me, except the Father which hath sent me draw him.' In Acts 13:48 I read this: 'And as many as were ordained to eternal life believed.'

In 2 Thessalonians 2:13 you find, 'But we are bound to give thanks alway to God for you, brethren beloved of the Lord, because God hath from the beginning chosen you to salvation through sanctification of the Spirit and belief of the truth.' Then in his letter to Timothy Paul says: 'Who hath saved us, and called us with an holy calling, not according to our works, but according to his own purpose and grace, which was given us in Christ Jesus before the world began' (2 Tim. 1:9).

But especially I want to emphasise again that great statement, which I have already quoted, from Romans 9:20–3. The apostle Paul, preaching this great doctrine of the eternal decrees of God, imagines somebody in Rome asking a question, and saying: I do not understand this. It seems to me to be contradictory, to be unfair. If what you are telling me about these decrees is true, it seems that God is unjust. The questioner says to Paul, 'Why doth he yet find fault? For who hath resisted his will?' (Rom. 9:19).

And Paul's reply is, 'Nay but, O man, who art thou that repliest against God? Shall the thing formed say to him that formed it, Why hast thou made me thus? Hath not the potter power over the clay, of the same lump to make one vessel unto honour, and another unto dishonour? What if God, willing to shew his wrath, and to make his power known, endured with much longsuffering the vessels of wrath fitted to destruction: and that he might make known the riches of his glory on the vessels of mercy, which he had afore prepared unto glory.'

That is the apostle's answer. That is the scriptural answer. That is God's answer, therefore, to us and for us while we are in this world of time. It is beyond us. We cannot grasp the ultimate working of God's mind. It is no use asking, Why this? and, Why that? Why did God raise up Pharaoh? Why did He choose Jacob and not Esau? Why does He punish us if all things are determined and decreed? The answer is, 'Nay but, O man, who art thou?' You are pitting yourself against the mind of God. You are forgetting how small you are, how finite you are, how sinful as a result of the fall. You have to leave the ultimate understanding until you arrive in glory. All you have to do here in time is to believe that God is always consistent with Himself, and to accept what He has plainly and clearly told us about His eternal decrees, about what He has determined and decided before He ever created the world.

And, above all, realise that if you are a child of God, it is because God has determined it, and what He has determined about you is certain and safe and sure. Nothing and no one can ever take you out of His hands, or make Him forgo His purpose in respect to you. The doctrine of the eternal decrees of God before the foundation of the world! He knew me. He knew you. And our names were written in the Lamb's Book of Life before the world was ever made, before you and I or anybody else ever came into it.

Let us bow before His Majesty. Let us humble ourselves in His holy presence. Let us submit ourselves to the revelation that He has so graciously been pleased to give.

10

Good Angels

Before we come to deal with the doctrine of creation there is still another doctrine which we have to consider. We are approaching these great biblical doctrines in an order which seems to me to be quite inevitable. We are concerned with God – not with man, as the present tendency is. We are concerned with God's revelation of Himself. We have considered His being, His person, and His character. We have arrived at the great doctrine of the Holy Trinity, and then, naturally, we have asked the question: What has God done? And we have seen that before God actually did anything, He determined certain things, and planned what He was going to do. God's actions are not haphazard or accidental; there is nothing contingent about them. God, being God, by His very nature (if one may speak with reverence) must work in a given way, and the Bible tells us that He does so.

So, then, the next step I think, quite logically, is this: What was God's first action? We use the term 'first' because we obviously speak from the standpoint of time. It is very clear in the Bible that before God made the world, or before He made anything in connection with men and women, He first of all brought into being those heavenly intelligences which are called angels.

I know that some authorities take the doctrine of providence before the doctrine of the angels; but I think that that is the wrong order, because we see very clearly in the Bible that angels were in existence even before the creation of the world. So I would argue that the doctrine of providence must come later, because it has to do with this world, and with men and women in the world.

Let me ask a question at this point: How often have you heard either a sermon or an address on the biblical doctrine of the angels?

How often have you considered this doctrine or meditated upon it? I ask those questions in order that I may ask another: Why is it that we tend to neglect certain parts of the biblical revelation? Why is it that even as evangelical people we seem to be content with the minimum of doctrine? Why are we only interested in the doctrine of salvation? It more and more seems to me that we rob ourselves of a wealth of truth because we do not isolate these doctrines and hold them up for our study and contemplation. As I suggested at the very beginning, any kind of Bible study which does not arrive at doctrine is probably going to be useless to us in the end, and I think the result is very often that we may never have considered what the Bible has to tell us about angels.

The term 'angel' means 'messenger'. It is a word that is not only used with regard to angels, and its use to describe angels indicates that they are sent as messengers. It was used by the Son of God Himself. He, as we have seen, was undoubtedly the Angel of the Covenant, to whom several references are made in the Old Testament literature. But now we are concerned with what is meant by 'angels', these bright intelligences, these beings of whom we read in the Scriptures. So let us first of all, therefore, consider certain general points about them.

The first thing we learn about the angels is that they are created beings, and that is why we put them in this particular place in the order of the doctrines. The first chapter of the epistle to the Hebrews draws a distinction between the Son of God and the angels. The angels, while they are spiritual beings, are nevertheless created beings. They have not existed from eternity as God the Father, God the Son, and God the Holy Spirit have existed. Indeed, Paul in Colossians 1:16 very definitely teaches that they were created by the Son. He says, 'For by him were all things created, that are in heaven, and that are in earth, visible and invisible, whether they be thrones, or dominions, or principalities, or powers' – and those, as we shall see, are descriptive terms of angels – 'all things were created by him, and for him.' So we start by realising that angels are beings that were created by God before He created the world.

Now another point that has often been discussed in the long history of the Church is the question as to whether or not the angels have bodies. The question arises because they are referred to as spirits, in the same way as people, after their death, are referred to as spirits. For example, in 1 Peter 3:19 there is a reference to 'the spirits in prison'.

These are people not in the body, and that has sometimes led some people to think that the angels have no bodies. And yet on the whole I am in agreement with those who say that this is probably false teaching and that angels have bodies. They have spiritual bodies, as we shall eventually have spiritual bodies, and as our Lord's human frame became a spiritual body, a glorified body, after His resurrection. Angels have a body which is appropriate for their spiritual condition, and thus you can account for what are called 'apparitions' or the 'appearances' of angels to different people.

But at the same time we must remind ourselves that the angels can appear in the form of human beings. In Genesis 18, for instance, we are told about the three men who appeared before Abraham, and there are other examples of the same thing. And yet in the story of Samson's father and mother and the angel, there was obviously something unusual about the appearance, because the angel was able to move in a way that an ordinary, physical, earthly frame cannot move (Judg. 13).

Then another question which we are bound to face is: Are the angels sexless? Are they divided into male and female? This is a question that must be of interest to us, the children of men. We cannot speak dogmatically, but in Matthew 22:29–30 we are given evidence with regard to this. You remember our Lord's answer to the Sadducees when they tried to trap him with the case of the woman who had married seven brothers. Our Lord told them that they were ignorant of the Scriptures, and that they did not understand, 'For,' he said, 'in the resurrection they neither marry, nor are given in marriage, but are as the angels of God in heaven.' In addition, however, we must notice that the angels are always referred to as 'he', as if they were masculine.

Another thing we know for certain about the angels is that they never die, and my evidence for that is to be found in Luke 20:36 where we are told, again, of those who have passed on to the resurrection, 'Neither can they die any more: for they are equal unto the angels . . .' And then we are told in Hebrews 2:9 that our Lord 'was made a little lower than the angels for the suffering of death'. If he had not been made lower than the angels he could not have suffered death, from which we deduce again that the angels do not and cannot die; they are immortal.

Then the last general point about the angels is their status. We have seen already that they are inferior to the Son, the Lord Jesus Christ. But it is equally clear, on the other hand, that they are superior to man. We have seen that our Lord was made a 'little lower than the angels', and the same words are used in the eighth psalm with regard to man: 'What is man, that thou art mindful of him? and the son of man, that thou visitest him? For thou hast made him a little lower than the angels, and hast crowned him with glory and honour. Thou madest him to have dominion over the works of thy hands . . .' (vv. 4–6). So as we think of the angels, we realise that they are inferior to the Godhead, inferior to the Son in particular, but in a realm above man, greater than man in many respects.

Next we must consider certain names which we find attached to the angels, certain designations which they are given in the Scriptures. They are referred to, as I have already reminded you, as 'spirits', but we also find them described like this in Ephesians 1:21: 'Far above all principality, and power, and might, and dominion . . .' Now when those terms are used, they are always used of angelic beings, both good and bad. When Paul, in Ephesians 6:12, talks about wrestling 'not against flesh and blood, but against principalities, against powers, against the rulers of the darkness of this world', he is referring to angelic beings, evil angels.

Another term that is used of the angels is 'holy' angels (Luke 9:26). We also have a description of them in 1 Timothy 5:21 as 'the elect' angels – we shall return to that term 'the elect' later, but some angels are described in that way while others are not. Then they are often described as 'ministering' angels, and we have that crucial statement in the last verse in Hebrews 1, where they are described as 'ministering spirits' – 'Are they not all ministering spirits, sent forth to minister for them who shall be heirs of salvation?'

Now as we are dealing with this question of the names and designations we must, of course, refer to those beings who are described as 'cherubim' (e.g. Ps. 99:1; Ezek. 10:1–22) or 'seraphim' (Isa. 6:2), and, also, we must consider those that are described in Revelation 4 as the 'living creatures' or 'the beasts'. We cannot now go into all the evidence, but I think we can take it that these terms are synonymous, and all these names probably refer to the same beings. We speak with comparative ignorance; we are told very little about them. But we are told that they have the appearance of different animals, though generally the face of a man. They seem to be composite beings, at any rate in their representation.

What, then, are they? Well, there is no doubt that they belong to this generic category of angels, but they are very special beings. They seem to stand for and to typify redeemed and glorified mankind. They seem to be symbolic of the highest properties of created life, and there can be little doubt but that their main function is to minister to us. And it is a most glorious thought that human nature, eventually, when salvation is completed, is to be so exalted that we shall dwell in the presence of the Godhead itself! If you keep your eye on every reference to the cherubim and the seraphim and these beasts or living creatures, you will find that they always dwell right in the presence of the Godhead; and the biblical teaching is that that is the future for which you and I are destined. They are symbolic of our ultimate salvation and glorification, and of our eternal existence in the immediate presence of the glorious God.

Now I believe, therefore, that there is a very real significance in the statement which we are given in the third chapter of Genesis. We are told that when the man and his wife had been turned out of the Garden, cherubim were placed there at the east end of the Garden of Eden – cherubim and a flaming sword. I think that there is profound significance in that; the flaming sword is to prevent man from entering back again into Paradise. He can never go back on his own. There is only one way back, and it is the way that has been opened by the Lord Jesus Christ. Yes; but we should thank God that in addition to the flaming sword there were the cherubim, as if to say, at one and the same time, 'You shall not come back; you shall come back. You shall not come back on your own, but you will come back – it is by another way, but you will return.' The presence of the cherubim indicates to me that those who have been thrown out shall also be brought back again. Let us leave it at that. It is a great and abstruse subject and we are told very little. But we are told that much, and it is our business to lay hold of it, to rejoice in it, and to praise God for it.

The next question which we must take up about the angels is their number. How many angels are there? The answer in the Scriptures is that there are very many, they are countless in number. Our Lord said, when His disciples would have defended Him, that, if He chose, He could command twelve legions of angels to defend Him (Matt. 26:53). You remember, too, that we are told that the shepherds at His birth heard 'a multitude of the heavenly host', suggesting an innumerable company (Luke 2:13), and, indeed, in the fifth chapter of the book of Revelation we are told that such is the case, that there are thousands upon thousands, a great, mighty host, a myriad of those angelic beings (Rev. 5:11).

And that, of course, leads us in turn to the next question which is: Are there orders among the angels? Are they all identical? Are they equal in power and in authority, or have they orders and ranks? It seems quite clear that there is a division both in status and in work. For instance, we read in the Scriptures of one who is described as the 'archangel', the chiefest of all, the supreme. The word 'archangel' only appears twice, but it is important to notice it. In 1 Thessalonians 4:16 we read, 'For the Lord himself shall descend from heaven with a shout with the voice of the archangel, and with the trump of God.' And the other reference is in the epistle of Jude, the ninth verse: 'Yet Michael the archangel, when contending with the devil he disputed about the body of Moses, durst not bring against him a railing accusation, but said, The Lord rebuke thee.' I think, taking these verses together, that we must come to the conclusion that the archangel, therefore, is the one who is also referred to as 'Michael'.

Two angels are given specific names: the first, as we have just seen, is Michael the archangel, who is also referred to in Daniel 10. Michael seems to have had a special relationship to the children of Israel. He was the one who fought for them against the Prince of Persia (Dan. 10:13); they seem to have been allotted to him as his special care. He is their protector, and his special work is to guard them. Then the other angel who is mentioned by name is Gabriel, and we are told of him that he stands in the presence of God, waiting, as it were, to be given a message. And he was given messages. It was he, you remember, who was sent to tell Mary of all that was to happen to her, and of how she was to become the mother of the Son of God (Luke 1:26); and we are told that it was he also who gave the message to Zacharias (Luke 1:19). Thus we see that he had a special function with regard to the coming of our Lord into this world.

There is obviously, therefore, some kind of order, some kind of divisions among the angels. Indeed, we notice that in all God's work that feature is a characteristic, and you have it even among the evil angels, 'principalities ... powers ... rulers of the darkness of this world ... spiritual wickedness in high places' (Eph. 6:12). There is a kind of gradation, and undoubtedly there is the same gradation among the other angels. And that brings us to the whole question of their power. The Bible is explicit about this – they are very great in power. We are told of the mighty angels, that they 'excel in strength' (Ps. 103:20). Their power is undoubtedly greater than human power; they are not only superior in dignity and in status, they are also undoubtedly superior in power.

But from our standpoint, perhaps the most important point of all is that the angels are clearly divided into two groups. The very term 'elect' angels, which I have quoted from the first epistle to Timothy, suggests that there are angels that are not elect, that are lost. In other words, we are reminded that there are good angels and bad angels. We read in Matthew 25:41 about 'the devil and his angels'; they are the evil angels, those who, as we have seen, are referred to as 'evil spirits', and we have looked at the designation applied to them in Ephesians 6.

First, however, we must deal with the good angels, and what we are told about them is that they dwell in heaven. We are to be 'like the angels of God in heaven', our Lord says (Matt. 22:30), and we shall refer frequently to the statement in Matthew 18:10 which reads, '. . . their angels do always behold the face of my Father which is in heaven.' It is clear, therefore, that the dwelling-place, the place of existence of these good angels, is in heaven round about the throne of God. Then the great question is: What is the business or purpose of these good angels? What do they do? And it is very interesting and most enlightening and encouraging to consider this wonderful doctrine.

Let me remind you of certain general things which we are told about their occupation. We are told, first, that they spend their time in adoring God and the Lamb. Read again the fifth chapter of the book of Revelation, and you will find that they are singing His praise, worshipping Him and adoring Him. That is the thing that comes first; that is what they delight in; that is what, as it were, they live for. And let us remember again that verse from Matthew 18, that in heaven they 'always behold the face' of the Father. Now there is no doubt but that the meaning of this term 'beholding the face' is that they are watching, as it were, for some indication of His will and of His pleasure. They are servants, and they are waiting. They are looking at Him; they are not lazy; they do not need to be roused. They are always looking for the slightest indication of the will of God. 'They do always behold the face of my Father.' We must start with that. As we come to consider what they do, let us remember that they are anxious to do this great work, like dogs on the leash, as it were, waiting to be let loose in order to do it.

Then there is something else that the angels are very busy about. I never read this next point without having a still more glorious understanding of my salvation. We are told that they spend a good deal of their time in looking into this question of our salvation. Let me give you my authority. Peter, in talking about our salvation says, 'which things the angels desire to look into' (1 Pet. 1:12). It is something so marvellous, and so wonderful, that these created angelic spirits, who have always spent their eternity in the presence of God, are, as it were, looking on at this thing which is most astonishing to them, and which surpasses everything else.

Couple with that statement the one in Ephesians 3:10 where Paul actually tells us that it is through the Church that God is going to show to these angelic beings, these principalities and powers, the wonders of His Christ. I have said that the angels are superior to man – yes; but did you know that were it not for you and me, for those who are redeemed, they would know nothing about the grace of God? It is only where the grace of God is concerned that the angels are looking into it. They are astonished at it. 'What is this?' they ask. 'This is the most wonderful thing of all!' They spend their time in looking into it, studying and inquiring into this marvellous salvation.

Then the next thing we are told about them is this – let us bear it in mind always – they not only behold the face of God, they are not only looking into salvation, but they are looking at us. In 1 Corinthians 11:10 Paul uses these words: 'For this cause ought the woman to have power on her head because of the angels.' You remember that Paul is considering the question of women praying without their heads being covered. Apparently some of the women in the church at Corinth were taking part in prayer with their heads uncovered, and the apostle tells them that that is quite wrong. A woman should have her head covered to show that she is under the authority of the man; and in addition to that, Paul says, she should be covered because of the presence of the angels. In other words, the Scripture teaches that when Christians meet together, and when they gather together in prayer, then the angels of God are present, and the women are to be covered when they take part in public prayer because of the presence of the angels. It is a tremendous and remarkable thing. Let us bear it in mind.

Finally, and this is the point that I am the most anxious to emphasise, the Bible teaches us that God uses the angels as the instruments of His will. Let me give you some of the ways in which He has done, and still does, this. First of all, we are told that the law was given to the Children of Israel through the medium of the angels. We read in Hebrews 2:2, 'If the word spoken by angels was stedfast, and every transgression and disobedience received a just recompence of reward; how shall we escape . . .?' That was a reference to the giving of the law, and there are similar verses in Galatians 3:19 and Acts 7:53.

Another function of the angels is to reveal God's purposes. It was through angels that God revealed to Abraham His purpose with regard to Sodom and Gomorrah (Gen. 18), and He revealed His will to Jacob more than once in the same way. Gideon also was told God's purpose for him through an angel, and in the New Testament Zacharias was told about the birth of his son, who became known as John the Baptist, through an angel that appeared to him when he was in the Temple. We have already considered the function of the angel Gabriel, and of Michael; and let me remind you also that it was an angel who told Joseph that he need not worry about the condition of his espoused wife Mary. It was an angel, also, who told him to flee to Egypt, and an angel who told him to come out of Egypt.

But again I would say that the most comforting, and the most wonderful aspect of this teaching is what we are told in the Scriptures of the way in which God uses the angels to bless and to care for His own people: 'Are they not all ministering spirits, sent forth [called forth] to minister for them who shall be heirs of salvation?' (Heb. 1:14). What, after all, is the greatest function of the angels? It is to minister to you and to me – to minister to the heirs of salvation.

What, then, do they do? Well, it seems to me from this biblical teaching that I am entitled to say that the angels are used by God with respect to us and to our salvation. From the very beginning right up to the end they help to prepare us. For example, in the account of the conversion of Cornelius in Acts 10, we are told that as Cornelius was praying one day an angel suddenly appeared to him and began to give him a 'preview', as it were, of his own salvation, and to tell him what he should do in order that his salvation might be realised. I think we are entitled to deduce from that that the angels may play a much bigger part in preparing us for our salvation than we have ever realised. You know those odd things that occur – you happen to meet somebody; you had not intended going to a place of worship, but you happened to meet somebody . . . and so on.

But not only that. We find that the angels protect us. Psalm 91:10–11 says, 'There shall no evil befall thee, neither shall any plague come nigh thy dwelling. For he shall give his angels charge over thee, to keep thee in all thy ways.' Do you remember how Daniel was cast into that den with the lions, yet came out quite unscathed? This was his explanation: Do not be surprised, he said to the king, 'My God hath sent his angel, and hath shut the lions' mouths' (Dan. 6:22).

But the angels not only protect us, they also give us guidance. In Acts 8:26 we are told that the angel of the Lord said to Philip, 'Arise, and go toward the south . . .' and these directions, given by the angel, led to the conversion of the Ethiopian eunuch.

And then I understand from Acts 27:23-4 that angels are sometimes used by God to cheer us and to give us comfort and consolation. The apostle Paul told his companions on that ship, which was already in a shipwrecked condition, 'For there stood by me this night' – notice – 'an angel of God, whose I am, and whom I serve' (Acts 27:23). The angel had a message for Paul. He had been sent by God to cheer the apostle. And there is very little doubt also but that it was the angels who enabled that poor, frightened servant of Elisha to realise that though the enemy was coming with great might to attack them, they were also surrounded by an unseen host that would destroy the enemy. Read the story for yourselves in 2 Kings 6.

But angels are also used by God to give us deliverance. In Acts 12 we read of Peter being arrested and thrown into prison; but what happened to him? 'And, behold, the angel of the Lord came upon him, and a light shined in the prison: and he smote Peter on the side, and raised him up, saying, Arise up quickly. And his chains fell off from his hands. And the angel said unto him, Gird thyself, and bind on thy sandals . . .' And then the angel went and opened doors and gates and Peter simply followed him. He was delivered from prison by an angel. All that is marvellous and wonderful, is it not? That is what angels do for us while we are in this life.

But there is something more which I trust will give great comfort and consolation to many people who may perhaps have been thinking with fear and dread of the end of their life in this world – afraid of the physical aspect of death. But we need not be, for we read in Luke 16:22-3, 'And it came to pass, that the beggar died, and was carried by the angels into Abraham's bosom: the rich man also died, and was buried; and in hell he lift up his eyes, being in torments, and seeth Abraham afar off, and Lazarus in his bosom.' The angels prepare us at the beginning, they watch over us and protect us and guard us and deliver us, and do all these things – yes. And when we come to die they will be there to receive our spirit and to take us to Paradise. That is the teaching of the Lord Jesus Christ Himself. Never again, Christian people, imagine that when you come to die you will be going into some awful loneliness as a disembodied spirit to an unknown world. Not at all. The angels of God will be there to receive you, and to conduct you, and to take you to be with the Lord in Paradise. What a wonderful thing!

Shame on us Christian people that we neglect the doctrine of the angels, that we do not read our Scriptures thoroughly and wholly. We are not told that angels take care of unbelievers when they die, for we read that the rich man 'died and was buried'. We are not told that any angels came to receive him. Furthermore, I must point out here that it does not seem to me to be the case that the Bible teaches a doctrine of what has sometimes been called a 'guardian angel' for every one of us. I think that that is not a true deduction. All we know is that the angels are looking after us for God in this way, but there is no specific teaching that to every single person there is a specific guardian angel; that is quite immaterial. What is important is that the angels do for us all the things that we have been considering.

The good angels have still two more functions. First, we are told that they execute God's judgments on God's enemies. What a great chapter Acts 12 is! It was an angel that delivered Peter, as we have seen, but in verse 23 of that same chapter we read, 'And immediately the angel of the Lord smote him, because he gave not God the glory' – that is a reference to King Herod who, arrayed in royal apparel, had delivered a great oration to the people. And they praised him and said, 'It is the voice of a god, and not of a man,' and he let them say it, and, 'Immediately the angel of the Lord smote him . . . he was eaten of worms, and he gave up the ghost.'

And that brings us to their final work, which is this: the good angels, we are told, function at the final judgment. Do you remember our Lord's explanation of the Parable of the Tares? 'As therefore the tares are gathered and burned in the fire; so shall it be in the end of this world. The Son of man shall send forth his angels, and they shall gather out of his kingdom all things that offend, and them which do iniquity; and shall cast them into a furnace of fire.' The angels are going to do that. Or again in verse 49: 'So shall it be at the end of the world; the angels shall come forth, and sever the wicked from among the just.' And then again in Matthew 24:30–1: 'And then shall appear the sign of the Son of man in heaven: and then shall all the tribes of the earth mourn, and they shall see the Son of man coming in the clouds of heaven with power and great glory. And he shall send his angels with a great sound of a trumpet, and they shall gather together his elect from the four winds, from one end of heaven to the other.' They will gather the elect together, to meet Him and to begin their glory with Him.

Paul says something similar in 2 Thessalonians 1:6–8: 'Seeing it is a righteous thing with God to recompense tribulation to them that trouble you; and to you who are troubled rest with us, when the Lord Jesus shall be revealed from heaven with his mighty angels, in flaming fire taking vengeance on them that know not God . . .' And that is the end of it all. There they are before the creation of the world and of man, and theirs shall be that last action, as it were, in severing the evil from the good, destroying the evil, collecting together the elect, and bringing them to Him who has died for them, and purchased them and whose they are and whom they serve.

I think you will agree with me that we neglect the biblical teaching about the angels to our own loss. Had you realised that all this was true? True for you and true for me! Do not attempt to seek into something that is a mystery, but believe the biblical teaching. That is God's Word, and that is what it teaches about the angels, and about their relationship to us. They are ministering spirits of God, appointed and sent to minister to us, the heirs of heaven. Whether you and I realise it or not, the angels are doing this for us. It may be that we shall go through this life without seeing an angel in any form, but whether we see them or not, we can be absolutely certain that this is the work which they are doing for us. They are caring for us, they are watching over us, they are protecting us, and sheltering us. They often deliver us, and they are used by God to help us in this way.

Let us take hold of the biblical teaching. Let us not rob ourselves as we do. Let us look into this great Word and receive it as it is, and we shall find things that will amaze us, and fill us with a still greater sense of wonder as we come to know our marvellous God and His wondrous love towards us.

11
The Devil and the Fallen Angels

We must continue with the doctrine of the angels, because, unfortunately, all that which we have considered together about the holy angels does not exhaust what the Bible tells us about these spiritual powers that dwell in the heavenlies. In addition to those beings who help us and care for us, there are others who are our greatest enemies. They are opposed to us and set against us, and obviously, therefore, we must consider the teaching of the Bible concerning them. There are many reasons for doing that. It is quite impossible to understand human history without considering what the Bible has to tell us about these fallen or evil angels. We cannot hope to understand man as he is today, we cannot hope to understand the world, apart from this. And it increasingly seems to me that the essence of the error which most people seem to make, even in the history of this twentieth century to which we belong, is that they fail to consider the biblical doctrine of the devil and his angels.

But it is also a most practical doctrine from the standpoint of the individual Christian's personal experience. I find more and more in my pastoral experience, as I am privileged to interview people, and to help them in their personal fight of faith, and in their personal problems, that the essence of the trouble so frequently is that such people have not realised the powers that are set against them. So often I have to deal with people who have been sent to a psychologist, a psychoanalyst, or somebody like that, and whose problem very frequently is simply that they have without realising it been besieged and attacked by the devil. And the essence of the treatment, and of the cure, is to enlighten them with respect to this; to make them see that what they have attributed to themselves and their personal sin and failure (perhaps even mental disease), is really to be attributed only to this mighty antagonist who is described in the Bible as the devil. So that, strange though it may sound, to understand the biblical doctrine of the devil and his angels can be a most comforting and releasing doctrine.

So then let us look at it as it is unfolded to us in the Scriptures and we start at once with the one who is described as the devil. Here is one to whom reference is made in the Bible from the very beginning to the end, from Genesis to Revelation. Constantly, running right through, there are references to the devil and his captives. At this point again, as we have done earlier, we need to ask why it is that those of us who are evangelical Christians so infrequently study this doctrine and fail to give it its due place and attention in our Christian life. I maintain seriously that it is our failure at this point that surely must account for many of the pitfalls into which we fall so readily, not only in our personal experiences, but in our evangelism, and in many other respects. For if the devil can but keep us asleep, he will fill us with a false zeal, causing us to confuse the flesh and the spirit, and thus when we appear to be most zealous we can unwittingly be most under the influence of the enemy.

So, what has the Bible to tell us about the devil? First of all, let us consider some of the names that are applied to him in the Scriptures. He is referred to as 'Satan', and the word Satan means 'adversary'. He is also referred to as the 'devil', and that means 'slanderer', one who slanders us. He is also described as 'Beelzebub', which means that he is the prince of the devils. He is described as 'Apollyon', and as the 'angel of the bottomless pit'. He is called the 'prince of this world' and the 'god of this world'. He is described as the 'prince of the power of the air, the spirit that now worketh in the children of disobedience' (Eph. 2:20). He is referred to as the 'dragon', as a lion, as 'Lucifer, that old serpent', and, perhaps one of the most significant names of all, as the 'evil one'.

Now you will often find in the New Testament that whereas in the *Authorised Version* the word 'evil' is used, it is probably true to say that it should be the 'evil one'. Sometimes you will find 'wicked' when it should be 'wicked one'. There are those who say that when we pray, 'deliver us from evil' (Matt. 6:13), it should be 'deliver us from the evil one'. And when John, in the last chapter of his epistle, says that the 'whole world lieth in wickedness' he is undoubtedly saying that the whole world lies in the 'evil one' (1 John 5:19). And in the same way in John 17 when our Lord prays his high priestly prayer, 'I pray not that thou shouldest take them out of the world, but that thou shouldest keep them from the evil,' it should be translated 'from the evil one' (John 17:15). It is a most important term – the evil one.

The second thing that the Bible tells us about the devil is that he is a person. This is most important at the present time, because it has been the fashion for at least a century not to believe in the devil as a person. This is true not only of those who are unbelievers but also of many who call themselves Christians. They say they believe in the power of evil, or an evil influence, or a kind of lack in us, but they have a feeling that to believe in a personal devil is to be very much behind the times. But that is thoroughly unbiblical, because the Bible, as I shall show you, teaches us that the devil is a person. For myself, there is one proof that is more than sufficient in and of itself, and that is the accounts we have in the Gospels of the temptations of our Lord. Now obviously our Lord's temptations came from somewhere, and when people say that temptation to evil is something which arises solely from within, and from a certain lack of power or positive qualities in us, they have no explanation to offer of the temptations of our Lord. (See Chapter 24 on the person of Christ.) It was a person who tempted our Lord, and our Lord addressed him as such; it was the devil who spoke to Him, and He spoke to the devil (Luke 4:1–13) – not an influence but a person. Furthermore, we find the same thing shown quite clearly in the book of Job in the first chapter, where the devil appears quite clearly as a person and addresses God. And God addresses him.

The biblical teaching is in no doubt at all about this. Our Lord, turning to certain Jews one day said to them, 'Ye are of your father the devil, and the lusts of your father ye will do' (John 8:44). How often you find the phrase, 'the wicked one' – 'then cometh the wicked one' (Matt. 13:19) – and that phrase, let me emphasise again, is very significant. Indeed, all these names that are applied to the devil assert in different ways that he is a person. Now I must not stay with this, but you notice that there is always a kind of parallelism in false doctrine. In dealing with the doctrine of God we had to point out that God is personal, but that people have been trying to describe God as some Force or some Energy. They have said that He is some great mind behind the universe and have denied the personality. The same error, you see, has been committed with regard to the evil one.

And what applies to the devil also applies to those who follow him, those who are described as 'devils' or 'demons' or 'fallen angels'. You remember, for instance, the conversation between our Lord and the legion of devils that were in the poor man of Gadara. They spoke to our Lord and made a request. They not only said, 'My name is Legion,' but asked that they might be allowed to enter into the swine – again revealing that they have definite personalities. So we must realise that apart from the sin that is in us, and the evil of our nature as the result of the Fall, we are confronted by a person outside us who is tracking us down, a person who has a kingdom, of which he is the head, and which is highly organised, and his one great concern is to destroy the work of God. We have referred to the great statement in Ephesians 6:12 – 'against principalities, and against powers, against the rulers of the darkness of this world' – that is the kingdom, the organised kingdom of Satan, the evil one.

Then, of course, at the very beginning of the human story, in the first chapters of Genesis, we are given positive evidence that the devil is a person, because he came and tempted Eve and led to the Fall. Indeed, if you want one other proof I would suggest that the very term the 'Holy Spirit' who is a person, suggests the opposite – 'evil spirit', the evil one, who is also a person and who tries to counterfeit all that God does. That is something, then, which we must never forget. It is of vital importance to realise that there is this person set over against the kingdom of God and His Christ, and all that belongs to it.

Next we must come to a very important and difficult question: What is the origin of the devil? The Bible asserts the fact of the devil, and of his personality. Where has he come from? Now we are not told much about this in the Bible, which is generally concerned simply to state things about the devil and his activities. The devil's origin seems to be assumed in Genesis, but I think there can be very little doubt but that in Ezekiel 28:11–19 we are given an account of the devil. Now it is clear that in the whole chapter two persons are being dealt with. The first is the king of Tyre. But certain of the descriptions in verses 11–19 obviously are not descriptive of any human being; they arise above that to another.

That is typical of Scripture. We see it in the prophecies concerning the coming of the Lord Jesus Christ. The prophecy is often put in that kind of dual form; it refers partly to some king or to some prince, but in addition there is a further suggestion about the Messiah. There are many examples of that in the prophecies of Isaiah, and in other prophecies – an immediate reference, but then in it and above it a remote reference – and here in Ezekiel, it seems to me, we have exactly the same thing. These verses, then, clearly refer to Satan and his origin, and there are certain things in them which we must emphasise.

The first thing we are told about Satan is that he was created: '. . . the workmanship of thy tabrets and of thy pipes was prepared in thee in the day that thou wast created' (v. 13); 'Thou was perfect in thy ways from the day that thou wast created, till iniquity was found in thee' (v. 15). The devil has not existed from all eternity; he is not an eternal being; he is a created being. There was a time in the history of the Church when that needed to be emphasised very powerfully, because there were those who taught that evil was eternal, that Satan was eternal, and that there were two gods, the good and the evil god. But that is an unscriptural idea. The devil is not eternal – he was made by God. Not only that. We are told that he had great power and ability. You get that in verse 12: 'Thou sealest up the sum, full of wisdom, and perfect in beauty.' That was the devil as he was made by God. He seemed to sum up perfection.

He is also described, you notice, as the 'anointed cherub that covereth . . .' (v. 14). Now this is a very significant statement – 'the anointed cherub'. You remember that in dealing with the angels in an introductory manner in the last chapter, we pointed out that the cherubim are undoubtedly the highest form of being, and that their special function is to worship God, and to present to Him the worship of the entire universe. You see that in the four beasts in Revelation 4. They are the representations of man worshipping God, and, therefore, of the whole universe worshipping God – the 'living creatures'. Well now, here we seem to have an indication that the devil was originally made by God as the anointed cherub, the chief of all cherubs. The suggestion is (and it is only a suggestion) that when God created this being he meant him, as it were, to represent the whole universe in its praise, worship and adoration. He was the anointed cherub – this cherub that 'covereth'. Does it not remind us of the Ark of the Covenant, shielded by the wings of the cherubim, still with the idea of worship and of adoration? There is much in Scripture that leads one to the conclusion that the devil was the brightest of all the angelic beings, given this position of superiority in which he was the head of the whole created universe in representing worship and adoration unto God.

You see also that we are told that he was 'in Eden the garden of

God' (Ezek. 28:13). But that is not a reference to his being in the Garden of Eden when he tempted Eve and Adam, and they fell, because the description given here of this Eden, the garden of God, does not tally at all with the description in Genesis. Here is an Eden which is characterised not so much by fruit as by precious stones, and in verse 13 a list is given of these stones. Now many saintly men reading this passage have meditated upon it and perhaps have speculated a little, and they have suggested an explanation that cannot be proved. But I mention it to you for what it is worth, and it seems to me that there is much to be said for it. It is suggested that the devil and his angels were present at the original creation of the world and it was when the devil and his angels fell, that a calamity took place which reduced this first world into a condition in which it had no form and was void, and necessitated the creation which is described in the first chapter of the book of Genesis. We will come back to that later on, I just mention in passing that Eden, the garden of God, to which reference is made here, may well be a reference to that first original creation of God.

And then we are told here in verse 15 that the devil was perfect in all his ways, but that, alas, he did not keep that first estate: 'Thou wast perfect in thy ways from the day that thou wast created, till iniquity was found in thee.' Then in verse 17 we read, 'Thine heart was lifted up because of thy beauty, thou hast corrupted thy wisdom by reason of thy brightness.' This bright, angelic, glorious being was perfect in beauty, but he became lifted up and consumed with pride. Instead of leading the worship and adoration of God, he desired to be worshipped himself, and to be equal with God, and thus he raised himself against God, sinned against God, and was cast down and cast out by God. That seems to be the teaching of Ezekiel 28, and in Isaiah 14 you find something similar. Verses 12–15 of Isaiah read: 'How art thou fallen from heaven, O Lucifer, son of the morning! how art thou cut down to the ground, which didst weaken the nations! For thou hast said in thine heart, I will ascend into heaven, I will exalt my throne above the stars of God: I will sit also upon the mount of the congregation, in the sides of the north: I will ascend above the heights of the clouds; I will be like the most High. Yet thou shalt be brought down to hell, to the sides of the pit.' That undoubtedly is a reference to the same thing.

Now, you notice, the Bible does not tell us how all this became possible. It does not explain to us how all these thoughts ever entered into the heart of Satan, the devil. It simply tells us that they did. The Bible gives us no explanation as to the ultimate origin of evil, and I suggest to you, therefore, that if you waste a second of your time in trying to speculate about that you are guilty of a lack of faith, because faith means to be content with the revelation given. It is beyond us. We cannot understand it. Theologians have speculated and have said that because the devil was perfect he must have been perfectly free, and perfect freedom in itself contains within itself the possibility of choosing against God. All right. Still, it does not seem to me to explain the ultimate origin of evil; all we do know is that the devil was created, as we have seen, then that evil entered his heart, and he rebelled against God, and was cast down.

What do we know further about him? Well, we are told a good deal in the Bible about his power, and what we learn about it is not surprising in view of what we have been told about his origin. Peter tells us that the devil is like a 'roaring lion' (1 Pet. 5:8). He is described as 'leviathan' (Isa. 27:1), and the 'dragon' in several places in Revelation. I wonder whether you have ever noticed, when you have gone through your Bible, that there is the suggestion that the power of Satan is even greater than the power of the archangel? In Jude 9 we read, 'Yet Michael the archangel, when contending with the devil he disputed about the body of Moses, durst not bring against him a railing accusation, but said, The Lord rebuke thee.' Even Michael the archangel speaks to the devil in that way – he does not 'bring against him a railing accusation'; he does not treat him with contempt, as if he were a nonentity. Even Michael says, 'The Lord rebuke thee.' You will find the same suggestion in 2 Peter 2:10–11.

There is no doubt at all about the power of the devil being greater than human power. Our Lord Himself described Satan as the 'strong man armed' who 'keepeth his palace, his goods are in peace' (Luke 11:21). And you will recall that the devil is as powerful as this (I must come back to it, but I just mention it to make this section complete at this point): that he is able to influence our bodies. You remember what he did to Job? And Peter tells us that our Lord 'went about doing good, and healing all that were oppressed of the devil' (Acts 10:38). Then you remember what Paul tells us about himself and the 'messenger of Satan' that was sent to buffet him (2 Cor. 12:7). Yes, the devil can affect and influence our bodies.

What is his status? He is described as 'the god of this world' (2 Cor. 4:4). He is the 'prince of the power of the air' (Eph. 2:2). He is the evil one, the concentration of evil; all evil, as it were, is centred in him; he is the head and all evil seems to emanate out of him. Indeed, we are told in the Scriptures that he is the one who controls the power of death (Heb. 2:14). And in Matthew 25:41 we read that our Lord refers to the 'devil and his angels', again showing that he is powerful.

Now I emphasise all that for this reason: if there is one lesson we should learn above all others from this consideration, it is that we should never speak loosely or flippantly about the devil. I am often appalled as I hear good Christian people referring jocularly to the devil. The Bible never refers to him in that light and flippant manner; it emphasises his power, his status. Nevertheless, let me hasten to say, his power is limited, he is not all-mighty. In the first chapter of Job we are told that God, as it were, gave the devil permission to do certain things to Job, but he put a very definite limit upon them, and the devil could not go beyond that.

There is a mystery at this point; ultimately the devil acts within the power of God, and yet the Bible teaches quite clearly that for some inscrutable reason that we cannot understand, God seems to accord to the devil a certain status and position. He allows him to do certain things; these very names and distinctions are applied to him. God in His eternal wisdom has allowed the devil to maintain a certain amount of power until the end, and yet that power is ultimately under the control of God. It is His permissive will that allows it, and the devil, as in the case of Job, was only allowed to go so far and no further (Job 1:12; 2:6).

Where does the devil exist? Where is his place? Where does he work? Well, we read in many places that he dwells in 'the heavenlies'. He is the prince of the power of the air, and yet we read of him 'going to and fro in the earth, and walking up and down it' (Job 1:7). This again is an important point, and to me a very comforting one. The devil, because he is a created being, and because he is finite, is limited and can therefore only be in one place at a time. Yes, but he is a deceiver, and because he has so many emissaries and because he is represented by his agents everywhere, he deceives us into thinking that he is everywhere at the same time. But he is not. He is not omnipresent.

What is the character of the devil? The things that characterise him supremely are his pride, pride above everything else; then malignity; then subtlety; then deceitfulness. Another term applied to him by our Lord Himself is 'murderer': 'He was a murderer from the beginning, and abode not in the truth, because there is no truth in him. When he speaketh a lie, he speaketh of his own: for he is a liar, and the father of it' (John 8:44). That is his character – a deceiver, a liar, a whisperer, a murderer; one who hates God and is full of subtlety and pride.

Then the Bible speaks about the 'works of the devil'. John tells us that Christ came to destroy the works of the devil (1 John 3:8), so what are his activities? Well, these are shown in his attacks upon the Son of God: his one great objective always is to destroy the work of God and to set himself up as God. So the first activity of the devil recorded in the Bible is the fall of man (Gen. 3). But if some of you have doubts (which you should not have) about the historicity of Genesis 3, then you will find your answer in 2 Corinthians 11:3 where Paul says, 'as the serpent beguiled Eve'. And what he did there, of course, was to produce in Adam and Eve antagonism to God: 'Hath God said?' (Gen. 3:1). The suggestion was that God was unfair, that God was keeping them down. Everything opposed to God – that is his activity.

And then because Adam and Eve listened to him, and fell, the devil became the one who controlled the power of death. I have already reminded you of that statement in Hebrews 2:14. It is a difficult verse to understand, because ultimately the power of death is in the hands of God, but it seems to me to mean this: the moment man listened to the devil he put himself under the power and under the dominion of the devil, and thereby the sentence of death was pronounced upon him. And the devil, as it were, claims this sentence of death, because one who breaks the law automatically belongs to the devil and is in the territory of the devil, which is the territory and the dominion of death. And it is only in that sense that the devil has the power of death.

Then we are told, of course, that he controls all unbelievers, all who are not Christians, in their lives and in the whole of their activities. Our Lord says that they are the children of the devil, (John 8:44), and John says that 'we are of God, and the whole world lieth in wickedness [the evil one]' (1 John 5:19). Then Paul, in 2 Corinthians 4:4, describes the devil as 'the god of this world', while in Ephesians 2:2 he describes him as 'the spirit that now worketh in the children of disobedience'. We have seen, too, that our Lord describes him as 'the strong man armed' who keeps constant control of those who are unbelievers.

How does he do this? Well, the first thing he does is blind them to the truth. 'If our gospel be hid, it is hid to them that are lost,' says Paul, 'in whom the god of this world hath blinded the minds of them which believe not . . .' (2 Cor. 4:3–4). And that is the trouble with every many and woman in the world today who is not a Christian. They are lost, not because they are scientists or philosophers, not because they have gigantic brains, or have read more than other people who call themselves Christians, but because the devil, the god of this world, has blinded their minds to the truth, and does not allow them to see that he is hiding it from them. That is the only explanation of why there is a single person in the world who does not believe in God or in His Christ. Then the second thing the devil does is to order and control the lives of these people: 'the spirit that worketh in the children of disobedience'. He is the father of lust and desire and evil in every form in the life of the ungodly.

If, then, that is what he does to unbelievers, what are his activities with respect to believers? The Bible describes him as our 'adversary' – one who is always opposed to us in every way. He is also our accuser; he is essentially the accuser of the brethren. He accuses us to God, and he accuses us to ourselves. What does he do in particular? First, he resists our works and our activities. In Zechariah 3:1 you will find, 'And he shewed me Joshua the high priest standing before the angel of the Lord, and Satan standing at his right hand to resist him.' Daniel 10:13 tells us that the prince of the kingdom of Persia resisted the archangel Michael. Paul writes about the 'messenger of Satan sent to buffet him' – to prevent his preaching, and doing his work as he would like to do it. Then in 1 Thessalonians 2:18 Paul says, 'Wherefore we would have come unto you, even I Paul, once and again; but Satan hindered us.'

Satan also discourages us. He is always waiting to devour us (1 Pet. 5:8), to try us and to deceive us. 'Satan hath desired to have you,' said our Lord to Peter, 'that he may sift you as wheat' (Luke 22:31). He tempts us with his wiles, his snares, his fiery darts, his deceits and his suggestions; he excites our passions; he affects our minds. He is responsible for most of our moodiness, our depressions, our sense of hopelessness and our sense of despair. Indeed, you can be certain of this – every time you are turned in upon yourself, and find yourself looking at your weakness, your failure, your disability, or anything else in yourself, when you are looking at yourself like that, it is always the devil. I do not hesitate to say that the devil turns men and women in upon themselves, knowing that when they are looking at themselves they are not looking at God, and so he produces all these moods and depressions within us. He even affects our bodies, as I have already reminded you (Job 2:7; 2 Cor. 12:7). He can produce sickness and illness; he has the power to do so and he uses it. Later on in the series I hope to come back to these things; I just tabulate them for you at this point.

How does the devil do all this work? He does a great deal of it directly himself, but he also does it through his angels. We have seen already that the Lord refers to 'the devil and his angels' (Matt. 25:41), and in 2 Peter 2:4 we read, 'For if God spared not the angels that sinned, but cast them down to hell, and delivered them into chains of darkness, to be reserved unto judgment . . .' There were certain angels that sinned as well as the devil, and God has cast them down.

In other words, those whom the Bible refers to as demons or as devils, or as unclean spirits, are undoubtedly fallen angels, these angels that sinned against God with the devil, the angels that followed him, that 'kept not their first estate' (Jude 6). These are the devil's angels, his emissaries, his agents, the instruments that he uses to do his work. These are the principalities and powers and 'rulers of the darkness of this world', the 'spiritual wickedness in high places' (Eph. 6:12). All these are fallen angels. They must be – what else can they be? The devil cannot create; he cannot produce such followers; he cannot produce his own angels, because he is only a created being himself. No. The demons or the devils are those who followed this 'anointed cherub' and have been cast out by God.

That, then, is in its essence the biblical doctrine of the devil and of the fallen angels, and we are confronted by this adversary. But we cannot finish without emphasising this: we must never forget that the devil's power is limited; it is under God. Christ in His life, His death and His resurrection, has already vanquished the devil. And we, as Christian people, should be enabled by the Lord to resist, and we can, for James tells us, 'Resist the devil, and he will flee from you.' It is not that we refer to him disparagingly, nor that we bring against him a railing accusation or regard him as a joke. No! But in the power of the risen Lord we can resist, knowing that we can defeat him, we can withstand him. We are told in Revelation that the saints 'overcame him by the blood of the Lamb, and the word of their testimony' (Rev. 12:11).

How important it is to remember both sides. We must never be light or flippant; we must never be foolhardy. There is always the adversary. Yes, but we need not spend our lives in a craven fear of him, mighty as he is. 'Greater is he that is in you, than he that is in the world' (1 John 4:4). So, as we see the truth about the devil, let us realise more than ever the truth about our God, and about His Christ.

12

The Creation of the World

We come now to the doctrine of creation proper – that is, as we usually consider it. We have, actually, been dealing with it in the doctrine of angels, where we saw that God created the heavens as well as the earth; and now we are looking at the creation of the earth and all that is in it.

As we approach this doctrine, there are certain general points that need to be made. First, we are not given a fully detailed account or philosophy of creation and yet we claim that the account which we are given is wholly accurate. The Bible claims that it is from God. We read in Hebrews 11:3, 'Through faith we understand that the worlds were formed by the word of God, so that things which are seen were not made of things which do appear.' God gave an account of the creation to Moses or someone else; so it is not man's ideas or theories. The biblical account does not, however, claim to explain everything.

Second, we must be clear about what creation means. It has been defined as, 'That free act of God whereby He . . . in the beginning brought forth the whole visible and invisible universe without the use of pre-existing materials, and thus gave it an existence distinct from His own and yet always dependent on Him' (Berkhof). Now we hold to that as against other theories that have been put forward. There are those who believe that matter itself is eternal; while others believe in the spontaneous generation of matter and its spontaneous development. Other views are that God simply worked into form matter which already existed or that matter is just an emanation of the divine substance. *Pantheism* teaches that matter is but a form of God – that it *is* God. On the other hand, those who believe in *dualism* say that God and matter are eternal; while some teach that the world was produced by an antagonistic spirit, another god or demiurge.

But the biblical doctrine is clear: God made everything out of nothing. The world has a distinct existence but it is always dependent upon God. 'By him,' says Paul, 'all things consist' (Col. 1:17).

The third general observation is that the Bible does not give a reason for creation. It did not happen as the result of a need in God; there was no necessity for it. Neither was it because of His love. It was a free act according to His will and glory and, ultimately, we do not know the reason why.

Fourth, the question is often raised: Are there two accounts of the creation, one in Genesis 1 and one in Genesis 2:4 and following? The answer is, No! Genesis 2:4 does not pretend to be an account of creation. It is the beginning of the account of man's history and it starts with the typical formula for that – 'These are the generations . . .' (compare Gen. 5:1).

Those, then, are the general observations and we now turn to consider what it is that the Bible teaches. First, it tells us that *creation was the work of the triune God.* In general it is attributed to the Father, but Scripture makes it clear that it is also the work of the Son. We read in John 1:3, 'All things were made by him,' and in 1 Corinthians 8:6, 'But to us there is but one God, the Father, of whom are all things, and we in him; and one Lord Jesus Christ, by whom are all things, and we by him'. Paul also says, in his letter to the Colossians, 'For by him were all things created, that are in heaven, and that are in earth, visible and invisible . . . all things were created by him and for him' (Col. 1:16).

Creation is also the work of the Holy Spirit. Genesis 1:2 says, 'And the Spirit of God moved upon the face of the waters.' And we read in Isaiah 40:13, 'Who hath directed the Spirit of the Lord, or being his counsellor hath taught him?' So it is the perfect work of the Three-in-One – out of the Father, through the Son and in the Holy Spirit. Or, as it has been expressed: the being is in the Father, the idea is in the Son and life is in the Spirit.

Second, we must see what the Bible teaches us about *the time of creation.* In the Bible's great opening words, we read, 'In the beginning God . . .' We are told in many places that there is no time with God and that the world and time started together. Now all this means that there was a beginning, but when we come to the questions: What was before? or, Why did it happen when it did?, our only answer can be that we do not know.

Third, there is the interesting matter of the *words that are used in the Bible with regard to creation.* First is *bara'* which means calling into being without the aid of pre-existing material. This word is used only three times in Genesis 1, and only of God's activity in the Old Testament. *Bara'* is never used in connection with existing material and always describes divine activity. See Genesis 1:1, 21, 27. Second is *'asah* which means to prepare out of existing material, a word which is used to describe the work of most of the days of creation: Genesis 1:7, 16, 25, 26 and 31. And the third word is *yatsar* which means to fashion out of pre-existing material. This is used in Genesis 2:7. However, these terms are obviously interchangeable.

Our fourth subject for consideration is *what exactly happened at creation?* Here at once we come to the problem of the relationship between the first two verses of Genesis 1. What is their interpretation? There have been two main answers. One is that these verses describe the two steps of one process; while the other says that there was a gap between the two verses. In the second view, verse 1 tells of the original creation of heaven and earth with perhaps Satan and angels dwelling in it. Then came a calamity and a destruction as a result of the fall of the angels and verse 2 tells of the work of reconstitution and reconstruction.

There are, it seems to me, two points in favour of the second interpretation. First, the words 'without form, and void' are suggestive of waste and destruction. That is the meaning in Isaiah 24:1, 'Behold, the Lord maketh the earth empty, and maketh it waste, and turneth it upside down.' And Jeremiah 4:23 reads: 'I beheld the earth, and, lo, it was without form, and void.' The second interpretation would also explain the whole problem of the geological strata. But Christians are divided on all this and we cannot prove it either way.

Second, still under our heading of what exactly happened, we must look, of course, at the details in the biblical account of the days of creation. On the first day, light was created; the light and darkness were separated and so day and night were constituted. Light would seem to mean luminous ether, or electricity – the sun is the light-bearer.

On the second day there was also a separation. The firmament was established by dividing the waters above and the waters below. The word 'above' refers to the clouds, while the 'firmament' means an expanse.

On the third day, there was a separation of sea and dry land, and the vegetable kingdom of plants and trees came into being. These are three types: grass; herbs, vegetables and grains; and fruit trees – all 'after his kind'. There are two points to be observed here. The first is that *God* did this and the second is that 'after his kind' in verse 12 means that the species are separate and do not evolve out of each other.

The fourth day saw the creation of the sun, moon and stars as light-bearers. Their function is to divide day and night; to act as signs of the change of weather, of future important events, and coming judgment; to affect the change of seasons and the succession of days and years; and to serve as lights.

The fifth day saw the creation of birds and fishes. Notice again, in verse 21, the words 'after their kind'. Once more, this is an indication of different species.

On the sixth day, first, the animals were created. Notice also the use of the words, 'God made' and again, 'after his kind', and 'after their kind' in verse 25. Then, second, in verse 26 we read of the creation of man and this is special.

There is a parallel to be seen between the work of the first three and the last three days:

Day 1
The creation of light

Day 4
The creation of light-bearers

Day 2
The creation of the expanse
and the separation of the
waters

Day 5
The creation of the birds of the
air and fish of the sea

Day 3
The separation of water and
dry land and the preparation
of the earth as a habitation for
man and beast

Day 6
The creation of the beasts of the
field, cattle and creeping things
and man.

And finally we are told that on the seventh day God rested and contemplated His work: He looked at creation as an artist does, and was satisfied with it.

The next matter for us to deal with is the exact meaning of the word *day*. There are two main views. The first is that it means a twenty-four hour day and the second is that it means an extended period of time.

There is considerable disagreement on this subject among people who are equally good Christians, and the correct meaning cannot finally be proved either way. In favour of the second view is the fact that in the Bible, the word translated in Genesis 1 as 'day' does not always mean the twenty-four hour day. In verses 5, 16, and 18 of Genesis 1 it refers to the daylight hours, while in verses 5, 8 and 13 it means light and darkness, and in Genesis 2:4 it means the six days of creation.

Then in other passages in the Bible the same word means an indefinite period of time, as in 'the day of trouble' (Jer. 51:2), or 'the day of the Lord' (Isa. 13:6; Joel 3:14), and, of course, in 2 Peter 3:8 we read, 'One day is with the Lord as a thousand years, and a thousand years as one day.' This last reference, however, is not relevant to our discussion, as Peter's purpose is to show the differences between eternity and time.

On the other hand, in favour of the twenty-four hour day is, first of all, the fact that this is the primary meaning of the Hebrew word. Second, there is the importance of the phrase 'evening and morning' throughout Genesis 1. How is this repetition to be explained? The question at once arises: If you take a day to mean an extended period, then how do you explain this evening and morning? If you take the point of view which says that in the creation of the world God had taken millions of years to do something that is described here as having been done in a day, and then there followed an evening in which there was darkness and nothing apparently happening and then another extended period and so on, then how do you account for these extended evenings as well as mornings? What was happening during these millions of years of evenings? Furthermore, you have to answer the seemingly impossible question: How could life – vegetable and animal life – exist at all during this extended period of millions of years of darkness and absence of light? Not only that, it seems perfectly clear that the last three days in the account in this first chapter of Genesis were determined by the sun and therefore were twenty-four-hour days. From the moment that the sun comes into being and determines the difference between day and night, surely all must agree that now at any rate we are dealing with twenty-four hours. So if the other theory is right, then we are asked to believe that the first three days mean an extended period, but the last three days mean only twenty-four hours, and obviously there is nothing in the account itself to suggest that the word has a different meaning. I cannot prove that there is no difference, but it surely is a very strange thing that you should have this sudden change in meaning when the description is identical in both the first and the last three days.

But it seems to me that the most important argument of all is what we are told about God resting on the seventh day and beholding with satisfaction the work that He had done. Notice, too, the importance that is attached to that in the Scripture and particularly, of course, in the question of our observing and keeping the seventh day. In Exodus 20 we read, 'Remember the sabbath day, to keep it holy . . . For in six days the Lord made heaven and earth, the sea, and all that in them is, and rested the seventh day: wherefore the Lord blessed the sabbath day, and hallowed it' (vv. 8, 11). And that is repeated several times in the Scripture.

Now at that point, of course, there can be no discussion at all. The reference is to a day of twenty-four hours. The Sabbath which they were told to observe was not to be an extended period, it was to be a day of twenty-four hours and the reason given is that after God had made the world in six days, He rested upon the seventh. It does not say that He rested for an extended period of millions of years.

Well there, it seems to me, is the evidence with regard to both these theories. I think I have been making it plain that as far as I myself am concerned (it is only an opinion, I cannot prove it to you) I cannot see how we are entitled to interpret this term 'day' in any other sense than by saying that it means twenty-four hours. The difficulties of the other suppositions make it, to me at any rate, quite impossible.

But I would remind you again that great and learned and devout Christians have held and do hold the other view. Thank God that our salvation is not determined by our view on this particular question. So I trust we will all look at the evidence, bearing that all-important truth in mind. I think it is right and important that we should look at these things but to be dogmatic or to insist that one bit of evidence can certainly prove our case, is to make ourselves ludicrous.

So, let us go on to another question. 'What about all this,' says someone, 'and modern science?' Now as I said at the beginning of this series of discourses, they are not meant to be lectures in apologetics and I want to emphasise that again. Indeed, were I to consult my own feelings I would not do what I am proposing to do now. But, after all, I know full well, having been a student myself and a student of science and biology, that many Christian people do get into trouble about these matters. So I regard it as a part of the function of a Christian minister to try to help. I know that as he does it he is exposing himself to attack from both sides, but that really is immaterial. It is our business to help one another as far as we can. Let me make it quite plain that I am not asserting that I am able to prove much, but, at any rate, I think I can disagree with some common and popular assumptions.

So then, what about all this and modern science? Now certain things can be said without any fear of contradiction and here is the first: *this problem, the dispute between science and the Bible, is one which is greatly exaggerated.* The trouble, generally, is due to the fact that, on the one hand, what poses as science is not science but merely opinion and supposition and, on the other hand, what is regarded as biblical is very often not the biblical teaching. So if you have a false conception of the Bible and science, then obviously you will very easily manufacture a great dispute between the two. The trouble is due very largely to the fact that people will persist in quoting errors as facts and suppositions as truth. But I would always assert that I am not aware of any real contradiction between the teaching of the Bible and true, established scientific facts. Now that is the most important thing of all.

It is most astounding to observe the way in which the Bible makes statements which come into the realm of science. It has often been pointed out that if you compare the book of Genesis with some of the accounts in Egyptian and Babylonian literature of the origin of life and of the world and of man, the contrast is simply incredible. There you have myths and superstitions, exaggerations and gross statements which patently are impossible and ridiculous. There is nothing like that in the Scripture. If you put the Bible over against literature which is more or less of the same date, the difference is truly remarkable. And that, I think, is an important bit of evidence.

Now I have already reminded you in passing – but it is important to repeat it again – that even in the time of the book of Job it was known that the earth is a globe. The Bible never says that the earth is flat. In Job 26:7 you read this: 'He stretcheth out the north over the empty place, and hangeth the earth upon nothing.' Now if the book of Job is (as is probably the case) about the oldest book in the world, stemming from remote antiquity, we must ask the question: How was a thing like that known? Who would ever have thought it out or imagined it? It is clearly something that was revealed by God Himself. It is up to date. It is modern science, if you like. It is a description of the earth as a globe.

Then another thing which has been pointed out quite often is that the very order of creation which is given in the first chapter of Genesis is identical with the order that the modern scientist gives us – I mean the modern scientist who is not a Christian and who rejects the Bible.

And then there is another very striking point, namely, that it has been discovered in this present century that there are only four blood groups, that the whole of mankind can be divided into these four groups, and that all of them can be derived from just two persons. Then you remember that the apostle Paul told the people at Athens that God 'hath made of one blood all nations of men ...' (Acts 17:26). Finally, you get a contrast between the greater light and the lesser light in the book of Genesis. In other words, they realised that there was a difference between the sun and the moon, which is a very striking fact.

'But then,' says someone, 'what about the statements of geologists who tell us that one layer was put down and then another layer on top of it and so you have the various strata? This has caused a great deal of trouble; many Christian people have been very perplexed about it and many theories have been put forward in an attempt to reconcile the Bible with this supposed evidence from geology.

Some have put forward the theory that Genesis does not claim to be a scientific treatise, but is just allegory or poetry, that the Bible does not pretend to be scientifically accurate but is a typical, poetical, allegorical way of describing creation. To this the answer is, of course, that there is not a trace of poetry in these early chapters of Genesis. The form is not poetical at all. It claims to be history. It claims to be giving facts, and the history that follows immediately and directly out of it is certainly true history and not allegory.

Then others say, 'Well, of course this is a myth,' and a myth, they tell us, is something which embodies religious truth. It is a statement which is not of necessity true in and of itself, it is historical in a sense and yet not historical. A myth does not give information about what actually happened, but reveals a religious meaning and truth. But the moment you say that Genesis 1 is a myth, you are in difficulties about the Person and the teaching of the Lord Jesus Christ, because in His teaching about divorce, He referred to the creation of man and woman. He based His whole argument upon the fact that this is literal history. This leads us on to lay down another proposition. It is that you must be always careful in case, in attempting to solve one difficulty, you are not creating a more serious one. We shall come back to that later.

Then another way of trying to answer the geological question is to introduce that old conception that a day means a long period, the argument with which we have already dealt. Now here, it again seems to me, you come back to two possibilities: one is that restitution theory, to which I have already referred, which states that there is a gap between verses 1 and 2. That seems to me to be an explanation which would be adequate. I am not saying it is the correct one, but it does seem to answer most of the difficulties. But if you do not accept that, you must remember that, after all, the geologists are not all agreed and that it is still possible that they are mistaken. I cannot prove that, but we must always bear it in mind as a possibility. The fall of man may itself have produced such a cataclysm upon the earth that it would account for most of the problem. We know that God cursed the ground because of the sin of man. What was the limit of that cursing? What exactly took place then, and what took place at the flood? The answer is, of course, we just do not know, but it is possible that there, somehow, something happened which adequately accounts for these different layers of which the geologists speak. But, ultimately, there are certain matters about which we have to say that we do not know; it is the only honest and safe position to take up.

But we can say that science is very much more humble today than it was at the beginning of the century. There have been great changes and admissions in scientific attitudes and standpoints. The position, for instance, with regard to astronomy today is very different from what it was earlier and that is something that is admitted by all competent investigators in this field. So it seems to me that there is one rule here: let us always be careful to differentiate between theories and facts, suppositions and proofs. When people say, 'Science has done so and so,' make certain that they are giving you a fact and not merely putting forward the theory of a particular scientist.

But at the same time, let those of us who are Christians be very careful to face facts when they are put before us. We must never be guilty of obscurantism. We must never refuse a fact because it makes things difficult for us, we must never try to invent facts, and we must not put forward theories which are patently not true. For instance, there was a man who once attempted to defend the Genesis account by saying that he believed that when God created the world He actually created these geological strata, and even created the fossils in them. But that seems to me to be making the whole position of the Bible ridiculous and futile. We must never just bury our heads in the sand and say, 'Well, I shall go on saying this whatever else may be said!' We must be open-minded and ready to face real evidence, sifting it and examining it but always remembering that scientists are human beings, and that, like ourselves, they are sinful human beings. So when you are asked to believe that because a man is a scientist, he is a pure intellectual, has no prejudices at all and is consumed by a passion for truth to the exclusion of everything else, well, remember that that just is not true. Scientists, like the rest of us, are full of error and of failure. Indeed, they are some of the most opinionated people in the world today, dogmatism is certainly not confined to pulpits! You get it in scientific laboratories, on the radio and in books.

Now this brings me to suggest a word or two about the vexed question of evolution. I say once more that if I were to consult my own inclinations and feelings I would not be doing this. For the past thirty-seven years or so I have had to read, for various reasons, this argument about evolution, and I am more than tired of it. And yet, of course, I know that it is a live and burning issue with so many. I know that many young people in schools and colleges and other places are being taught things as if evolution has been proved beyond any doubt at all. So I feel that for those reasons, if for no other, I must just again make one or two comments, though from the standpoint of biblical doctrine there is no necessity for me to do so.

Now when you come to this question of evolution, you must start with a definition. Evolution as it is commonly and popularly understood means this: life is something that generates itself; it is a force and a power in and of itself and it produces one type out of a previous type; we start with something utterly simple and undifferentiated and from that something more involved and complex evolves and that in turn evolves into something still more complex and on and on you go up and up the scale from one point to another.

There are many groups of people who believe in evolution, and the commonest and the largest group of all comprises atheists who exclude God altogether – the so-called *atheistic evolution*. But there is also a theory sometimes called *deistic evolution*. Proponents of this view say, 'Yes, we believe in God and we believe that God created matter at the beginning, but having created matter He did no more about it. He put the power into matter and matter has done the rest itself. God, as it were, wound up the watch and having done so He put it down and it has gone on by itself. All the great changes leading up to man, they say, have happened, as it were, automatically out of this power.

And there is a third group who hold the view which is called *theistic evolution*. Now these are the people who are Christians – they are believers in God, and at the same time they believe in evolution. You will find them among both Roman Catholics and Protestants – including evangelical Protestant Christians. They say that the development of these different types and species has gone on, but God has been guiding it and has intervened frequently in the process. So they are different from the deists – they are theists and they emphasise the activity of God.

Now I do not want to stay with this, I would simply like to make these comments. The first thing we always have to remember is that evolution is only a theory. Nobody can prove it. Indeed, there are many different theories (which do not agree with one another). If you want to know one of the best attacks that is available upon Darwin's particular theory I would recommend you to read (and it may astound you that I should quote such a name and such a man) Bernard Shaw's introduction to his drama *Man and Superman* for a devastating criticism of Darwin's particular brand of evolution. Shaw believed, you see, in another type of evolution.

I have often said this when I have been involved in discussions, and I pass it on to any who may be troubled by people who talk rather glibly about evolution: the next time anyone comes to you and begins to dangle this word 'evolution', just stop and put this question: 'Which particular brand or theory of evolution do you believe?' And I think you will find that in nine cases out of ten you will be introducing them for the first time to the knowledge that there is more than one theory. So there are many theories and an interesting argument is going on among their advocates; but nothing is proven. Furthermore, none of the theories really explains the origin of everything. Scientists talk about a great planet that began to cool – but where did the planet come from? They talk about this primitive slime, this protoplasm, but where did that come from? Where did the gases come from that have cooled? And so on. There is no explanation of ultimate origin. They admit that quite frankly. And yet it is rather important. Not only that, they have completely failed to explain why any changes should take place at all. Why should that undifferentiated slime or protoplasm become more complicated and involved; what made it do it? They do not know. There is a complete failure to explain the changes, still less to explain why the changes should always be upward.

Geologists talk a great deal *about* the evidence provided by fossils and so on. However, it is a fact that the geological records show that there is a fixity of types. A type is always the same in the geological record. Another thing the records show is that every new type appeared suddenly. There was no gradual evolvement of a new type; you suddenly find a new type quite complete. And the third point about the geological record is the scarcity of evidence for the so-called missing link. If one type does gradually and almost imperceptibly turn into another, then you would expect to find some evidence in these deposits of some of these intervening stages and they simply cannot be found. The missing link is a potent argument.

Again, if you are interested in my personal opinion, I shall put it like this: quite apart from my believing the Bible to be the inspired and authoritative word of God, on scientific grounds alone I have never been able to accept the theory of evolution. The difficulties I am left with, if I accept the theory of evolution, are altogether greater than the few residual difficulties I am left with when I accept the biblical record. But lest you may think that this is simply my own opinion, let me read you one or two statements from some authorities in these matters for you to see how I substantiate my statement. There was a biologist called Delage, who believed in evolution, and this is what he said: 'One is or is not a conformist (that is to say, a believer in evolution) not so much from motives deduced from natural history as from motives based on personal philosophic opinion.' Here is a man who believes in evolution and he says what really determines a man's view is not so much his scientific knowledge as his scientific opinion. He goes on to say; 'If one takes his stand upon the exclusive ground of fact, it must be acknowledged that the formation of one species from another species has not been demonstrated at all.' And that was a man who believed in evolution and was a great biologist.

Another scientist has said, 'Darwinism is more a religion than a science.' It is, he says, not so much a question of scientific fact as of a person's ultimate outlook. In this way, he says, the idea of evolution has become a sacred conviction of thousands, a conviction that no longer has anything to do with unbiased scientific research. This point of view was echoed by Professor D. M. F. Watson who once said in a broadcast, 'Evolution itself is accepted by zoologists, not because it has been observed to occur, or can be proved by logically coherent evidence to be true, but because the only alternative, special creation, is clearly incredible.' You see, he did not have the facts to prove his theory, but because he could not believe in this idea of a God who creates, then he believed in evolution.

I could go on quoting to you. Others – Sir Arthur Keith, for instance – admit that evolution is 'a basic dogma of rationalism'. Then let me give you just one other statement. A Fellow of the Royal Society (and to be a Fellow of the Royal Society is the greatest distinction a scientist can have in this country or in any other) once remarked that it is 'professional suicide' for a biologist to attack evolution. In other words, it is a dogma involving feeling and heat, and a man who ventures, even in spite of these facts, to say that he does not believe in it is a man who is more or less committing 'professional suicide'. But there are certain great names in the realm of science who have never accepted it. Sir Ambrose Fleming, Sir William Shelton, and many others whom I could mention to you. But let me just give you two final quotations: the only statement, writes one biologist, that science can make is to make her feel that she knows nothing about the origin of man. We have reached, says another, 'a stage of very general scepticism'.

And, therefore, we must realise that all that is being taught and constantly asserted is nothing but a theory, without proof. It is a form of dogmatism, an anti-God religion. That does not apply, of course, to the theistic evolutionist, but, speaking generally, it describes the others.

This, therefore, makes it doubly distressing that all too often the media refuse to allow the anti-evolution view to be stated. This, of course, just confirms the prejudice that is involved. In spite of these admissions by various scientists, the prejudice is such that the other side is not even allowed to speak for itself. Thus it seems very clear that we are facing, not a problem of science, but a problem of a spirit and an attitude that is antagonistic to God, and whose concern, as some of these scientists have been ready to admit, is to prove that the earth could not have started as the Bible says.

Here, therefore, we leave this consideration of the relationship of the biblical account of creation to the popular and prevailing scientific opinion. I have not had time to deal with the theistic evolutionists, but I cannot understand people who are ready to accept the theory of evolution in the absence of proof to allow themselves to be placed in difficulty. Let us never compromise the truth of God to fit any scientific theory. The time will soon come when that scientific theory, if it contradicts the Bible, will be replaced by another. So we must never allow our position to be determined for us by the passing theories or current of so-called scientific opinion. Let us hold to the truth as it is revealed and ever, I repeat, with an open mind listen to facts that are placed before us. But let us shake ourselves entirely free from this pseudo-scientific dogmatism that so often masquerades in the guise of a truly scientific spirit.

13
Providence

In our consideration of these biblical doctrines we come now to a consideration of the biblical doctrine of providence. I think it is right that we should consider this doctrine before we deal with man in particular, because it follows on, in logical sequence, from the doctrine of creation. Now perhaps the best way of describing what we mean by providence is to define it in terms of its relationship to creation. We can put it like this: creation, as we saw, means calling into existence something which did not exist before. So if that is creation, then providence means the continuation, or the causing to continue, of that which has been called into existence. Creation brings things into existence, providence keeps them, or guarantees their continuation in existence, in fulfilment of God's purposes. The doctrine of providence does not just mean, therefore, that God has a foreknowledge of what is going to happen, but is a description of His continuing activity, of what He does in the world, and what He has continued to do since He made the world at the very beginning.

Now there can be no doubt at all but that this doctrine at the present time is a very important one for us to consider. Every biblical doctrine, of course, is important, and we must not take any single one for granted, but if you look at the long history of the Church, you will find that in different times and in different centuries some doctrines assume a particular importance. The great doctrine in the early centuries of the Church was, of necessity, the doctrine of the person of Christ. It had to be. That was the doctrine that was most attacked, so the Church placed its maximum emphasis upon it. At the time of the Reformation it was the doctrine of justification by faith only, and so on, at different times. It behoves us to lay very special emphasis upon particular doctrines, and I am prepared to assert that perhaps in this twentieth century of ours the most important doctrine in many ways is the doctrine of providence.

Now I hope that no one will think that I am arguing that the doctrine of providence is more important than the doctrine of the incarnation or the atonement; that is not my point. I am simply saying that there are certain reasons why we must pay particular attention to this doctrine. Let me give you my reasons. The first is the state of the world at this present time, especially the state of the world during the whole of this century up to now. This doctrine of providence is the stumbling-block to a large number of people who are outside Christ and outside the Church. They say, 'I cannot believe your doctrine, I cannot believe your gospel. You say that God is a God of love, well, look at the world; look at the things that have happened in the world; look at these two world wars! How can you reconcile something like that with a God of love, a God who you say is all-powerful, so powerful that there is nothing He cannot do if He so chooses? How can you explain all this?' So you see, the very historical situation in this century concentrates attention immediately upon this great doctrine of providence.

Then another thing that has focused attention on the doctrine of providence is what we call 'special providences'. Now special providences are special interventions of God on behalf of individuals or groups of people. For instance, at Dunkirk during the War a kind of mist came down to protect the soldiers while at the same time the sea was unusually calm and smooth, and many people in this country were ready to say that that was a providential act of God. They said that God had intervened in order to save our troops by making it possible for them to be brought back into this country. There are also those who would say the same thing about the wartime defence of Malta. Then, of course, it has been customary and traditional in this country to say that the same thing happened at the time of the Spanish Armada: that what really accounted for the destruction of that fleet was the change in the direction of the wind.

Furthermore, there are people who claim special providences in their own personal lives. 'It is most amazing,' they say. 'Do you know, this is what has happened to me . . .' – and they describe to you how certain things seem to have been arranged particularly in order to suit their special circumstances! And then, when you tell them that they cannot say things like that, they resent the whole doctrine of providence.

Another reason why it is important to be clear about this doctrine in this century is that most of the thinking of men and women today seems to be determined by what is called a 'scientific outlook'. It is undoubtedly the fact that large numbers of people do not even begin to consider the great message of Christianity because, they say, 'Your whole message includes the idea of miracles and these interventions of God. For those who take a scientific outlook, as I do, towards the whole of life, such things are a sheer impossibility, and if your gospel contains the supernatural, I just cannot begin to consider it.'

And the last reason I would adduce is this: you cannot begin to talk about prayer, answered prayer, without at the same time introducing the doctrine of providence. So we must consider this doctrine because many other matters presuppose it.

What, then, does the Bible tell us about the doctrine of providence? Again, we are looking at a very difficult subject. The particular doctrines of salvation that we shall be considering are very simple in comparison with a doctrine like this. It is one of those inscrutable doctrines and there is a hymn which reminds us of that. 'God moves in a mysterious way, his wonders to perform,' says William Cowper, and, 'Blind unbelief is sure to err.' And not only blind unbelief, but lack of faith, but a desire to understand that which is impossible, are certain to lead us into trouble if not into error. Therefore let us approach the doctrine of providence with reverence and humility, going as far as Scripture takes us, but not going beyond that.

Now the Bible teaches everywhere, very clearly, as I shall show you, that God is in control of all things. Psalm 104 is enough, in and of itself, to establish that doctrine. There is no limit to what He does. Psalm 103:19 also says, 'The Lord hath prepared his throne in the heavens; and his kingdom ruleth over all.' Everywhere. And the Bible teaches us that first of all, as over against deism, to which I have referred, that doctrine which regards the universe as a kind of watch made by the watchmaker, wound up by him, and then put down to run itself out. But the doctrine of providence contradicts that, and I rather like the comparison which was once used to show the difference. The doctrine of providence tells us that the universe, and everything within it, is like a great ship which is being piloted from day to day, hour to hour, minute to minute, second to second, by God Himself. Furthermore, of course, it is over against pantheism also, which says that God is everything, and in everything, and that therefore you cannot differentiate between the universe and God Himself. The doctrine of providence contradicts both these views.

How, then, do we find this doctrine in the Bible? Well, first of all we find it in a number of very direct statements in the Scriptures. I shall give you a list of them later on. Then another very powerful argument for the doctrine of providence is based upon the fact of prophecy. It would not be possible for a man inspired by God to predict what is going to take place, perhaps in several hundreds of years, unless God controlled everything. Prophecy is not merely foreknowledge, it is a guarantee – that the prophesied events are going to happen because God is in control.

Then another great argument, as we have seen, is derived from answers to prayer. If we did not believe that God controlled everything, there would be no point in praying – we would not pray for sunshine, we would not pray for rain; we would not pray for health and for the control of disease. Prayer, in a sense, would be ridiculous if we did not believe in the doctrine of providence. And that is why deists do not believe in prayer. Pantheists do not pray; there is no purpose in it. But those who believe in the doctrine of providence obviously pray because the very idea of that doctrine immediately leads to prayer.

And our last general argument is the argument from miracles. Were it not that the doctrine of providence is true, if it were not the case that God has His hand upon everything, and is controlling everything, then miracles simply could not take place at all.

So then, what exactly do we mean by providence? I cannot think of a better definition or description than this: 'Providence is that continued exercise of the divine energy whereby the Creator upholds all his creatures, is operative in all that transpires in the world, and directs all things to their appointed end.' We shall consider the biblical proof for that statement later on. Now there are three elements in this idea of providence, and we must differentiate between them in thought as well as in practice, though, of course, the three tend to work together. You can look at the three aspects of providence from different angles. The first is the aspect or the element of *preservation* – 'that continuous work of God by which He maintains the things which He has created, together with the properties and powers with which He has endowed them.' Now this is most important. The Bible teaches that God preserves everything that He has made. It is a continuous work. Some have tried to say that this doctrine of preservation simply means that God does not destroy the work He once made, but that is not preservation. It means more than that; it means that He keeps everything in being.

Others, too, have misunderstood this doctrine. Incidentally, the great Jonathan Edwards, one of the greatest theologians that the Christian Church has ever known, that great American who lived two hundred years ago – if ever you find anything written by him buy it and devour it! – Jonathan Edwards himself almost fell into error about this. It is an error which says that preservation means a continuous process of creation, so that God is continually creating, anew and afresh, everything that exists, and everything is kept going by being created in this way from moment to moment. But that is not really preservation, as I understand it, and as it has been traditionally understood. So we will put it like this: everything that has been created by God has a real and permanent existence of its own, apart from the being of God, but that must never be taken to mean that it is self-existent, which belongs to God alone. If things were self-existent they would not need God in order to keep going. That is the difference. God has created a thing, and He keeps it alive. He upholds all things, and they continue to exist as the result of a positive and continued exercise of His divine power.

Notice how Psalm 104 puts it in verses 28–30: 'That thou givest them they gather: thou openest thine hand, they are filled with good. Thou hidest thy face, they are troubled: thou takest away their breath, they die, and return to their dust. Thou sendest forth thy spirit, they are created: and thou renewest the face of the earth.' Now God does not create these animals of the earth constantly. What He does is to keep life, to preserve what He has already created. Paul, of course, puts this exactly in Acts 17:28: 'For in him we live, and move, and have our being.' He means the same thing in Colossians 1:17: 'And he is before all things, and by him all things consist.' They are preserved, they are kept going by Him. It is stated still more strikingly in Hebrews 1:3: 'upholding all things by the word of his power'. He has not only made them, He upholds them. There is nothing in the universe that would continue to go forward if God were not upholding it. So we must never think, therefore, of the universe as something which God created and then allowed to work itself out; that is deism.

Second, there is the governmental aspect of providence. This means the continued activity of God whereby He rules all things to a definite end and object, and does so in order to secure the accomplishment of His own divine purpose. 'The Lord reigneth; let the earth rejoice' (Ps.

97:1). He is the King of the universe. He is the Lord of lords. Everything is under His control: 'his kingdom ruleth over all' (Ps. 103:19). 'The nations are as a drop of a bucket, and are counted as the small dust of the balance' (Isa. 40:15). That is the idea of government. Or take the mighty statement in Daniel 4:34–5:

> And at the end of the days I Nebuchadnezzar lifted up mine eyes unto heaven, and mine understanding returned unto me, and I blessed the most High, and I praised and honoured him that liveth for ever, whose dominion is an everlasting dominion, and his kingdom is from generation to generation: and all the inhabitants of the earth are reputed as nothing: and he doeth according to his will in the army of heaven, and among the inhabitants of the earth: and none can stay his hand, or say unto him, What doest thou?

The governmental aspect of the doctrine of the providence of God is of vital importance and runs through the Bible from the beginning to the end. 'His purposes shall ripen fast, unfolding every hour,' says William Cowper. There is an end to this creation, a purpose, an object. Everything is leading up to God's determined purpose for it.

The third aspect of providence that I must emphasise is what has generally been called the aspect of *concurrence*. It means 'the co-operation of God and His divine power with all the subordinate powers according to the pre-established laws of their operation, causing them to act and to act precisely as they do'. If you like, it means the whole idea of the relationship of second causes to God's ordering of all things. The Bible teaching is that God works in and through the second causes which He has made. We are all clear, I take it, about secondary causes. We find, do we not, that everything that happens has a cause; certain things lead to certain other things. You see that right through the whole of nature. One thing produces another. Now those are the second causes, and the biblical doctrine of providence teaches the existence of second causes. But it is very, very clear in its emphasis that the second causes do not operate automatically or independently. God works through them. They have their own operations, but God is over all these operations.

Now it is important to emphasise this point, because so many people today speak of the powers of nature as if they were something independent. But they are not. There are powers and laws in nature, but not apart from God. God is in direct relationship to them, and uses them and orders them and manipulates them; so we hold the two ideas at one and the same time – the reality of secondary causes, but their dependence upon God and His control of them.

This is a mystery, of course. This is the difficult aspect of this doctrine – how can these things be true at one and the same time? But the Scriptures teach it. You will find it in Psalm 104:20, 21 and 30. Amos 3:6 says, 'Shall a trumpet be blown in the city, and the people not be afraid? shall there be evil in a city, and the Lord hath not done it?' Matthew 5:45 tells us, '. . . for he maketh his sun to rise on the evil and on the good, and sendeth rain on the just and on the unjust'. In other words, these things do not happen automatically as the result of the secondary causes or laws of nature. God is behind them. He is working in them and through them. He is not divorced from them.

So there, briefly, are the three aspects of providence. You can think of them like this: the idea of preservation makes us think of the being of everything that is. The idea of government tells us that this being is guided, and the doctrine of concurrence tells us about how the activity is guided. Being, guidance, and activity.

Then the next question we come to is this: In what way is providence exercised? Or, to put it another way: What are the objects of providence? Now here it is customary to divide providence into *general* and *special*. We have just seen that throughout the Bible we are taught that the whole of the universe is being controlled by God. This is general providence. He not only made it, He keeps it going, and He is controlling it.

Then you come to special providence, which can be thought of in three ways. First of all it is God's care for each separate part of the universe in its relationship to the whole. There are abundant Scriptures to prove that. Psalm 104 is nothing but a great elaboration of that point. God not only controls the whole universe, He controls the brooks and the streams and the trees and plants as well – not only general but also particular.

Special providence also means that God has a special care for all rational creatures: animals and human beings. Throughout the Bible we are told that God controls the existence of all people, evil as well as good. That is why He causes His sun to rise and the rain to fall upon all types of people. God is thus related even to sinners, even to men and women who deny Him and do not believe in Him. Scripture teaches that they are not outside a relationship with God.

But, of course, above all, special providence means God's special care for His own people, and what He does for them.

So let us come now to the scriptural statements and the scriptural principles. First, the Bible tells us that God's providence is exercised over the universe at large. Psalm 103:19, which we have already quoted, says 'his kingdom ruleth over all'. We find it also in Ephesians 1:11: 'the purpose of him who worketh all things after the counsel of his own will'. God is controlling all things everywhere – the heavens and the earth, and under the earth. He has a purpose behind it all.

Second, God's providence is exercised over the physical world; I refer you to the whole of Psalm 104, and also, again, to Matthew 5:45.

Third is God's controlling providence over the brute creation, over the animals. We see that again in Psalm 104 and also in Matthew 6:26, where we read about the birds that 'they sow not, neither do they reap, nor gather into barns; yet your heavenly Father feedeth them', while in Matthew 10:29 we are told about the sparrows: 'and one of them shall not fall on the ground without your Father'.

Fourth, we are told that His providence is exercised over the affairs of nations; you will find that in Job 12:24, 'He taketh away the heart of the chief of the people of the earth, and causeth them to wander in a wilderness where there is no way.' Or again in Acts 17:26 we read, 'And hath made of one blood all nations of men for to dwell on all the face of the earth, and hath determined the times before appointed, and the bounds of their habitation.'

Fifth, we are told that God providentially governs a man's birth and his lot in this world. We read in 1 Samuel 16:1, 'And the Lord said unto Samuel, How long wilt thou mourn for Saul, seeing I have rejected him from reigning over Israel? fill thine horn with oil, and go, I will send thee to Jesse the Bethlehemite: for I have provided me a king among his sons.' And Paul says about himself in Galatians 1:15–16, 'But when it pleased God, who separated me from my mother's womb, and called me by his grace, to reveal his Son in me, that I might preach him among the heathen . . .'

In the sixth place, we find that God's providence determines the outward successes and failures in human life: 'For promotion cometh neither from the east, nor from the west, nor from the south. But God is the judge: he putteth down one, and setteth up another' (Ps. 75:6–7).

The seventh is this: that God governs things which appear to be accidental, or apparently insignificant. My favourite text to prove that is the first verse of Esther 6, where we are told that the king 'could not sleep'. 'Dear me,' says someone, 'surely that has got nothing to do with God's providence!' But read the book of Esther, and you will find that it is a crucial point. It is made quite clear that the king could not sleep that night because God kept him awake. So Mordecai was saved, and Esther and her people were saved, through the instrumentality of God causing this insomnia – something apparently trivial and seemingly accidental.

In the eighth place, God's providence protects the righteous. Read Psalm 4:8: 'I will both lay me down in peace, and sleep: for thou, Lord, only makest me dwell in safety,' says the psalmist. Why? The Lord had protected him. Indeed, that is shown beautifully in both Psalms 4 and 5.

And God supplies, in the ninth place, through providence, the needs of His people: 'But my God shall supply all your need according to his riches in glory by Christ Jesus,' says Paul in Philippians 4:19.

And tenth and last, you will find that every single answer to prayer which is in the Scriptures is just a statement that God providentially orders things in this way for His people.

Now that brings me to what is called 'extraordinary providences', or, in other words, miracles, for miracles come under this heading of providence. A miracle is an extraordinary providence. 'What is the difference between ordinary and extraordinary providence?' asks someone. I would answer that question like this: in ordinary providence God works through second causes, in accordance with the laws which He has placed in nature. But in extraordinary providences, or miracles, God works immediately, directly, and without the secondary causes. A miracle is God working, not contrary to nature, but in a supernatural manner.

People often get into trouble about this question of miracles because they start by thinking that a miracle is something contrary to nature. But that is quite wrong, and it is wrong because their idea of nature is wrong; they have forgotten that God works in nature. It is simply that God has two different ways of working. Generally He achieves His purposes through the secondary causes; but sometimes He does it directly, and that is a miracle. God is working, as we have been seeing at length, in everything, always and everywhere; so that when you have a miracle, it is still God working, but working in a different way; and to deny the possibility of miracles is to say that God is confined, or bound, by His own laws.

Some people, of course, insist that miracles are impossible because they break the laws of nature. If such people believe in God at all, they mean that God is now bound by the laws which He Himself has placed in nature, and can do nothing about it. They reduce God to a position subservient to His own law. But this denies the doctrine of God all along the line. There is also a tendency, among certain people, to believe in miracles only when they think they can explain them!

Let me illustrate that by a story. I remember once, a man, a deacon, coming to talk to me about his minister; he had been rather troubled about the call of this minister to his church, because he was not quite certain about the soundness and the orthodoxy of this man. But he came to me with great glee and delight one day and said, 'You know, our minister now believes in miracles.'

'What has convinced him?' I asked. 'What is your evidence?'

'Well,' he said, 'he was preaching on Sunday night and he told us that some recent discoveries made in the region of Sodom and Gomorrah have revealed that there were certain substances there which might very well account for what is described in the Old Testament.' So his minister now believed in miracles! But in fact he still did not believe in miracles, for if you can explain a thing scientifically it is no longer a miracle. By definition, a miracle is something that you cannot explain.

Someone else once said that an astrologer had discovered that just about the time – the person talking to me was really quite excited about this, and he was an evangelical – that the children of Israel were crossing the Red Sea, the sun and the moon were so positioned that it was more than likely that a sort of gale had arisen that drove back a part of the Red Sea. So it was possible that the children of Israel had passed over on dry land after all. And this man fondly thought that he was a believer in miracles now! No, no! You will notice, perhaps, that there is a tendency to do this at the present time. It just means that such people are not happy in their belief in miracles, and that they really do not accept the biblical doctrine. A miracle by definition is supernatural. It cannot be explained in terms of the ordinary operation of the laws of nature or of secondary causes. It is God's direct and immediate action.

I think that the real trouble with regard to a belief in miracles is due to the fact that people always will approach them from the standpoint of science or of nature, instead of from the standpoint of God who is all-mighty and who governs and controls everything. The danger in this century is to deify nature, to regard it as some absolute power with which even God cannot interfere. It is an utterly false notion.

Once we have the right idea of God's providence, I think most of our difficulties with regard to miracles should be removed.

Now we must mention one or two difficulties which people sometimes have with regard to this doctrine of providence. They say that they are ready to believe in providence in general, but they cannot quite understand the idea of a special providence, and they say they have two reasons for this. The first is that God is surely too great and too all-mighty to be troubled and worried by the details of our petty little problems. The second is that the laws of nature make such an interference impossible. But the Bible teaches us that God *is* concerned with the details of our lives. He answers the prayers of His people, in detail, in very small matters, and He encourages us to take all things to Him. Paul says, 'Be careful for nothing; but in every thing by prayer and supplication with thanksgiving let your requests be made known unto God' (Phil. 4:6). As for that second objection, the biblical teaching denies it utterly. Scripture teaches this special providence of God positively, and miracles, of course, prove it to the very hilt.

But, after all, the great problem is this: if God does govern and control everything, then what is His relationship to sin? All I can do, in answer, is to lay down a number of propositions that are clearly taught in the Scriptures. The first is that sinful acts are under divine control, and occur only by God's permission and according to His ultimate purpose. If you want proof of that you will find it in the case of Joseph and his brethren. 'It was not you that sent me hither,' said Joseph, 'but God' (Gen. 45:8). God permitted their sinful act and controlled it. You will find the same teaching about the death of our Lord as it is expounded by Peter on the Day of Pentecost (Acts 2).

The second is that God restrains and controls sin. In Psalm 76:10 we read, 'Surely the wrath of man shall praise thee: the remainder of wrath shalt thou restrain.'

The third is that God overrules sin for good. Genesis 50:20 puts it like this: 'But as for you, ye thought evil against me; but God meant it unto good, to bring to pass, as it is this day, to save much people alive.' God overruled the sin, and He did exactly the same in the case of the death of our Lord.

My last proposition is that God never causes sin, nor approves of it; He only permits, directs, restrains, limits and overrules it. People alone are responsible for their sin. The first chapter of James gives that particular teaching clearly.

Let us finish with two general points. The first is to me one of the most comforting of all. I cannot but believe, having read the Bible, that ultimately the whole of providence is for the sake of God's people. If you want a proof of that it is in Romans 8:28: 'All things work together for good to them that love God.' It seems perfectly clear to me that, ultimately, God is thus concerned with everything for the sake of His own people, and everything else is being manipulated for our benefit and for our good. It is a wonderful thought, and I commend it to you. As you read your Scriptures keep your eye on that – providence really is concerned about salvation, and everything is kept going in the world for the sake of God's people. Were it not for His people, everything would be destroyed. All others – all sinners – are clearly going to be destroyed. They are preserved and kept going because of God's people and because of God's salvation.

My other point is this: be careful – it is a warning! Always be careful in your application of any particular event. Let me explain: whenever anything good happens to us or to our country we are all very ready, are we not, to say that it was undoubtedly an act of God – the providence of God. I have explained what the doctrine of providence teaches, but I would warn you that it is dangerous to particularise about any particular thing. Take the famous case of Dunkirk. I am not going to express an opinion as to what happened at Dunkirk; I do have an opinion but I shall not give it. All I would do is show you that if you do claim it was an act of God, you must do so in the light of the following. In 1934 German Christians – and very fine Christians among them – issued this statement: 'We are full of thanks to God that He as Lord of history has given us Adolf Hitler, our leader and our saviour from our difficult lot. We acknowledge that we, with body and soul, are bound and dedicated to the German State and to its Führer. This bondage and duty contains for us as Evangelical Christians its deepest and most holy significance in its obedience to the command of God.' That surely makes us think, does it not? Here is another declaration of theirs in 1933: 'This turn of history,' they said, referring to Hitler's coming into power, 'we say God has given him to us, to God be the glory. As bound to God's word we recognise in the great events of our day a new commission of God to His Church.'

Now those people were absolutely sincere; they were absolutely genuine. They were evangelical Christians, and they believed that! So I think you will agree that we must be a little cautious when we come to make particular claims. Or again, someone in Moscow once said of Stalin, 'He is the divinely appointed leader of our armed and cultural forces, leading us to victory.' It is a very simple thing to persuade yourself that God has an unusual and a special interest in your country. Let us be very careful lest we bring God and His cause into disrepute by unwise and injudicious claims. Sometimes during the Second World War we had the National Days of Prayer, but terrible things happened almost the next day. Do remember that. My point, then, is this: the doctrine is plain and clear, but let us be judicious and cautious, and have a great concern for the glory and the name of God when we claim any particular event as an instance of His special providence either with regard to us or our country.

14
The Creation of Man

We are studying these biblical doctrines in their chronological and theological order, and so we come now, of necessity, to a consideration of the biblical doctrine of man. We started by considering what the Bible tells us about the being of God, and we confessed that we have no knowledge of Him apart from what we have in the Bible. So we had to start with the doctrine of Scripture and Scripture's own doctrine about itself, and then we looked at what it tells us about God, and about what God has done; and that took us to the doctrine of creation. That in turn led us to consider how God maintains what He created. That was the doctrine of providence which we were considering together in the last chapter.

Now, having done that, we must concentrate in particular upon man, because that is the special concern of the Scriptures. They have been given to us in order that we might arrive at a knowledge of the truth concerning ourselves and our relationship to God. We must, therefore, start with a hurried glance at what the Scripture tells us about the origin of men and women, and it describes that in terms of His creation. A number of things strike us at once with regard to this biblical account and we referred to two or three of them, in passing, when we dealt with the doctrine of creation, indicating that we would have to return to them more particularly when we came specifically to deal with the doctrine of man.

It is clear, as you read the account in the first chapter of Genesis — and it is equally true of the second — that the Scriptures' own account of the creation of man gives the obvious impression that something special was taking place, something distinct, something which must be emphasised. There is a kind of pause here, and in most Bibles it is put as a separate paragraph. All of this is designed to remind us of the uniqueness of what was now going to be done. But in addition to that general emphasis, certain things are put before us in particular. For instance, we are told that before the creation of man, God said, 'Let us make man in our own image, after our likeness' (Gen. 1:26).

It is quite clear – and it seems to me to be the only adequate explanation – that the three Persons of the blessed Trinity held counsel together before man was created. It is quite inadequate to suggest that this phrase, 'Let us,' is simply a kind of plural of majesty such as that used by royal personages who say 'We' instead of 'I'. That is something that is not done in Scripture. God generally refers to Himself in the singular; but here we have this plural. Neither can it be argued, surely, that this was a kind of conference or consultation which God had with the angels; there is no suggestion of that anywhere in the Scriptures.

No, it has generally been agreed from the very beginning that this is undoubtedly a reference to a conference between God the Father, God the Son and God the Holy Spirit. Now that is something unique; we have not had that with regard to the creation of anything else. Having made these other things, there was a kind of pause, and the three blessed Persons held counsel together and said, 'Let us make man in our image, after our likeness.'

So then, the second thing that we are told is that man was made in the image of God. You remember that in other cases we keep on reading the phrase 'after their kind', but there is no such phrase here. Man was not created after any kind, and is not told to reproduce after any kind. There is this peculiar something about him, that he was made and created in God's image and after His likeness.

Then we are told something else in Genesis 2:7: 'And the Lord God formed man of the dust of the ground, and breathed into his nostrils the breath of life; and man became a living soul.' In other words, in the case of man, there is a distinction of the elements which compose him; there is a distinction between the body and the spirit, the material and the immaterial parts. Again, it is something unique, something that we have not met before. God took of the dust of the ground and out of that He made man's body. But He did not take hold of anything in order to put the soul in man; He breathed into his nostrils the breath of life. So the important thing to observe here is the distinction of the elements that compose man and his being.

And the other thing, of course, that is emphasised is the exalted position that was at once given to him; he was made lord over the whole of creation, over all nature, over all creatures, and all the beasts. We shall have to return to that later, I simply note it here in order to emphasise the uniqueness of man in all this process of creation.

Now once more I am afraid we must turn aside for a little, as I indicated we should, to the vexed question of evolution. There are many, as you know, who believe that man has just evolved out of the animal. Whether they say that man has evolved out of some ape-like creature, or whether they say that the apes and man have both come from a common stock, it does not matter. The theory in general is, as we have seen, that he originally evolved out of some animal, thus denying this doctrine of the special creation of man.

But I must show you, without going back again to the argument of evolution, that this theory with regard to man is something that very definitely and specifically contradicts the biblical teaching. There is, I repeat, this pause in the Bible, and I regard it as being very significant. If man had evolved out of the animals, then there would not be this pause between the creation of the animals and the account of the creation of man; the account would have gone on directly from one to the other. But the Bible pauses, and it says that God did a unique thing; there was a conference between the three Persons of the Trinity. Why say that, if it was just a continuation of the previous process? It seems to me to be quite unnecessary.

Then, as I have just reminded you, the Scriptures tell us, and they emphasise it, that God made man out of the dust of the earth, so the question I would ask is this: If man has evolved out of some previous creatures, why not say so? Why say specifically that He has been made out of the dust of the earth? Surely if the theory of evolution were true, then this statement about man being made in that way is misleading, and so we could charge the Scriptures with misleading us, and apparently deliberately misleading us, which is, of course, quite unthinkable.

Now it is no use trying to argue that people at that time did not know about the doctrine of evolution, because if you believe at all in divine inspiration, then that argument will not hold up for a second. But there are other points which we must notice in this connection, and the first is man's essential difference from all animals. At once we are told certain things about man which mark him out as being essentially different from every type of animal. He has self-consciousness;

he has moral freedom; he clearly is capable of abstract thought; and he is capable of religion and worship. There is not a suspicion of those things with regard to any of the animals, but from the start the Bible emphasises – and we can substantiate and corroborate what it teaches – that these are peculiar qualitative differences between man and all types of animals, even the highest type.

Then another point, which is extremely important from the standpoint of doctrine, is this. The theory of evolution tells us that man has not only evolved, but that it is always an upward process, from the primitive and the simple to the more highly organised and involved, moving steadily in the direction of perfection. It tells us that man started way down, scarcely to be differentiated from the animal, and then he grows further and further away from the animal, until eventually he is perfect.

But the Bible, of course, tells us the exact opposite; the Bible tells us that man started, as it were, on top and then fell from that. It teaches this doctrine of the fall, and, as I shall have to show many times, the doctrine of the fall is a vital part of the biblical doctrine of salvation. That is why it is so important that we should be clear about these things and see why we cannot accept this idea of the evolution of man. The whole biblical case for salvation rests upon the fact that man, who was made perfect, fell and became imperfect – which is the exact opposite of the doctrine of evolution. So we really must fight at this point. The doctrine of the evolution of man from the animals, and the denial of his special creation by God, involves us at once in a denial of the doctrine of the Fall, and therefore puts us in serious trouble with regard to the doctrine of salvation.

'Yes, but wait a minute,' says someone, 'what about the person who is a theistic evolutionist?'

Well, all we say is that first and foremost on purely scientific grounds he has to establish that human beings have evolved in the way that the theory tells us. You remember what theistic evolution means – it is a theory that says that man's body has evolved out of the animal but that the soul was put in specially by God. But there is no evidence or proof for that; indeed, the evidence, as we saw, is against it. But in addition to that, the doctrine of theistic evolution does not solve our problem at all; it still leaves us with the great problem of the fall; we still have to explain that. So theistic evolution, which attempts to reconcile what goes by the name of science, but is merely the theory of evolution, with the scriptural teaching, is unnecessary because it finally does not help us.

The next thing the Bible tells us, and tells us categorically, is that the human race is one. It teaches very clearly the doctrine of the unity of the entire human race. It tells us that the whole of mankind has come from two people, Adam and Eve. The Bible does not in any way equivocate about this, it just states it. Nobody will deny that that is stated in Genesis, but it is not only stated there, and I want to emphasise this very particularly because some people suggest that it is only to be found in those early chapters of Genesis. It is something which is also stated elsewhere in the Scriptures. Take, for instance, Deuteronomy 32:8: 'When the most High divided to the nations their inheritance, when he separated the sons of Adam, he set the bounds of the people according to the number of the children of Israel.' Again, the whole incident in connection with the Tower of Babel, in Genesis 11:1–9, obviously teaches the same truth – that here was this unit which then became divided and separated. And then the apostle Paul said the same thing to the people of Athens: 'And hath made of one blood all nations of men . . .' (Acts 17:26).

But why are we so concerned about this and why are we emphasising it so much? Again, we have to do so because other central, crucial doctrines depend upon this very idea. I remember once being in a conference with a number of scientific Christians who were tending to be dominated by their scientific brethren, and their one concern was simply to get out of their difficulties with regard to the first three chapters of Genesis. But it was a very simple thing to show them, and indeed to convince them, that their problem was not only with the first three chapters of Genesis; they also had to face Romans 5. The whole argument in that chapter is that the human race is one, that it has all come out of Adam, so that when Adam fell the whole race fell with him. So, you see, we cannot afford to play fast and loose with these theories.

Now I emphasise it in this way because I think that there is nothing so dangerous to faith, or so fatal, as to be afraid of supposed science. If you start accommodating at one point you will be denying another doctrine at some other point. The whole doctrine of Romans 5 is based upon the unity of the entire human race in Adam, and the unity of all Christians in Christ. Read it for yourselves and you will work out that parallel: 'Therefore as by the offence of one judgment came upon all men to condemnation; even so by the righteousness of one the free gift came upon all men unto justification of life' (Rom. 5:18);

and you find exactly the same thing in 1 Corinthians 15:21-2. So we must insist upon this doctrine.

And, of course, in a very interesting way it is increasingly being found that what the Bible has always taught and asserted can now be corroborated by evidence outside the Bible. Let me put some of it to you for your consideration. Scientists, even today, have to admit that the human race is but one species; there are obviously different families but there is only one species. And they simply cannot account for this; they are in difficulties about it. Take, for instance, the people who were found in North America and South America when Columbus and others got there. According to the scientific theory, it was very difficult to explain their likeness to us, since the animals they supposedly evolved from were unlike the animals from which people in Asia were supposed to be descended.

Then there is the fascinating evidence which historical research and knowledge provide of the history of the migrations of people. You have probably read about this many times – how the various tribes moved away from central Asia, some travelling north, and some westwards to the Mediterranean area. And with that let us put the fact, which is quite established and undoubted among anthropologists, that however widely separate and different races may be, most of them have certain common traditions, the tradition of a flood, for instance, and the tradition of a fall. Now the evidence of the history of the migrations of people, plus these common traditions, point conclusively to the fact that there seems to have been a common ancestry for all the families of mankind somewhere in central Asia. This is not my theory, nor simply that of Christian people. It is the theory of anthropologists, who study man and try to find out the truth about him. All of this goes to corroborate and substantiate the biblical teaching about the unity of the entire race.

Then there is the evidence provided from the study of languages – philology. This evidence is most important. Did you know that most of the so-called Indo-Germanic languages can be traced to a common primitive tongue? The nearest approach to it that is extant today is ancient Sanskrit, but they all, including English, can be traced back in that way. Not only that. There is very good evidence, it seems, for saying (I am simply passing on to you now the results of what the experts have found) that ancient Egyptian may very well be the connecting link between these Indo-European languages and the Semitic languages. In other words, philologists have been able to trace all these languages back to a common source. It is a most fascinating theme. Those of you who know different languages have probably often noticed how practically the same word in French and in Latin, in English, and in the Celtic language, is used for the same thing, and you have got to explain what the common origin is for these words. And it all points back, you see, to the original unity of the race.

Then there is a very powerful argument from what is called the 'psychology of man', which means that wherever you find a man, you always find a creature of the same type, of the same kind; he has the same instincts, the same desires. One may be absolutely illiterate and another very sophisticated, but it is amazing to note how similar they are in what they want and in what they like and what they do. So then, it is very important for us, particularly in the light of the biblical teaching about our unity in Adam and our unity in Christ, to hold on to the teaching of the unity of the race.

We consider next the constitutional nature of man, and the great question here is whether 'soul' and 'spirit' are one or two. There are two main theories: first, *dichotomy* – man as body and soul; second, *trichotomy*, that man has a body which is material, a soul, which is the principle of animal life, and a spirit which is the God-related, rational and immortal element.

The arguments for dichotomy are, first: the terms for 'soul' and 'spirit' are used interchangeably in Scripture.

Second, the words 'spirit' and 'soul' are both applied to animals. In the book of Ecclesiastes we read, 'Who knoweth the spirit of man that goeth upward, and the spirit of the beast that goeth downward to the earth?' (Eccles. 3:21). The apostle John wrote, 'And the second angel poured out his vial upon the sea; and it became as the blood of a dead man: and every living soul died in the sea' (Rev. 16:3).

Third, in the book of Revelation the disembodied dead are referred to as 'souls', not 'spirits'. Revelation 6:9 talks of 'the souls of them that were slain' which were under the altar, and, in the famous passage about the millennium in Revelation 20:4, we read of 'the souls of them that were beheaded' reigning with Christ.

Fourth, you find also that the very highest exercises of religion and of worship are ascribed to the soul rather than to the spirit: 'What shall it profit a man, if he shall gain the whole world, and lose his own soul?' (Mark 3:36). 'Thou shalt love the Lord thy God with all thy heart, and with all thy soul, and with all thy mind, and with all thy strength' (Mark 12:30). The part that is engaged in worship and in relationship to God is not referred to as spirit but as soul. Then you remember how Mary in her song says, 'My soul doth magnify the Lord . . .' (Luke 1:46). In Hebrews 6:19 you have, 'Which hope we have as an anchor of the soul, both sure and stedfast, and which entereth into that within the veil.' In James 1:21 we read about 'the engrafted word, which is able to save your souls', not spirits; and in the same way you will find that death is sometimes described in the Scriptures as giving up the 'soul', and sometimes as giving up the 'spirit', or the 'ghost'.

Fifth, the immaterial element of the dead is sometimes described as soul and sometimes as spirit. Take, for instance, those two passages in Revelation to which I have referred; they describe the immaterial element as 'the soul'; but in Hebrews 12:23 we read about 'the spirits of just men made perfect'.

So there is difficulty about this. Man is described in Matthew 10:28 as body and soul, but in other places as body and spirit (Eccles. 12:7; 1 Cor. 5:3–5). In other words, it does seem clear from the Scripture that the two terms are frequently interchangeable, and the conclusion we draw from that is that man seems to be two elements only: body, and soul (or spirit).

'Yes,' says someone, 'but what about 1 Thessalonians 5:23?' 'And the very God of peace sanctify you wholly; and I pray God your whole spirit and soul and body be preserved blameless unto the coming of our Lord Jesus Christ.' And then in Hebrews 4:12 we read, 'For the word of God is quick, and powerful, and sharper than any two-edged sword, piercing even to the dividing asunder of soul and spirit, and of the joints and marrow, and is a discerner of the thoughts and intents of the heart.' 'Now, then,' continues the questioner, 'there it is specifically, twice over – body, soul and spirit; soul and spirit separated and regarded as distinct.'

Well, the reply of those who believe in the dichotomy or the bipartite idea is that two passages like that must obviously be taken in the light of the whole of Scripture, and if the whole gives the impression that there is essentially no difference between the two, then these verses must be explained in a way which does not divide them. So they go on to say that neither of these verses really proves that the two things are distinct substances or essences, any more than Mark 12:30 shows that there is a difference between mind and soul, as, for instance, 'Thou shalt love the Lord thy God with all thy heart, and with all thy soul, and with all thy mind, and with all thy strength.'

Now people are agreed that the mind and the heart – the thinking and the affections – are a part of the soul, but our Lord Jesus Christ seems to differentiate between them. So it is suggested that the separation of the soul and spirit may have a similar purpose. Thus what is emphasised in the 1 Thessalonians 5 passage is the wholeness of the sanctification: the entire person is to be sanctified and preserved blameless. And in Hebrews 4:12 the emphasis is upon the thoroughness with which we are searched: the Word of God differentiates even between the 'thoughts and intents', it goes right down to the very depths.

What, then, do we say about all this? I am afraid that once more I have to say that I cannot decide which of the two groups I belong to. Neither theory can really be proved, but we can say that the Scripture does draw a *distinction* between spirit and soul, even if it does not say that there is a *difference* between them. There may be a distinction without a difference. Let me put it like this: certainly the Scriptures teach us that the spirit is that part of the spiritual or immaterial element in each of us which is related to God, and is capable of receiving the operation of the Spirit of God through His word. Spirit is that which puts us into relationship with God and enables the Spirit of God to act upon us. If there is only one immaterial element, then a part of that immaterial element is called spirit, and it is that which, as it were, links us to God, whereas the soul is the part of the immaterial element which animates the body, which renders us capable of thinking and willing and feeling. It is also the seat of the affections. It is that part of us which links us to the body and enables us, through the body, to communicate with other people.

You may not be satisfied with that explanation, but it is an attempt at a compromise. In other words, you must agree that there is a distinction between spirit and soul, but whether you must press your distinction to the extent of saying that they are two essentially different things is something about which I personally am not convinced. So we might say that man *has* spirit but *is* a soul. You will find that the term 'soul' is often used instead of the personal pronoun, and often about the whole personality. You will find that the number of people who went to Canaan, was such and such a number of 'souls' (Gen. 12:5), or that the number of 'souls' who went down to Egypt was sixty-six (Gen. 46:26), and so on. So I am afraid we cannot arrive at any finality, but, at any rate, it is good for us to notice that the material and the immaterial element together make up the person, and that the immaterial element has this distinction of spirit and of soul.

Having said that, let us consider briefly the relationship between body and soul. Again, we have to say that we do not know exactly what this is; we do know, however, that they are organically and vitally related. We know that they act on each other and that they affect each other. The Scriptures teach us these things quite plainly, though they do not tell us what the relationship is in detail. But certain things are clear. I remember once listening to the famous Sir Arthur Keith delivering a lecture, and he said, amid much glee and great applause, that he had dissected many human bodies, but still he had never discovered an organ which he could describe as the soul. To which the reply is, of course, that we start by saying that the soul is immaterial, that it is not something you expect to find when you have dissected a body. But it is there and it animates the body.

Furthermore, we know that though the soul normally uses the body as the instrument by which it expresses itself and does what it wants to do, it can exist apart from the body, and when the body is buried in the grave the soul goes on and still exists, and can exert itself without the body. So that while it uses the body, it is not a part of it; it is not solely dependent upon it. There is a vital organic relationship between them, but exactly what it is is left for us as a great mystery.

One final question: What is the origin of the soul in each individual? Every person born into this world has a soul, but where does it come from? How are our souls a part of us? Once more, the answer is that we do not know. 'But, if you do not know,' asks someone, 'why are you concerned about it?' The answer to that is that we shall soon be dealing with the doctrine of original sin, and you cannot deal with that without considering something of the origin of the soul. The question we shall be up against is this: How does the sin of Adam affect me? What is my exact relationship to him? We believe that every soul born into the world is born in a fallen condition. How did it fall? When? If we really take these doctrines seriously we cannot avoid these questions. And another reason for considering this question is that we shall be looking at the person of the Lord Jesus Christ and we shall teach that He had a human soul. Where did He get it from? Did He get it from Mary? You see, the question is bound to arise.

Now at this point I shall just give some headings. There are those who believe in the pre-existence of the soul – that we have all existed before and come back into this world. There is no biblical evidence for that view whatsoever, but many people have read Wordsworth, his great Ode in particular, and they think:

But trailing clouds of glory do we come
From God, who is our home.

Plato taught it, and there is often an admixture of Platonism and philosophy in religion without people realising it.

Then there is another idea, called *traducianism*. This means that the soul, with the body, is propagated by human generation; that the soul of the newborn infant has been derived from its progenitors, from its parents, that as its body is given to it in that way so is its soul. What is there in favour of this theory? Well, here are some of the things that are generally said: first, God breathed into man once only, we are never told that it was repeated, and that from thereon man is told to replenish the earth, and so on.

Second, we are not told that Eve's soul was a special creation or that God breathed into the body that He made out of the side of Adam. We are also told that God ceased from the work of creation after he had created Adam and Eve. There are also some very interesting biblical statements about the descendants being in the 'loins' of their fathers. We are told in Hebrews 7:9–10, for example, that when Abraham was paying the tithes to Melchisedec, Levi being in the 'loins of Abraham' was himself paying the tithes to Melchisedec. That is called the doctrine of seminal identity, and a very fascinating doctrine it is to think out. Then we are told that there are analogies – that you get this kind of thing in the vegetable and animal world – and it is said that it is the only way in which you can truly explain family traits in physical appearance, in characteristics, and in mental faculties.

There are certain objections to this theory. First, the soul seems to be regarded as something material, does it not? It seems to be something that can be divided up into different parts, and you raise the questions: Does the soul come from the father or the mother, or both? And in what state did it exist in the father or mother if it were preexistent there? And, second, there is grave difficulty, again, about the person of our Lord if he derived His soul from man.

Then the other theory with regard to the origin of the soul is what is called *creationism*, which teaches that each individual soul is the immediate creation of God and that we do not get our souls from our parents. Our body comes from our parents, but at some point or other – nobody knows when – whether it is in the earliest beginning of the human foetus or later, when the child becomes viable, or when it is born, the soul is put into it. To me there is a very grave objection to this theory. It is this: if the soul is an immediate creation of God, where does its tendency towards sin and evil come from? It means that God must be the author of moral evil.

Or if you say that the body alone comes from the parents and that what accounts for original sin is that God puts this pure soul into a sinful body which is sure to cause the soul to sin, then you make God the indirect author of moral evil and of sin. If God creates each soul separately, where does original sin come in? How do you account for it? You see, the traducian idea is not in difficulties about that; it says that we were all, as it were, in the loins of Adam when he sinned, and we have therefore all inherited our fallen nature directly from him. Creationism, while it is right in its views of the nature of the soul, leaves us in grave difficulties about original sin, and almost seems to teach that God has somehow produced something that is evil, which is unthinkable.

I therefore sum it up like this: when we face a question like that, it is vitally important that we should approach it with humility, with reverence and godly fear. We must be careful not to go beyond what the Scripture tells us – and I believe that at that point we have reached something which we cannot understand or explain. But we can say certain things quite definitely: God does not create anything which is evil – that is certain. God cannot create a sinful soul. We are equally clear from the Scriptures that human depravity is inherited – 'I was shapen in iniquity; and in sin did my mother conceive me,' says the psalmist (Ps. 51:5). And we are equally certain that the humanity or the human nature of our Lord and Saviour Jesus Christ was not guilty of sin and was not sinful in any way.

Now I trust I have made my attitude towards this clear. This last matter, and the previous one, are obviously not essential to our salvation. But if we are desirous, as I am sure we all are and as we all ought to be, of understanding, to the fullest possible extent, the doctrines that are clearly and plainly taught in the Scriptures, then we have to raise certain questions, even though we may not be able to give final answers. So I would say in conclusion that we should not spend too much of our time with these problems. Let us not fall into the error of so many philosophers, of wasting a lifetime over them, because we will end where we began. Let us above all be careful of becoming 'party men' with regard to these things. When we cannot arrive at finality, let us never belong to any party – if indeed we should ever belong to a party about anything. But about these matters, certainly, as I said, let us be humble, and let us be content to go only as far as Scripture takes us; but also let us always be anxious to go as far as Scripture does take us.

What a mystery is man! What a mystery is his being! Here we are in these bodies, and yet we have this immaterial part. We are made by God and we are made for God, and though we may not understand exactly how it all happens, thank God that about the things that are essential to salvation there is absolute clarity. But we thank God who has so endowed us with faculties that we can raise questions, and see their significance, even if we cannot always answer them.

15

The Divine Image in Man

Having looked at man's creation, his constitution and some of the problems arising therefrom, we come now to consider the great question of what is meant by man being created in the image and likeness of God. Our first reason for considering this is Scripture itself – let me give you a number of verses which deal with it.

First are the verses in Genesis 1:26–7: 'And God said, Let us make man in our image, after our likeness: and let them have dominion over the fish of the sea, and over the fowl of the air, and over the cattle, and over all the earth, and over every creeping thing that creepeth upon the earth. So God created man in his own image, in the image of God created he him; male and female created he them.'

Next are two verses in Genesis 5 – verses 1 and 3: 'This is the book of the generations of Adam. In the day that God created man, in the likeness of God made he him . . . And Adam lived an hundred and thirty years, and he begat a son in his own likeness, after his image; and called his name Seth.'

Then there is Genesis 9:6 where we read, 'Whoso sheddeth man's blood, by man shall his blood be shed: for in the image of God made he man.' This is a most important text. The context deals with the question of murder, and ultimately the scriptural teaching about murder is that it destroys the image of God. Whenever, therefore, you consider the question of capital punishment, you should bear that in mind, as it is a most potent argument with regard to it.

Then another important reference is found in James 3:9: 'Therewith [James is referring here to the tongue – 'a little member'] bless we God, even the Father; and therewith curse we men, which are made after the similitude of God.' It is the same idea once more. Two other references are clearly very important: Ephesians 4:24, 'And that ye put on the new man, which after God is created in righteousness and true holiness'; and the parallel statement in Colossians 3:10: 'And have put on the new man, which is renewed in knowledge after the image of him that created him.'

Now you may wonder why I gave the quotation from James before giving the ones from Ephesians and Colossians. My reason for doing so is that the last two verses have references to 'the new man'; while the previous quotations all refer to man as he is apart from regeneration, and I shall explain later the significance of drawing that distinction. However, in the light of those scriptural quotations – and there are others which I shall refer to – it is, of course, our duty to face this whole question as to what the Bible means by our being made 'in the image and likeness of God'. We have no right to read the Scriptures without attempting to discover what they are saying. The fact that a subject is difficult is not an excuse for not trying.

But in addition to that, there is another reason that I would commend to you, which compels us to consider this matter, and that is a doctrinal reason. I mean by that that there are other doctrines which of necessity raise this doctrine of the image of God in each man and woman. For instance, the whole doctrine of man himself forces us to consider this doctrine. The great questions today are: What is man? What is the matter with him? What has gone wrong with him? How do you explain life as it is in the world today? That is called *anthropology*, the knowledge and study of man. It is a rapidly developing study, and is obviously most important. So clearly – and this is especially true of those of us who accept the biblical revelation and are Christians – we cannot begin to explain the world and what we are doing in it, unless we are clear about our origin, and our essential nature and being.

Then in addition to that, of course, the doctrine concerning the person of the Lord Jesus Christ compels us to look at this question of the image of God in man. We assert that He was truly man, but what does that mean? What do we believe about His manhood? What do we assert concerning His human nature? Obviously, therefore, without having some sort of idea of this, we cannot hope to be clear about our *Christology*, our understanding or our knowledge of Christ Himself.

Furthermore, of course, the whole doctrine of salvation raises this problem acutely: What exactly happens in the rebirth? What is the difference between an unregenerate and a regenerate person? What is the difference between the regenerate person and Adam? Those are questions which are bound to arise. If we are at all anxious to know what it is that Christ has done for us, and the position in which He has placed us; if we are interested in any sense in what is called 'biblical psychology', then this question of the divine image faces us even as we begin to approach the subject.

Finally, there is one other reason for considering this doctrine, which I would describe as a general reason. The whole biblical revelation, in which God reveals Himself to man in order to reconcile man and to restore him to Himself, obviously proceeds upon the fact that man was so constituted originally as to be capable of becoming the subject of such revelation and redemption. If we believe, as we do, that God has granted us a revelation as to how we can know Him again, and be reconciled to Him, and be redeemed from our sins, and prepared for heaven and for glory, if we believe that this is possible, then we are at once suggesting that there is something in us which renders us capable of that; there is something there, if you like to use the theological term, some 'point of contact' which revelation can address, and which makes each of us susceptible of redemption, renovation and deliverance.

These, then, are the main reasons for considering this great subject. Of course, it has been considered in the Church from the very beginning. There has been much argument concerning this throughout the centuries, especially at the time of the Protestant Reformation, because the Reformed doctrine of the image of God is very different from that of the Roman Catholics; and if you want to be a real controversialist in that respect, I think it is well to concentrate on that particular point. Over and above their practices, it is their doctrine to which we should object most strongly, and this was, therefore, very much in the forefront at the time of the Protestant Reformation, as it has been ever since.

However, I am not going into the history; I should very much enjoy doing so, but I must not, because it does not strictly come under the heading of biblical theology. But the history of this doctrine is extremely fascinating – how some have said that the 'image' means man's body, and that the 'likeness' means his spirit, and so on. But we must leave that, and confine ourselves rather to a positive exposition of what the Scriptures teach. Once more, I must preface this by saying that the subject is a very high and a very difficult one, and, again, there are certain respects at which we cannot arrive at finality. But with this, as with the other doctrines we have considered, it is our duty to go as far as we can, and not to be dogmatic when we are not in a position to be so.

So then, there are certain things which can be said, and here is the first. It is generally agreed that *there is no real difference of meaning between 'image' and 'likeness'*. You notice that the two terms were used in Genesis 1:26 – 'Let us make man in our image, after our likeness.' If you go through the scriptural references you will find that the terms are used interchangeably, sometimes 'image', sometimes 'likeness', and mean exactly the same thing. This is obviously for the sake of emphasis, and to bring out the greatness of this subject.

And man's greatness is, perhaps, our supreme reason for considering the doctrine at all. I am never tired of pointing out that to me one of the great tragedies in the modern world is man's failure to realise this. That sounds strange in an age when man is worshipping man; yes, but what he worships is totally unworthy of the biblical conception. The real trouble in the world today is that man does not know who he is and what he is; he does not realise his own greatness. For instance, the theory of evolution is an utter insult to man from the standpoint of the biblical account – man is great and glorious and wonderful in the mind and conception of God.

Now this term 'image' or 'likeness', of course, conveys to us the idea of a mirror and a reflection. Paul uses it in that way in 2 Corinthians 3:18 where he says, 'But we all, with open face beholding as in a glass the glory of the Lord, are changed into the same image from glory to glory, even as by the Spirit of the Lord.' Charles Wesley's hymn puts it,

> Changed from glory into glory,
> Till in heaven we take our place.

We all, says Paul, are able to look upon Him, in Christ, without the veil that covered the face of Moses, the veil that still stands between the Jews and the realisation of this. We with 'unveiled', with 'open' face are able to behold, and as we do so, God's image, as it were, is formed upon us, and is reflected back again; and as we go on looking the image becomes more and more glorious. That is the idea of image, so that fundamentally when we talk about being made in the image of God, we mean that God made us in such a way that we are some kind of a reflection of God. We must not be too mechanical in our notions, but we cannot get nearer to it than that; that man as made by God was a kind of reflector of something of the divine glory itself. That is the essential idea.

The next principle that I would emphasise is that *this term is used after the fall, as well as before the fall*. That is a very vital point, as we shall see. Take those scriptural quotations and you will find that the bulk of them come after the fall. So the image of God was not entirely lost when Adam and Eve sinned and fell. There have been schools of thought that have taught that. There have been unworthy and inadequate notions of the image which have suggested that when man sinned everything that belonged to the image of God in him disappeared, and in the rebirth what was entirely lost is given back. But these scriptural quotations demonstrate very clearly that the term 'image' is used after the fall as well as before. In other words, when man fell he lost something, he lost an aspect of the image, but he did not lose the entire image; something essential to the image still remains. And that at once suggests that there are certain elements in this image of God which are to be found in each person.

The next point I make is this one – and here we come to my reason for putting the quotation from the epistle of James before the other two. I have a feeling (and I am not alone in this) that *it is somewhat misleading to define the original image of God in man in terms of what we are told about regenerate man*. The quotations from Ephesians 4 and Colossians 3 are descriptions of what we become when we are regenerate, when we are saved, when the life of God has come into us. Now I suggest that while those two quotations may tell us something about the image of God in man, it would be very wrong to determine our idea of the image at the beginning, before the fall, in terms of these quotations.

I say that for this reason: I think I can demonstrate to you from the Scriptures that what happened in regeneration is not merely that we are restored to the condition that Adam was in before he fell, but we are advanced beyond that: 'Where sin abounded, grace did much more abound' (Rom. 5:20). Yes; as Isaac Watts has put it,

> In Him [in Christ] the tribes of Adam boast
> More blessings than their father lost.

Salvation, redemption, regeneration do not merely put us back where Adam was; we are in a much higher position. So here again, you see, the doctrine of the image is very important from the standpoint of the doctrine of salvation, and we must be very careful that we interpret it correctly. So while we will still use those two quotations, they will not determine our exact definition of what is meant by the divine image.

And my last general principle is that clearly *there is a difference between man as he was made at the beginning by God, and the manhood or the humanity of the Lord Jesus Christ*. If you take those verses at the beginning of Hebrews 1, you will find this: Christ is the 'express image of his person'. All the effulgence of the glory is in Him. That cannot be said about man. Man is, as it were, a created copy – Christ is the image. He is indeed the very express, essential image of God Himself. That will be important to remember when we come to deal with the person of the Lord Jesus Christ.

Next we must go on to say that it seems clear, therefore, that there are two main elements in this idea of God's image in us. Often these two elements have been described as the *natural image* and the *spiritual image*. The great Jonathan Edwards, for instance, said that 'the natural image consists very much in that by which God in His creation distinguished man from the beasts, namely, in those faculties and principles of nature whereby he is capable of moral agency.' That is the natural part of man. The spiritual and moral part, he said, consisted in that moral excellence with which man at the beginning was endowed by God. You see the difference between the natural and spiritual aspects? Let me put it like this: you can say that the image consists of a man's intellectual and moral nature, and his original moral perfection. His intellectual and moral nature – that is the natural; his original moral perfection – that is the spiritual.

Here it might be well to quote the teaching of John Calvin as he was able to explain perhaps more clearly than anybody else at that time the essential difference between the Reformed and the Roman Catholic views. He puts it like this: 'The seat of the image in man is the soul, though some rays of it shine even in the body.' And when he comes to define the image, he says that it really means man's original integrity, his unity, his uprightness, his straightness. But he says as well that 'the image of God extends to everything in which the nature of man surpasses that of all other species of animals'. You see, they are all really saying the same thing. The divine image in man, they are saying in effect, means everything in man as a natural being that differentiates him from the animal. But there is more than that; in addition to that, man had an original righteousness, and that is the spiritual aspect.

So having given you some definitions in general, let me now come to consider it in a little more detail, because clearly we can divide it up. What is this image of God in which man was made at the beginning? What is this likeness of God? First of all, it obviously refers to the soul or the spirit – our spiritual nature, our spirituality. Or you can use this term as well, as a concept – our 'invisibility'. We look at one another and in one sense we see one another, but in another sense we do not. We, none of us, see the essential self of anybody, nor of ourselves. You have never really seen yourself. I wonder if you have ever thought of that? Try to think of yourself and what you look like; you cannot really do it. That is because our essential being, our personality, is invisible. When you look at another person you are seeing certain manifestations of that person but you are not really seeing the person.

Now man in that sense – let us say it with reverence – is like God. God is invisible – 'No man hath seen God at any time' (John 1:18). You remember how, in dealing with the doctrine of God, one of the points we made was that of His invisibility? And that, in a sense, is true also of us; our soul or spirit is invisible. And at the same point we must refer to our immortality. As originally made and created, Adam and Eve were not subject to death. And again, you remember, that was something which we said was true of God, according to the scriptural teaching.

But then, second, we would put what you may call our psychical powers and faculties; the powers and faculties of the soul. You noticed I said 'psychical' and not 'psychic'. I am not interested in psychic phenomena, but very interested in the psychical. It means everything that pertains to, or belongs to, the soul, and these, it is generally agreed, are a part of the divine image. I mean things like this: that we are rational and moral beings; that we have intellect, we can think; that we have a will and can desire; and the intellect and the will have their powers and their propensities. Our capacity to reason and to think, to analyse and to meditate is a reflection of the same thing, in an eternal degree, in God. And it is unique to human beings, you do not find it anywhere else.

We also have self-consciousness. We are conscious of ourselves. Again, we have to predicate that about God. And our self-consciousness, our self-awareness, our inability to get rid of the self – all that is a part, again, of the divine image. And perhaps well worthy of very special emphasis at this point is our capacity for self-contemplation and analysis; that surely is something that belongs to human beings. Man can contemplate himself, he can examine himself and analyse himself. This is an astounding faculty, and we must all at times have wished we had not got it. But you cannot be a person without it and it is a part of the curse that the fall has brought upon us that we cannot get rid of ourselves, and we cannot stop contemplating and analysing ourselves. Even in a fallen condition we proclaim to ourselves our own original greatness by this very capacity.

The third feature of the divine image we will put in this form: it is intellectual and moral integrity revealing themselves in (to use the words again of the Ephesians and Colossians passages) knowledge, righteousness and holiness. Man was made intellectually and morally in such a way that there was a kind of integrity about him, nothing false, nothing imperfect, nothing wrong. There was a straightness, an uprightness. There was a truth. His nature was one; it was balanced; it was exactly what it was meant to be: moral and intellectual integrity, expressing themselves in 'righteousness and true holiness' (Eph. 4:24).

Next, fourth, I come to something about which there has not always been agreement, and it is the question of the body. Does the body in any way share in this divine image? And for myself, I am prepared to say that it does. In saying that, I am not referring to the material substance of which the body is made, but rather to the body as a fit organ of the soul, the instrument of the soul, the thing through which the soul and the personality express themselves, and therefore, ultimately, the instrument through which we exercise dominion over the lower creation, and especially over the animals. Now this is, of course, the most difficult aspect of all, and we cannot be sure, as I say, but there are many suggestions in the Scriptures that in a sense we have been made like unto God, even in the matter of the body.

'But,' says someone, 'I thought you taught us that God is Spirit and you have emphasised His invisibility.'

Yes, but you remember that Paul tells us that our Lord, before the incarnation, was in the form of God (Phil. 2:6). Also, speaking to the Jews one day, our Lord told them that they had not heard God's voice at any time, and then went on to say, 'nor seen his shape' (John 5:37). There are suggestions here about the form of God, though He is Spirit, about the kind of shape of God.

Furthermore, we are told in Philippians 3 that we await Christ's coming from heaven who, says the apostle Paul, 'shall change our vile body, that it may be fashioned like unto his glorious body' (Phil. 3:21) – this spiritual body. Our Lord is in that spiritual body now, and obviously – because He is in glory, and because we, when our bodies are changed and glorified, shall be in glory – then at that point there will be a likeness. We do not know yet what we shall be, says John, but we know this, that when we see Him, 'we shall be like him' (1 John 3:2). And I suggest to you that the likeness will include the body – the glorified body, it is true – but that makes me suggest that the original human body bore something of this. So I would suggest that the image partly expresses itself and manifests itself in our physical being.

Then the fifth and last feature of the divine image and one which I want to emphasise is this: the image of God shows itself also in man's dominion over the earth. There is no doubt at all but that that is a part of the divine image. It is there that man partly reflects God's lordship and sovereignty over everything. You notice how there is a suggestion of this in Genesis 1:26: 'And God said, Let us make man in our image, after our likeness: and let them have dominion over the fish of the sea, and over the fowl of the air, and over the cattle, and over all the earth, and over every creeping thing that creepeth upon the earth.' The moment the image is mentioned that function is mentioned, so that surely it is a part of the image of God in man that he does exercise this lordship. Consider also Psalm 8 in the same connection: 'O Lord, our Lord, how excellent is thy name in all the earth! who hast set thy glory above the heavens. Out of the mouth of babes and sucklings hast thou ordained strength because of thine enemies.' Then the psalmist goes on, 'When I consider thy heavens . . . what is man [in the light of all this] that thou art mindful of him? and the son of man, that thou visitest him? For thou hast made him a little lower than the angels [and some would tell us that the right reading there is, 'For thou hast made him a little lower than God'], and hast crowned him with glory and honour. Thou madest him to have dominion over the works of thy hands . . .' Having this dominion, this control, this rule over creation, is a part of the glory and honour. What God is to the whole universe He has made man, as it were, to creation.

So having looked at it like that in detail, let me gather it up in this way. The essential elements in the image are those which man cannot lose without ceasing to be man; they are those qualities and powers of the human soul that remain always. But there are other elements, which we may call 'accidental' elements, which a man can lose and still remain man. In other words, when man sinned and fell he did not lose the whole of the image, he retained the essential elements, but he lost the accidental elements. We must be very clear about this. When man fell, he did not cease to be man. His essential manhood remained, and that retains that part of the divine image in which he was originally created.

Therefore it is important that we should emphasise this. We must never confine our idea of the image of God in man merely to man's original righteousness and holiness. People have often done that, and it has landed them in grievous trouble with regard to other doctrines. They say, you see, that the divine image in man simply meant his original righteousness and holiness; when he fell, therefore, he lost it all. But that is not so. The natural element in the divine image must be emphasised, because, as Scripture has taught us, it persists after the fall. It was there in Genesis 5; it is there in Genesis 9, and it is there in the third chapter of James. Man, even in sin, retains those elements and aspects of the divine image; they are an essential part of human nature. If he lost those he would no longer be human.

Very well then, we can say this: the essence of the soul endowed with the faculty of knowing and willing – the general congruity and analogy between the nature of God and the nature of man – and man's dominion over the creatures, survives even the fall, but man's moral conformity to God was lost at the fall. The rational, the intellectual, and those general elements survive the fall, but after he sinned, his moral conformity to God was lost, as we shall see as we go on to consider the doctrine of the fall.

So, the question which we must ask at this point is this: What was man's original state if all those things are true? Now there are two main dangers here. One is the danger of exaggeration and of making Adam into a kind of Colossus. The other is the danger of underestimating grievously what he was, and here evolutionists again come in and describe him as some kind of half savage half beast. Both are wrong. What we must say is this: man as he was originally made was clearly connected with the earth, but he was also connected with God.

Second, God made him His representative in the world.

Third, he was obviously intelligent and able to understand. God brought the animals to him and asked him to name them, and it was Adam who gave the names to all these animals and creatures (Gen. 2:19–20). He could differentiate and distinguish; he knew the right type and kind of name to give, and they are names that carry meanings and tell us something about the character of each animal. So he was obviously gifted with a high intelligence. We gather also that he was happy. He worked without toil. He exercised mastery over the world. He obtained his sustenance from the vegetable kingdom without toiling for it. And he was clearly in a state of familiarity with the animals.

What was his relationship to God? It was one of filial dependence, the dependence of a child, a son. He gave God implicit obedience, and, most importantly, his communion, his fellowship, his intercourse with God was entirely without fear. What, also, was his spiritual condition? Here is an important subject. Again, there has been much error with regard to this. We are told that when God made everything, man included, 'God saw everything that he had made, and, behold, it was very good' (Gen. 1:31). In Ecclesiastes 7:29 we are told that God made man upright. This is not only a reference to his physical frame, but also to his essential moral and spiritual constitution.

Now that means, it seems to me, that there was never any conflict in man at the beginning between his lower and his higher elements, between his physical and his spiritual elements. The Roman Catholics say there was – that from the beginning the body was always a danger to man, and God had to give man an extra gift to safeguard him against being dragged down by his lower nature. That is the Roman Catholic idea of the image. In other words, a kind of capacity for sin was already there before man fell. But that is something which the Scripture does not teach. There was no conflict at all; there was perfect harmony between body and spirit. The conscience surely proves that. Every time our conscience accuses us it is a proof that man was originally sinless. We have a feeling that we should not have sinned, that it was wrong to sin. Yes, that is a memory, a recollection of man's original, sinless condition.

Another negative is this: we must not think of Adam as just being in a state of innocence. Some people think of him as if he were just a child – though a man, a child in outlook and mentality – and say that he was morally neutral. He was neither good nor bad, they say; he had not sinned, he was nothing, neutral. But the Bible does not teach us that. The Bible teaches us that man was in a state of positive holiness and true righteousness. That is where the quotations from Ephesians and Colossians are important. Salvation must at any rate bring us back to that, and more.

So then, you ask, what is the difference between Adam before he fell and man in regeneration and salvation? I suggest to you that the difference is that these things were present in Adam in germ, in embryonic form. They were not fully developed. They were there, and as they were they were perfect. They were perfect in part but not in degree. In other words, man was perfect as far as he had gone, but there was room for development. There was nothing imperfect in him at all. You can have a perfect acorn, and a perfect oak tree. It is a different perfection, and yet they are connected to each other. The fact that the acorn is not an oak tree does not mean that it is imperfect. No. It is a perfect acorn, and all the potentialities of the perfect oak tree are there in the perfect acorn. Adam and Eve at the beginning was surely like that. The knowledge, the righteousness, and the true holiness were there in germ and in embryo, in perfect form, but they were not yet fully developed. In other words, man was on trial, he was on probation. He was in a preliminary condition, which could lead either to infinitely greater dignity and glory or could terminate in a fall. We know it actually did terminate in a fall, but it could have gone on growing and developing until it was in full bloom and perfect.

So that is how God made man. He put him in that condition in the Garden, and He made a covenant with him. He told him that if he obeyed His laws, then he would go on growing and developing to that final, complete perfection; on the other hand, if he did that which God had prohibited him to do, if he broke God's commandment, he would fall and lose certain blessings.

Very well; at this point we must leave it – man created in the image of God, with these intellectual, moral, rational faculties, yes. But over and above that, this original righteousness and holiness. There he is, placed in the Garden, lord of creation, reflecting something of God even in his form, in his very body, and with these two great possibilities – if he remains in correspondence with God, an everlasting development in his perfection until it becomes absolute; on the other hand, if he rebels and does not go God's way, the possibility of a fall. Thus God made man in His own image and after His own likeness. Such was man at the beginning, and in spite of the fall, in spite of sin, elements of that remain today. That is the tragedy of the world. That should be the greatest impulse and motive to evangelism. In a sense, our first message to man should be to realise who he is, what God made him, and then what he has done to himself and has made himself.

16
The Fall

You will remember that in our last study we ended by looking at man as he was to be found created in the image and likeness of God, and dwelling in Paradise. We considered the character and nature of his being. We examined, as far as is possible, in the light of scriptural teaching, what this image of God meant. We found that man was in correspondence with God, in fellowship with Him, reflecting something of His glory. Happy, carefree, able to live without toil, eating of the fruits of the Garden, he was in a state of bliss. He had righteousness, an uprightness, a moral being and character corresponding to the God with whom he was thus in fellowship.

But now, obviously, when we look at man today, we see something very different, the whole picture is entirely changed. And the question to which we must address ourselves therefore is: What has produced this change? We look at man's present moral and spiritual, and even physical, condition and, I repeat, we see something entirely different. We are confronted by a new series of phenomena with regard to life and death. We see the corruption of human nature, and the whole character of human life in this world, and so, of course, the first question which the gospel, and the preaching of the gospel of Jesus Christ, must always ask is just that: What is the matter? What went wrong? If we talk about a salvation, why is it needed? You cannot escape this whole doctrine of man and of sin.

Now many explanations have been put forward in an attempt to account for the state of man and of the world as we know it at present. I must not keep you with these, although many of them are worthy of careful examination in order to refute them. I try not to do that more than I am bound to because I am anxious to keep to a positive exposition of the biblical teaching. And yet it is necessary that we should just refer to these other theories and ideas in passing, if only for this reason – that there are people who sometimes think that if a preacher does not mention a thing, it means he has never heard of it! I would, therefore, like any 'intellectuals' who may be considering these doctrines with us to know that though we do not spend a great deal of time with these things, it is not because we are not aware of them, but that we find it more profitable to be positive rather than negative.

However, having said that, let me just mention one or two. There is a very old theory which goes back to a time even before the Christian era, which says that there are two equally great principles in life: the principle of good and the principle of evil; the technical term for that is *dualism*. Dualism states that good and evil are of the very essence of life, and even that there is a god who controls the evil as well as a god who controls the good. There have been various ramifications of that; you will find these ideas in some other religions, and that is why it is important that we should know of their existence. But we have already dealt with dualism in previous lectures, and have rejected it because not only is there nothing to suggest that teaching in the Bible, it cannot be substantiated from an examination of people or of life.

Another attempted explanation is the theory which works itself out in the theory of evolution – that man is only an animal, and that what we witness in life and the world, therefore, is nothing but a manifestation of certain animal qualities and characteristics. I need not go into this again because in refuting the theory of evolution we have already answered this particular idea.

Then when you come to theories which are not based upon evolution or upon this principle of good and evil, but are prepared to look at man in and of himself, there are again a great variety of explanations. There are those who would say that what the Bible calls evil and sin is just a kind of resistance that is an essential part of human nature, put there by God in order that we might have something to overcome, and that by overcoming it, we might grow. Now that is the great principle of all exercise, is it not? You lift up weights in order to develop your muscles; the resistance of the weight is the thing that develops them.

Then there are other theories which regard sin merely as the absence of some positive qualities, the absence of knowledge, the absence of understanding. It is said that what the Bible calls sin and evil are just negative conditions, and that if only men and women had more knowledge and were better educated and more cultured and better trained they would get rid of all this. It is put like this, for instance: 'You must not say about a man that he is bad; what you should really say is that he is not good.'

Well, you see the kind of theory that has been put forward. There are very many, but they all, more or less, boil down to the ones that we have already considered. I shall have to return to this later when I come to consider the doctrine of sin a little more directly, but I think I have done enough to show that man and woman, face to face with this problem, as with every problem, always do their utmost to avoid the plain and clear teaching of the scriptures; and therefore they invent and imagine these theories which they cannot substantiate in any way whatsoever.

But over and against all that, we are confronted by the biblical doctrine of the fall of man, the biblical explanation of the present state of man and of the world. And in a very interesting way you will find that this biblical idea has penetrated into various other religions, and even into folklore, in a sense confirming the biblical history about the unity of the human race and the fall of man. Wherever men and women have gone, this story, this idea, of the fall, has somehow or other accompanied them, thereby providing very striking evidence for the truth we are about to consider.

Now the biblical account of man's present condition is found in that great chapter at the beginning of the Bible – the third chapter of Genesis. What is this? Is it history or is it not? Is what we read there the plain, unvarnished, historical fact, or is it not? This is obviously a crucial question, and therefore you have people suggesting that it is not history but allegory, that it is not really true and did not happen like that. They say it is a wonderful story which is designed to give us in a pictorial manner an account of man's gradual change. That is one way in which people have tried to avoid the clear statement which is made here.

Then there are others who say that it is not so much an allegory as a myth. A myth, they say, is a story which expresses religious truth. It is not actual history, but the ideas it contains, they say, are true.

Human ingenuity and imagination has exercised itself very much throughout the centuries. People say that the serpent was not really an animal. It was just a kind of symbol, a symbol that, according to some, is meant to represent covetousness. But no, say others, the serpent is a symbol of sexual desire. Others say that it is a symbol of erring and straying reason, and still others that it is a symbol, a figure, to represent Satan himself. In other words, they do not believe in the literal serpent. But even those who accept the serpent have their difficulty – they struggle with the question as to whether the serpent ever spoke or not.

Now I mention all these difficulties, these objections that have been put forward, in order that we may consider them all together. What do we say about these matters? Well, the obvious thing is that this whole chapter is given to us as history; there is no suggestion of allegory. It offers itself to us as plain, unvarnished fact, and if you begin to say that it is not history, or that parts of it are not history, you will find yourself in an utterly contradictory position. For instance, we are told in verses 14 and 15 about the punishment that followed Adam and Eve's sin, and if you do not accept that, then you have to shed a great deal of the Bible because the consequences that followed, and which are described here, have continued ever since, and the entire teaching of the Bible with regard to man is dependent upon that being fact. So if a part of Genesis 3 is fact, why not the whole? And therefore it seems to me that the only possible thing to do is to accept it all as fact.

Personally I am in no difficulty at all about that. The moment you believe in God, the moment you believe in the devil, then you are entitled to expect miracles, you are entitled to expect things that are supernatural. The Bible says that, and it is the ultimate answer to people who are in trouble over miracles. The moment you believe in God as the Bible depicts Him, you really should not be in any trouble about miracles, and it is exactly the same over this question of the serpent speaking. If you believe in the devil as the Bible depicts him, then you should have no difficulty in believing that he has power even to make a serpent speak. So all this difficulty not only contradicts what we have already agreed about, but, it seems to me, is quite unnecessary.

But over and above that, I want to call your attention to certain other Scriptures which clearly teach that what we have in the third chapter of Genesis is literal history. Take, for instance, Job 31:33: 'If I covered my transgressions as Adam, by hiding mine iniquity in my bosom' – this supports the historicity of Genesis 3. Then take Hosea 6:7. In the *Authorised Version* it reads like this: 'But they like men have transgressed the covenant,' and it is generally agreed, and you will find it in both the *Revised* and the *Revised Standard Versions*, that it should read like this: 'But they like Adam have transgressed the covenant.'

But there is a still more important verse in 2 Corinthians 11:3 where the apostle writes, 'I fear, lest by any means, as the serpent beguiled Eve through his subtilty, so your minds should be corrupted from the simplicity that is in Christ.' You notice what Paul says: 'as the serpent beguiled Eve' – he treats Genesis 3 as historical fact. The apostle claimed to be divinely inspired and what he wrote was therefore without error, yet that is what he said. And you have still another reference in 1 Timothy 2:14 where the apostle deals with the question of women teaching in the Church, and things of that kind. This is what he says, 'And Adam was not deceived, but the woman being deceived was in the transgression.'

In other words, it always seems to me to be very pathetic when people, in the interests of some supposed scientific knowledge, feel that they must dismiss the historicity of Genesis 3 and say that it is only a myth, or something like that, or that parts of it are true and parts are not, and then imagine that they have solved their problems! But if you do that, you are creating tremendous problems for yourself. What do you make of these statements in other parts of Scripture? As we have already seen, if you begin to play fast and loose with the scriptural teaching at any one point, you will find that your whole system will be shaken. And therefore, though – again one has to say it – there are certain things one does not understand, yet for myself I have no difficulty whatsoever in accepting this third chapter of Genesis as being literal, actual history.

Very well then, accepting it like that, let us examine Genesis 3 and see what it tells us. The first thing is that evil, sin and temptation came from the outside; they came from Satan, using the serpent. The thing I am anxious to emphasise is that there was nothing in man himself that produced that fall into sin. There was no physical cause. There was nothing sensual in man that brought it about. This temptation came to man entirely from the outside, and he had perfect free will to decide what to do with it. That is a most important point which is of the very essence of the biblical teaching. We must get rid of all the ideas that say that something in the body, in the human frame, in a man's flesh, some form of natural desire, dragged man down.

As we saw, the Roman Catholic doctrine about the image does suggest that very strongly. Its view is that man always had a kind of struggle, that the animal, the bodily part of man, always had a tendency to pull him down, and that God gave him the extra gift of original righteousness in order to enable him to keep at bay this other part that was always tending to pull him down. The Bible says nothing of the kind. Man was perfectly balanced; there was nothing within him at all to drag him down. Sin came entirely from the outside, and that is vital to our doctrine, as we shall see, time and time again.

What, then, were the steps to the fall? I am now simply reminding you of what we are told in Genesis 3. The first thing was that the serpent attacked the woman, not the man. You see the significance of that in some of the quotations I have already given you. We shall not go into that now; we shall come to it some other time perhaps. But the Bible emphasises it, not only in this chapter but elsewhere, and this is what happened. The woman began to listen to the slanders of the devil against God; she began to doubt God's word and God's love. Then, you remember, she began to look at the thing which God had prohibited, and, having looked at the fruit, and having seen that it was good to eat, she began to desire it and to lust after it, and that in turn led her to a definite act of disobedience. She deliberately broke God's commandment and did the thing that God had told her and Adam not to do. Then Adam, on being offered the fruit, took it from her and ate with her. So they were both in the transgression – the woman first, followed by the man.

So the question that arises is: What made them do this? Ultimately, of course, we cannot answer that question. Nobody has been able to answer it. The most we can say is that man's moral constitution, his being made in the image of God, and his possession of free will, at any rate held the possibility of his disobedience, but beyond that we cannot get, even as we could not arrive at any ultimate explanation of how Satan himself originally fell. You notice that ambition came into it, and ambition taking on a particular form: a desire for a short road to divine knowledge.

Now I am most anxious to emphasise that, because I am never tired of saying that the ultimate trouble with most false doctrines, and especially with most false doctrines of sanctification, is that they are trying to arrive at something by means of a short cut, and you will see that that was the original cause of man's downfall. God had got His programme for Adam and Eve, which was one of development in fellowship with Him, and ultimately they were going to arrive at this position; but the devil came along and said, 'You need not go that way, you need not take all that time about it. Just do what I am telling you and you will be there at once' – a short cut. The short cut always appeals to us. We always have a feeling that God's way is too slow and too laborious, and you will find that most cults are based upon this idea of offering you something by an easy and quick method – always much more rapid, simple and direct than the biblical method.

And the second thing, of course, was this – insinuated doubts of God's love. What was the result of this? Well – I am still talking, not of the actual consequences but of the result in their minds – it led to a transgression of God's law, and to a departure from God. Perhaps we can sum it up like this: it was a refusal on the part of Adam and Eve to submit themselves to the will of God, and to have God determine the course of their life; it was their determination to settle this for themselves. The essence of what took place was that they pushed on one side God's plan, God's purpose, and substituted their own idea and their own method. The famous Professor Emil Brunner has quite an interesting analysis, a psychological analysis, if you like, of what took place. He puts it like this: there were three elements – the desire for the fruit, then the whispered doubt about God, which seared and inflamed the desire still more, and then, finally, ambition turned the scale. First there was the original desire, then the serpent played on that by this whispered doubt, but still there was hesitation. Then ambition came in – 'You can be like God, you will know everything . . . if only . . .' And the ambition proved too much. It tilted the balance and they fell.

The one other point to which I would like to call your attention is the extraordinary correspondence between what is described here in Genesis 3, and what John tells us in his first epistle. In chapter 2:15 he says, 'Love not the world.' Then he divides up this love into 'the lust of the flesh, and the lust of the eyes, and the pride of life'. In Genesis 3 there is the desire, and then seeing that the fruit was good to look upon – the lust of the eye; then this pride of life, the ambition to be great, to be marvellous and wonderful. The same elements! Indeed, as I have already suggested, they reappear throughout the Bible and are worked out everywhere.

But to all that, I would add two special points, and here they are: sin is only possible, and was only possible to man at the beginning, because he had a free spiritual personality. Sin is not possible for an animal. In the most extraordinary way, man's being made in the image of God made sin possible for him, because of his free personality, because of his free will. The very fact that Adam and Eve were made in the image and likeness of God, in and of itself, exposed them to this possibility. No more than that, but it certainly did that.

Then the second point I would like to put for your consideration is this one: we know, and we have discovered from the Scriptures, that angels have also fallen, but you notice we are never told anywhere in the Bible that the angels, the fallen angels, are going to be redeemed. Salvation is only for man, and you may have asked yourself why. The angels fell as man fell. Why should there not be salvation for angels as well as for man? And I myself am very ready to accept the explanation which has been put forward, which is that in the case of man, the temptation and the fall came, as I have just been reminding you, from the outside. It is not an excuse, and yet it does make a difference. When Satan fell, he fell because of something within; the temptation did not come to Satan outside himself. What it was we do not know, but there is at any rate that difference. And is it possible, I wonder, that God in His infinite grace and kindness, has drawn that distinction? Because man was subjected to subtlety, to beguiling, to the malign angelic power of this fallen angel, is it possible that God had mercy and compassion and pity, and provided a way of salvation, which He did not provide in the case of the angels? I leave it for your consideration.

Let us come now to a practical point: What were the results of this disobedience, this transgression of God's law and commandment? They are described here very clearly. The first thing we are told is that Adam and Eve became conscious of their flesh (Gen. 3:7). This is an extraordinary thing. Man, as he was made originally by God, was quite unselfconscious about his body (Gen. 2:25). The man and the woman were naked, and that was no trouble to them at all. But the moment they sinned, the moment they fell, shame developed and they tried to cover themselves with fig leaves.

The Scripture emphasises that because it clearly has great significance. We must be careful as we note it, because there are two dangers confronting us. There is the danger of making too much of the sex element in sin, and there is the danger of making too little, but the Scripture specifically calls our attention to it. The first thing that happened was that Adam's and Eve's bodies became a problem to them, and have been a problem ever since. One difference between a man and an animal is that an animal is not conscious of its own body in the way that man is. It is of the very essence of man's sinful condition that the body which was given to him by God, and which in a sense is a reflection of God's own glory, the form of God, as we have seen, has become a problem. One of his greatest problems is that there is this sense of shame in connection with it.

Then the next thing which is emphasised is their sense of guilt. The moment they ate the fruit, they knew they had done something wrong. They were immediately condemned within themselves and became guilty. The next thing is that they began to develop a fear of God, and instead of running to God when they heard His voice in the cool of the evening, they ran away (Gen. 3:8). Before that, to hear the voice of God had been the highest bliss possible. They had been in perfect correspondence. They had no craven fear of God, they ran to Him. Now they ran away from Him. And their fear of God persisted. Another way of putting that is to say that they lost their fellowship with God, and their sense of fellowship with God – the thing they had glorified in above everything.

The next thing that is emphasised is that they clearly underwent a spiritual death. They were in an entirely new condition, and in that state, we are told, they were driven out of Paradise, out of the Garden, and were not allowed to return there by their own volition. You remember the flaming sword that guarded the way to the tree of life and barred their entry into the Garden (Gen. 3:24)?

But in addition to that, you find that they were in an entirely new relationship to nature. There had been no toiling before but now Adam had to toil, he had to sweat; it was by the sweat of his brow that he had to earn his bread. Difficulties and obstacles would rise in nature; he would have to tame nature and overcome the thorns and the briars and all the other problems (Gen. 3:17–19).

Moreover, we find that Adam and Eve had clearly undergone a perversion in their moral nature; you see that at once in the story of Cain that follows. There was a perversion in Cain's very nature which he inherited from his parents.

And the last consequence that is noted here is that of physical death. Now we just touched upon this on a previous occasion. Let me put it like this: there was no need for man to die. If he had obeyed God, and had continued living his life in correspondence with God, he would never have undergone physical death. It was possible for him, therefore, not to die. But the result of the fall was that now it was not possible for him not to die. It is put like this in Latin: the original condition was *posse non mori*; now it is *non posse non mori*. Now he must die. It is impossible for him not to unless there is some special intervention. The Scripture puts that in this way: Adam is told that he must return to the dust from which he came (Gen. 3:19); that would not have happened but for this sin. And that is confirmed in Romans 5:12: 'Wherefore, as by one man sin entered into the world, and death by sin . . .' Death came in that way by sin and as the result of sin.

Now those are the things that immediately resulted, but, again, there are certain things that we must be very careful to observe. You notice that although all that happened to Adam and Eve, they did not immediately lose all their intellectual power – indeed, man has never subsequently lost his intellectual power. He retained that. Go on and read the next chapters in Genesis, and you will find how he became musical, built cities, developed a great civilisation. He did not lose his intellectual power, nor immediately die physically. Indeed, there does not seem to have been any immediate physical change.

In other words, the effects of sin were delayed both physically and mentally. There was subsequently a very great decline in man's intellectual, moral and all his other faculties, as we see described in Genesis 6; but it did not happen at once. Sometimes people think that the moment Adam sinned and fell, he fell as far as man can go. But he did not. He fell in the essential way I have described, but there was a decline and a degradation consequent upon it. He did not die physically at once; he died some time later. And the same delayed result is true of his mental and moral qualities.

So then, let me sum up the results in this way: certain legal results happened at once. Man immediately came under condemnation and was punished by God, whereas formerly he had only been blessed. Spiritually, he immediately fell from his original righteousness. There was not a second's delay. The moment he sinned, he lost that uprightness, that correspondence with the moral character of God. And, equally, he was separated from God at once. His fear came in, and the various other things of which I have reminded you. But the physical consequences followed more slowly. In other words, I am emphasising that when man fell, he did not cease to be man; he did not lose any of his essential qualities or attributes. His intellect, his power of self-analysis, his understanding, his will, all these things remained. But he lost his original righteousness and his fellowship with God. He became fearful, he hid himself, he became ashamed, 'self-conscious' in a bad sense – he did not know what to do with himself.

Such is man as the result of the fall. What can we say about him? Well, the best description I have ever read or heard was made by an old Puritan, John Howe. He said that man, as the result of the fall, reminded him of some of these great buildings which you see in London, and in various distant countries. Once there was some great palace which has now fallen to ruins, and there is a sign outside which says, 'Centuries ago, such and such a king once dwelt here.' Now, as a result of the fall, it is written over man, 'Here God once dwelt.'

We have been considering one of the most profound and most awful truths that men and women can ever face. That is why all people, and that is why the world, are as they are today. From that great beginning to this – 'Here God once dwelt.' What a terrible, what an awful, what a calamitous thing is sin.

17

Adam's Posterity and Original Sin

In the last lecture, we began our consideration of the doctrine of the fall of man. We looked at the modern world and we saw that there is a very great difference between the picture we see there and the picture that we considered earlier when we looked at man as created by God in His own image and likeness and set in the Garden of Eden, in Paradise. And we considered together the account which is given in the third chapter of Genesis of what produced the difference – the fall of man, the first sin. We went on to trace some of the immediate consequences, some of the things that happened at once in the case of Adam and Eve; but we did not quite finish our consideration of these consequences. There were certain other consequences that followed immediately. There was, for instance, the curse that was pronounced upon the serpent. You find that in Genesis 3:14–15:

> And the Lord God said unto the serpent, Because thou hast done this, thou art cursed above all cattle, and above every beast of the field; upon thy belly shalt thou go, and dust shalt thou eat all the days of thy life: and I will put enmity between thee and the woman, and between thy seed and her seed; it shall bruise thy head, and thou shalt bruise his heel.

We do not stay with that, but to make our record complete, it is right to notice that that was a direct and immediate consequence of the sin and the fall of man.

Then, you will remember, certain consequences follow in the case of woman. These are described in verse 16: 'Unto the woman he said, I will greatly multiply thy sorrow and thy conception; in sorrow thou shalt bring forth children; and thy desire shall be to thy husband, and he shall rule over thee.' That is a most important statement, obviously, and one which is very significant. It is something which has been true ever since then and it is important for us to realise the significance of that fact. Birth was never originally meant to be as it is. It is one of the consequences of the sin and the fall of man.

And the other immediate consequence was that the ground was cursed. You will find that in verses 17 and 18: 'Cursed is the ground for thy sake; in sorrow shalt thou eat of it all the days of thy life; thorns also and thistles shall it bring forth to thee; and thou shalt eat the herb of the field.' And then the passage goes on to say something which we considered earlier: 'In the sweat of thy face shalt thou eat bread.' Because of man's fall, the very earth was cursed and thorns and briers came into being, increasing man's toil and effort, confronting him with a perpetual problem. The earth is constantly tending to return to a wilderness condition. If you cease to cultivate ground, it very soon reverts in that way. Now all that is a consequence of the fall. The apostle Paul takes up this very important point: 'The creature was made subject to vanity, not willingly, but by reason of him who hath subjected the same in hope' (Rom. 8:20). There we are reminded of this vital fact in connection with the whole life of the world. This curse that follows the fall of man has affected creation, and creation is not today as it was at the beginning, nor as it will be again when evil and sin are removed out of the world.

Those, then, were the immediate consequences of the fall. But now we come on to consider another vital aspect of this great doctrine. We have to consider the effect of sin and the fall upon Adam's posterity – not now upon Adam himself, but upon all who have come out of him. The best way, perhaps, of approaching this subject is, again, to put it like this: we are face to face with the fact of the universality of sin. Now this is something that is agreed upon by all. They do not all call it sin; some are not willing to call it that. But in various ways all people, whether they are Christians or not, have to admit that there is something wrong with man everywhere, wherever you find him. It does not matter how primitive he may be, whether he is civilised or uncivilised. Something in man is clearly lacking, there is something which causes misery and unhappiness. The Bible calls that, and so do we, therefore, the universality of sin.

Now this is something which we have to explain. It behoves anybody who is interested in the world and in man to explain this fact, this phenomenon. Earlier, I mentioned in passing that there are those who have their explanations. The most popular of all, I suppose, is the one that bases its case upon the theory of evolution, and would say that man is imperfect because he is not yet fully developed. He has just come out of the backwoods. He has not yet sloughed off all the relics and the vestiges of his bestial past. It is just his immaturity. (We have already considered this view, and given our answer.) Others say the cause is lack of knowledge, yet others, lack of good economic and social conditions, and so on. Many reasons are put forward and we have no time to stay with them and to refute them. We can simply say that they are all inadequate. They are contradictory and all of them are clearly too superficial to explain the problem by which we are confronted.

Now this fact of the universality of sin is asserted throughout the Bible. To illustrate this, let me simply select certain well-known passages more or less at random. Take the great statement in Isaiah 53:6, 'All we like sheep have gone astray.' All of us. But in many ways, of course, the classic statement of this doctrine is the one in Romans 3. The apostle goes on repeating it: 'There is none righteous, no, not one' (v. 10). '. . . all the world may become guilty' (v. 19). 'All have sinned, and come short of the glory of God' (v. 23). There is no exception – Jew and Gentile, Barbarian and Greek. It does not matter, the whole world, man in his totality lies guilty before God. It is a vital doctrine, essential for a true understanding of the biblical doctrine of salvation. James says exactly the same thing: 'For in many things we offend all' (Jas. 3:2). Again, it is universal. John in his first epistle says it twice over in the first chapter: 'If we say that we have no sin, we deceive ourselves, and the truth is not in us . . . If we say that we have not sinned, we make him a liar, and his word is not in us' (1 John 1:8, 10).

There, then, are some typical biblical statements and we sum it up by saying that the Bible asserts that the entire world is guilty of sin. But the Bible goes further and says that sin has not only affected all men and women, but has also affected their entire nature, that every part of their being is involved – body, soul and spirit.

And, of course, the question that arises at once is: How has this come to pass? But before we take that up, it may be a good thing at this point to be clear in our minds as to what exactly we mean by sin. What is the character of sin? What is sin as the term is used and taught in the Scripture itself? Well, let us summarise it in this way: first of all, the Bible teaches clearly that *sin is a special kind of evil*.

Now you can have evil which, in a sense, is not sin. Evil can be something general, something physical perhaps – calamities and things like that. That is a manifestation of evil but not of necessity of sin. The difference between them is that sin is moral or ethical evil; not evil in general, but a particular kind of evil.

Now the Bible has quite a number of terms to describe sin. A word that it uses very frequently means 'missing the mark' or deviating from the right way. Another word means an absence of integrity, of being true and whole, a want of rectitude, a departure from the appointed pathway. It is a most important distinction. Yet another word carries the meaning of a revolt, a rebellion, a refusal to subject ourselves to rightful authority. It means a positive transgression of law and a deliberate breaking of a covenant. Now it is very important that we should always realise that sin includes all these various things and others also.

Another biblical word translated as 'sin' means 'guilt', and that is an important consideration. Another term means unfaithfulness and even treason: it is not merely that we are unfaithful but that we are guilty of treason. Another word, which is often used in Scripture to cover this idea of sin, is 'vanity' or emptiness, futility. Peter talks about our 'vain conversation' inherited by tradition from our fathers (1 Pet. 1:18). Paul, in Ephesians 4, writes of doing things in the vanity of our minds (v. 17) – vanity is a very common biblical conception of sin. But then, finally, we are told that sin means a perversion or a distortion of nature – something that has been taken and twisted and perverted. Those, then, are some of the words that are used in the Scriptures to cover this idea of moral and ethical evil.

Now the second thing that the Bible teaches about sin is that *sin has an absolute character*. The Bible always puts up good and evil as entire antitheses. It does not know anything at all in between them. In the Bible, a thing is either black or white, there is never a grey. There is no communion between light and darkness, good and evil, God and Belial. The quality of sin is an absolute quality, it is actually, positively bad. Sin is not merely the absence of good, it is a positive something and it has a clearly defined character. There is no mean between two opposites, said Aristotle, and that can be applied here. There is no gradual shading from evil to good. A thing is either good or it is evil.

The third thing that the Bible stresses is that *sin is always something that is directly related to God and His will and His law*. The Bible always defines sin in terms of our relationship to God. That is where the biblical concept of sin must be differentiated so sharply from moral ideas which do not derive from the Bible. God is always involved and what makes sin sin is that it is a wrong relationship to God. It is men and women in a condition in which they do not love God and do not live entirely for God's glory and honour.

The fourth biblical emphasis is that *sin is something that is in the heart of men and women, not something on the surface of their life, but right down in the very depths*. It is out of the heart that 'proceed evil thoughts, murders, adulteries' and so on (Matt. 15:19). And the heart in the Bible does not merely mean the seat of my affections, it is not merely something on the surface of my life, it is not merely the way in which I manifest my personality, but it is the very centre or root of my personality. Now sin is resident there, says the Bible.

Another way of saying that is, fifthly, that *sin does not consist of actions only but essentially it is a condition*. Now there are those who have defined sin only in terms of actions, and they have forgotten that it is a condition before it manifests itself in acts. In other words, sin can be thought of in terms of layers: first of all we are in a sinful state and condition, and because of that we tend to develop the sinful habits of which we are so constantly guilty. Then, because we are creatures of sinful habits, we indulge in deeds or in particular acts of sin. So it is superficial and quite unbiblical to think of sin only in terms of particular actions.

And, lastly, the Bible always includes in its descriptions and definitions the fact that *sin is guilt and pollution*. Again, the pollution is a state, the condition, but guilt is a part of sin and according to the Scriptures guilt is sinful in and of itself. One of the best comprehensive definitions of sin I have ever encountered is this: sin is lack of conformity to the moral law of God, either in state, disposition, or act. That is a summing up of it all. So the great questions are: Why are we all guilty of sin? How have we become guilty of sin? What accounts for the universality of sin? There are, of course, many who think that this can be explained in various ways – a point we have already touched upon. The Bible tells us that it is all due to the sin of Adam, that all this has resulted directly as a consequence of that original sin which we have been considering together. But there are those who do not accept that. They say that we are all born into the world in a kind of neutral condition, but that we immediately see the bad example that is set by others and we imitate it and thereby sin.

But that is a denial of the biblical doctrine of original sin. That does not connect sin directly with Adam but says that Adam left a bad example which was followed by others and this process of imitation has continued ever since. But we must not think of sin like that if we want to be biblical. Neither must we think of it merely in terms of some kind of inability or disability. No, the Bible connects sin directly with that first sin of Adam.

Now, if that is so, the question arises as to how that sin of Adam has affected the whole of his posterity. And here there have been two main explanations which we must of necessity consider. The first, which is generally called *the realistic theory*, is that sin is universal because the whole of human nature was in Adam. Entire humanity was resident in him. Therefore, it argues, when Adam sinned and fell, the whole human nature fell with him. But not only that, it all fell in Adam at that one moment.

Now you will remember that when we were trying to look at the character or the nature of the soul, we had to ask whether the soul is something that passes from parents to children in a kind of semi-physical manner or whether each soul is a special creation of God. This realistic theory holds to the view that the soul is something that is inherited from our parents and, you remember, it introduces the argument which we describe as the argument of *seminal identity*. In Hebrews 7:9–10 we are told that Levi, who was yet unborn, paid tithes to Melchisedec in Abraham. Abraham, you remember, paid tithes to Melchisedec. Yes, says the author of Hebrews, and when Abraham paid those tithes, Levi ('who was in the loins of his father') was therefore paying the tithe himself. That is the theory of seminal identity. Now the realistic theory of original sin makes use of that argument. It says that the whole of mankind, all of us, were in the loins of Adam when he sinned and because we were in the loins of Adam, as Levi paid tithes in the loins of Abraham, so all of us sinned when Adam sinned his original sin at the beginning. That is the biblical basis for this particular view as to how sin has become universal.

Now there are certain difficulties about this theory. One immediate difficulty is that it does, of course, as I pointed out in the previous discussion, tend to materialise the soul. It almost of necessity must regard the soul as something material which somehow or another can pass physically from parents to children. That is the argument that has generally been brought against it and up to a point I admit the cogency of that argument, and yet it does not seem to me to be a conclusive objection.

There is another difficulty. If this theory of seminal identity is true and we have all sinned in Adam because the whole of human nature was in him, then why does the Bible teach as clearly as it does that we are only responsible for Adam's first sin? Why are we not responsible for all his sins? Furthermore, why are we not responsible for all the sins of all the children of Adam and of all the people who have come out of Adam ever since and of all our forefathers right down until we were born? The Bible does not say that we are responsible for all those sins. Its teaching is that we are responsible for this one sin of Adam that produced the fall. But according to that theory, in a sense – and I admit that this argument is a powerful one – the Bible really should teach that we are responsible for all the sins of all our ancestors.

And the other difficulty with regard to the theory is that it does present a certain problem about the person of the Lord Jesus Christ Himself. If human nature is something that is divisible like this and is derived by a physical process from parent to child, does it not follow, almost of necessity, that the human nature that our Lord received was therefore sinful? If we believe in this common unit of human nature in Adam which has been divided up since, it is hard to see how you can avoid that difficulty.

The second theory as to how Adam's sin has affected his posterity tells us that we have all inherited this sin and that sin has become universal because Adam was not only the natural head of the human race, but that God made a covenant with him and appointed him as the representative of the human race. It says that God made man and said in effect, 'Now, you are going to represent the whole of humanity, and I will make a covenant with you. If you do what I tell you I will bless you and you will grow and develop and eventually you will reach full maturity. But on the other hand, if you fail, not only will you fail, but all who come out of you and all whom you represent will fail in the same way.' This is called the *covenant theory*. It says that Adam was a kind of federal representative of the entire human race, that God appointed him as such and that, therefore, anything that Adam did had consequences for all who came out of him. For instance, we send a man to parliament to represent us and when a member of parliament votes he not only votes for himself, he votes for us – his constituents, the people whom he represents. He is our representative in parliament.

Or take another illustration. An ambassador represents a whole country and if he should be guilty of some error, the whole country will bear the consequences. If he should blunder and the country go to war, though we did not agree with what he did, we all suffer. He was our representative and he acted for us. Now that is the covenant idea which says that Adam was the federal representative of the entire human race and for that reason his sin was imputed to all of us and we all suffer the consequences.

Now there are certain advantages about this second theory. One is that it does explain very clearly why only the first sin of Adam is imputed to us. There is no need to impute any further sin because it was that one sin that made Adam lose his position. That one sin alone was sufficient. This theory also avoids the difficulty with regard to the person of the Lord Jesus Christ because the Scripture teaches us, as we shall see, that the Lord Jesus Christ was not a human person. He is a divine-human person. There is something unique in Him. He is not one in series with all the rest.

Well, again, if you are interested in my personal opinion, I must admit that I find it very difficult to be entirely on the one side or the other. There is a great deal, as I said before, about the doctrine of seminal identity which appeals to me. We cannot avoid that explicit statement in Hebrews 7:10, and it does seem to me that if it is a fair argument there, it is a fair argument here. At the same time, I admit that there are those great difficulties about that doctrine of seminal identity to which I have already referred and there are aspects about this second idea of Adam as our federal representative which greatly appeal to me. I dislike compromise but I do not quite see why, in a sense, we cannot adopt both views.

At any rate, whichever of the theories is true, or if both are true, the fact is, according to the Bible, that it is from Adam directly and from that first sin of Adam, that universal sin has come. Now the way in which this is generally described is this: it is called the *doctrine of original sin*. Now what do we mean by this? First of all, let us get rid of certain very common misunderstandings of this doctrine and especially misunderstandings of the meaning of this word 'original'. It does not mean, and must never be allowed to mean, that sin belonged to the original constitution of human beings. It specifically did not and we were at great pains earlier to emphasise that. It does not mean that sin is due to something that was originally a defect in man's constitution.

What it does mean, first of all, is that sin is derived from the original root of the human race — Adam — that all sin has come out of Adam. Or, to put it negatively, it asserts that sin does not originate from our imitation of the examples of others who have gone before us or whom we see, but that it is something that now inheres in human nature from birth, that we are all born in this condition. It has been derived in that way from the original root and therefore we are born in sin, 'shapen in iniquity' (Ps. 51:5).

And the other thing which we must emphasise about it is that it is something which is the inward root of all the sins that we actually commit and which defile us. It is original in the sense that it comes, as we have seen, right out from the centre of our being and our personality.

But we must go on to point out that there are two parts to original sin. The first is *original guilt*. The second is *original pollution*. According to the Scriptures we have inherited those two things from Adam and from his sin, and I want to emphasise this very carefully because you will find that there are many people who believe in original pollution but who reject the doctrine of original guilt. 'Yes,' they say, 'it's quite true to say that we have inherited this pollution from Adam,' but they say that they regard it as unjust and unrighteous, and impossible to reconcile with the love of God, to say that we are actually guilty of Adam's sin, that we have inherited guilt from him as well as pollution. But this, as I want to show you, is the biblical doctrine. It asserts that we have been born under the penalty of the law and of justice and that we deserve this penalty and punishment, that we are actually guilty of Adam's transgression.

Now people do not like this. They say that we are not guilty until we have done something wrong, that we have been born with this inherited inability or disability, this bias even, towards wrong but that, they say, is not guilt. The moment you have done something, then you are guilty, but not until then. Or some people, going a little further and becoming a little more biblical, say, 'Yes, we are guilty, but what we are guilty of is our polluted natures. We are not guilty of the actual transgression of Adam, but because we've inherited a polluted nature from him we're in a guilty condition, because to be polluted is to be guilty.' Now the Bible, I would assert, does not teach either of these views. It teaches, rather, that we are actually guilty of the sin that was committed by Adam.

Now the great, classic passage on this is Romans 5:12–19:

Wherefore, as by one man sin entered into the world, and death by sin; and so death passed upon all men, for that all have sinned: (For until the law sin was in the world: but sin is not imputed when there is no law. Nevertheless death reigned from Adam to Moses [when the law was given], even over them that had not sinned after the similitude of Adam's transgression, who is the figure of him that was to come. But not as the offence, so also is the free gift. For if through the offence of one many be dead, much more the grace of God, and the gift by grace, which is by one man, Jesus Christ, hath abounded unto many. And not as it was by one that sinned, so is the gift: for the judgment was by one to condemnation, but the free gift is of many offences unto justification. For if by one man's offence death reigned by one; much more they which receive abundance of grace and of the gift of righteousness shall reign in life by one, Jesus Christ.) Therefore as by the offence of one judgment came upon all men to condemnation; even so by the righteousness of one the free gift came upon all men unto justification of life. For as by one man's disobedience many were made sinners, so by the obedience of one shall many be made righteous.

How anybody can dispute or deny that passes my comprehension! It is so clear and the apostle goes on repeating it. Great teacher as he was, he repeats himself and repeats it and repeats it because he knew that men and women in sin are natural philosophers and would not like the doctrine, and would object to it and would try to argue against it.

But let me put the argument to you like this. You notice that in this paragraph the apostle is drawing a parallel and what he is saying is really a further exposition and explanation of what he has been saying in the first ten verses of this great chapter. He is magnifying the grace of God in Christ. He is showing how we owe everything to Christ, everything is given freely by His grace and we are justified by Him and by Him alone. So this is Paul's argument: How are we justified? Well, like this: without doing anything at all we are justified because God imputes to us the righteousness of Jesus Christ. His action, not mine at all, is imputed to me, and you notice the way in which Paul brings that out? He says: I've got a perfect illustration here. You know that when Adam committed that one sin, though we had not committed it, it was imputed to us all. In exactly the same way, this action of Christ is imputed to us, though we have done nothing, and we are justified by it.

But, you notice, Paul goes into particulars. He says here, 'Wherefore, as by one man sin entered into the world, and death by sin; and so death passed upon all men, for that all have sinned.' He says, in effect: I can prove this to you. For until the law came, which was given to Moses, sin was in the world, but sin is not imputed where there is no law.

'Well then,' you may ask, 'if sin isn't imputed how was it that all these people died?'

Here is the answer: 'Nevertheless death reigned from Adam to Moses, even over them that had not sinned after the similitude of Adam's transgression.' In other words, all these people who have died, from Adam to Moses, died, not because of anything that they had done, but because of that sin of Adam's. The law had not yet been given and sin is not imputed where there is no law, but these have died because of the sin of Adam which was imputed to them. It is that one sin that brings death upon them.

Conversely, he says, and gloriously, this great action of the Son of God is imputed to me. I have done nothing. He has done it all. But it is imputed to me because He was my federal representative or because I was in His loins, whichever you like, but you see the parallel. Now what I am anxious to stress, therefore, is that the Bible thus teaches plainly and clearly this doctrine of original guilt and if we are to have a complete conception of the doctrine of original sin we must be careful to emphasise this original guilt quite as much as the original pollution which we have also inherited, and which I hope to go on to consider with you.

But I do commend to you again that great fifth chapter of Romans. It displays the grace of God in Christ in our salvation in a most astounding manner, but the whole argument is really dependent upon our acceptance of the doctrine of original guilt as well as original pollution. Once more, in the light of all this, I would ask you, with me, to consider the greatness of God's grace and love in dealing with us as He does in Christ Jesus.

18
Original Pollution

We resume now our consideration of the biblical doctrine of original sin. It is a great and vast subject, and in the last chapter we were only able to deal with a portion of it. We are considering in general the consequences of Adam's sin, Adam's original sin and transgression, which meant his fall, and in him and through him the fall of the entire human race. Then we considered the consequences in Adam himself, and the consequences which befell him immediately and we went on to a consideration of the effect of this on the progeny of Adam. We saw that this subject of original sin is divided into two main sections, or, to put it another way, there are two main aspects of the matter. The first is original guilt, and we have been considering that. We are all held guilty and responsible for that first sin of Adam; it is imputed to us, to our account.

We come now to consider the second aspect of this doctrine, and that is what is known as *original pollution*, because, you remember, the moment Adam sinned, two things happened at once. One was that he became guilty, and the second was that changes took place in him; he was not the same as he had been. Now the doctrine of original sin says that both of these consequences devolved upon us also, so that we are guilty of original pollution as well as original guilt.

What, then, do we mean by this term original pollution? Well, first and foremost, obviously, it means in us what it meant in Adam – the absence of that original righteousness which Adam had. He was made in the image and likeness of God, and a part of that was that he was righteous with a righteousness corresponding to the righteousness of God Himself. But Adam lost it, so that all of us are born with an absence of original righteousness. Not only that. We are also born

200

with the presence within us of a positive evil. There are those two aspects to this matter of pollution.

Now we must examine this a little further. This pollution, from which we all suffer as the result of that first sin, is not merely a disease; it is a sinful and, therefore, a guilty condition. We are guilty because we are polluted. It is something which must be regarded, therefore, partly in a legal manner. Another thing we must be careful to observe about it is that we must not say that it means that there has been a change in the substance of the soul. By 'the substance of the soul', I mean its constitution. As we have seen, we do not know what that constitution is, but we must be very careful not to say that there is any change in the soul. It is, rather, a change along the lines which I shall elaborate.

But let us consider another negative before we do that. We must not consider it, either, as merely a privation of something which we once had. The pollution is not merely negative. It does not just mean the absence of something in the soul. No, it is something which is positive, a positive inherent disposition towards sin. This pollution is something active. It is not merely that we are not what we ought to be; we are positively what we ought not to be. We saw that, of course, in the last chapter when we were considering some of the biblical terms and definitions with regard to sin. Modern psychologists do not like this. They say that what we call sin is merely the absence of certain qualities. You must not say a man is positively bad; what you mean is that he is not good; sin is negative. But the Bible says that sin is positive. It is not the absence of goodness, it is the positive presence of evil and of badness. And that is something which we must emphasise because from the very beginning it is emphasised, constantly, in the Scriptures themselves.

How, then, does this condition, this absence of original righteousness and the presence of positive evil, manifest itself in fallen humanity? How does it manifest itself in all of us? And here again there is a twofold division which is taught and emphasised right through the Bible. The terms generally used are these: first, it shows itself in what is called *total depravity*, and, second, in *total inability*.

So let us look at these separately. What do we mean by total depravity? This, again, is a term that is often attacked. Indeed, alas, there are even Christians who dislike it, almost invariably because they do not know the meaning of the term. They attach a false meaning to it, and then say that they cannot abide this idea of total depravity. If, however, you ask them what they mean by it, they will probably give you one or the other of the following false definitions.

First, we do not mean by total depravity that all men and women are as thoroughly bad and depraved as they can possibly be. Now you generally find that people who dislike the idea of total depravity define it in that way. But no reputable theologian has ever defined total depravity like that. I most certainly do not and neither do the Scriptures.

Second, it does not even mean that men and women in their fallen state have no innate knowledge of God, because they have. They are totally depraved and still have a sense of God within them.

Third, it does not mean that men and women do not have a conscience; therefore, it does not mean that they have no knowledge of good and evil. People in a state of total depravity do have a conscience, and they recognise the difference between good and evil.

But I still have not finished my list of negatives. Total depravity does not mean that men and women are incapable of recognising or admiring virtues, or that they are incapable of disinterested feelings and actions. You notice why I am emphasising these negatives. 'Ah,' says the modern psychologist – and so, unfortunately, do many Christians also – 'I cannot abide this doctrine of total depravity, it cannot be right.' They say, 'Look at many people who are not Christians; they have ideas of virtue, they try to do good, they may be idealistic.'

Quite right! It is not a part of the definition of total depravity to deny that. And the last negative is that we do not mean by total depravity that every unregenerate person will indulge in every form of sin.

'So then,' asks someone, 'what does it mean?'

Well, positively, it means that man in his fallen condition has an inherently corrupt nature, and the corruption extends through every part of his being, to every faculty of his soul and body. It also means that there is no (observe the adjective) *spiritual* good in him. Yes, there is plenty of natural good, there is natural morality, he can recognise virtue and so on. But there is no spiritual good whatsoever. That is what it means.

Or, to elaborate a little more: someone in a state of total depravity, every unregenerate person, is at enmity against God and God's holy law. That is always the great characteristic of total depravity. To put it another way, all that person's powers are misused and perverted. Now let me give you the Scriptures to prove this. The first clear statement of all this is to be found in Genesis 6:5: 'And God saw that the wickedness of man was great in the earth, and that every imagination of the thoughts of his heart was only evil continually.' That is a most amazing, comprehensive statement; I commend a very careful study of it. But consider also Psalm 51:5: 'Behold, I was shapen in iniquity; and in sin did my mother conceive me.' There again is an account of this total depravity – 'shapen in iniquity', 'conceived in sin'.

Then take Jeremiah 17:9: 'The heart is deceitful above all things, and desperately wicked: who can know it?' But I suppose in many ways the classic statement of this doctrine of total depravity is in the seventh chapter of the epistle to the Romans. There it is in all its fulness, with the variation in the use of the terms describing man as the result of sin. I shall not, at this point, go into an exposition of that chapter; I am simply concerned to show you that its definition of total depravity is complete and perfect. But listen also to Romans 8:7: 'Because the carnal mind is enmity against God: for it is not subject to the law of God, neither indeed can be.' Another terrible statement of the same thing.

Paul again, in Ephesians 4:17–18, talks about the Gentiles being '. . . in the vanity of their mind, having the understanding darkened, being alienated from the life of God through the ignorance that is in them, because of the blindness of their heart.' What an astonishing statement that is! Or listen to Paul writing to Titus: 'For we ourselves also were sometimes foolish, disobedient, deceived, serving divers lusts and pleasures, living in malice and envy, hateful, and hating one another' (Titus 3:3). What a terrible description of depravity as the result of sin!

Notice that Scripture, in some of the passages that I have quoted to you now and earlier, Scripture, in order to make this thing perfectly plain and clear, uses a number of terms to describe this pollution, and we must be familiar with them. I trust that no one is bewildered as to why we are going into all this. The obvious explanation is that no one can have a true or adequate understanding of the scriptural doctrine of salvation, not one of us can appreciate our own salvation truly, unless we realise the nature of the disease, the condition, out of which we are to be saved by the gospel. In other words, we must understand the truth about ourselves in sin. We can never really know the love of God until we realise this. The way to measure the height of God's love is first of all to measure the depth of our own depravity as the result of the fall.

So Scripture, in order to bring this right home to us, uses a number of terms and here are some of them. It talks about *the flesh*, about *concupiscence* and the *old man*. It talks about *the law in our members*; about *the body of sin* and *the body of death*. It talks, too, about *the carnal mind*. There are other terms, but those are the chief ones, and I think it is probably correct to say that in general all those terms mean and describe the same thing. The important one – I suppose the most important of all, because it is the one that tends to be most misunderstood – is the term *flesh*. What does the Scripture mean by this?

Now the Scripture uses this term in three main ways; first, it uses flesh to describe the body, the physical body. Second, it sometimes uses the word to stand for the whole person – 'That no flesh should glory in his presence' (1 Cor. 1:29). That does not mean no physical body, it means that no person shall glory in his presence. So flesh sometimes means the entire personality. The third meaning may be described as the ethical meaning of flesh, or even the spiritual meaning, and this is the one which I am anxious to deal with now.

But I can imagine someone asking, 'You tell us that the word flesh is used in three different senses, how am I to know which of them is being used at any given point?'

The answer to that is not, I am happy to tell you, that you should have a knowledge of Greek, but that you should know the context. The Greek does not help you a bit; it still uses the same term. The only way we can tell which of the meanings the word carries is through the context, and the context, if we allow it to speak to us, will invariably make this quite clear.

So let us consider the ethical meaning of the term flesh. It is very important to realise that the word does not mean the body when it is used in this ethical way. The trouble with us is this flesh of ours – this is the thing that causes all our trouble, says the Bible. That is the argument of Paul in Romans 7, and when he says that, he is not thinking of the body. This is obviously important because the whole idea of monasticism was based on that false understanding. Men became monks, and they half starved themselves and mutilated their bodies, because they thought that sin resided in their physical frames, and that the thing to do was to keep the physical body down; and if they did that, they thought, all would be well.

But Scripture does not mean the body in this context. I can easily prove that in this way: if you read the lists that are given in various parts of the Bible with regard to the operations of the flesh, you will find that some of the things mentioned have nothing whatsoever to do with the physical body. Take, for instance, Paul's famous list in Galatians 5:19–21, where he puts it like this: 'The works of the flesh are manifest, which are these; Adultery, fornication, uncleanness, lasciviousness.' All those are definitely connected with the flesh, the physical part of our selves. But then Paul goes on, 'idolatry, witchcraft, hatred, variance, emulations, wrath, strife, seditions, heresies . . .' Now heresy has nothing at all to do with the physical frame; it is a sin in the realm of the spirit. But these are all catalogued together as 'works of the flesh', which, I think, is enough to prove that flesh when it is thus used in an ethical sense must never be taken to mean the physical frame, the animal part of our being.

Or let me put that positively in this way: flesh in the Scripture is almost invariably opposed to the spirit, and especially to the Holy Spirit within us. So flesh means the working of that nature which we have inherited from Adam, that which is entirely natural, and which is entirely without the influence of the Holy Spirit upon it. That is one definition, but take another. The flesh in this ethical sense is 'the principle, or the seat of the principle, which in fallen human nature resists the divine law and wars against the spirit'. 'The flesh lusteth against the Spirit, and the Spirit against the flesh' (Gal. 5:17). Or, if you like a still simpler definition, the flesh has been described as 'human nature in its estrangement from the divine life'. I think that is as good as any.

But perhaps the best way to understand this term 'the flesh' is to take that famous statement which our Lord made to Nicodemus, 'That which is born of the flesh is flesh; and that which is born of the Spirit is spirit' (John 3:6). Now when our Lord said, 'That which is born of the flesh is flesh,' He was not simply thinking of our physical frame. No, He was telling Nicodemus that he, a leader in Israel, was still thinking in a fleshly manner, still thinking 'after the flesh', in ways devoid of the Spirit. Flesh, in other words, is the human race as self-evolved and as self-continued; it is the human race without the Spirit of God. There, then, is our main definition of this term that is used so frequently in the Scriptures. And what we are told about our state in a condition of total depravity is that we are in the flesh and acting according to it.

Now one of the main characteristics of our life as the result of that influence is that it is a life which lacks balance, and this is a most important matter. Man consists, as we have seen, of body and soul — or, of body, soul and spirit. (See chapter 15). Now we saw that when he was first made by God, man was in a perfectly balanced condition. That part of him which was related to God was there and functioning; that part which included his mind, his understanding, the rational part of him, which enabled him to communicate with others round about him, there it was, working perfectly, and the body was perfect. Yes, but the important thing was that the parts were working together in a state of perfect harmony.

I often feel in the matter of illustrations that I am somewhat crippled, because I am afraid that so many people do not have sufficient agricultural background to their lives to understand what I am saying. But if you have ever seen a dairymaid milking a cow (in the days when they used to milk with hands and not with these machines they now use) you would often find that the dairymaids used to sit on little three-legged stools, and it was always a trouble if one leg was shorter than the others, or if one leg suddenly broke. Now man at the beginning was like that little stool; there was perfect balance, each part fulfilling just its right function and no more.

But what has sin done? It has upset the balance. This condition of being 'in the flesh' means that the balance has gone. Formerly the spirit controlled everything, it kept the balance. Man in the right relationship to God functioned perfectly in his spirit, in his soul, in his body; the body was kept in its place. You remember that Adam and Eve were naked and everything was all right. The moment they sinned they became ashamed of their bodies, and they tried to cover themselves. You see, the body had immediately got out of proportion, and that was the beginning of this modern sex mania, this consciousness of sex, this thinking about it, reading about it, suggesting things to it, looking on it from the outside. And man in this fleshly condition, in this state of depravity, has become utterly lopsided.

Paul describes him in Ephesians 2:3 as guilty of being controlled by 'lusts of our flesh, fulfilling the desires of the flesh and of the mind' — something which people forget. Everybody recognises lusts of the flesh, but according to the apostle Paul, lusts of the mind are as bad as lusts of the flesh. For man was never meant to be controlled by his mind, any more than he was meant to be controlled by his body. He was meant to be controlled by the spirit. But that has been lost as the result of sin and the fall, and man, if you like, has become eccentric, he is not at home, he is lopsided, he has not got his balance. Some people are controlled entirely by their bodies — eating and drinking, and various other things. Yes, but others who are not guilty of that, can be equally in a state of lust, and equally in the flesh, because they are controlled by their earthbound minds, by their own thoughts, by the philosophies of men, not by God's revelation and not by God's Spirit.

And that is why you will find that the Bible seems to teach everywhere that the ultimate sin is intellectual pride. It was the great trouble with the Greeks. Their pride was the pride of intellect, and they would not listen to the gospel. That is why at times it seems a very much easier thing that a man who is guilty of lusts of the flesh should be saved, rather than a man who is guilty of intellectual pride. It is equally terrible, if not more so, in scriptural definition.

Other characteristics of man in a state of total depravity are these: first, he is controlled by self instead of by God; it follows of necessity. The original sin – temptation – was put in that form, was it not? An appeal was made to human pride: Why should you be subservient to God? Why should you allow God to keep this from you? Why don't you assert yourself? (Gen. 3:1–6). Eve fell to the temptation, Adam followed, and the result has been this most amazing thing – that man is a victim of himself! You yourself, and I myself, are our greatest enemies. The curse of life is that we are all self-centred. We live for self instead of for God, and thus we are selfish, we are jealous, and we are envious. As Paul puts it, we are 'hateful, and hating one another' (Titus 3:3). Why? Because we are out for ourselves. Instead of living to God, in worship of Him and to His glory, we have all made ourselves gods. We are revolving round ourselves, and our little planets collide with other planets, and thus there are quarrels, there are clashes and disputes and differences. Man as the result of this depravity has become egocentric and he cannot get away from himself.

And, of course, this leads in turn to the misuse of all our faculties. We are meant to use them to the glory of God, but now we use them for our own glory. They were never meant for that, so they are being abused, and the result of persistent abuse is that wrong habits develop and, eventually, our faculties become defective. The Scripture teaches us that this can happen even to the conscience; the conscience can be 'seared with a hot iron' (1 Tim. 4:2), and it may get into such a state, because of ignorance, that it misleads us. We may think we are right when we are wrong. The conscience needs to be educated. And that is why you will find the conscience of a man in a pagan country speaks differently from the conscience of a man who has been educated in virtue and in morality.

The final and ultimate depravity is that we are all slaves of Satan. Not only has our own nature become twisted and perverted in the way we have seen, but still more terrible is the fact that we have become the slaves of the devil. Our Lord described us by nature apart from regeneration as children of the devil. He said, 'The lusts of your father ye will do' (John 8:44). We belong to the kingdom of darkness. Or again, our Lord said, 'When a strong man armed keepeth his palace, his goods are in peace' (Luke 11:21). Unregenerate mankind is nothing but the goods of the devil. What a terrible state we are in by nature as the result of Adam's original sin and transgression – total depravity!

Then the second effect of original sin and pollution is *total inability*, and this has reference, obviously, to our spiritual powers. The Bible teaches that man is totally incapable and I emphasise both terms. Again, this does not mean that he cannot perform any natural good. Of course he can. It is obvious. It does not mean that he is incapable of civic good and righteousness, because of course he is, and history proves that. Indeed, it does not even mean that he is not capable of an external kind of religion; he is capable of that. A man can be very religious and yet we still say of him that he is totally depraved and totally incapable. How do you show that? Well, he is totally incapable in the sense that all his actions are defective, good though they may be in many ways, because they are not prompted by a love of God, and by a concern for the will and glory of God. So though actions may be morally good in and of themselves, they are useless because their motive is not true.

Let me put this still more specifically. When we say that man is totally incapable we mean that he cannot do any act which fundamentally meets with God's approval, or which meets the demands of God's law. 'There is none righteous, no, not one . . . For all have sinned, and come short of the glory of God' (Rom. 3:10, 23). All the goodness of the world is as 'filthy rags' (Isa. 64:6). All the goodness of the world is as dung, and refuse, and loss; ultimately it has no value because it cannot win God's approval or satisfy His law.

But by total depravity, or total incapability, we also mean that man cannot change his fundamental preference for sin and self. He cannot change his nature. He cannot get rid of the depravity which I have been defining. I go further. He cannot make even an approach to such a change, to getting rid of it. He can do nothing about his fallen condition, his fundamental total depravity and inability. Even beyond that, I must say this: he has no appreciation at all of spiritual truth. I find that stated in 1 Corinthians 2:14 where Paul says, 'But the natural man receiveth not the things of the Spirit of God: for they are foolishness unto him: neither can he know them, because they are spiritually discerned.' Read that chapter very carefully and you will find that the apostle's entire case is that the natural person, this person who is in the condition of flesh, not only cannot change his nature, but also has no understanding or appreciation of spiritual truth.

Why is this? Well Paul answers his own question in the second chapter of Ephesians where he tells us in the first verse that the natural or carnal person is 'dead in trespasses and sins'. Or take that statement in Romans 8:7: 'The carnal mind is enmity against God: for it is not subject to the law of God, neither indeed can be.' This is an absolute statement of total inability. Let me give you some other Scriptures. The new person in Christ is described in John 1:13 as one who is 'born, not of blood, nor of the will of the flesh, nor of the will of man, but of God'. I have referred already to our Lord's words, 'that which is born of the flesh is flesh; that which is born of the Spirit is spirit' (John 3:6), and in John 6:44 we read, 'No man can come to me, except the Father which hath sent me draw him.' Read again Romans 7, where Paul tells us what the natural man cannot do – he is quite incapable.

So there, then, we see these two great consequences of original sin – original guilt and original pollution; and the pollution manifests itself in these two terrible and terrifying ways – total depravity and total inability. And you notice that the essence of the definition of both the depravity and the inability is that they concentrate on describing man's spiritual state. It does not mean, let me emphasise this again, that every man is as bad as he can be. It does not mean that he is not capable of any sort of good at all. Why, even animals are capable of that; you see them sometimes doing kindnesses to one another, and showing consideration for one another. Of course! But the point is that there is no spiritual value in these things; they are of no value in the sight of God. Man can do nothing at all about his own salvation, he cannot change his nature. 'Can the Ethiopian change his skin, or the leopard his spots?' (Jer. 13:23).

There, then, according to the Bible, we see man as he is as the result of Adam's sin and the fall. He is guilty, he is condemned by the law of God, he is polluted, he is depraved, he is under the dominion of self and sin and of Satan, and he is utterly and absolutely helpless. He has no appreciation of spiritual truth, because of his depravity and because he is blinded by the god of this world who will not allow him to have that appreciation, even if he wanted it. 2 Corinthians 4:3–4 says, 'But if our gospel be hid, it is hid to them that are lost: in whom the god of this world hath blinded the minds of them which believe not, lest the light of the glorious gospel of Christ, who is the image of God, should shine into them.'

So there is man, and again I would remind you of that great statement as we look at him – 'God once dwelt here'! What a calamity that sin of Adam was! What a terrible, devastating thing! What awful consequences have devolved upon man! What can be done about such a creature? Is there any hope for him? Is there anything we can say to ourselves as we look at man as he is as the result of sin and the fall? We have not flinched. We have not tried to protect or to shield ourselves. We have allowed the Scriptures to speak to us, and we have seen this horrible picture, this awful photograph of ourselves as we are born into this world. Is there no hope?

Well, thank God, we all know the answer – there is! Into that awful condition there came a cross, and the thing, I think, that will fascinate us and charm us throughout eternity is this: that the promise came through the very God against whom man rebelled. And still more amazing and remarkable is that it came almost immediately after man had rebelled, for the promise was given to Adam and Eve even before they were thrust out of Paradise; the promise was given to them even in the very Garden where in their utter folly they had listened to the devil and, alas, brought all these horrible consequences upon themselves. Even then, without any delay, this amazing God whom we worship and adore, in His everlasting and eternal love gave the promise that the seed of the woman would bruise the serpent's head (Gen. 3:15). There was going to be a deliverance, a Saviour, a salvation; and God's universe, man supremely, would not only be restored to what it had been before, but to even something beyond, for –

> In Him the tribes of Adam boast
> More blessings than their father lost.
>   Isaac Watts

And so we shall go on to consider that ultimate, crucial act which made all that possible, in which the Son of God gave Himself and 'bare our sins in his own body on the tree, that we, being dead to sins, should live unto righteousness' (1 Pet. 2:24).

19

Redemption: the Eternal Plan of God

'According as he hath chosen us in him before the foundation of the world, that we should be holy and without blame before him in love: having predestinated us unto the adoption of children by Jesus Christ to himself, according to the good pleasure of his will' (Eph. 1:4–5).

Before we continue with our study of biblical doctrines it would be good, perhaps, for us to remind ourselves of the exact point at which we have arrived. We started with the general proposition that we find it difficult to understand both the world and ourselves. We have within us a sense of God, and yet that in itself is not enough to bring us to a knowledge of Him, and we came to the conclusion that if we really are to know anything truly about God or ourselves or our world, we must of necessity come to the Bible, this book which we say is the Word of God, inspired by Him, and infallible. And therefore we submit ourselves to it, realising that there are many things that we cannot understand, but that we have come with minds made receptive by the operation of the Holy Spirit upon us.

The first thing we find as we do this is that God has been graciously pleased to reveal Himself, and we have considered that revelation. Then we went on to think about what God has done, the creation of the heavens and earth and the various orders of beings that He has brought into existence. But we concentrated upon man, and saw that God created man and woman perfect; He made them 'in our [God's] image, after our likeness' (Gen. 1:26). We tried to consider what the Bible tells us about this and there we saw man and woman in Paradise, without sin, perfect, and enjoying a life of communion with God.

Then from that, we looked at men and women as they are today;

we looked at ourselves, as we know ourselves to be, and the great question is: Why are we as we are now, if Adam and Eve were like that? So that led us to a consideration of the doctrine of the fall and that is the point at which we have arrived. We saw that all men and women are as they are because of the fall. Adam and Eve disobeyed God and that led to their fall (Gen. 3); and in working out the doctrine of original sin, as it is called, we saw that men and women, as the result of this, are in a fallen condition. They are guilty before God, their very nature is polluted and perverted, and they are quite helpless – helpless especially in the matter of returning to God and of arriving at a knowledge of God (Rom. 5:12). You remember we summed it up by putting it like this: that you look at a man or woman today and you say, with that Puritan John Howe – 'God once dwelt here.' Man is a ruin, a ruin of his former self. And there we looked at him, driven out of Paradise, out of the Garden of God, and eating his bread by the sweat of his brow; and we saw all that is so true of him now, and of human nature as the result of sin.

But we were glad to end on a note of hope. We found that in the third chapter of Genesis, in which we are given the account of the fall, of its immediate consequences and of some of the remote consequences also, there is, after all, a hope: before God thrust Adam and Eve out of the Garden He gave them a promise. It looked at that moment as if everything was irretrievably lost. Adam and Eve, having listened to the devil in the form of the serpent, had made themselves the slaves of the devil, under his power, unable to resist him and helpless in his hands. It looked as if man's future was altogether lost and hopeless, but, even there, God flashed into the gloom and darkness a ray of light. He addressed the serpent and pronounced a curse upon him, telling him that there would be warfare between him and 'the seed of the woman'; that he would pierce, as it were, the heel of the woman's seed, but that his own head would be crushed; and there lay the one gleam of hope.

So now we proceed to consider what exactly is meant by that hope. Having faced the history of men and women from their original perfection to their degradation and pollution, in a state of sin and guilt, we asked: Is there no hope for them? And the answer is: Yes, there is. In other words, we are beginning to consider the biblical doctrine of redemption or of salvation. In many ways it can be said, of course, that this is the central theme of the whole Bible, and yet all that we have considered hitherto has been absolutely essential. It is because so many frequently fail to consider that mighty background that their conception of the doctrine of salvation is often incomplete, and even fallacious at certain points. It is only as we truly understand something of the nature and character of God and the condition of men and women in sin, that we can understand this grand doctrine of redemption. Therefore it is but right that we should have spent all that time in considering these great doctrines that lead on to it.

However, here we are now, face to face with this great central doctrine. Obviously it is very comprehensive, and we shall have to divide it up under various headings. But we will not do that now. I am anxious, rather, that we should take a general look at it. Here, again, is a procedure which I advocate very strongly. It is a very wise thing, a very biblical thing, to take a general view like this of the doctrine of redemption before coming to its particular aspects; and as we do so, we shall find that certain things stand out very prominently and gloriously, and we must grasp them and take a firm hold on them.

Let me give you a number of headings. First: *redemption is entirely of God*. What we have in the Bible is the record of God's activity in the redemption of man. Now that, of course, is something that you find at once, away back there in the third chapter of Genesis. The moment man had fallen and had found himself in this pitiable condition, and when he seemed to be absolutely without hope, the hope was given by God. It was God who spoke. And it was God who gave an outline of what He was proposing to do.

Now this can never be emphasised too strongly. The Bible, after all, is an account of what God has done about the redemption of man. It is *not* an account of man seeking for God. That has been, perhaps, the greatest of the heresies that have characterised so much of the Church and her teaching during the past hundred years. The so-called 'higher critics' were never tired of telling us, influenced as they were by the theory of evolution which they applied to the Scriptures, that the Old Testament was nothing but a record of man searching for God. But it is the exact opposite. It is the record of God's activity, what He has done, and what He is going to do.

We can put that very clearly like this. We saw that when God had made man in His own image and likeness, and had placed Him in the Garden, He made a covenant with him, which has generally been called, very rightly, the 'covenant of works'. God said to Adam, in effect: 'If you keep my commandment, if you do what I tell you and refrain from eating of that particular tree, if you refrain from doing what I have prohibited, you will go on growing and increasing in your perfection.' And so God made certain promises. Man's future was then contingent upon his own action; it was a covenant of works.

But then, you remember, man failed to keep the covenant; he rebelled against God. And the result was that he landed himself in that condition which we describe as one of total inability. So clearly God could no longer make a covenant of works with man. Man when he was perfect had failed to keep that covenant, so God obviously did not make another. In the light of what we have already seen, it was impossible. But, we thank God, it was not left at that and the biblical doctrine of redemption is an account of what God has done about man.

Or, to put it another way, it is not a question of what man can do to placate God. The Bible does not tell us that. There are some people who seem to think that the message of the Bible is one which tells us what we have to do in order to please this God whom we have offended. That again is quite wrong. The Bible tells us about what God has done in order to reconcile us to Himself. I want to put that very strongly. Not only is God not unwilling to receive us, it is He who goes out of His way to seek us. So if we want to grasp the biblical doctrine of redemption we must once and for ever get rid of that notion which has been instilled into the human mind and heart by the devil, who is God's adversary and our adversary, and who tries to make us believe that God is against us. But the Bible's message is that 'God so loved the world, that he gave his only begotten Son . . .' (John 3:16).

Indeed, let me go even further and put it in this extreme form: the Bible does not even tell us that the Lord Jesus Christ needs to placate God for us or has done that for us. You still find people who hold that view. They say that there is God in His justice and in His absolute righteousness, and then they depict the Lord Jesus Christ as pleading with God on our behalf, and beseeching Him to forgive us. You will find it in certain hymns and choruses. But it is quite false to the biblical teaching, which can be summed up in what Paul says in 2 Corinthians 5:19: 'God was in Christ, reconciling the world unto himself, not imputing their trespasses unto them.' The biblical case is not that Christ, as it were, has to appeal to God to change His mind. It was God who sent Christ; it was God Himself who took the initiative. So we can never emphasise too frequently or too strongly this first proposition, which is that redemption and salvation are entirely of God, and that the Bible is nothing but a record of what God has done, is doing, and will do about us men and women and our salvation.

The second principle is this: *salvation is all of grace*. It was all done in spite of man's rebellion, in spite of man's arrogance, in spite of his folly and sin. You go back to that account in Genesis 3 and that is what you will find. Adam and Eve foolishly disobeyed and rebelled, and there they were, frightened and alarmed when they heard the voice of God, and they hid themselves; their instinct was to get away from God. But it was God who called after them, who called them to come back.

Now that is the whole case of the Bible: this gracious action on the part of God, who does not turn His back upon us and upon the world because of sin and disobedience and the fall, but who, in spite of the fact that we are so undeserving of His love and His mercy and His compassion, looks upon us with a pitying eye, and speaks to us in terms of grace and of love. You remember that when we were considering the character of God we emphasised this character of grace. Grace means 'undeserved favour', and that is the essence of the biblical message. The hymn writer says,

> Great God of wonders! all Thy ways
> Are matchless, godlike, and divine.
>   Samuel Davies

There is nothing comparable to the grace of God, to the way in which He looks upon us and upon the world, in spite of what we have done, and gives us these promises. We have no claim upon the love of God. We have forfeited it. Salvation is all of grace.

The next point that the Bible makes very clear about this doctrine of redemption is that *it was all planned before the foundation of the world*. Now this is most important. Read what Paul says about it in the first chapter of his letter to the Ephesians. Redemption is not an afterthought. It was not something that God thought of after man fell and because man fell. To say that is to contradict the Scripture. The Bible all along keeps on referring to this as something that was conceived before the world was made. Before man was ever created, this plan of redemption was clearly in the mind of God.

Here again we are confronted by a great mystery. There is a sense in which it is impossible for us to grasp it. We are so bound by time, we are so accustomed to seeing everything in a kind of time sequence! We think chronologically and it is quite inevitable that we should do so.

But God is outside time. God sees the end from the beginning and all things are always in His presence. It is a staggering thought, and yet here it is, very plainly taught everywhere in the Scriptures: 'According as he hath chosen us in him before the foundation of the world . . .' (Eph. 1:4). Now you will find that certain people give the impression that God is continually having to modify His plan and His purposes because of things that are done by man, but this is something you can never substantiate from the Scripture. Before anything was made, the plan, the idea of redemption, was already present in the mind of God.

The next thing we go on to is something that we should consider with adoration, praise and worship, and it is this: *the three Persons of the blessed Trinity took part in this plan and purpose of redemption.* There can be no question at all but that the Scriptures teach that before the foundation of the world a council with respect to man took place between the three Persons of the Trinity – the Father, the Son, and the Holy Spirit. And there in that eternal council they seem very clearly to have divided up the work of redemption, so that we can describe the Father as the originator, the Son as the executor and the Holy Spirit as the One who applies what the Son has achieved.

But it is also very clear that in particular an agreement, even a covenant, was made between God the eternal Father and God the eternal Son. It is quite clear, according to Scripture, that the Son has been made the 'heir of all things' (Heb. 1:2), which means that everything in this world was given to Him, that it was, as it were, made over to Him. And everything that happens in this world and on this earth belongs, therefore, to His domain. In His high priestly prayer in John 17, our Lord reminds His Father, 'As thou hast given him [Christ] power over all flesh . . .' (v. 2). That is the same idea. God the Father hands the world as it is to the Son, and He gives Him power over all. The eighth psalm not only refers to man, it refers in a very special way to the Son of God Himself:

> What is man, that thou art mindful of him? and the son of man, that thou visitest him? For thou hast made him a little lower than the angels, and hast crowned him with glory and honour. Thou madest him to have dominion over the works of thy hands; thou hast put all things under his feet: all sheep and oxen, yea, and the beasts of the field; the fowl of the air, and the fish of the sea, and whatsoever passeth through the paths of the seas.
>
> Verses 4–8

But beyond that, we see clearly in the Scriptures that for the purpose of redemption God the Father has made the Son the head and the representative of a new humanity. Take, for instance, what we are told in Romans 5, where we are given the contrast – 'As in Adam . . . so in Christ.' The apostle works this out and his teaching is that Adam, as we have seen, was the head and the representative of mankind, but now, for the purposes of redemption, God has appointed a new head and a new representative, and that is His own Son. He could not appoint a man, obviously, because all men had fallen in Adam, and God cannot appoint fallen man as a representative. If man in a state of perfection had failed, how much more so must man in Adam, and in a state of imperfection, fail.

So now you see why the incarnation was an absolute necessity. There was no one on earth with whom God could make His covenant, there was no one whom he could pick out and make a head and representative. So He took His own Son, whom He was going to send into the world in the likeness of sinful flesh, and appointed Him as the head and the representative of this new humanity. You find that in Romans 5 and, equally definitely, in 1 Corinthians 15:22: 'For as in Adam all die, even so in Christ shall all be made alive.' It is the same contrast between Adam and our Lord. And, of course, you find the same teaching in Psalm 2: 'Thou art my Son; this day have I begotten thee' (v. 7), with the other things that follow from that.

The next step in this compact, or covenant, between the Father and the Son was that God the Father gave God the Son this people whom He would raise at the last day. Read, for instance, John 6, and you will find that our Lord constantly refers to that and He says He must not lose anything that God has given Him. It is very clear, again, in John 17, in that high priestly prayer. Our Lord constantly repeats that He is doing all this for the sake of those whom the Father has given Him. 'Father, the hour is come,' he says, 'glorify thy Son, that thy Son also may glorify thee: As thou hast given him power over all flesh, that he should give eternal life to as many as thou hast given him' (John 17:1–2). And He goes on repeating the phrase: 'I have manifested thy name unto the men which thou gavest me out of the world' (v. 6). And then He reminds His Father, 'While I was with them in the world, I kept them in thy name: those that thou gavest me I have kept, and none of them is lost, but the son of perdition; that the scripture might be fulfilled' (v. 12). So that is another part of the compact.

Then you have another reference to it in Hebrews 2:13 where the Son says, 'Behold I and the children which God hath given me.' So clearly there was an arrangement concerning the people who had been given to Him. He is the head of this people, this new humanity, the redeemed.

But further, we see that God not only gave Him the people, He also gave Him a certain work to do with respect to them. Again in John 17 we read, 'I have glorified thee on the earth: I have finished the work which thou gavest me to do' (v. 4). So the Father, in eternity, gave the Son a certain work to do and then, having given it, He sent Him to do it. 'God so loved the world, that he gave his only begotten Son' (John 3:16). 'God sent forth his Son, made of a woman, made under the law' (Gal. 4:4), and there are many other similar statements. And, indeed, in a most marvellous way we are actually told that the Father even prepared a body for Him. There is a reference to that in Psalm 40, and you will find it quoted in Hebrews 10:5: '. . . a body hast thou prepared me.' So that is the essential teaching; it was the Father who sent forth the Son.

The next, the fifth general heading, I would suggest is that *this plan and scheme of redemption is a definite plan*. There is nothing incidental or contingent about it. It is a perfect plan, and it was all perfect before the very foundation of the world. God had mapped it out in eternity, and then had put into operation in this world of time. You cannot read the Bible without noticing in a very particular way the time element. Everything that has happened up till this moment has happened according to God's plan and programme.

There are some most astonishing examples of this, and it is most fascinating and encouraging to consider some of these instances and to work them out in detail. For instance, God actually told Abraham of the four hundred years which his descendants would spend in the captivity of Egypt (Gen. 15:13–16). Then the time of the flood was known to God. When He first gave His commandment to Noah to start building that ark, when the world began to scoff and say: Where is the promise of this judgment that you are speaking about?; God knew, and, at the prescribed moment, it happened (Gen. 6–7). And the same is true of the time when He chose a man called Abraham and founded a nation in him (Gen. 12:1). We will be considering this again in detail but all these things happened at precisely the time which God had appointed for them. And so as you go along with all the history of the Judges and the Kings and the Prophets, you find that it is all according to this perfect plan and it is all perfectly timed.

And this brings us especially, of course, to that great statement which we have already quoted in part: 'But when the fulness of the time was come, God sent forth his Son, made of a woman, made under the law . . .' People have often asked, 'If God gave that promise away back there in Eden, why did He wait so long before He sent His Son?' It is an idle question to ask. But God has His great purpose in it all. It is very easy to suggest many reasons why God did not send His Son until the exact moment when He did send Him. It seems to me to be more and more clear that He did this in order that He might first show men and women their utter helplessness. The law had to be given in order that they might see that they could not keep it. An opportunity had to be given to Greek philosophy to do everything that it could do; an opportunity had to be given to Roman law and Roman ideas of justice and of government. Everything that men and women could think of for redeeming themselves and their world had already been tried and had failed before God sent His Son.

God knew that from the beginning. If we are told that 'he that believeth shall not make haste' (Isa. 28:16), how infinitely more true is that of God, who sees the end from the beginning. So I emphasise that it is a perfect and definite plan, complete and entire. The apostle Paul in Romans 11 does not hesitate to speak about a time when the 'fulness of the Gentiles be come in. And so all Israel shall be saved' (vv. 25–6). Now God had known all this from the foundation of the world. The plan was entire and He gave these revelations of it to His servants so that they could write about it and we can read about it. God knows the number of the fulness of the Gentiles; He knows the number of Israel; He knows the number of this new humanity that is in Christ Jesus. The plan of redemption is an entire plan: a perfect, definite plan, down to the smallest detail.

The next thing I want to emphasise about it, the sixth principle, is *the absolute certainty of the consummation of this plan of redemption*. This is one of the most glorious and encouraging things that we can ever consider together. I thank God that that is made very clear even in Genesis 3. When God pronounced His curse there upon the serpent and announced the warfare between the seed of the woman and the serpent, He made it plain that this enemy who had brought man, who was perfect, down to the dust and to shame and degradation, was going to be utterly defeated and destroyed.

And the Bible keeps on reminding us of this. In its last book it gives us a picture of the consummation of it all, when even the devil himself shall be cast into the lake burning with fire and shall be destroyed to all eternity. Whatever the appearances may be, however much they may suggest the contrary at different times and in different epochs, God's plan is certain. Nothing can frustrate it, nothing can prevent it from being worked out to the smallest detail. That is, of course, the major theme of the Bible. We are given an account of the end as well as the beginning. The whole thing is there; we can rest assured that no power of man nor of earth nor of hell can ever prevent what God purposed in this eternal council before the foundation of the world.

Then the next heading – and again it is something that is emphasised in Ephesians 1 – is that *this purpose of God in redemption applies not only to man but to all things*. It applies to the world itself, and, as we have just seen, it includes what God has purposed even with regard to His enemies. Paul says, 'Having made known unto us the mystery of his will' – it was there in His purpose but it was a hidden mystery and we would not have known it if He had not been pleased graciously to make it known to us – 'according to his good pleasure which he hath purposed in himself' – it is all of grace, it is all His love. Why? – 'That in the dispensation of the fulness of times' – there it is again – 'he might gather together in one all things in Christ, both which are in heaven, and which are on earth; even in him' (Eph. 1:9–10).

Now that is the plan. I am afraid that many of us are often tempted to think of salvation only in terms of ourselves or only in terms of a number of individuals. We must never do that. This great purpose of God includes the heavens and the earth. All things, everywhere, come within His purpose, even to the extent of determining beforehand the final state and destiny of Satan and evil and all that belongs to his territory. There will be a final destruction, and there will be 'new heavens and a new earth, wherein dwelleth righteousness' (2 Pet. 3:13), which will be the grand result of the work of redemption of the Son of God.

And that brings me to my eighth point, which is that *this great plan of redemption always centres in the Lord Jesus Christ*. Paul tells us that God's purpose is to 'gather together in one all things in Christ, both which are in heaven, and which are on earth' – and he repeats himself – 'even in him' (Eph. 1:10). I shall have occasion again to go on emphasising and repeating that. I put it here as a principle, because I am afraid that certain people very definitely teach that some form of redemption is possible apart from the Lord Jesus Christ. You will find in certain 'Notes on the Scriptures', a teaching which says that a time is coming when the dispensation of grace will have finished and a new dispensation of law will come in, and people will be saved by keeping the law and will not be saved if they do not keep it.

Now I do not hesitate to assert that that is a completely erroneous conception, and a contradiction of the Bible. There is no mention of any salvation anywhere in the Bible except in and through the Lord Jesus Christ. There is only one gospel; there is only one way of salvation. The saints of the Old Testament are saved in Christ as much as you and I are, and all who will ever live must be saved in Christ or not at all. It is in Him that God is going to reconcile everything, and there is no other way of reconciliation. We cannot emphasise that too often or too strongly.

To put it another way, we call this book the Bible, and we divide it into two portions, the Old Testament and the New Testament. What does this mean? It means that the Old Testament and the New are both concerned about the same person, and that is the Lord Jesus Christ. The Old Testament is the preparation, the promise, the prophecy of His coming. There, back in Genesis 3, you have it; the whole thing is put so plainly. Who is the seed of the woman that is going to crush and bruise the serpent's head? It is none other than the Son of God, and He did it upon the cross on Calvary's hill. The Old Testament from beginning to end points to Him.

Then what is the New Testament but the glorious fulfilment of every type and shadow? He is the substance of all the shadows. He is the great antitype of all the types. He is the fulfilment of everything that God had indicated He was going to be. So there is the Bible – Old Testament, New Testament – but it is all in Christ. The plan, the purpose, the way of redemption are always in Him.

And that brings me to my last heading, which is that *this purpose of God in redemption has been revealed to mankind in various covenants*. Now I do not enter into that now; I hope to go on to consider this question of the covenants in our next study. But God, in His great condescension, in His infinite grace and kindness, has not only determined upon this plan of redemption, He has done something else which in a way is still more extraordinary and marvellous: He has made agreements with men. The almighty and eternal God, the sovereign Lord, turns to men and women who have sinned and rebelled against Him and begins to tell them what He is going to do. And, as we shall see, when He did that with Abraham, He not only told him what He was going to do, He confirmed it with an oath in order that man might have a certain and sure hope (Heb. 6:17–20).

So then, we have taken a kind of synoptic view of the biblical doctrine of redemption. We have looked at it in general. We have surveyed the whole landscape, as it were. We have looked at it from beginning to end, and have seen that God in His kindness and love and mercy and compassion, and in His infinite grace, looked upon men and women when they deserved nothing but hell and destruction, and gave them the promise of their wonderful redemption that would finally be consummated in His own eternal Son, our Lord and Saviour Jesus Christ. Therefore to Him, and to Him alone, must of necessity be all the praise and all the honour and all the glory!

20
The Covenant of Grace in the Old Testament

We continue now with our consideration of the biblical doctrine of redemption or salvation. We have seen that man, having failed to keep God's law and commandment, became the slave of Satan, dead in trespasses and sins, and that had he been left to himself his condition would have been entirely hopeless. But God, in His infinite grace and love and mercy, looked upon man in pity, and informed him of His great plan of salvation. And we have considered the general character of this great plan of redemption. I ended by saying that God revealed it to man in the form of a covenant that He made with man. This is commonly called the covenant of redemption or the covenant of salvation, and that is to be our special theme now – the way in which God has made known His gracious purpose to save man from the guilt and pollution which resulted from listening to the suggestion of Satan.

Now the great word we must consider is this word *covenant*. It is a word that God used when He was speaking to Abraham (Gen. 17). What is a covenant? Well, it can be defined as an agreement or a pact which is entered into by two parties, the two parties generally being more or less of equal standing. People often make covenants today; they make them, for example, with respect to giving gifts towards good causes. There is also the Covenant of the League of Nations or the Covenant of the United Nations. A covenant is generally confirmed by some kind of solemn ceremony – you take an oath, or there is perhaps a religious service. And in the covenant the two sides bind themselves to the fulfilment of certain promises given on the basis of certain conditions.

In the Bible you will find covenants made between men – David and Jonathan made a covenant, and it was on the basis of equality. But when you come to God and man, clearly there is of necessity a difference; the idea of covenant undergoes some modifications. This difference appears especially in the *Authorised Version* of the Bible in this way: the word is sometimes translated as 'testament' and not as covenant. So we talk about 'Old Testament' and 'New Testament'; and you will find the word 'testament' in 2 Corinthians 3:6 and also in other places.

Now it is generally agreed that the word which stands for this idea should always be translated as covenant except in one instance, and that one exception is Hebrews 9:16–17, where clearly it must be translated as testament for it refers to a person dying and making a will. But apart from that one instance you will find that the other translations, the *Revised Standard Version*, for example, always translate it as covenant rather than as testament.

I emphasise that for this reason: the translators of the *Authorised Version* had a very definite object in view when they used the word 'testament'. Their purpose was to emphasise the priority of God. When God makes a covenant with man, there are not two partners of equal standing, but God is *giving*, as it were, His covenant to man. So the translators thought that it was more like a testament than a covenant, and chose to use that word. Strictly speaking, they were wrong, but they certainly did emphasise this idea of the priority of God over against the idea of man as an equal. They did it also because they could see very clearly that in Hebrews 9 the word means a testament, and as it can be argued that ultimately all the blessings that come to us under the covenant of grace come as the result of the death of the Lord Jesus Christ, there is a sense in which we do inherit everything as the result of His last testament. So there was that much at least to be said for their translation. Furthermore, they were undoubtedly partly influenced by the fact that the Latin word for all this is *testamentum*, and they were dependent partly upon the Latin translations of the Scripture.

However, the thing that we must keep in mind is that the priority of God must be emphasised. The covenant is a gift from God which has been ushered in by the death of Christ, and because it comes from God it is something which is certain, and inviolable, and unbreakable. And yet we must hold on to this idea of a covenant, because God in His wonderful love and grace and condescension chose to reveal His purposes in this particular way. He called man to Himself and He chose to make an agreement with man. God need not have done that, but He has done so. In spite of human rebellion, sin and arrogance, God, as it were, called man in and said, 'I want to make an agreement with you.' In a way, there is nothing that so displays the wonderful love and grace and kindness and condescension of God so much as this teaching in the Bible with regard to His making covenants with men.

Now we have already seen that God originally made a covenant with Adam. You remember that He put him into the Garden and told him that if he did certain things he would have a certain reward. That is called a covenant of works, because Adam's inheritance of this promise was entirely dependent upon his works, upon what he did. But, you remember, Adam broke the covenant; he failed, and landed himself and his posterity in the terrible plight that we have been describing. So, from there on God has made a new covenant, which is called the *covenant of grace*.

Clearly, as we have seen, God could not make another covenant of works with man. If man, in an ideal position and while perfect, could not keep the covenant of works, what would be the object of making another covenant of works with fallen man? So the Bible tells us that God did not do this but that He made the covenant of grace. And yet in this covenant, God has introduced a condition. He has made His promises. He has told us what He is making possible for us. But He does make a demand upon us. He tells us that we are only going to receive and enjoy these promises if we have faith, and we have to accept this condition voluntarily before we will enjoy the blessings. But furthermore, God has also told us in the covenant that He Himself is going to do something which makes it possible for us to derive these benefits, and that is why it is called the covenant of *grace*.

Now let me divide that up a little. God, I say, has made certain promises, so what is the great central promise that He has made in the covenant of grace? Well, it really can be put in this way: He has promised to be a God unto man. That is the great promise – 'I will be to you a God.' You see the importance and the significance of this? God had been the God of Adam, but Adam sinned against Him and fell; he became the slave of Satan and broke the connection with God. And the remarkable and astounding thing is that God turned to man and assured him in the covenant of grace that He would find a way, that He had a way, whereby He could still be a God to man. 'I will take you to me for a people, and I will be to you a God' (Exod. 6:7).

Make a note of that because as you go through your Scriptures you will find that that is the great promise that is repeated time and time again. You will find it in Jeremiah 31:33; 32:38–40. You will find it in Ezekiel 34:23–5; 36:25–8; 37:26–7. You will find it in 2 Corinthians 6:16–18, in Hebrews 8:10; and, in a marvellous way, in Revelation 21:3 where we read this: 'The tabernacle of God is with men, and he will dwell with them.' That is the final state. So you see that that is the very essence of God's promise in the covenant of grace – that what had been broken by sin and the fall was going to be restored. And the supreme blessing therefore, the ultimate blessing, the blessing of blessings, is that God is my God, and that I have a right to say 'my God'. And the whole of salvation is included in that.

I must not stay with that now, but how often do we forget that? How often do we tend to define salvation in terms other than that? Yet the greatest thing a human being can ever say since the fall is this: 'God is my God.' And the greatest blessing of all is to know for certain that God is saying to you, 'I am your God'; 'I will be to you a God.' That is what He has promised.

But the covenant also includes certain other things. God has promised certain temporal as well as spiritual blessings. He especially promised those under the old dispensation, and let us never forget that the temporal blessings are meant to be pictures of, and to symbolise, the spiritual blessings.

He has also promised, obviously, a way of justification. God cannot be my God, and I cannot say 'my God' unless I am justified, unless my sin is forgiven, unless my sin is removed, and unless I am adopted and made a child of God. This is all implicit in the promise that God is to be my God. Indeed, it includes the promise of life eternal, the giving of the Spirit, and the full application and working out of redemption in my sanctification and ultimate glorification. The promises in the covenant of grace include all this, and we are called upon to respond by faith, by the desire for all this, and by faithfulness and obedience to God in these new conditions.

So I have tried to give you an omnibus definition of what we mean by the covenant of grace. We can put it like this: the covenant of grace is that arrangement between the triune God and His people, whereby God carries out His eternal purpose and decree of redemption by promising His friendship. The promise is full and free salvation to His people upon the basis of the vicarious atonement of the Lord Jesus

Christ, who is the mediator of the covenant, and His people accept this salvation by faith. It is the promise of God's friendship, of His being our God, of entry into intimate relationship with Him, and knowing Him, and it is all made possible by Jesus Christ.

But the thing I want to consider now is this: this great covenant which God has made with man, this covenant of grace, can be divided up into two dispensations, or, if you prefer it, two administrations. This one great covenant has been administered in two different ways, the way that is described in the Old Testament and the way that is described in the New Testament. You notice what I am saying? There is only *one* covenant of grace and I hope before we finish this study to prove that to you.

What, then, are the ways in which the covenant of grace has been dispensed under the old dispensation? Well, you go first of all to Genesis 3:15. If you are interested in the technical term, it is generally called the *protevangel*. In other words, there is a kind of foreshadowing of the whole gospel in Genesis 3:15. Now to me this is one of the most fascinating and thrilling things anyone can ever encounter. Here is this great book; we divide it up and we call it the Old Testament and the New Testament and we all know what we mean by that. But, you know, if we were to be strictly accurate we would not describe it in that way. The real division of the Bible is this: first, everything you get from Genesis 1:1 to Genesis 3:14; then everything from Genesis 3:15 to the very end of the Bible. What you have up until Genesis 3:14 is the account of the creation, and of God's original covenant of works with man, and of how that failed because man broke it. Beginning with Genesis 3:15 you get the announcement of the gospel, the covenant of grace, the way of salvation, and that is the whole theme of the Bible until you come to the last verse of the book of Revelation. That is the real division of the Bible.

But, of course, we talk about the Old Testament and the New Testament because we want to emphasise the two main ways in which this one great covenant of grace has been administered, and here it is beginning in Genesis 3:15 – 'And I will put enmity between thee and the woman, and between thy seed and her seed; it shall bruise thy head, and thou shalt bruise his heel.' Now the whole of the gospel is there. It is there in this almost cryptic form, in this very undeveloped form, but it is there.

Let us work it out. What does God tell us in Genesis 3:15? Well, first of all that He was going to put enmity between the serpent, and the woman and her seed. Hitherto, you see, there had been no enmity between them; but the serpent had beguiled Eve, so they were very friendly together, and the woman was now under the dominion of the devil. Had God not done something, that would have been the end of the story. But God came in and He said, 'Now I am going to break that friendship; you were meant for friendship with me, not with the devil, so I am going to put enmity between you and the devil, and between the devil and you.' That was the first announcement of salvation; man cannot be saved while he is a friend of the devil and an enemy of God. He must be a friend of God; therefore he must become an enemy of the devil.

The second thing, therefore, that is implied is that God was going to give man power and grace to fight the devil. Man had already been defeated by him, and was his slave. Man must have help and strength, and God promised him that. God promised to be on man's side in this fight against the enemy. He applied the promise also to the 'seed' – 'between thy seed and her seed'. That is most important. It was not a temporary promise given there in Eden; it was to continue until it had achieved its ultimate purpose.

You notice also that God said that the quarrel was to go on not only between woman and her seed, and the devil, but also between the seed of the woman and the seed of the serpent. In other words, mankind was here divided into two sections – those who do not belong to Christ belong to the devil, they are the children, the seed of the devil. So humanity can be divided into the seed of God and of Christ, and the seed of the devil, and there is a fight between them – all announced in Genesis 3:15.

Then you notice that we are given the promise there of the certainty of the triumph of God and His way. The serpent was going to be bruised, his head would be bruised, he would be destroyed. Cannot you see that there is the prefiguring of Calvary? It was there he was put to an open shame, it was there he was defeated – all promised in the protevangel. And ultimately there is this idea which we can see so clearly in the light of subsequent Scripture, that the real seed of the woman is none other than the Lord Jesus Christ Himself (Genesis 3:16). Now there was the first announcement of this covenant. God did not call it a covenant at that point, but it was a foreshadowing of the covenant that later was made more explicit.

But, second, let us come to the covenant made with Noah. You will find that described in the ninth chapter of the book of Genesis, after the flood. God promised here that He would never again destroy the earth and all flesh by means of water, by the return of such a flood. He furthermore guaranteed that there would always be a succession of seedtime and harvest, cold and heat, summer and winter, day and night. God promised that that would continue, come what may. He also promised that the forces of nature would be bridled. In other words, the effects and results of sin and the fall were checked, they were held in balance in the covenant made with Noah.

In the same way, the powers of evil were put under a greater restraint, and man was not allowed to be as violent as he had been, and as he would like to be, against other men. Man was protected against the violence both of man himself and of beasts. Read it for yourself in Genesis 9. And it was all confirmed and sealed by the sign of the rainbow in the cloud.

Now the thing I want to emphasise here is this: the covenant made with Noah was not a new covenant of grace. The covenant of grace was adumbrated in Genesis 3:15. This did not interfere with that at all, but simply introduced certain subsidiary promises and ordinances. The covenant with Noah was not a new covenant in the ultimate sense of grace and redemption. It was simply a temporary legislation, it was what is sometimes called *common grace*, as distinct from the special grace which ensures our spiritual salvation.

Then, thirdly, there was the covenant made with Abraham. That is what you find in Genesis 17, and it was here that God first explicitly and clearly stated His purpose of redemption in the exact form of a covenant. What do we find here? Well, we find that here for the first time, in any definite manner, we have the beginning of a kind of church. There was a separation between the people who belonged to God and those who belonged to the world. There had been a kind of family worship before, in houses or tents, and so on, but something new was introduced in the covenant with Abraham. God chose a particular man, a particular family, and made a promise to Abraham and his descendants – and to nobody else. There was this separation; there was the formation of a unique body, a special people of God.

This is most important. Notice also the emphasis placed upon Abraham's faith, upon his response. It was by his faith that he entered into the covenant and began to receive the benefits and the blessings. And notice, too, the spiritual character of the blessings that were promised to him. Over and above the promise concerning the land, etc., there was the great promise of a spiritual seed, that all the nations of the world were going to be blessed in him.

Now if you want to work that out, just read the epistle to the Romans, chapters 3, 4 and 5, and the epistle to the Galatians, chapter 3, which I shall quote shortly. You see that in his covenant with Abraham, God was giving Abraham justification. We are told in the epistle to the Romans that Abraham was justified by faith, justified in a spiritual sense – justified from sin, he was forgiven, he was adopted into God's family, and made the father of the faithful, the father of all believers. And then, in addition to that, there were also temporal blessings. We can never place too much emphasis upon the covenant made with Abraham. If you keep your eye on the references to Abraham in the subsequent parts of the Bible, you will find that this covenant is absolutely crucial. It is the great, explicit, original promise which God adumbrated in Genesis 3:15, but here stated explicitly.

Then we must move on, of course, to the covenant at Sinai, the Sinaitic covenant, the covenant made through Moses, which you will find in Exodus 19 and following. Now this is most important. Here the emphasis is placed especially upon the fact that this covenant was a *national* covenant, and from here onwards the church and the nation became one. So to belong to the nation of Israel was to belong to the church, and you could not be put out of the church without being put out of the nation. A man who transgressed the law was put to death. He was not merely punished in a spiritual sense, he was literally put to death, put out of existence, put out of the nation as well.

Then, of course, at Sinai great prominence was laid on the giving of the law. But I do want to make it very plain that the giving of the law did not mean that, in any sense whatsoever, God was re-establishing a covenant of works. I have already shown you the sheer impossibility of that. What is the point, I ask again, of making a covenant of works, of telling a man that he can save himself if he does certain things, when man had failed to do that in Paradise! No! The giving of the law did not mean a return to a covenant of works. The children of Israel made the terrible mistake of thinking it did; that was their error. It did not mean that. It was simply given in order that the life of the nation should be regulated in certain respects, and also for certain other reasons.

In the covenant at Sinai God gave to Moses the ceremonial law and all the typical sacrifices and services in connection with the Temple – the burnt offering, the various other offerings, and the appointment of certain people set apart as priests. And we have also the promulgation of the fact that the gospel, the great covenant of grace, was to be preached now in symbols and in types. These are meant to show us the demands of God upon us, and also, at the same time, to remind us of God's great promise of forgiveness and of salvation.

The law as a rule of life you can divide in a threefold manner – the moral law, the civil law and the ceremonial law, that is, the certain great, fixed principles of morality, the special legislation for the life of the nation, and the laws governing the ceremonies and the ritual. Now I want to emphasise that the making of this subsidiary covenant with Moses on behalf of the children of Israel at Sinai in no way whatsoever interfered with the covenant of grace that had already been given to Abraham, and that had previously been hinted at in the Garden of Eden. Now let me explain that, because there are some people who regard this as an entirely new covenant. But it was not; and I prove it in this way: in Romans 4:13 we read, 'For the promise, that he should be the heir of the world, was not to Abraham, or to his seed, through the law, but through the righteousness of faith.' This is most important. Listen again to Galatians 3:17: 'And this I say, that the covenant, that was confirmed before of God in Christ, the law, which was four hundred and thirty years after, cannot disannul, that it should make the promise of none effect.' In other words, Paul's great argument in Romans and Galatians is that the subsidiary covenant made with Moses at Mount Sinai, did not interfere to the slightest extent with the great covenant of promise and of grace that God had made with Abraham.

'But,' says someone, 'what about Galatians 4:21–2 where we read, 'Tell me, ye that desire to be under the law, do ye not hear the law? For it is written, that Abraham had two sons, the one by a bondmaid, the other by a freewoman.' And Paul goes on to say that this is an allegory, for these are two covenants. Does that not teach that there was a subsidiary covenant? To which the answer is this: it cannot mean that, because if it did, it would mean that in Galatians 4 Paul contradicts his own great argument in Galatians 3 and in Romans 4.

But quite apart from that, the context surely makes it quite clear. Paul's only purpose in Galatians 4 is to differentiate between the natural Israel and the spiritual Israel. It is his way of denouncing the wrong understanding of the Jew, who argued that to belong to Israel in the flesh meant that of necessity you belonged to the true seed of Abraham. But it does not. There was an earthly agreement, and there was a heavenly agreement, and it is the heavenly agreement that saves. After all, the promise God made to Abraham, in a sense, included Ishmael and Esau, did it not? All these people were circumcised, yes; but they were not the children of faith, they were not the true children of promise. They belonged to the realm of the flesh. God explained that to Abraham even in Genesis 17.

Very well then; the covenant made through Moses when the law was given, did not in any way interfere with the covenant of grace, but was simply meant to do two things. First, it was meant to increase the consciousness of sin, it was meant primarily to do that. 'Moreover,' says Paul, 'the law entered, that the offence might abound' (Rom. 5:20). He makes the same point in Romans 4:13: 'For the promise, that he should be the heir of the world, was not to Abraham, or to his seed, through the law, but through the righteousness of faith.' And in Galatians 3:17 Paul says, 'And this I say, that the covenant, that was confirmed before of God in Christ, the law, which was four hundred and thirty years after, cannot disannul, that it should make the promise of none effect.' So that is the first great argument – that the law was given in order to show the exceeding sinfulness of sin, in order to convict the nation, and all nations, of the utter hopelessness of a man dealing with his own sinfulness.

So the second purpose of the law we can put as Galatians 3:24 puts it: 'Wherefore the law was our schoolmaster to bring us unto Christ, that we might be justified by faith.' You see, the original covenant was the covenant which teaches justification by faith; that was the covenant God made with Abraham and his seed. That is the fundamental thing. What was the point of the law? It was to bring us to that, to act as a kind of teacher, a pedagogue, to act as a coach – it showed us the utter necessity of Christ and our absolute need of him. The law was never given as a means of salvation in itself.

You notice that I am emphasising this with considerable feeling, and I do so because you will find certain Bibles with notes, and certain books on the Bible, which would teach that God told the children of Israel that they could save themselves if they kept the law, that He provided the law in order to give them another way of saving themselves. But as we have seen, that is an utter contradiction of the teaching of Scripture.

We have, then, been dealing with the ways in which the great covenant of grace was administered and revealed to the people under the old dispensation. That leads on, of course, to the new dispensation which is the way that God has revealed and perfected, re-ratified and fulfilled the promise, and all that is contained in the covenant in and through His Son our Lord and Saviour Jesus Christ.

So let me try to summarise, therefore, what we have been considering thus far. First of all God made with man – perfect man, man in the image and likeness of God – a covenant of works. Man was to inherit eternal life, with the possibility of communion with God, if he kept the commandment, the law. Man fell – he broke God's law; sin, pollution, and degradation followed.

Now since then God has only made one fundamental covenant with man, it is the covenant of grace; and He revealed that great covenant of grace in the Old Testament in the ways that I have been describing.

So I think we have all probably learnt one thing, and I trust have seen it more clearly than we have ever seen it before. Christian people have often expressed surprise that the early Church decided to incorporate the Old Testament with its new literature, and they say, 'I do not see why, as a Christian, I need to be bothered about the Old Testament.' Well, if anybody still feels like that, I have failed and failed lamentably, because I have tried to show that the same great fundamental message is there in the Old, as in the New. And if we want to know about God's great purpose, we must delight in tracing it from the very beginning in the Garden of Eden, right the way through until we come to our Lord. We must see the marvellous plan of God as it unfolds in the old administration of the covenant of grace, and the new administration of the same covenant. The gospel begins, not in Matthew 1:1, but in Genesis 3:15. Let us never forget that, and so let us go to our Old Testament and look for the gospel. You will find it there almost everywhere in a most astounding manner, and it is our business, as well as our privilege, to seek it and to rejoice in it as we find it there.

21

The Covenant of Grace in the New Testament

'God, who at sundry times and in divers manners spake in time past unto the fathers by the prophets, hath in these last days spoken unto us by his Son . . .' (Heb. 1:1–2).

We have dealt so far with the old dispensation of the covenant of grace, and we have seen, you remember, that it is only one covenant. It has been administered or dispensed in two ways – the old and the new dispensation, or, if you prefer another term which is seldom talked of now, 'economy', but both are aspects of the same covenant of grace. It was made and given in full to Abraham, as it is recorded in Genesis 17, but we saw also that it had been guaranteed, and indeed laid down quite clearly in Genesis 3:15.

Furthermore, in looking at the old dispensation of this covenant we also saw that God made other subsidiary covenants with respect to the nation of Israel, but we must be careful to emphasise that none of those further covenants interfere with, deviate from, or even interrupt the covenant of grace given to Abraham. Apart from that covenant there is no hope at all for any of us.

So we come now to the *new* dispensation of the covenant of grace – the word 'new' simply means a new administration of the same covenant – and let us again remind ourselves of God's purpose in this covenant of grace. Through sin and the fall men and women lost their knowledge of God, they were estranged from Him, and God's purpose of redemption was to bring us back to know Him. And as we look at the working out of the new economy of this covenant, we shall see how all this has been done in and through our Lord and

Saviour Jesus Christ. It is important, first of all, that we should establish clearly that we are still dealing with the same covenant, so let me give you these proofs.

The first, as we have seen, is that there is but one covenant of grace and it is the same covenant in the Old Testament as it is in the New. We notice that the great promise made in the Old Testament: 'I will be their God' – the promise made to Abraham in Genesis 17:8 – is mentioned several times in the New Testament. It is one and the same promise. I hope we are clear about this. The greatest thing, let me repeat, that can happen to anybody is to say, 'My God'; nothing is to be compared with this and it is the New Testament term as well as the Old.

The second proof is that you find the same kind of blessing in the Old Testament and in the New. Take Psalm 51 and see what David prays there: 'Create in me a clean heart, O God; and renew a right spirit within me' (v. 10), and he wants to have the joy of his salvation restored to him (v. 12). We might spend a good deal of time on this point, but we must not, in order to move on. However, sometimes Christian people speak very wrongly of the kind of spiritual experience that was enjoyed by the Old Testament saints. There is a tendency to say that we have this experience but that they had nothing. You would be very surprised to hear that the psalmist is further on spiritually than you are! The type and kind of blessing is exactly the same in both Testaments. Notice that I am referring to the *type* and the *kind* of blessing; there is a difference, and I am coming to it. But the same blessing is in the Old Testament; it is a spiritual blessing and Psalm 51 alone is proof.

The third proof is that the Bible teaches very clearly that there is only one gospel; the gospel is the same in the Old Testament as it is in the New. Again, I am surprised when a preacher does not see it in the Old Testament, for if a man does not see it there, I doubt if he understands the gospel in the New Testament. Take the gospel that was preached by God in the Garden of Eden and also the promise made to Abraham; that is the essence of the gospel. Look at all the types and shadows, look at the various offerings described in Leviticus and elsewhere. Look even at the very furniture of the tabernacle. All these things preach the gospel; they are the types of the gospel and its message.

It is most important that we should grasp that whenever we read the Bible. Listen to the teaching of the prophets, look at the great passages in Isaiah and in Jeremiah, and, indeed, in all the prophetic books. The statements of the gospel are the same in both Testaments. Consider, too, the specific statements made by Paul in Galatians 3:8 where he speaks of God justifying the heathen through faith. He says, 'And the scripture, foreseeing that God would justify the heathen through faith, preached before the gospel unto Abraham, saying, In thee shall all nations be blessed.' Surely this statement in and of itself is enough to show that there is only one gospel – though there are further statements of this in the same chapter.

My fourth proof is that there are a number of direct statements which tell us that the Old Testament saints are now in the kingdom of God in exactly the same way as we are, and share all the blessings of God with us. Take, for example, Luke 13:28: 'There shall be weeping and gnashing of teeth, when ye shall see Abraham, and Isaac, and Jacob, and all the prophets, in the kingdom of God, and you yourselves thrust out.' Then take another illustration, and a most important one. In Romans 11, in his great teaching about the oneness of the people of God, Paul addresses the Gentiles and says,

> For if the firstfruit be holy, the lump is also holy: and if the root be holy, so are the branches. And if some of the branches be broken off, and thou, being a wild olive tree, wert graffed in among them, and with them partakest of the root and fatness of the olive tree; boast not against the branches. But if thou boast, thou bearest not the root, but the root thee.
>
> Verses 16–18

In other words, the Gentiles are put into the same tree; they have been grafted in. It is not a new tree, it is the old one; some branches are taken away, others are put in. It is the one lump and it is the lump that matters; we belong to the lump. Verse 24 in the same chapter states, 'For if thou wert cut out of the olive tree which is wild by nature, and wert graffed contrary to nature into a good olive tree: how much more shall these, which be the natural branches, be graffed into their own olive tree?'

So the argument in Romans 11, obviously, is that the old and the new economy all belong to the same tree, it is the one kingdom, the one covenant of grace, one salvation. Then in Galatians 3:14 we read, 'That the blessing of Abraham might come on the Gentiles through Jesus Christ; that we might receive the promise of the Spirit through faith.' There it is once more, and we find it again in verse 29, 'And if ye be Christ's, then are ye Abraham's seed, and heirs according to the promise.' What a tremendously important chapter the third chapter of Galatians is!

But now go on to Ephesians 2:11–13 where we read,

> Wherefore remember, that ye being in time past Gentiles in the flesh, who are called Uncircumcision by that which is called the Circumcision in the flesh made by hands; that at that time ye were without Christ, being aliens from the commonwealth of Israel, and strangers from the covenants of promise, having no hope, and without God in the world: but now in Christ Jesus ye who sometimes were far off are made nigh by the blood of Christ.

The Gentiles are 'made nigh' to the covenant of grace, as Paul puts it in verse 19: 'Now therefore ye are no more strangers and foreigners, but fellowcitizens with the saints, and of the household of God' – the same terms as those made to Abraham.

It is clear and unmistakable and Paul is not content with saying it once, he must repeat it again, in Ephesians 3:6, where he says, 'That the Gentiles should be fellowheirs, and of the same body, and partakers of his promise in Christ by the gospel.' Paul always claimed that that was the special message delivered to him, that the Gentiles are to be fellow heirs with those chosen in the nation of Israel; they are joined together in this receiving of the blessings of the kingdom, for the promise is in Christ by the gospel.

Then look, too, at Hebrews 6:12–13 – I have just chosen some of the relevant texts – 'That ye be not slothful, but followers of them who through faith and patience inherit the promises. For when God made promise to Abraham, because he could swear by no greater, he sware by himself . . .', and verse 18 states, 'That by two immutable things, in which it was impossible for God to lie, we might have a strong consolation, who have fled for refuge to lay hold upon the hope set before us.' This refers to the promise that God made to Abraham, with an oath that accompanied it, as something that is meant to strengthen our faith in the new dispensation, under the new economy.

In Hebrews 11 you will find that the great argument there about faith is a very extended and wonderful exposition of this selfsame point. The writer winds up his argument in verses 39 and 40 by saying, 'And these all, having obtained a good report through faith, received not the promise: God having provided some better thing for us, that they without us should not be made perfect.' His point is that both they and we are all going to be made perfect together. A total unity is established between these Old Testament saints that we have been reading about and those under the new dispensation. These are explicit and specific statements that all of us, new and old, have the same benefits of salvation.

My fifth proof is that clearly, according to the Scriptures, there is only one way of obtaining salvation and all those blessings, and that is the way of faith. All the Old Testament saints believed explicitly in God, and they exercised faith. In Habakkuk 2:4 we read, 'The just shall live by his faith.' This is the theme and the message of the Old Testament from beginning to end, and, as in Hebrews 11, it is reiterated in the New Testament. Paul, quoting from Habakkuk, says in Romans 1:17, 'The just shall live by faith'; and this is the theme of all his epistles.

But Paul puts it still more clearly and specifically in Romans 4:23–5, where, referring to Abraham, he says, 'Now it was not written for his sake alone, that it was imputed to him; but for us also, to whom it shall be imputed, if we believe on him that raised up Jesus our Lord from the dead; who was delivered for our offences, and was raised again for our justification.' It is clear that we receive justification by faith, exactly as Abraham received it by faith. So once more under this heading, read again from the end of Hebrews 10 through chapter 11 to the beginning of chapter 12. It is the same truth, elaborated at length.

The sixth and last proof is that there is only one mediator under the two dispensations; the same mediator, the Lord Jesus Christ – 'the Lamb slain from the foundation of the world' (Rev. 13:8). Take the promise made to Adam about the seed of the woman. God says that salvation is going to happen in that way, and other Scriptures prove that the seed of the woman is no other than the Lord Jesus. He is the mediator in the Old Testament types, all point to Him, the prophecies all point to him, it is always the Lord Himself.

In John 5:39 our Lord Himself says – to me this is still more wonderful – 'Search the scriptures; for in them ye think ye have eternal life: and they are they which testify of me.' That is a perfectly clear and explicit statement, but He repeats it in verse 46: 'For had ye believed Moses, ye would have believed me: for he wrote of me.' He and He alone is the mediator. Listen to Him again in John 8:56: 'Your father Abraham rejoiced to see my day: and he saw it, and was glad.'

But let us go further on to Acts 10:43 where Peter is preaching in the house of Cornelius: 'To him give all the prophets witness, that through his name whosoever believeth in him shall receive remission of sins.' Or again, Paul writes in Romans 3:25, 'Whom God hath set forth to be a propitiation through faith in his blood, to declare his righteousness for the remission of sins that are past, through the forbearance of God.' He alone was and is the only mediator, and He alone can justify what was done under the old dispensation.

The writer of Hebrews tells us, 'And for this cause he is the mediator of the new testament, that by means of death, for the redemption of the transgressions that were under the first testament, they which are called might receive the promise of eternal inheritance' (Heb. 9:15). You notice the argument: those who were under the first testament can only receive the promise of eternal inheritance through Him who is the mediator of the new testament. So there you have six proofs designed to show that there is only one covenant of grace which is the same in the New Testament and the old.

Now, second, we must look at differences in the two dispensations. There are, for instance, certain things which are characteristic of the Old Testament and not of the New. In the Old Testament everything points forward to Christ: the promise looks foward to Him. Another characteristic of the Old Testament is the types and shadows, the foreshadowing adumbrations and hints, which is the form the promise takes under the first dispensation. All these refer to the specific covenant made with Abraham, and are confined to one nation only, to Israel. It is of Israel that God says in Amos 3:3, 'Can two walk together, except they be agreed?' They were His special people.

So let us put all this positively under three new headings. First, we must emphasise the superiority of the new dispensation of the one covenant over the old dispensation of the same covenant. The old was mediated through the servants, Abraham and Moses, but the new has been mediated through the Son of God. Hebrews 3:5–6 makes this very clear: 'And Moses verily was faithful in all his house, as a servant, for a testimony of those things which were to be spoken after; but Christ as a son over his own house; whose house are we, if we hold fast the confidence and the rejoicing of the hope firm unto the end.'

Second, the truth in the old dispensation was partly revealed and partly hidden in the types and shadows. But in the new dispensation it is clearly revealed in the incarnation of Jesus Christ, in what He did, taught and accomplished and in the work of the Holy Spirit. The mystery that had been concealed is now being shown in the New Testament language.

Then third, in the new dispensation it is not only clearly revealed, but the revelation has been, of course, increased and made more clear by the incarnation of the Lord Himself and the work of the Spirit. You will see this in Hebrews 1:1–3:

> God, who at sundry times and in divers manners spake in time past unto the fathers by the prophets, hath in these last days spoken unto us by his Son, whom he hath appointed heir of all things, by whom also he made the worlds; who being the brightness of his glory, and the express image of his person, and upholding all things by the word of his power, when he had by himself purged our sins, sat down on the right hand of the Majesty on high.
>
> Hebrews 1:1–3

The revelation is now complete, full and final, it is all in Him. 'For in him dwelleth all the fulness of the Godhead bodily', says Paul to the Colossians, and, 'In him are hid all the treasures of wisdom and knowledge' (Col. 2:9, 3).

This leads me to the fourth way in which the new dispensation is superior to the old. Under the old dispensation the revelation was largely carnal and material in form, whereas now it is entirely spiritual. You see this in Hebrews 9 where the writer, speaking of 'the first covenant' (v. 1), says,

> Which stood only in meats and drinks, and divers washings, and carnal ordinances, imposed on them until the time of reformation. But Christ being come an high priest of good things to come, by a greater and more perfect tabernacle, not made with hands, that is to say, not of this building; neither by the blood of goats and calves, but by his own blood he entered in once into the holy place, having obtained eternal redemption for us.
>
> Hebrews 9:10–12

Fifth: the old dispensation, as we have seen, was for one people only. Now it is no longer confined, it is for all nations everywhere; it is for the world.

The sixth superiority is that the old dispensation was clearly preparatory, while the new is final. The whole purpose of Hebrews is to demonstrate the finality of the cross. Nothing can be added, nothing needs to be added, for everything is in Him.

Then, seventh, under this new economy the Holy Spirit has been poured out. He had not been poured out under the old dispensation but he came upon specific men to enable them to accomplish given tasks. Undoubtedly God's people were made children of the kingdom because of the work of the Holy Spirit in them and upon them, but He had not been poured out in the way He was at Pentecost. The result is that the blessing is greater in scope under the New Testament. There is greater knowledge, greater understanding, and therefore greater enjoyment of these blessings. Abraham only saw these things 'afar off' (Heb. 11:13), though seeing them afar off, he rejoiced (John 8:56). We do not see afar off. We see in the clear fulness of the day, and therefore our joy is greater.

The difference between the old and the new dispensation is the difference between a child and a mature person. This is extremely important and we can look at it like this: the child is as much the child of the parent at the age of one year as at the age of forty years. The relationship does not change, but as the child grows and develops, knows the father better, and enters into an enjoyment of that relationship with a greater degree of understanding than before. That, it seems to me, is the essential difference between these two dispensations of the one covenant of grace. They are children; we are mature. In a way they could not be this greater thing. As Hebrews 11:40 puts it, 'God has provided some better thing for us, that they without us should not be made perfect.' But they enjoy it with us; they could not then, they do now.

Having seen, then, something of the superiority of the new dispensation over the old, let us sum it all up, and emphasise it. There is only one covenant of grace and it all centres around the Lord Jesus Christ. The old points forward to Him; the new reveals Him and holds Him forth to us in person. He alone is the fulfilment of everything that is promised from Genesis 3:15 onwards. It is all in Him. The original covenant with regard to redemption was fully and clearly made with Him.

Sometimes you hear people saying that the Bible is not a book, but a library of books. I think I know what they mean but, you know, this sort of thing is wrong, it should never be said. This is really one book. It was written by different men, at different times and in different places, but there is only one book and one message; it is one book with one theme, about one person. Let us follow our fathers, who always talked about 'The Book'. For that is what it is, not a library of books. It is infinitely greater, that is the glory of it, and these different men were used by the Holy Spirit to write this one book, inspired by the Author.

This leads me to the last point I would make. It is that while it is true to say there is only one covenant, it is equally true to say that the covenant was originally made between the Father and the Son. Man, having fallen, was not in a position to make a covenant with God, so God made it with His Son, and you and I come into this covenant. His Son is our representative, our mediator, our surety, our guarantor; what He did, He contracted to do. This is perfectly clear.

But what did He contract to do? First, He contracted to keep, to honour and to fulfil the covenant of works which was first broken by Adam in the Garden of Eden.

Second, He contracted to deal with the results of the fall, of the sin and the pollution of man. Obviously we cannot be reconciled to God until that is done.

Third, He guaranteed the performance on our part of all the duties devolved on us in the covenant. God promised, on the condition that certain obligations are fulfilled; the Son contracted to do this so that this covenant might become possible. He guaranteed to do this on our part.

What, then, does all this involve? I will simply give you three headings:

The Son must become the second man, the second Adam, and that is precisely what He is called in 1 Corinthians 15:45, 47. In verse 45, Paul says, 'The first man Adam was made a living soul; the last Adam was made a quickening spirit.' Then in verse 47 we read, 'The first man is of the earth, earthy: the second man is the Lord from heaven.' So He is the 'last' Adam and the 'second' Adam.

Second, He must assume our place; He must take our nature upon Himself – 'made of a woman, made under the law, to redeem them that were under the law, that we might receive the adoption of sons' (Gal. 4:4–5); and He must present us faultless in the presence of God (Jude 24).

Lastly: He must undertake all our obligations. Obviously, the covenant cannot be carried through by us, so He must undertake all the things that God demands from us.

Our consideration, therefore, of the covenant of grace shows God's plan, purpose, redemption and salvation. It leads us to Christ and from every direction it points to Him. So in our next study, we shall be happy to start upon our consideration of the biblical doctrine of our Lord Jesus Christ.

But let me emphasise and impress upon you the importance of

coming to this doctrine about that blessed person in the way we have done. So often you find people beginning with redemption and salvation, rushing immediately to the person of our Lord, not realising that He is the final statement, the truth of this great covenant of grace that God promised in the Garden of Eden and specifically and explicitly stated to Abraham. Does this not cast a great light upon the Old Testament, and show the importance of studying it as well as the New Testament? Let us read it constantly, looking for this covenant of grace as set forth in types and shadows which show that everything is pointing to Him. And I trust that from the blessings we all hope to enjoy, from the realisation of that great covenant, we will all be helped to know the Old Testament in a deeper way than hitherto.

22
The Lord Jesus Christ

At the end of our last study on the doctrine of the great covenant of grace, we ended by emphasising the fact that the covenant, in both its dispensations, always points to the person of our Lord and Saviour Jesus Christ. So we have come now to our consideration of the biblical doctrine concerning Him. While this is obviously not the starting-point of biblical doctrine, it is certainly its centre. The truth concerning the Lord Jesus Christ is the central and the most stupendous fact in the history of redemption. It stands out as the unique event in all history. This truth concerning Him is the biggest and most astounding event of all.

Not only that. We have seen several times already that all history points to Him and to this event. Everything until this points forward, everything that has happened since points backward; it is indeed the turning point of history. That is recognised if only by our calendar. By dividing up history into BC and AD, we pay tribute to the fact that this is undoubtedly the central and the most important event that has ever taken place. So we are forced, for every reason, to consider this doctrine. The Bible itself makes it very plain and clear that the whole essence of the Christian position is dependent upon the person of the Lord Jesus Christ.

Now that is in many ways what you will call the 'differentia' of Christianity. That is the thing that separates the Christian faith from all other religions. Their founders, while important, are not absolutely essential to them. If Buddha had never existed you could still have Buddhism. If Muhammad had never lived you could still have Islam. In other religions it is the teaching that matters and the person is not essential; other persons might have done it equally well, and the teaching would remain unaffected.

But that is not the case with the Christian faith. Christianity, as has often been pointed out, is Christ Himself. He is not only central, He is absolutely vital, and therefore we have to see that we are concerned primarily and always with Him. This is something that I shall have to emphasise, of course, time and time again, but the touchstone of anybody's profession of the Christian faith is, of necessity, such a person's relationship to the Lord Jesus Christ. What proclaims at once that so many people who call themselves Christian are not Christian is that Christ as a person is not at all essential to them.

I am referring here to people who think that a Christian is just a good man or woman. Obviously, you can be a good man without even mentioning the Lord Jesus Christ; but in Christianity He is vital, and if the truth concerning Him is not the truth, the whole position vanishes. Now that is something that one cannot overemphasise. The Christian faith is entirely concerned about Him, who He is, what He has done, and what He has made available and possible for us. And therefore you see the vital importance of our being quite clear in our minds, and absolutely right about all these things.

So I make no apology for putting it as dogmatically and as bluntly as that. To me, those who apologise for saying such a thing are very doubtful Christians, if, indeed, they are Christians at all. There is an intolerance about the Christian faith, expressed like this by the apostle Paul: 'But though we, or an angel from heaven, preach any other gospel unto you than that which we have preached unto you, let him be accursed' (Gal. 1:8). And we must say the same thing. The truth is clear, it is well defined, it is perfectly definite, and we must be certain, therefore, with regard to what we believe about Him. It is not enough to say, 'I believe in Christ.' What do we believe about Christ? What is the teaching about Him? That is what now concerns us.

Now the New Testament itself exhorts us to do this. Why do you think the four Gospels were ever written? Surely there can be no hesitation about answering that question. They were written, God caused men to write them and guided them, through the Spirit as they did so, in order that the truth concerning the Lord Jesus Christ might be known exactly. All sorts of false stories were current in the first century. There were apocryphal gospels and in them things were being ascribed to Him, and He was reported to have done and said things, which had never happened. So the Gospels were written in order to define the truth, in order to exclude certain falsehoods, and these other facts plainly and clearly. Luke, in the introduction to his Gospel, says that, and you will find that John, at the end of his Gospel, virtually says the same thing: 'But these are written, that ye might believe that Jesus is the Christ, the Son of God . . .' (John 20:31).

But not only do the Gospels tell us that, there are also several sections in the other parts of the New Testament which specifically make the same point. Take the first epistle of John, for example. Why was that written? Well, undoubtedly, for one major reason, and that was to counteract the false teaching that was current, the teaching that denied that Jesus Christ had come in the flesh, that docetism, that false doctrine. And therefore I make no apology not only for calling your attention to this doctrine, but also for defining certain things clearly, and pointing out certain errors which we must avoid.

Let me also warn you, before we go any further, that we are not only dealing with a great and mysterious subject, but with one which makes demands upon us and upon our thought and our attention. But it is essential, and I am anxious that I should deal with the case of anybody who may be thinking, 'Well I really have not much time to be interested in doctrine like this. I am just a simple believer in the Lord Jesus Christ.' If you take that position you are utterly unscriptural! It was because such simple Christians were ready to believe false teachers, and, indeed, did believe them, that so many of the epistles had to be written, with their stern warnings against the terrible danger to the soul of believing these wrong teachings and false ideas concerning our Lord and Saviour Jesus Christ.

It is not enough to say, 'I believe in Jesus Christ.' The New Testament asks you questions when you say that. It asks, 'What do you believe about Him? Is He man only? Is He God only? Did He really come in the flesh or did He not? What did He do? What is the meaning of His death?' The New Testament is concerned about definitions, and there is nothing, I suggest, that is further removed from its teaching than to say, 'It is all right; so long as you believe in the Lord Jesus Christ it does not matter very much what you say in detail.' The 'detail', as I am hoping to show you, is all-important and absolutely vital.

Furthermore, not only is all that stated in the New Testament, but if you read the subsequent history of the Christian Church, you will find that in the first three or four centuries heresies kept crowding in, and the Church had to meet together to define or to reject certain ideas. So various discussions and councils were held which were very largely engaged in safeguarding this great central doctrine of the person of the Lord Jesus Christ. So we must study the doctrines as we value our souls and our salvation, and, we must have a desire to be clear in our conceptions and to be able to give a reason to others for the hope that is in us (1 Pet. 3:15).

So then, what are the general statements made by the Bible concerning this person? What does it tell us about Him, as it focuses attention upon Him and compels us to consider Him? First, it says that He is the fulfilment of all the Old Testament prophecies and promises. The great central statement of that is in 2 Corinthians 1:20: 'For all the promises of God in him are yea, and in him Amen, unto the glory of God by us.' They come to a focus, to a point, in Him.

Now I cannot take you through all these promises and prophecies in detail. Let me simply pick out some which clearly are the most important, in order to establish this point. For instance, as we have seen, He is the fulfilment of the promise that was given in the Garden of Eden where God says that the seed of the woman shall bruise the serpent's head (Gen. 3:15). There is also the promise given to Abraham in Genesis 17 about the seed. Paul refers to this in Galatians 3:16: 'He saith not, And to seeds, as of many; but as of one, And to thy seed, which is Christ.' Again, we have already considered that, so let us look also at some others that we have not considered.

Take, for instance, the promise given in Genesis 49:10: 'The sceptre shall not depart from Judah, nor a lawgiver from between his feet, until Shiloh come; and unto him shall the gathering of the people be.' That is a tremendous promise, and a most vital statement, and it was literally fulfilled in the coming of the Lord Jesus Christ. It is a fact of history that the sceptre and lawgiver did remain with Judah until AD 70, and then, with the destruction of Jerusalem, and the casting out of the Jewish nation among the nations, that has no longer been the case. The sceptre of the lawgiver remained there until He came, and then it departed, in that external sense. And likewise this statement: 'and unto him shall the gathering of the people be' obviously has been fulfilled, and only fulfilled, in the Lord Jesus Christ. Though born 'of the seed of David according to the flesh' (Rom. 1:3), all nations have come to Him. He is the Saviour of the world.

Then look at the prophecy in Daniel 9:24–6:

Seventy weeks are determined upon thy people and upon thy holy city, to finish the transgression, and to make an end of sins, and to make reconciliation for iniquity, and to bring in everlasting righteousness, and to seal up the vision and prophecy, and to anoint the most Holy. Know therefore and understand, that from the going forth of the commandment to restore and to build Jerusalem unto the Messiah the Prince shall be seven weeks, and threescore and two weeks: the street shall be built again, and the wall, even in troublous times. And after threescore and two weeks shall Messiah be cut off, but not for himself: and the people of the prince that shall come shall destroy the city and the sanctuary; and the end thereof shall be with a flood, and unto the end of the war desolations are determined.

Again, this is a most vital prophecy. It is always agreed that 'weeks' here mean weeks of years, and, therefore, we are told that there shall be this seventy weeks of years, meaning altogether four hundred and ninety years. First of all we are told that there will be seven weeks of years, forty-nine years before the city would be rebuilt, and so it happened exactly. Then that there will be sixty-two weeks, which comes to four hundred and thirty-four years, after the rebuilding of the city, and then the Messiah will appear. Work it out and you will find that it coincides with the coming of the Lord Jesus Christ. And then we are told that there is to be a period of one week, seven years, and that halfway through this He should be cut off, three and a half years. Now there you see again is another great prophecy, not only pointing to Him but obviously clearly fulfilled in Him.

Then take a number of prophecies with regard to His birth. First of all we are told something with regard to the time of His appearance. The verse I have already quoted from Genesis 49 does that, and so do the verses from Daniel 9; and you will find in the prophet Haggai the prophecy, 'The glory of this latter house shall be greater than of the former' (Hag. 2:9), referring to the fact that He did not appear in the former house but would appear in this latter one. And then there is a very vital statement in Malachi 3:1 where the prophet says, 'Behold, I will send my messenger, and he shall prepare the way before me: and the Lord, whom ye seek, shall suddenly come to his temple, even the messenger of the covenant, whom ye delight in: behold, he shall come, saith the Lord of hosts.' That is very significant, and I shall refer to it again later. Furthermore, you remember that in Micah 5:2 we are given an exact prophecy with regard to the place of His birth – that it is to be in Bethlehem. We are told also that He was to be of the tribe of Judah, and of the house and family of David – read Jeremiah 23:5–6, and you will find such a statement.

Then in Isaiah 7:14 we are told that He is to be born of a virgin. Now I am strongly tempted to stop and deal with this. There is

considerable discussion about it because the *Revised Standard Version*
has dropped the word 'virgin' and refers to a 'young woman'. However, we must press on, and I do not think I should pause to go into
the evidence with regard to that now. But I can assure you that
scholarship is quite clear that it is an unjustifiable change, and it really
does mean 'virgin'. The essence of the argument is this: the prophet is
promising a sign, and a sign is obviously something unusual. Now it
is not an unusual thing that a young married woman should have a
child. That would not be a sign. But if a virgin has a child it is unusual
and it is a sign. So apart from the meaning of words, the whole context makes it perfectly clear that it must be a virgin. Furthermore, if
you believe that the Scriptures are inspired – and we agreed about
that earlier – then we have no problem because we are told specifically in Matthew 1:22–3 that that verse in Isaiah was indeed a
prophecy that our Lord would be born of a virgin. I shall come back
to that fact in a subsequent lecture.

Then again Malachi 3:1 says that He would be preceded by a
forerunner, and we know that our Lord was preceded by John the
Baptist. So all these prophecies, and others, meet in the Lord Jesus
Christ, and what is still more interesting is that not only have they
been fulfilled in Him, they never can be fulfilled in anybody else. Now
this is most important if you are ever discussing this matter with a
Jew, because the fact is that the genealogies of the tribes and the
families have been lost. This means that in the future it will be impossible to establish that anyone claiming to be the Messiah is the Messiah. No longer can any genealogy be traced in the way that it has
been traced in the case of our Lord and Saviour Jesus Christ.

But now let us look at a number of prophecies which point out the
characteristics of the Messiah when He comes. We are told that He is
to be a king and the conqueror of a universal empire. Psalm 2:6,
Psalm 45 and Isaiah 9:6–7 all make this point. And yet the extraordinary thing is that He is not only to be a king and a conqueror, He is
also to be 'despised and rejected of men; a man of sorrows, and
acquainted with grief' (Isa. 53:3). And it was because they failed to
realise those two things that His own countrymen did not recognise
Him when He came. They were looking for the king only; they had
forgotten these other aspects. But the prophecy combines the two and
our Lord does also.

Prophecy also tells us that He is to be 'a light to lighten the Gentiles', a most astounding thing to have said to the Jews. But it was said

many times in the prophecy of Isaiah, in chapters 42:6 and 60:3, and in other places. We are also told in Isaiah 53 that His death is to be vicarious; and when we come to look at the doctrine of the atonement, we shall see that it was vicarious and substitutionary. We are told that He will enter into the city of Jerusalem riding on an ass (Zech. 9:9), and you remember how that was fulfilled. We are told that He is to be sold for thirty pieces of silver, and that with His price a potter's field will be purchased (Zech. 11:12–13). We are told that lots would be cast for His garments (Ps. 22:18). We are told that He will be given vinegar to drink in his sorrow (Ps. 69:21). We are even told that He will utter certain words on the cross, 'My God, my God, why hast thou forsaken me?' (Ps. 22:1). Psalm 22:6 says that His hands and feet will be pierced, and Zechariah 12:10 adds, '. . . they shall look upon me whom they have pierced, and they shall mourn . . .' And we are told in Isaiah 53:9 that He will make His grave with the wicked and with the rich in His death and we know that He was buried in the tomb of Joseph of Arimathaea.

Then there is a whole group of prophecies concerning His work – for instance, His work as a prophet. Deuteronomy 18:18 tells us, 'I will raise them up a Prophet from among their brethren, like unto thee' – that was said to Moses. And from there onwards the children of Israel were looking for that prophet, and the Jews often asked whether Christ was the one. We are told that He is also to be a priest. You will find that in Isaiah 53:10 and in Daniel 9:24. And we are told that He is to be a king. Read the great prophecy in Daniel 2:44–5. The stone 'cut out of the moutain without hands' that smashes every other kingdom and that conquers and fills the whole world is a prophecy of our Lord who would one day come as a king. And so His work is prophesied – Prophet, Priest and King.

So the first great statement of the Bible concerning Him is that the prophecies point to Him, and that He is their fulfilment. But, second, the Bible also exhorts us to consider Him, because He is the only one by whom we can be reconciled to God, and by whom we can know God. We read in Hebrews 12:24 that He is 'the mediator of the new covenant'. He said Himself, 'I am the way, the truth, and the life: no man cometh unto the Father, but by me' (John 14:6). Anyone who says a thing like that must be looked at and considered. If we value our salvation and want to know God we must listen to such a person. Then after His resurrection He said, 'Thus it is written, and thus it behoved Christ to suffer, and to rise from the dead the third day: and that repentance and remission of sins should be preached in his name among all nations . . .' (Luke 24:46–7). Nothing could be clearer than that. And then Peter, when he was on trial, claimed for Him, 'Neither is there salvation in any other: for there is none other name under heaven given among men, whereby we must be saved' (Acts 4:12). And there is the statement made by Paul in 1 Timothy 2:5: 'For there is one God, and one mediator between God and men, the man Christ Jesus.' That, then, is the claim that is made for Him everywhere: that it is in Him, and in Him alone, that we know God and are reconciled to God, and in Him alone, therefore, can we be saved.

The third great reason which the Bible gives us for considering Him is that He holds all things in His hands. All power has been given to Him in heaven and in earth (Matt. 28:18). He has all might and dominion and authority. In Revelation 5 we are told that He is the only one who can control and open the seals. There was no one strong enough to break the seals of the book of history except the Lion of the tribe of Judah, the Lamb that once was slain. But He can do so, and He does so. In 1 Corinthians 15:25 we are told that He must reign till God has put all His enemies under His feet; again, in Ephesians 1:22–3 we are told specifically that 'God hath put all things under his feet, and gave him to be the head over all things to the church, which is his body, the fulness of him that filleth all in all.' It is a staggering and a stupendous thought that all history is in the hands of this person. Everything that happens in this world is under His control – everything without exception. He is the Lord of glory and the Lord of history, and He sits at God's right hand in the authority and the glory of God.

And then the final reason which the Bible gives us for considering Him is that He is the one by whom the world is going to be judged, and this is where we are all vitally concerned. He claimed this Himself. In John 5:27 He says, '[The Father] hath given him authority to execute judgment also, because he is the Son of man.' Paul in preaching to the learned Athenians says, God 'hath appointed a day, in the which he will judge the world in righteousness by that man whom he hath ordained; whereof he hath given assurance unto all men, in that he hath raised him from the dead' (Acts 17:31). The Father has committed all judgment unto Him. Read the book of Revelation; you see the same thing again portrayed in its symbols and in the wealth of its imagery. The Lord of history will be the Judge of the whole world.

Those, then, are the general reasons given by the Bible why all people should consider Him. Consider Jesus! Look at this person! So we accept the invitation. What else does the Bible tell us about Him? Now here we come to the first subdivision of the biblical doctrine concerning the Lord Jesus Christ: it is what is commonly called the *doctrine of the incarnation*. Here, obviously, is a wonderful subject. Let me first lay down some of the general principles.

Here we come to the greatest mystery of all time, the mystery in which we are told that 'the Word was made flesh and dwelt [tabernacled] among us' (John 1:14).

The apostle Paul states the same truth in 1 Timothy 3:16 in these great words: 'And without controversy great is the mystery of godliness: God was manifest in the flesh, justified in the Spirit, seen of angels, preached unto the Gentiles, believed on in the world, received up into glory.' Now in the doctrine of the incarnation we are concerned, of course, with the first part of that statement: 'Great is the mystery of godliness: God was manifest in the flesh . . .' So what does this mean? Let me just give you a definition at this point and then in our next study we shall consider it in greater detail. But let us be clear about the comprehensive statement; it is that the eternal Son of God has taken on Him, or has taken unto Himself, human nature.

Notice what I am saying. I am not saying that when Jesus of Nazareth was born in Bethlehem a new personality came into being. That is not true. That is rank heresy. The doctrine of the incarnation says that the eternal second Person in the blessed Trinity entered into time and into the world, took unto Himself human nature, was born as a babe, lived a life as a man, and appeared in 'the likeness of sinful flesh' (Rom. 8:3). Now there I am making the most vital statement of all. I hope to go on to break it up, to show you the importance of making this statement, and safeguarding it against various errors. But the essence of the statement is that the one who was born was not coming into being, was not starting His existence as a person. No! It was this eternal Person, the Son of God, who now assumed this form and entered the life of man in the world.

There are numerous great statements in the Scriptures which put it like that, and which emphasise that. The most notable, of course, which we shall have to consider in greater detail later, is that great passage in Philippians 2:6–8; but there are many prophecies in the Old Testament which put it in the same way. Malachi says, 'But unto you that fear my name shall the Sun of righteousness arise with healing in his wings' (Mal. 4:2); and we have considered all those other statements which talk about His coming or His appearing. It did not start at Bethlehem. He came from eternity, from the bosom of the blessed God Himself, and entered into life and into time and into history in that particular form.

We must leave it at that point now. But you notice the progression of ideas, the progression of our thoughts? Something must be done by God before man can be saved. We have the assurance in the covenant that it will be done and the covenant points to this person. He is at the centre of the Bible. It asks us to consider Him for the reasons I have given you. And as we come to look more closely, we shall see what a glorious and astounding truth it is and why it had to happen in the way it did. Then we shall go on to consider the details, which will involve a consideration of the doctrine of the virgin birth. After that, we must consider what we are told about His deity and His humanity, and how these two are reconciled, or exist together, in the one person. And so we shall be plunging right into the midst of this most wonderful and most glorious doctrine concerning the mystery and the marvel of the person of the Lord Jesus Christ.

23
The Incarnation

We have now begun to consider together the biblical doctrine of the person of Christ. That, as you notice, I put under the general heading of the doctrine of redemption, and I think one must do so. We have looked at the person of our Lord, in dealing with the doctrine of the Trinity, but specifically, when considering the doctrine of redemption, we must, of course, concentrate upon the person and the work of our Lord and Saviour Jesus Christ.

And we have seen that when we do come to consider Him, we are at once confronted by the first particular doctrine wih respect to Him, and that is the doctrine of the incarnation. We have made the general statement that the eternal Son of God, the second Person in the blessed Holy Trinity, took unto Himself human nature. We said that this did not mean that a new personality came into being, but that God the eternal Son became incarnate. We saw, too, that it was necessary to take that statement, that general statement, and to break it up, because it is something that has been so frequently misunderstood; and as our salvation and our eternal destiny depend upon our relationship to the Lord Jesus Christ, what can be more important than that we should be clear and certain in our ideas and in our thoughts concerning Him.

Furthermore, of course, Church history shows very clearly — indeed, before you come to Church history, the New Testament itself shows us — that the devil is concerned about nothing more than to lead people astray with regard to the person and the work of our blessed Lord and Saviour Jesus Christ. That is why we can take no risks, and we cannot content ourselves with a mere general statement of the doctrine of the incarnation. We must break it up and analyse it;

we must show what it does and what it does not say, lest any of us should inadvertently fall into error.

I propose, therefore, to make the following series of statements. The first is this: the doctrine of the person of our Lord, and the doctrine of the incarnation in particular, show us again the all-importance of the doctrine of the Trinity. Now we considered that doctrine earlier and as we come to consider it now, we shall see why it was so important for us to have considered it then. The whole Christian position, in a sense, depends upon the doctrine of the blessed Holy Trinity. If we do not believe in that we cannot be Christian; it is impossible. Someone who does not believe in the Trinity cannot be a Christian because he cannot believe in the doctrine of redemption. Therefore as we talk about the person of the Son we see how important it is always to realise that God exists in three Persons – Father, Son and Holy Spirit.

The second statement is that the doctrine of the incarnation asserts not that the eternal triune God became flesh, but that the second Person in the triune God became flesh. The Scripture puts it like this: 'The Word was made flesh' (John 1:14). Now this is surely something which we must emphasise. We often speak rather loosely, I am afraid, in talking about the incarnation, and many of our hymns tend to do the same thing. But to me it seems always to be wise not to say that God became man. That is a loose statement which we had better not use. We often do say that, but believing as we do in the Persons of the Trinity, what we should say is that the second Person in the Trinity was made flesh and appeared as man. If we merely say, 'God became man', then we may be saying something that is quite wrong, and if people believe something wrong as the result of our statement, we cannot really blame them. We must be particular and we must be specific and we should always be careful what we say.

The third statement is that the doctrine of the incarnation does not say that it was merely an appearance or a form that was taken on by the second Person in the Trinity, but that it was indeed a true incarnation; He did come in the flesh. I emphasise that because in the very early years of the Christian Church there were people who went into errors and into heresy about this. The so-called Gnostics said that our Lord had the mere appearance of flesh; He had a phantom body, an appearance of a body. But the doctrine of the incarnation does not say that. It says it was not an appearance, it was real; it was a true incarnation; the Word *was made flesh* and dwelt among us.

Point number four is again a negative one. The doctrine of the incarnation does not say that it was merely the divine nature that somehow became united with human nature and so formed a person. It is not that; it was the second Person Himself, the Person, who became flesh. Now there were many in the early ages of the Church, and they have persisted throughout the centuries, who have not understood that. Their view of Jesus Christ is of divine nature and human nature forming a new person. That is not the truth. It was the second, eternal Person in the Trinity who took human nature. You see the significance of that? We have already seen, you remember, that the doctrine of the incarnation does not teach the creation of a new person. It teaches that He took on to Himself flesh and appeared in this world in the likeness of man – not a new person, but this eternal Person.

So the next point, then, is that the doctrine of the incarnation does not teach, neither does it involve the idea, that a change took place in the personality of the Son of God. There was a change in the form in which He appeared, there was a change in the state in which He manifested Himself, but there was no change in His personality, He is the same Person always. In the womb of the virgin Mary, and lying as a helpless babe in the manger, He is still the second Person in the Holy Trinity.

The next definition I put like this: we must never so state the doctrine of the incarnation as to give the impression, therefore, that we say that the Son of God was changed into a man. That is why that phrase about God becoming man is misleading. We have seen that John 1:14 says, 'The Word was made flesh, and dwelt among us,' and that very phrase 'was made' has often caused people to think that the Son of God was changed into a man. This is partly due to the fact that it is not really the best translation. Instead of saying, 'The Word was made flesh,' what we really mean is that He *became* flesh, or that He *took on* flesh. The idea of 'making' gives the impression of being 'changed into', but that is wrong.

In other words, the way in which the Scripture generally puts it is this: in Romans 8:3 we are told that He came 'in the likeness of sinful flesh'. That is better. Or take it as it is put in 1 John 4:2: 'Hereby know ye the Spirit of God: Every spirit that confesseth that Jesus Christ is come in the flesh is of God.' Jesus Christ has not been changed into a man; it is this eternal Person who has come in the flesh. That is the right way to put it.

The next principle is that our Lord did not merely take the *appearance* of human nature; it was true human nature. Let me explain. We have accounts in the Old Testament of angels appearing to various people and we are told that they appeared in human form. Now when we say that the angels appeared in that way, we are not talking about an incarnation, but an appearance. The angels did not change their nature, they did not add to it in any way, they just took on that form. Indeed, we saw earlier, you remember, that our Lord Himself appeared in that way; we spoke about the Angel of the Covenant. The Angel of the Covenant in the Old Testament is undoubtedly the Lord Jesus Christ Himself, and He appeared more than once to various people in the form of a man. That is what we call a *theophany*. Now theophany is entirely different from incarnation. Theophany means that an angelic or a divine person appears in this form for the time being, but the doctrine of the incarnation asserts that the Lord Jesus Christ has taken on human nature itself – not its appearance but real human nature.

There are many statements which say that; let me give you two. Hebrews 2:14: 'Forasmuch then as the children are partakers of flesh and blood, he also himself likewise took part of the same.' He really did take unto Himself human nature. 'For verily he took not on him the nature of angels,' says verse 16 of that same chapter, but He 'took on him the seed of Abraham.' That is what He has taken on. Take also 2 John 7 where we read that 'Many deceivers are entered into the world, who confess not that Jesus Christ is come in the flesh.' There is no doubt at all but that John wrote his three epistles in order to counter the dangerous heresy which had arisen, and which denied that He really had come in the flesh, asserting that it was a mere appearance. Some said that the Messiah entered into this man Jesus at His baptism and left Him on the cross, while others said that the whole thing was a phantom. Now the New Testament – John especially in his epistles – not only denies that, but denounces it as being the most dangerous error, the very lie of the antichrist, and therefore we must be certain that we are clear about these things.

That brings me to the next statement. The doctrine of the incarnation asserts that our Lord took unto Himself a full human nature. It was not merely partial, it was complete. He did not merely take a body to Himself. There have been people throughout the centuries who have taught that; they say that the Son of God only took on a human body. That is wrong. There are others who say that He took on a body and a kind of animal soul, but that the spiritual part of the soul was provided by the eternal Person. That is wrong also. The doctrine of the incarnation teaches that He took on Him complete human nature, body and soul, including spirit, that He was truly man. I shall have to emphasise this again, but it has to be stressed at this point.

And my last point under this general heading is that He took on this complete human nature from the Virgin Mary. That means that we must not say that a new human nature was created for Him. Some people have taught that God created a new human nature for His Son, and that this human nature merely passed, as it were, through Mary. That is wrong. The doctrine states that He derived His human nature from His mother, the Virgin Mary. It was not a new creation. He did not bring His human nature with Him. He received it from her. And therefore, as the Scripture often emphasises, He is truly of the seed of Abraham and of the seed of David. Here it is in Matthew 1:1: 'The book of the generation of Jesus Christ, the son of David, the son of Abraham.' Now if a special human nature had been created for Him, He would not have been the son of David nor the son of Abraham. But He was both, because His human nature came from His mother, the Virgin Mary. Again, let me emphasise that what He had was not a human nature that was merely like ours but not really a part of ours, not organically related to us. He actually did receive our nature. Go back again to those verses in Hebrews 2:14–18. He really does belong, therefore, to the human race, He is one with us.

Now I must not stop with this, tempted as I am to do so. I am concerned about it because the doctrine of our redemption ultimately depends upon it. If He had not taken our human nature, He could not have saved us. As Hebrews 2 argues so clearly, because we are partakers of this flesh and blood, he had to partake of the same. It was the only way in which He could save us. So we cannot afford to take any risks about this doctrine. We cannot afford to say, 'It does not matter what your precise statement is.' That is to be utterly unscriptural. We must be precise and clear and certain and definite in all our statements, otherwise, without knowing it, we may make the doctrine of our own redemption quite impossible.

So, having established that, we now return to the mystery of the incarnation, and at once the question arises: How did all this come to pass? How did this extraordinary thing become actual? And that, of course, leads us immediately to the doctrine of the virgin birth. I do trust that we are all observing the order in which we are taking these truths. I conceive it to be my main function in these addresses to show you that order as it is worked out in the Scriptures; the details, the facts, you can derive from the Scriptures themselves.

And so by logical inevitability we arrive at the doctrine of the virgin birth. What is this? Well, the Apostles' Creed, the first creed of all, the first great confession, puts it like this: 'He was conceived of the Holy Ghost and born of the Virgin Mary.' Now here is, again, one of those great subjects which is full of mystery; it is a doctrine that has been much debated and argued about and misunderstood and frequently denied; and people seem to find great difficulty with it.

Therefore, as we approach it, there is nothing, it seems to me, more important than that we should bear in mind everything we have considered in all our previous lectures. If you have agreed with me in what I have been saying in them, you should have no difficulty about the doctrine of the virgin birth. If you really have agreed about the doctrine of God and the doctrine of the Trinity; if you really have believed what I have said about the doctrine of the Scriptures as being the infallible Word of God inbreathed by the Holy Spirit and not merely human ideas; if you have agreed with all I have said about miracles and the supernatural, and how all this is inevitable when God acts and deals with this world, then, I repeat, there really should be no difficulty about the doctrine of the virgin birth.

And it is, of course, a fact that the people who have difficulty with this doctrine are the very people who have difficulty with the doctrine of Scripture and with the doctrine of miracles. They are in trouble about the doctrine of the incarnation because they set up their puny minds as the ultimate test of all truth, and because when they cannot understand a thing they will not believe it.

But surely we must be in agreement that in all these matters we are outside the realm of natural human reason and understanding. We started at the very beginning with the whole concept and category of revelation. We know nothing apart from that. I do not put forward theories and philosophies; I start on this premise – that what I am announcing is what God has done, what God has revealed. I know nothing apart from what I find in the Bible. I am entirely shut up to it; I am utterly dependent upon it. And therefore it is my business to come to it as a little child. 'The world by wisdom knew not God' (1 Cor. 1:21); so, if that was true and is still true, then I must depend upon this book, I must accept its authority, I must receive its statements, even though my little mind cannot always understand them. That is the frame of mind and the appropriate attitude to adopt as we come to consider this extraordinary and amazing and yet glorious doctrine of the virgin birth.

What, then, do the Scriptures teach? What are we told? There are two portions of Scripture which are the basis of the doctrine of the virgin birth. I always feel one should start with the statement in Luke 1:26–38, because it gives us the announcement to Mary of the great thing itself. Notice the details in connection with that announcement; notice the facts, and how the angel came. You see, if you have not agreed with my account of the doctrine of angels, you are already in trouble; but if you accept that, then there is no difficulty about this at all, it is what we would expect.

Notice, too, what we are told about Mary's surprise, which of course was quite natural. It is obvious, is it not, from her very surprise, that she understood the significance of what the angel said to her. Here was an unmarried woman, a virgin, to whom this announcement was made, and at once she saw the difficulty, and did not hesitate to express it. How could she be the mother of a child when she had never known a man? And the angel gave her the explanation. He announced to her that this was something that was going to be done by the Holy Spirit Himself. He told her that she would be 'overshadowed' by the Almighty: 'The Holy Ghost shall come upon thee, and the power of the Highest shall overshadow thee: therefore also that holy thing which shall be born of thee shall be called the Son of God' (v. 35). 'Conceived of the Holy Ghost, born of the Virgin Mary', says the Apostles' Creed.

But then the account in the first chapter of Matthew, from verses 18–25, is equally important, and, surely, equally interesting, because there we are told what happened to Joseph. Joseph discovered that this virgin to whom he was betrothed was with child. He was confused and unhappy. He was a good man, a righteous and a loving man. He decided he would not make a public example of Mary, but he must of necessity put her away or he would not be keeping the law, so he was pondering about all this and about how he could do it, when the angel appeared to him in a dream. And what the angel did, of course, was explain to Joseph what was happening: 'Joseph, thou son of David, fear not to take unto thee Mary thy wife: for that which is conceived in her is of the Holy Ghost' (v. 20). He was given exactly the same explanation; and as we read the story I am afraid we often forget to observe the extraordinary faith of Joseph. He believed the angel's message; he accepted it without any demur, without any hesitation, and he proceeded to act upon it.

That is what we are told in the record, and it teaches us that the birth of the Lord Jesus Christ as a man is entirely the work of God. The doctrine of the virgin birth must always be considered first and foremost in a negative way, and what it says negatively is that He had no earthly father. He was not born of the will of man, nor of the will or the energy of the flesh. Let me put it still more strongly. The male human being did not enter into the question of His conception.

Now that is a very remarkable thing because, as we have seen already in working with the great doctrines at the beginning of the book of Genesis, the glory of God, as it were, is in the man, and the woman is under the man. You remember how we worked that out. But here the man is put on one side; he has nothing to do with it. You notice that the very word, the promise that was given by God to the man and the woman in the Garden of Eden was this: 'And I will put enmity between thee and *the woman*, and between thy seed and *her seed*; it shall bruise thy head' (Gen. 3:15). And so it proved. The man had nothing to do with it – the very one whom God had appointed lord of creation, and to whom he gave power over the woman, and to whom the woman is subject by God's own desire and ordination, as the result of creation and especially as the result of the fall. In spite of all that, when it came to the question of the incarnation, the male was put on one side and God used the woman only.

Surely, then, the significance and importance of that must be obvious to all – it is to emphasise again the total inability of man. Man, in the person of Joseph, is seen in his utter failure and incapacity. God took hold of human nature at its weakest, as it were, in order to produce out of it this human nature for His own Son. I have come across a very beautiful phrase which I think will help you to remember this: 'As the Lord's divine nature had no mother, so His human nature had no father.' I think that puts it very well. It was entirely the work of God. He took on Him human nature from Mary, but it was done through the instrumentality of the Holy Spirit.

'What happened?' asks someone. I cannot answer; no one can answer. That is the great mystery. But what we know is that the power of the Holy Spirit came upon Mary, and out of Mary, out of a cell in her body, the human nature of our Lord was made. We cannot go

further. It is a great mystery. But we have to go as far as that. It was
the operation of the Holy Spirit, and it was obviously done in such a
way that this human nature that the Son took unto Himself was sinless – you notice that the angel spoke to Mary of 'that holy thing [that
sinless, pure thing] which shall be born of thee . . .' (Luke 1:35). This
does not mean that Mary herself was made sinless and holy. It does
not even of necessity imply that any part of Mary was. All we know
is that something was taken, was cleansed and rendered free from all
pollution so that His human nature was sinless and entirely free from
all the effects and results of the fall. Such was the effect of the operation of the Holy Spirit upon her.

What, then, of this doctrine? What have we to say about it in general, especially having in mind those who find it difficult? I would
suggest once more that it is a doctrine which is quite inevitable if you
really do believe the doctrine of the incarnation. If you really do
believe that the babe in the manger in Bethlehem is the second Person
in the Trinity – and that is the truth – then I cannot see that there is
any difficulty about this doctrine of the virgin birth. Indeed, I would
find myself in much greater difficulty if I did not have the doctrine of
the virgin birth to believe. You see, the fact of the incarnation is so
unusual, so exceptional, so miraculous and mysterious, that I would
expect everything about Him to be the same; and so it proved to be.
To put it another way: the virgin birth was the sign of the mystery of
the incarnation. It was a kind of symbol of that mystery; there it was
in a tangible form – this virgin birth.

Everything about our Lord is mysterious. His coming into the
world was mysterious. His going out of it was mysterious. He did not
enter into life like anybody else; He did not go out of it like anybody
else. The resurrection was as unique as the virgin birth. It had never
happened to anybody before. He is the 'first begotten of the dead'
(Rev. 1:5); 'the firstborn among many brethren' (Rom. 8:29). The
resurrection was equally startling. So I would say to anybody who
stumbles at the virgin birth: Do you stumble in the same way at the
resurrection? You see, if we start with the doctrine of the incarnation
and realise what we are saying, if we realise that we are really speaking about the second Person in the Trinity, then surely you would
expect His birth to be entirely unusual and exceptional? And so it
was. He was exceptional from beginning to end.

But let me try to help you by putting it like this: If you do not
believe in the doctrine of the virgin birth, how do you account for his

sinlessness? Are we not entitled to put it like this: If He had been born in the ordinary way, of a father and a mother, then surely He would have been like every other person, He would have been in direct sequence, in the direct line, from Adam, and therefore it would be true to say of Him also 'as in Adam all die' (1 Cor. 15:22). He would have died in Adam, and He would have been guilty of original sin and of original guilt.

But the doctrine of the incarnation at once tells us that that is not what happened. A person, I repeat, did not come into being there. This person was the eternal Person, the second Person in the Trinity. When a husband and a wife come together and a child is born a new person, a new personality, comes into being. That did not happen in the incarnation. But given a father and a mother, you would have a person in the direct line from Adam and therefore sinful and fallen. The only way to have prevented that would be to say that some similar kind of operation to that performed by the Holy Spirit on Mary, should also have had to be performed on Joseph.

But surely that does not help us. If you are already in difficulties about this miraculous operation on Mary, then you are doubting it and it is still more impossible. No, if we really took a firm hold of the doctrine of the incarnation itself, that this blessed Person took unto Himself human nature that had to be sinless because He could not unite with anything that was sinful, then there was only one way for it, and that is that He had to be born not in the ordinary way of generation, but in this special way.

You will notice that the whole doctrine is surrounded by pitfalls and difficulties because when I put it like that, I am sure that many will think, 'Ah, I see! God created a special human nature for Him, did He?' No, He did not! I have already denounced that as heresy. He got His human nature from Mary, but it was acted upon by the Holy Spirit in such a way that it was rendered wholly free from sin and from all pollution.

And so we stand before Him. We stand before this mystery of godliness, God in the flesh! The strangest, the most amazing thing that has ever happened – indeed, I do not hesitate to say, the supreme act of God. It is so supreme that I expect it to be unusual in every respect, and I find the Scriptures tell me that it was. He was conceived of the Holy Spirit, He was born of a virgin named Mary. Man was entirely excluded; the male did not come in. Joseph is there ever to remind us of that. It was entirely the work of God. And let us realise and remember that it all happened so that we might be saved, that our sins might be forgiven. The Son of God became man that the children of men might become children of God.

24

Evidence for the Deity and Humanity of Christ

In our consideration of the doctrine of the virgin birth, we were looking at this babe in Bethlehem, of whom we assert that He is God the eternal Son. That obviously means that we must look a little more closely at what the Bible tells us about this person who came into the world as a baby, grew into a boy, developed into manhood, and set out on His public ministry. It is of vital importance that we should be clear with regard to the doctrine concerning Him; we have already adduced evidence to show the importance of that. So before we make any attempt to understand what the Bible teaches us about this great mystery, we must look at the evidence with which it presents us in order that we may arrive at an adequate doctrine of His person.

Now we find at once that the Bible tells us two main things. The first is that it makes many claims to the effect that He is divine; it asserts and teaches His divinity or, still more accurately, His deity. The evidence for this is voluminous and it could occupy a great deal of time, so we must just look at some brief headings at this point. You can look at the evidence and check it for yourselves at leisure; I simply want to classify it in order to make your study a little more easy.

The first evidence is that certain divine names are ascribed to Him. Indeed, altogether some sixteen names are ascribed to Him, each of which clearly implies His deity. Here are some of them. He is described as the 'Son of God' forty times; He is referred to as 'his Son' (God's Son); God refers to Him audibly as 'my Son'. So there in various forms is that title 'Son', 'Son of God'.

Then five times He is also referred to as the 'only begotten Son of

God'. You find it in John 1:18 – 'the only begotten Son, which is in the bosom of the Father' – and there are many others: a notable one is the parable of the wicked husbandman, when God says, 'They will reverence my son' (Matt. 21:37). The teaching there is perfectly clear, the words are uttered by our Lord Himself.

He is described in Revelation 1:17 as 'the first and the last', and in verse 11 of the same chapter as the 'Alpha and Omega', the beginning and the end. These are obviously terms of deity; there is nothing before the beginning and nothing after the end. Then Peter, preaching in Jerusalem – you will find it recorded in Acts 3:14 – refers to Him as the 'Holy One': 'But ye denied the Holy One and the Just.' Again, these are terms of deity.

Take also that great term 'the Lord' which is used of Him several hundred times in the New Testament. That word is equivalent to the Old Testament term 'Jehovah', which we have already considered together, one of the highest titles ascribed to God. Another term used for Him is 'the Lord of glory'. You will find that in 1 Corinthians 2:8: 'Had they known it,' says Paul, 'they would not have crucified the Lord of glory.' It is a most exalted term.

Then He is actually referred to as 'God'; Thomas says, 'My Lord and my God' (John 20:28). He is also described as 'Emmanuel . . . God with us' in Matthew 1:23; and there is a most remarkable statement in Titus 2:13 where He is referred to as our 'great God and Saviour Jesus Christ'. Again, another equally remarkable ascription is found in Romans 9:5: 'Whose are the fathers, and of whom as concerning the flesh Christ came, who is over all, God blessed for ever.'[1]

So there you have a number of names which are ascribed to Him, all of which are divine names.

But, second, the Bible also ascribes to Him certain divine attributes. You remember that when we were dealing with the doctrine of God we considered the divine attributes. Now you will find that those very attributes are also ascribed to our Lord. For instance, omnipotence: Hebrews 1:3 says that He upholds 'all things by the word of his power' – no stronger statement than that is possible – and that 'all things are put under him' (1 Cor. 15:27). There are others also which you can find for yourself.

Then omniscience is attributed to Him: in Matthew 11:27 we read,

---

1. For a full discussion of this text by Dr Lloyd-Jones see *God's Sovereign Purpose*, Banner of Truth Trust, 1991.

'No man knoweth the Son, but the Father; neither knoweth any man the Father, save the Son, and he to whomsoever the Son will reveal him.' In John 2:24-5 you will find the same claim: 'he knew what was in man'. It was not necessary for anybody to tell Him.

Then in a very extraordinary way omnipresence is attributed to Him also. In Matthew 18:20 it says, 'For where two or three are gathered together in my name, there am I . . .' In Matthew 28:20 He says, 'And, lo, I am with you alway, even unto the end . . .' And in John 3:13 there is a very striking statement: 'No man hath ascended up to heaven, but he that came down from heaven, even the Son of man which is in heaven.' He said those words while He was on earth – the Son of man who is 'in heaven'. And, indeed, the apostle Paul writes, He 'filleth all in all' (Eph. 1:23) – again, a very comprehensive statement.

Another divine attribute is His eternity: 'In the beginning was the Word' (John 1:1). We also have statements about His immutability: He cannot change. Hebrews 13:8 tells us, 'Jesus Christ the same yesterday, and to day, and for ever.' Then, of course, the Bible asserts His pre-existence. Colossians 1:17 tells us, 'And he is before all things . . .' In John 17:5 He prays, 'And now, O Father, glorify thou me with thine own self with the glory which I had with thee before the world was.' And again, in the great passage in Philippians 2:6 Paul asserts that He was in the 'form' of God before His incarnation.

Finally, to sum it all up, we have another comprehensive statement of His deity in Colossians 2:9 where Paul says, 'For in him dwelleth all the fulness of the Godhead bodily.'

Then, third, we go on to consider certain divine offices which He is said to hold and to fill. First of all creation: 'All things were made by him; and without him was not anything made that was made' (John 1:3). You find the same thing repeated in Colossians 1:16, and again in Hebrews 1:10. But we are also told that He preserves everything. Hebrews 1:3 refers to Him 'upholding all things by the word of his power'. And again in Colossians 1:17 you will find that 'by him all things consist'.

Notice also that He did not hesitate to claim the power to forgive sins. He said to the paralysed man, 'Thy sins be forgiven thee' (Mark 2:5). He also claimed power to raise the dead; you will find that mentioned several times in John 6:39-44, 'I will raise him up,' he said, 'at the last day.' The apostle Paul claims that He also has power to transform our bodies: 'Who shall change our vile body [or this body of our humiliation], that it may be fashioned like unto his glorious body, according to the working whereby he is able even to subdue all things unto himself' (Phil. 3:21).

Judgment, too, is committed to Him; read John 5:22–3: 'For the Father judgeth no man, but hath committed all judgment unto the Son.' Again, Paul makes that claim in Acts 17:31, and you also find it in 2 Timothy 4:1: 'The Lord Jesus Christ, who shall judge the quick and the dead.' So the power of judgment is given to Him, and also the power of bestowing eternal life: 'And I give unto them eternal life' (John 10:28). John 17:2 says the same thing: '. . . that he should give eternal life to as many as thou hast given him'.

The fourth piece of evidence for His deity is this: statements in the Old Testament which are made distinctly of Jehovah are, in the New Testament, ascribed to the Lord Jesus Christ and are definitions of Him. I shall not give you the words in full but I will give you the texts so that you can look them up for yourself: Psalm 102:24–7 (compare Hebrews 1:10–12); Isaiah 40:3–4 (compare Matthew 3:3; Luke 1:76); Isaiah 6:1, 3, 10 (compare John 12:37–8); Isaiah 8:13–14 (compare 1 Peter 2:7–8).

Now we can sum up all that by putting it like this: in the Old Testament the term 'Lord' is always used of God, except when the context makes it perfectly clear that it is used of a man in the sense of 'Sir'. In exactly the same way when the term 'Lord' is used in the New Testament, it is always used of the lordship of Jesus Christ – that is, His deity – except when the context makes it quite plain that 'Sir' is intended. So we have this tremendous fact that these specific terms which are used directly of Jehovah are also used of the Lord Jesus Christ.

Then the fifth piece of evidence is the way in which the names of God the Father and Jesus Christ the Son are coupled together. There are several examples of this. Christ Himself said, 'Go ye therefore, and teach all nations, baptizing them in the name of the Father, and of the Son, and of the Holy Ghost' (Matt. 28:19). Romans 1:7 speaks of 'God our Father, and the Lord Jesus Christ'. In 2 Corinthians 13:14, in the so-called 'apostolic benediction', we read, 'The grace of the Lord Jesus Christ, and the love of God, and the communion of the Holy Ghost, be with you all.' 1 Thessalonians 3:11 says, 'Now God himself and our Father, and our Lord Jesus Christ, direct our way unto you.' And, indeed, you will find it in James 1:1, 'James, a servant of God and of the Lord Jesus Christ . . .'

That brings us to the sixth bit of evidence: divine worship is ascribed to the Lord Jesus Christ. He accepted such worship from men and women when He was on earth. You will find that in Matthew 28:9 and in Luke 24:52. But you get it also by way of exhortation in 1 Corinthians 1:2 where Paul refers to 'all that in every place call upon the name of Jesus Christ our Lord . . .' That is worship. In 2 Corinthians 12:8–9 Paul tells us, 'For this thing I besought the Lord thrice . . .' – it is the Lord Jesus Christ, that is quite clear from the context. In Acts 7:59 we read of Stephen, as he was being stoned: 'And they stoned Stephen, calling upon God, and saying, Lord Jesus, receive my spirit.' Indeed, our Lord Himself already prepared us for all this when He said, 'That all men should honour the Son, even as they honour the Father. He that honoureth not the Son honoureth not the Father which hath sent him' (John 5:23). There are other instances, also, of worship ascribed to Him, and the claim in Philippians 2:10 is that a time is coming when 'at the name of Jesus every knee should bow, of things in heaven, and things in earth, and things under the earth.'

And that brings me to the seventh point, which is our Lord's own self-consciousness and His own specific claims to deity. I shall simply give you some of the references which I regard as most important, though there are many others. The first is found in Luke 2, in the incident described in verses 41–52, when He said that He must be about His Father's business or, 'about the things of my Father' – a most remarkable claim made when he was but a twelve-year-old boy. You get exactly the same thing at His baptism. When He went to John to be baptised, John remonstrated with Him and said, 'I have need to be baptized of thee, and comest thou to me?' Now our Lord did not reject that statement, but simply replied, 'Suffer it to be so now' (Matt. 3:14–15). In other words, He accepted John's words, and thereby acknowledged His superiority to John. And in this connection we notice again the voice from heaven that attested His deity (v. 17).

Then you find much the same kind of thing in the account of His temptation. The devil tempted Him like this each time – 'If thou be the Son of God . . .' – and He never said He was not. He accepted the devil's statement and proved to Him that He *is* the Son of God. Thus by accepting the statement He asserted and claimed His own deity. And He did so, of course, in many other ways. In the calling of the Twelve, for instance, He was clearly asserting it, and in giving power to them, in giving them the message and the power to cast out devils,

He was, again, claiming this uniqueness. And you also get it in the fact that He specifically said of believers in Him that, 'In my name shall they cast out devils' (Mark 16:17).

We find, too, that He made this unique claim of deity for Himself in the Sermon on the Mount. He did it by contrasting what they had heard from 'them of old time' with what He Himself said, (Matt. 5:21, 27, 33). And then there is the specific claim in John 8:58: 'Before Abraham was, I am.' Once more also I would refer you to that statement in Matthew 11:27 where He claimed unique knowledge of the Father. But in many ways the most important section of Scripture under this heading is to be found in John chapters 14-17. As you study them at your leisure, notice His claim to and His consciousness of His unique deity.

Then, the eighth piece of evidence is the virgin birth. This, of course, and everything that the Scriptures teach us about it, is again a proof of His deity. And to bring it all to its climax, the apostle Paul teaches us in Romans 1:4 that ultimately what proves and declares the Lord Jesus Christ to be the Son of God is His resurrection: 'declared to be the Son of God with power, according to the spirit of holiness, by the resurrection from the dead.'

There, then, we have looked in general at the great scriptural evidence for His deity. As I have said, it is voluminous, but we have taken a kind of synoptic view of it, and those are the main headings into which it can be classified.

But, of course, we must also move on to the second great claim, and see that the Scriptures also, equally definitely, teach His humanity. And we cannot arrive at an adequate doctrine of the person without again looking carefully at the evidence which is provided in the Scriptures for His humanity. Now we have already considered the first piece of evidence here; it, again, is the virgin birth, and all the arguments in connection with it. All those again establish the fact of His humanity – all the arguments about the precise nature of the doctrine of the incarnation, that it was not a phantom body, and so on, but that He really did take on human nature, that He was truly the son of the Virgin Mary, and that it was not an appearance but a fact; all those are our first proof.

The second, again, is provided by names. Take, for instance, what you read in 1 Timothy 2:5: 'For there is one God, and one mediator between God and men, the man Christ Jesus.' He is described as 'the man'. And you notice – you cannot have read the Gospels without noticing – the frequency with which the term 'the Son of man' is used about Him. It is used over eighty times! Now the Son of man, of course, is a very special term, and it has a very special significance. At this point, I am simply concerned to remind you, and to emphasise, that He is described in this way. That clearly is an indication of His humanity.

Then the third thing that the Scriptures make abundantly plain and clear is that He had a typical human, physical nature. Take that statement in John 1:14: 'The Word was made flesh', or 'became flesh'. Consider also the statements in Hebrews 2 that we considered in the last lecture, particularly verse 14, where we are told that because the children are partakers of flesh and blood 'he also himself likewise took part of the same'. Then another very striking bit of evidence under this heading is that He obviously looked like a man. Not only that, we also have evidence to prove that He looked like a typical Jew. You remember what we are told of the incident of the woman of Samaria meeting our Lord at the well, and how she expressed her astonishment that He should speak to her: 'How is it that thou, being a Jew, askest drink of me, which am a woman of Samaria?' (John 4:9). She had no idea who He was, but when He spoke to her she at once recognised that He was a Jew.

Then, under this same heading of His physical frame, the Scriptures teach us that He still had this human body even after His resurrection. When He appeared to the disciples, when Thomas was present in the room and He was anxious to prove to Thomas that He was the same person, He said, 'Reach hither thy finger, and behold my hands; and reach hither thy hand, and thrust it into my side: and be not faithless, but believing' (John 20:27). But we find a still more specific statement in Luke 24:39 where He told the disciples that He was not a spirit: 'For,' He said, 'a spirit hath not flesh and bones, as ye see me have.' So He still had a true human body, even after His resurrection.

Indeed, I can go beyond that: there is evidence in the Scripture to teach us that He still has His human body in glory. In Acts 7:55–6 we are told that Stephen saw the Son of man in the glory, and he saw Him as the Son of man. He is still the Son of man, and recognisable as such. Or again, Paul says in Philippians 3:21, 'Who shall change our vile body, that it may be fashioned like unto his glorious body . . .' His glorious body; it is still the same body glorified. That is a most remarkable statement and a striking piece of evidence.

That brings us to point number four, which is that like all of us He was subject to growth and development: 'And the child grew, and waxed strong in spirit, filled with wisdom: and the grace of God was upon him' (Luke 2:40). In the same chapter we read, 'And Jesus increased in wisdom and stature, and in favour with God and man' (v. 52). Hebrews 2:10 says, 'For it became him, for whom are all things, and by whom are all things, in bringing many sons unto glory, to make the captain of their salvation perfect through sufferings' – a suggestion of growth and of development. And, still more specifically, in Hebrews 5:8 we read, 'Though he were a Son, yet learned he obedience by the things which he suffered.'

The fifth evidence of His humanity is that here on earth he was subject to certain limitations in His knowledge. There is an instance of this in Mark 11:13 – the incident of the barren fig tree. We are told that our Lord came to it expecting to find fruit. He did not know that it had none. Also, in Mark 13:32 we read these most important and momentous words: 'But of that day and that hour knoweth no man, no, not the angels which are in heaven, neither the Son, but the Father.' He said specifically that He did not know the precise time of this day which is coming; not only the angels, but even He did not know it, only the Father. Now in our next study, when we come to the doctrine itself, we shall try to consider the significance of these statements about the humanity and deity of our Lord. I am simply providing you with the evidence, the material out of which the doctrine is formed.

So that brings us to proof number six, which is that He was subject to physical limitation. Again in John 4, in the instance of the woman of Samaria, we are told that he was weary. He sat down by the side of the well, and did not go with the disciples to buy provisions, because he was physically tired. We read that He fell asleep in the boat on the sea, in the stern of the vessel (Mark 4:36–41). We are told that going one morning to Jerusalem, He was hungry – the incident of the barren fig tree again. He was thirsty; we are told that upon the cross He said, 'I thirst' (John 19:28). He endured physical agony; He was in an agony in the Garden of Gethsemane. He was there sweating great drops of blood. And finally, of course, and conclusively, and most important of all, He actually, literally died; and His death – this physical limitation – is the ultimate proof of His humanity.

The seventh evidence is that He was tempted. We find this in Hebrews 2:18, in addition to the Gospel accounts of the temptation in the wilderness; and in Hebrews 4:15 it is put specifically like this – He was 'in all points tempted like as we are, yet without sin'.

Proof number eight is that He needed to pray. Now here is a great theme. Watch the frequency with which our Lord prayed, and ask yourself why. Why did He pray all night before He chose His disciples? He was constantly engaged in prayer; and as He came to face the end, He went into that Garden to pray, and asked the three disciples to pray with Him and for Him. The need of prayer is an absolute proof of His true humanity.

And then you can look at it like this, as the ninth proof: He was given power by the Holy Spirit. Though He is the eternal Son of God, He needed the power, which He was given. Listen to Peter in Acts 10:38: 'How God anointed Jesus of Nazareth with the Holy Ghost and with power: who went about doing good, and healing all that were oppressed of the devil; for God was with him.' God anointed Him with the Holy Spirit and with power. That, of course, is the significance, partly, of His baptism and of the descent of the Holy Spirit upon Him then. Notice, too, John the Baptist's statement in John 3:34 that 'God giveth not the Spirit by measure unto him' (v. 34) – He had the Spirit in all His fulness.

Evidence number ten is that He referred to God as His God. In John 20:17, we read, 'Jesus saith unto her, Touch me not; for I am not yet ascended to my Father: but go to my brethren, and say unto them, I ascend unto my Father, and your Father; and to my God, and your God' (John 20:17).

But what you also see there is again a great comprehensive claim – this is the eleventh point – that He really was human in every respect. Hebrews 2:17 says, 'Wherefore in all things it behoved him to be made like unto his brethren, that he might be a merciful and faithful high priest in things pertaining to God, to make reconciliation for the sins of the people.' That is a crucial statement and we shall come back to it again. I am simply asserting now that it claims that He was made like unto His brethren in all things, though, remember always, without sin; but in body and soul and spirit He was human. He said, 'My soul is exceeding sorrowful' (Luke 23:46). He was truly human in every respect.

And yet finally we must emphasise this fact that the Scriptures also remind us everywhere that though He was truly human He was also sinless. Now we have seen that the angel had already told Mary about this. He said, 'That holy thing which shall be born of thee shall be called the Son of God' (Luke 1:35). That is the first assertion of His sinlessness. But also our Lord challenged people to convict Him of sin: 'Which of you convinceth me of sin?' (John 8:46). Then let us consider some of the great claims that are put forward in the epistles, for example, the classic statement of Paul in 2 Corinthians 5:21: 'He hath made him to be sin for us, who knew no sin; that we might be made the righteousness of God in him.' And again there is the statement in Hebrews 4:15 which I have already quoted – '[He] was in all points tempted like as we are, yet without sin.' In Hebrews 9:14 we are told that He 'offered himself without spot to God'. No blemish; no sin; a perfect sin-offering, fulfilling the Old Testament type. In 1 Peter 2:22 we find Peter saying of Him, 'Who did no sin, neither was guile found in his mouth,' and 1 John 3:5 claims exactly the same: 'In him is no sin.'

Now there are other statements which are careful to tell us (and you notice the importance of believing in the full inspiration of the Scriptures, and the importance of every word) that He came in the '*likeness* of sinful flesh' (Rom 8:3). He did not come in sinful flesh. Paul goes out of his way to say that. So we can, perhaps, put it best like this: the Scriptures claim that He was truly human, but they never say that He was carnal. And this is a most important point, because carnality is not an essential part of humanity. Adam, as he was created perfect at the beginning, was truly human, but he was not carnal. Carnality is the result of sin, and the Scriptures therefore never say that Christ was carnal. So here again we see the importance of taking our doctrines in their right chronological and logical sequence, because we see that He took unto Himself human nature from Mary, as the result of the operation of the Holy Spirit upon her. He was truly human but free from sin.

Now I trust that no one is in any difficulty about the fact that He was subject to temptation, because this does not imply any defect in Him whatsoever. Of course, He could not have been subject to temptation if He had not become human: 'For God cannot be tempted with evil, neither tempteth he any man' (Jas. 1:13). So the fact that He was tempted proves that His nature was truly human nature. So we assert that He was subject to temptation but was at the same time sinless.

Indeed, we can go further and say that He was not even subject to the fall. You remember the famous statement which I quoted when we were dealing with this whole subject of sin: that it was not merely the case that it was possible for Him not to sin, but rather, it was not possible for Him to sin. And that is the essential difference between Christ and Adam; that is the difference between the first Adam and the second Adam. The first Adam was perfect. He had not sinned, but sin was possible. It was possible for Adam not to sin, but you could not say of him that it was not possible for him to sin, because he did sin. But of the Son of God we say that not only was it possible for Him not to sin – *posse non peccare*; it was also not possible for Him to sin – *non posse peccare* – because He is the Son of God. He is God-Man. Not only human but also divine. But still, because human, subject to temptation, and the devil did tempt Him. And so we see the importance of asserting at one and the same time the doctrine of His true humanity and yet also the doctrine of His complete sinlessness. In other words, it is not essential to temptation that there should be anything sinful in the one who is tempted. Temptation can be purely external, and the fact that it is so does not in any sense mean that it is no longer temptation. The devil tempted Him with all his might, in a way that nobody else has ever been tempted. It was a real temptation, but He at the same time was entirely free from sin, and it was not possible that He could or should fall. God sent Him to be the Saviour, and because of that there could not be, and there was no failure.

So we have looked in general at the evidence for His divinity and His humanity. We shall start our next study by showing that this person, of whom it is claimed that He is divine and human and that He is God the Son, nevertheless subordinated Himself to the Father. And then we shall consider what the Scripture tells us about His character, the nature of this person who is divine and human, and we shall attempt, in the light of the teaching of Scripture, to hold those two statements together.

25

God-Man: the Doctrine

In the last lecture we were considering a number of texts concerning the person of our Lord Jesus Christ, some clearly asserting His deity, others equally clearly asserting His humanity; but before we go on to the consideration of the doctrine itself, there is just one other piece of evidence that we must give, and that is the fact that the Scriptures very clearly teach His subordination to His Father. We shall not consider this evidence in detail, so I shall just give you headings, but you can easily discover the scriptural references for yourself.

The first is this: He said specifically that His Father (or 'the Father') was greater than He Himself: 'My Father is greater than I' (John 14:28).

Second, He is described as 'begotten of the Father': 'God so loved the world, that he gave his only begotten Son' (John 3:16). 'Thou art my Son; this day have I begotten thee' – how often is that repeated in the Scriptures (Ps. 2:7; Acts 13:33; Heb. 1:5; 5:5)!

Third, He told us that He lived because of the Father, or 'by the Father': 'As the living Father hath sent me, and I live by the Father; [or because of the Father]: so he that eateth me, even he shall live by me' (John 6:57). That is most important.

In the fourth place, He said that He had been sent by the Father. There are innumerable examples of this. 'And this,' said our Lord in John 6:39, 'is the Father's will which hath sent me, that of all which he hath given me I should lose nothing . . .'; or again, in John 8:29, He said, 'He that sent me is with me.' And he constantly repeated that.

In the fifth place, He said that he had received commandment from the Father as to what He was to do. John 14:31 tells us that, and so does John 10:18 – 'This commandment have I received of my Father.' In the same way – sixth – He said that He had received all His authority from the Father. 'For as the Father hath life in himself: so hath he given to the Son to have life in himself; and hath given him authority to execute judgment also, because he is the Son of man' (John 5:26–7). All this is indicative, you see, of His subordination to the Father.

In the seventh place, He said He could do nothing independently of the Father. He could do nothing by Himself. In John 5:19, for instance, we read, 'Verily, verily, I say unto you, the Son can do nothing of himself, but what he seeth the Father do: for what things soever he doeth, these also doeth the Son likewise.' That, again, is a very striking statement of His dependence upon, His subordination to, the Father.

Indeed, in the eighth place, He actually said that He had received His message from the Father. He said, 'I speak to the world those things which I have heard of him' (John 8:26); and He continued, 'I do nothing of myself; but as my Father hath taught me, I speak these things' (v. 28). 'The words that I speak unto you,' He told His disciples, 'I speak not of myself' (John 14:10). His words were given to Him by His Father.

He said the same, in the ninth place, about the works that He did. 'The Father that dwelleth in me, he doeth the works' – John 14:10 again. His words and His works were all given to Him by the Father, and what He did, He did because the Father had given Him this work to do. You will find it again in John 17:4: 'I have finished the work which thou gavest me to do.'

Tenth, He said that a kingdom, His kingdom, had been appointed to Him by the Father: 'And I appoint unto you a kingdom, as my Father hath appointed unto me' (Luke 22:29).

The eleventh argument is that we are told specifically by the apostle Paul, in 1 Corinthians 15:24, that at the end He will deliver up the kingdom to the Father, and then that He Himself will be subject to the Father, 'that God may be all in all' (v. 28).

Twelfth, in 1 Corinthians 11:3 there is a most important statement to the effect that God the Father is the head of Christ: 'But I would have you know,' says Paul, 'that the head of every man is Christ; and the head of the woman is the man; and the head of Christ is God.' You notice the sequence and the argument. The man is the head of the woman, Christ is the head of the man and God is the head of Christ.

Then, the thirteenth and last argument is that He said constantly that it was His work, His function, to lead us and to bring us to God; and there are innumerable statements to the same effect in the various New Testament epistles – 'in bringing many sons unto glory', says the writer of Hebrews (2:10). 'Now unto him that is able to keep you from falling,' writes Jude, 'and to present you faultless before the presence of his glory with exceeding joy . . .' (v. 24). So the work did not end with our Lord Himself; He takes us and brings us to God.

Now all these, of course, are indications of the subordination of the Lord Jesus Christ to the Father. But let me emphasise this: you will notice that every one of them has reference only to the incarnate Lord. Not one of them says any of these things about Him before His birth, before His incarnation. They are not descriptions of the pre-existent Word of God. That is a most important distinction.

So, then, having thus collected our evidence, we must put the doctrine like this. The Bible states that Christ was truly God but that He was also truly man, and we must be most careful to assert both these things, and to do so correctly. Now as we consider this great doctrine we must always be careful to guard ourselves against certain dangers. Those who are familiar with the history of the Church will know very well that the Christians of the first three to four centuries spent much time debating the doctrine of the person of the Lord Jesus Christ. All sorts of heresies came in. Very sincere, very genuine people, in an attempt to understand this amazing truth, began teaching what was clearly error, and several councils of the Church were held in order to correct them, and to define the doctrine.

So I would say once more that any Christian who says that he or she has no time for this sort of thing is not only displaying terrible ignorance, but is doing something that is exceedingly dangerous. Heretics were generally very sincere people, and some of them were very devout. Not only that. The New Testament itself warns us against heresy, and against the various antichrists and their teaching, so we must pay attention to these things. Let me, therefore, try to classify the particular dangers that we must avoid.

The first danger is that of denying the reality of His divine nature. That is one of a whole group of dangers propagated by the people who teach that He was only man. There were many such groups in the early Church and there are the Unitarians today. Now the people who fell into this error did so because they were anxious to safeguard the doctrine of what is called *monotheism* – the belief that there is only one God. As we have seen, they felt that if you asserted that Jesus

Christ is God, then you would be saying that there are two Gods, and if you say the Holy Spirit is God, you are asserting that there are three. So, in an attempt to avoid that, they went to this extreme of denying the deity of the Lord Jesus Christ, and that is heresy. And the whole purpose, in a sense, of the Gospel of John is to deny that particular error. John himself states it quite clearly. His object in writing his Gospel was that we might know that 'Jesus is the Christ, the Son of God' (John 20:31). This is an unmistakable assertion of His deity.

But the second group of errors, of course, goes to the opposite extreme; these deny the reality of His human nature. Many people, for instance, taught, and still teach, that Jesus was only a man but that the eternal Christ came upon Him at His baptism, continued in Him and worked through Him until just before He was taken to the cross, and then left Him, so that it was only the human Jesus that died. There were all kinds of refinements of this teaching, with which we need not be concerned, but we must emphasise the principles. They are all a denial of His true human nature – teaching that He had a phantom body, drawing a distinction between the eternal Christ and the human Jesus, and ideas like that. The first epistle of John was specifically written to counteract that error. John says that the test of the Holy Spirit is that, 'Every spirit that confesseth that Jesus Christ is come in the flesh is of God: and every spirit that confesseth not that Jesus Christ is come in the flesh is not of God: and this is that spirit of antichrist . . .' (1 John 4:2–3). So we must assert the reality of the human nature as well as of the divine nature.

Then the third group were errors and heresies that denied the integrity of the natures, the divine and the human. You may have heard of *Arianism* which was a great cause of trouble to the early Church. The error of the Arians was that they denied the reality of the divine nature. They said that this Logos, this Christ, was the first and the highest of all created beings. He was not God, but He was not man. He was something in between, the first created being, the highest of all the beings that God has ever created.

Then, on the other hand, there was once more a denial of the integrity of the human nature; people taught that Christ had a body and an animal soul, but that His mind and His spirit were not human. He was only human up to a point, they said. So they were not granting Him a full or a real human nature.

And the last group of false teachings with regard to His person were the denials of the unity of His Person. This is generally known as the *Nestorian heresy*. The Nestorians said not that He was one person with two natures, but that He was two persons. They said, 'He is God and man, a personal God and a personal man.' They were so anxious to emphasise the two sides that they went too far and said that He was two persons, God and man, instead of saying that He was one person with a divine and human nature.

And, as a part of that particular error, we must mention the case of those who denied that there is a distinction in the two natures. It is extraordinary how these views always contradict one another; people always will swing from one extreme right over to the other. It seems very difficult for most people to keep to the middle of the road, and to hold the two in balance. The Nestorians said, 'Yes, we must emphasise the divine and the human, and they went so far as to say He was complete God and complete man – two persons. Then at the other extreme was the heresy which taught that the two natures became blended into one nature. Instead of keeping the divine and the human separate, they had blended them together, and taught that there is a new sort of nature, partly divine and partly human. But that is equally heretical.

So then, as over and against all these errors, we claim that the Bible teaches that He is one person who has two natures. I can do nothing better at this point than to read to you the famous statement of the Council of Chalcedon of AD 451. This doctrine had been discussed, let me remind you, throughout the centuries. People had met at their councils and conferences, and, at last, they made this great comprehensive statement, which is not so much a definition, as a statement of certain things which are and are not true. They found it impossible, as we still do, to give an adequate statement of the doctrine, but because of all these errors, they laid down certain statements to safeguard the true position, and this is how they put it.

> Our Lord is truly God and truly man, of a reasonable soul and body, consubstantial with the Father according to the Godhead, and consubstantial with us according to the manhood; in all things like unto us without sin; begotten before all ages of the Father according to the Godhead, and in these latter days for us and for our salvation born of the Virgin Mary, the mother of God according to the manhood; one and the same Christ, Son, Lord, only begotten, to be acknowledged in two natures, inconfusedly, unchangeably, indivisibly, inseparably, the distinction of natures being by no means taken away by the union, but rather the property of each nature being preserved and concurring in one person and one subsistence; not

parted or divided into two persons but one and the same Son, and only
begotten, God, the Word, the Lord Jesus Christ.

What a glorious, what a magnificent statement! We rather tend to
think, do we not — at least some people do today — that we have
advanced a great deal since the fifth century; we are the wonderful
people of the twentieth century! Yet that is the sort of thing they
taught to Christian people in the fifth century. I hope we all
appreciate it! Christian people lacking all our educational facilities
and advantages were given truth like that. And you notice how comprehensive it is. It deals with practically all the errors and the heresies
which I mentioned to you, and it lays down these great propositions.
So that is the statement of the Council of Chalcedon of AD 451. Get
it and read it for yourselves. Notice that its emphasis is this: one
person, two natures, the two natures unmixed, joined but not mixed,
not fused, not intermingled, remaining separate, God and man.

But why is it so essential that we should assert these two natures?
Why did the early Church contend for it in this way, and why must
we? Well, we must assert the manhood because since man sinned,
the penalty must be borne in the nature of man. No one can bear
the penalty of man's sin except someone who is man Himself; it is
the only way to redeem man. Then the payment of the penalty
involves sufferings of body and of soul such as a man alone can
bear; sufferings which God could not bear. 'My soul is exceeding
sorrowful unto death' said our Lord in the Garden (Mark 14:34). The
suffering involved must include the body and the soul, so He had to
be a man.

And then He has to be a sympathetic high priest, argues the author
of the epistle to the Hebrews, and He can only be a sympathetic high
priest by having a human nature, by being 'in all points tempted like
as we are, yet without sin' (Heb. 4:15). It is because He is like us that
He is able to bear with us. He understands us, He knows our feelings
and our frailty. We have a high priest who has been 'touched with the
feeling of our infirmities' (Heb. 4:15). He knows us in that sense
because He has a human nature.

And in the same way the Scriptures tell us so often that He is an
example to believers. He is not an example to anybody else, but He is
an example to believers, for we are to follow in His steps, 'Who did
no sin, neither was guile found in his mouth: who, when he was
reviled, reviled not again; when he suffered, he threatened not' (1 Pet.

2:22–3). We are to follow Him. He is our example in Christian living. There, then, are the main arguments for the absolute necessity of the human nature.

But it is equally necessary that we must assert the Godhead or the divine nature, and for this great reason: in order that His sacrifice might have infinite value, He had to be God as well as man. Or I might put it like this: in order that He might render perfect obedience to God, without failure and without possibility of failure, He had to be God. Adam was perfect, but he fell. God made him perfect, in His own image and likeness, but he fell. So in order to ensure a perfect carrying out of the law, in order that He might bear the wrath of God redemptively, and free us from the curse of the law, without the fear of failure, it was essential that the Godhead should be combined with the manhood.

So, having said all that, shall we try to bring it to a focus by attempting to consider the mystery of His person? We have been saying extraordinary things, as we must if we are scriptural. We have been making these great assertions about His deity, about His humanity, about these two natures in this one person, and people have always asked: How is all this possible? Now, let me make it quite plain that I do not pretend that I can give an adequate or a full explanation. No one can. We are confronted by 'the mystery of godliness' (1 Tim. 3:16). It is beyond us; it is beyond reason; it is beyond our understanding. As we have had to say in connection with the doctrine of the Trinity, and with many other doctrines, it is not for us to understand; our business is to submit ourselves to the Bible.

Constantly, you see, we come back to that. In a sense, that is what faith is – that we accept this, that we are guided by this. We know nothing but what revelation tells us, and we do not desire to know anything beyond that. And there is, therefore, a point at which we must always cease to attempt to understand. We must cease trying to span the infinite with our finite reason, indeed with our sinful reason, and we must receive the truth as it is given, knowing that if we do so we shall progressively understand, and that when we go to glory we shall understand fully and finally. But here we must accept by faith. So let us approach this doctrine in that way, and with those preliminary observations very much in our minds.

Now it has often been suggested that certain analogies may help us to understand this, and if we remember that they are only analogies, they will help us, but they are not the complete picture and we must never press them too far. It has often been suggested, for example, that there is, in man himself, an analogy with respect to the two natures in the one person of our Lord. Man, after all, is body and soul. The body and soul are distinct and unmixed; they are separate and yet they are united together in one person. I can say, therefore, that I have a body and I have a soul. Everything that happens in the body, and in the soul, is essential to the person. For instance, if I have a pain in my body I say that *I* have a pain. It is really only in my body, but I say that I have a pain. And in the same way, if something happens in the realm of my soul and my spirit, I still put it in terms of myself. The things, you see, that happen in my body and my soul I ascribe to myself. From the two natures, as it were, I ascribe things to the one person.

In the same way, you notice that the biblical doctrine does that with our Lord and Saviour Jesus Christ. 'Had they known it,' says Paul to the Corinthians, 'they would not have crucified the Lord of glory' (1 Cor. 2:8). The Lord of glory! Now, in a sense, you cannot crucify God, but He had to have a human body before He could be crucified. Yet Paul does not say that His body was crucified, he says that 'the Lord of glory' was crucified. In other words, what happens in the one nature or the other is ascribed to the one person.

It always seems to me, also, that there is another analogy. I cannot recall ever having read it, but I put it to you for your consideration. I am rather helped myself by the thought of 'the old man' and 'the new man' in the Christian (Eph. 4:22–4). Here am I as a Christian, and I am aware of the old nature and the new nature. These two are not intermingled and fused, I am aware of them as distinct entities, yet they are both united in me. I, as a person, contain these two or these two are parts and expressions of me, my person and my personality. Now I am only using that analogy in order that we may have some sort of a glimmer as to the possibility of our Lord having two distinct natures within Himself, yet being one person, not two persons.

However, let me put it to you in terms of Scripture. There is no doubt that the most helpful Scripture with regard to this question is in Philippians 2:5–8:

> Let this mind be in you, which was also in Christ Jesus: who, being in the form of God, thought it not robbery to be equal with God: but made himself of no reputation, and took upon him the form of a servant, and was made in the likeness of men: and being found in fashion as a man, he hum-

bled himself, and became obedient unto death, even the death of the cross.

Now this passage has often been misunderstood. If I had been delivering these addresses, say, forty or fifty years ago, in the time of the new theology, so-called, and the 'kenosis' theory, I would have had to spend a great deal of time on these verses. The *Revised Version* unfortunately translates 'made himself of no reputation' as 'emptied himself', and that word 'emptied' has led to all the trouble. Incidentally, it is a bad translation; the *Authorised Version* is altogether superior there, as I hope to show you.

Now I often feel that people have got into trouble with this passage because they have forgotten the context. The passage begins, 'Let this mind be in you, which was also in Christ Jesus,' and the context is, 'Look not every man on his own things, but every man also on the things of others.' Paul is not setting out here to give a doctrine, as it were, of the person of Christ; he is giving a practical appeal about conduct. So what does he say? Well, take this word *form* – 'Who, being in the form of God' – what is this? Form is the sum total of the qualities that make a thing what it is. Take, for instance, a piece of metal; that piece of metal can be either a sword or a ploughshare, though it is the same metal. And when I talk about 'the form' of a sword I mean the thing that makes that piece of metal a sword rather than a ploughshare. So if I take a sword and smelt it down and turn it into a ploughshare, I have changed its form. That is a most important point.

Then there is this word 'being' – 'Who, being in the form of God' – that means that He already was in the form of God before He came into this world. He always was God. That is the assertion. Then take the phrase, 'thought it not robbery to be equal with God'. Now the *Authorised Version* is not quite so good here; the other translations are better: He 'did not regard it as a prize to be grasped at'; He 'did not regard it as something to be held on to at all costs'. No, He did not do that. He did not hold on to this form of Godhead, to this equality with God which He had. What, then, did He do? Well, instead of that, He 'made himself of no reputation'. He did not 'empty himself' of anything; He took another form.

And so the apostle says, in effect, 'Now you Philippians ought to be doing what He did. You are all of you looking after your own things and not the things of others. You ought to be very grateful that the Son of God did not do that. He did not hold on to His equality with

God; He made Himself of no reputation. He did not look on His own things; He looked on you and your needs, and He came down to earth in order to help you. You must do the same.' Notice the emphasis. Paul is not telling these Philippians to turn their natures into something else. No. He says, 'You must now humble yourselves, though you still remain what you are.' So our Lord did not empty Himself of anything. He did not empty Himself of His Godhead. But He did not hold on to the manifestations of that Godhead. He did not hold on to the power of the Godhead, as it were, to the assertion of it. No, as Paul says again in verse 8, 'he humbled himself'. He remained the same, but He came in this humble form. He came, Paul tells us, 'in the form of a servant'. Now, as we have seen, the form is the consummation of those qualities that make a thing what it is, so He really was a true servant. He came and lived as a real servant, though He was still God. He did not empty His Godhead out or cease to be God. What happened was that He did not go on asserting this equality, but came in 'the form of a servant'.

Now the apostle is obviously emphasising this point I am making, because why else does he say 'in the likeness of men'? If our Lord had left the Godhead behind and become a man, Paul would never have used that phrase; he would have said He was 'made a man'. But he does not say that; he says He was made 'in the likeness of men'. Then again, he says, 'And being found in fashion as a man'. Why these expressions? If He had emptied Himself of deity, if He had ceased to be God, Paul would not be talking about 'likeness' and 'fashion'; he would just say that He who was God also became man. Again, he does not say that, but what he does say is that though our Lord was still in the form of God, He became man also. Far from pouring anything out, He took something on.

That is the doctrine of the Scripture, that He who is still God, took the form of a servant, He was made 'in the likeness of men' and was found 'in fashion as a man'. He took on this something extra. He who was eternally God became man also. And He lived and did His work in this world as a servant. That is what Paul teaches. Let me give you a quotation from the great Dr Warfield which I think will help you: 'The Lord of the world became a servant in the world. He whose right it was to rule, took obedience as his life characteristic.' What a wonderful statement!

What, then, does all this mean? It means that there was no change in His deity, but that He took human nature to Himself, and chose to live in this world as a man. He humbled Himself in that way. He deliberately put limits upon Himself. Now we cannot go further. We do not know how He did it. We cannot understand it, in a sense. But we believe this: in order that He might live this life as a man, while He was here on earth, He did not exercise certain qualities of His Godhead. That was why, as we saw in the last lecture, He needed to be given the gift of the Holy Spirit without measure. That was why He found it necessary to pray. He had not ceased to be God. He said, in effect, to Nicodemus, 'The Son of man who is on earth and who is speaking to you is still in heaven' (John 3:13). Yes; but He chose to live as a man. He did not cease to be God, nor did He resign any part of His Godhead, but He was now living in this form as a servant and as a man.

And as we look at it like that, we see how it becomes possible that He could grow 'in wisdom and in stature, and in favour with God and man' (Luke 2:52). We see, too, how it was that He did not seem to know certain things at certain times, and yet clearly at other times asserted His Godhead and His unity with the Father, and said, 'Before Abraham was I am,' and so on. It was all true, and all this was happening at one and the same time. This eternal Son of God, who was still the eternal Son of God, having taken unto Himself this human nature; this one indivisible person, who had two natures instead of one, chose to, and actually did live as a man, taking the form of a servant and humbling Himself, becoming obedient unto death, even the death of the cross.

Ah, we have been looking at a great and wonderful and glorious mystery. I know of nothing, as I have emphasised repeatedly, more wonderful for us to contemplate and consider. Do you not feel your minds being expanded and stretched? Do you not feel that it is a great privilege to be allowed to look into such wondrous mysteries and glorious truths? God has given us His word that we might do so, not that we might skip over it lightly, but that we might delve into it and try to grasp what has happened. For the message is that God so loved you and so loved me that He called upon His Son to do all this. The Son did it, though He is eternal God. He went into the womb of Mary and was born as a babe and was put into the manger, still God eternal, the Son by whom all things were made. Yes, and He even endured 'such contradiction of sinners' (Heb. 12:3) and was spat upon and crucified, and died and was buried. And He did it all because it was the only way whereby you and I could be saved. The only way whereby our sins could be forgiven was that He should bear their punishment. The only way whereby you and I could become partakers of the divine nature was that He should have taken human nature. And having done so, He is able to give us this new nature and prepare us for heaven and for glory.

We have been contemplating the marvel and the mystery of the age, the thing that makes the angels in heaven astonished, the thing that they are looking into – God coming in the flesh and for sinners, vile and despicable sinners, rebels against God, to make them the children of God. Beloved friends, let us continue to look at Him, to consider Him, to look unto Him, and let us measure and estimate our spiritual life, not by feelings and experiences, but by our knowledge of Him and our love for Him. He is the centre of everything. 'This is life eternal, that they might know thee, the only true God, and Jesus Christ, whom thou has sent' (John 17:3). May God give us grace to do so.

26
Christ the Prophet

Before we continue with our consideration of the doctrine of the Lord
Jesus Christ, perhaps it would be good for us to remind ourselves of
our whole approach to the biblical doctrines. In our studies so far we
have realised the importance of the fact that each doctrine leads to the
next. You will see the value of that when talking to someone who is
not a Christian and who wants to know what Christianity is about. If,
as Peter puts it, you are to 'give an answer to every man that asketh
you a reason of the hope that is in you' (1 Pet. 3:15), and be ready at
all times to do so, you must know these biblical doctrines and must be
able to consider them, in order to be helpful to every person. So it is
easier for us if we know the logical sequence in which we can state
and present them.

If we do not like that approach to the subject, well, here are people
of the world, of modest living, with problems and upsets – and there
are plenty of such men and women – who endeavour to solve their
problems in various ways, through philosophy and reasoning and so
on. But if we are honest, we must admit that we cannot arrive at an
understanding and solution of the problems of life through these
means. I am in agreement with the great French mathematician and
thinker, Blaise Pascal, who said, 'The supreme achievement of reason
is to show us the limit of reason.' If we do not start from Pascal's position we are left to ourselves, groping in the darkness, and the modern
world does not know where it is going. Philosophers and teachers
admit it, if they are honest. What are we to answer?

Our answer is that we need light from another, and we claim that
we have that light. 'The world by wisdom knew not God,' says Paul in
1 Corinthians 1:21. People have always been conscious that there is a

God, but thought and reason cannot arrive at Him, so God has been pleased to give a revelation of Himself. We see it in history, in nature, in creation, but He has not spoken clearly in that way, though, in a sense, it is clear to all Christians. But men and women need something more and God in His infinite kindness has given something more. Our whole contention is that the Bible is the Word of God, hence it is a question of authority. Our entire case depends upon this book and this is the Word of God. We do not say that it contains the Word of God, but that it *is* the Word of God, infallible in all matters of faith and practice; there is nothing apart from what we are told in the Bible. So that was our starting point. We arrive at all our knowledge of the doctrine from this book. It is not what we think but what the Bible teaches.

Having reminded ourselves of this, let us now turn again to the great central point of all the revelation, the Lord Jesus Christ. We have looked at His person and now we continue with what the Bible tells us about His *work*. It was essential that we dealt first with the person, because we never can understand the work until we are clear about who He is.

Let me put it like this: when you come to the Gospels, you often notice the curious inability of the disciples to understand our Lord's teaching about His death. They did not understand Him and were confused and offended at things He said about His rising again; they could not grasp it. Why? Our Lord said just before His death, 'I have yet many things to say unto you, but ye cannot bear them now. Howbeit when he, the Spirit of truth, is come, he will guide you into all truth: for he shall not speak of himself; but whatsoever he shall hear, that shall he speak: and he will shew you things to come' (John 16:12–13). Why not tell them at once? The answer is that it is quite impossible to understand the work of the Lord Jesus Christ until we are clear about the person; indeed the disciples only understood the work of the Lord Jesus Christ in the light of the resurrection. It is my understanding of the person that enables me to understand the doctrine of His death and the atonement, which we are now beginning to approach.

So we come now to the work of Christ, which is defined in so many places in the Scriptures; He came into the world to reconcile us to God. We pointed out in the doctrine of the fall and its consequences that two main things are needful: reconciliation to God and restoration to that condition from which we fell with Adam. So the work of the Lord Jesus Christ is the work of reconciliation and restoration. He came specifically and deliberately into the world for that. Paul tells us in 1 Timothy 2:5, 'For there is one God, and one mediator between God and men, the man Christ Jesus.' So now we are going to look at Him as the mediator, at what exactly He has done and how He did it, at the way in which He is the One, as it were, who stands between God and man and brings them together.

There are three functions to His office and these have always been recognised and taught. He is Prophet, Priest and King, and it is foretold that we should consider Him in all those ways. Now, of course, in every one of the offices is also the other at the same time. He is a priestly Prophet, a royal Prophet, a prophetic Priest and a royal Priest, a prophetic King and a priestly King. He is one person and we cannot divide Him, but we must recognise that, in the nature of His work as mediator and redeemer, He does assume these three functions and they are very definitely given in the biblical teaching.

We see at once why it is necessary for Him to assume the three functions. We need a *prophet* because we need to be delivered and saved from the ignorance of sin. When we considered the doctrine of the fall and its consequences we saw that men and women had been left in a state of ignorance. The apostle Paul in particular describes the lost state of man in sin, when he says, 'This I say therefore, and testify in the Lord, that ye henceforth walk not as other Gentiles walk, in the vanity of their mind, having the understanding darkened, being alienated from the life of God through the ignorance that is in them, because of the blindness of their heart' (Eph. 4:17–18). 'The people that walked in darkness have seen a great light,' says Isaiah 9:2; the pictures are endless, as we shall see. Christ as Prophet, because we need to be delivered from the ignorance of sin.

But we also need to be delivered from the guilt of sin. So we need a *priest*; because of the guilt of sin we need someone who can appear on our behalf in the presence of God. So Christ has to assume the function of Priest.

And then, of course, we have to be delivered from the dominion of sin – and the Scripture puts it that we have been delivered. We have been translated from the kingdom of darkness into 'the kingdom of his dear Son' (Col. 1:13). He does that only as He assumes the function of *king*, with power and authority. Only as King can He set us free and place us in the kingdom over which He rules and of which we have become citizens.

But let us also look at it like this: Christ as Prophet, represents God with us; He speaks for God and from God to us. But as Priest, He speaks for us to God. He represents us with God, and that is equally necessary. Then as King He is the representative head of the new humanity.

It does seem to me to be always of the greatest spiritual benefit and value to consider our Lord and His work in this threefold way and there is nothing perhaps so helpful as to understand His work and glory. You see, in the Old Testament you have prophets, you have priests and you have kings, and these three functions were divided and set up in separate people. But the glory of the Lord Jesus Christ is that He in Himself alone combines all the offices – three functions in the one person, and this is something which makes us realise the grandeur, greatness and majesty of the person of our blessed Lord.

So let us look for a moment at the Scripture and see what it tells us about our Lord Jesus Christ as Prophet. What is a prophet? In the Old Testament he is constantly referred to as 'a man of God', a messenger from God, one who has been given a word to speak by God. We must not go into this now, because we considered it, in a sense, when dealing with the whole question of inspiration. The prophet gave his message from God in various ways, sometimes in a kind of trance; he was not clear about the mechanism but the message was quite clear. We read the words, 'the Lord spake to me and said', or, 'the word of God came to me in a dream suddenly'. So the prophet is a man who has been given a message by God to pass on to men and women for their instruction and enlightenment.

Another thing we must always bear in mind when considering the prophetic function is that it is not only confined to foretelling and prediction. We tend to use 'prophecy' in that sense only and it is a part of the prophetic office, but it is not the only part. In addition to *foretelling* there is the office of teacher and instructor – *forth telling*. The Old Testament prophets were not only confined to foretelling, a good deal of their writings show censure and blame of Israel. In addition to the foretelling, they were sent by God to warn people, to chastise and rebuke them, to remind them of the character of the law, and of God's promises. So we must remember that these aspects are as vital as the foretelling, and in our Lord Himself they were prominent.

Look for a moment at certain proofs given in the Scriptures of the fact that our Lord Jesus Christ is the Prophet. Look at Deuteronomy 18:15: 'The Lord thy God will raise up unto thee a Prophet from the midst of thee, of thy brethren, like unto me; unto him ye shall hearken.' That is one of the most basic texts in the Scripture with regard to the person of our Lord, and in the Gospels you suddenly find references to 'that prophet', in connection with the Lord Jesus Christ. People who heard His words and saw His miracles said, 'This is of a truth that prophet that should come into the world' (John 6:14). The whole nation was waiting for the coming of this Prophet, this teacher who would speak from God. Peter in preaching about Christ in Acts 3:19–26, refers to Moses' words in Deuteronomy 18 and goes on: 'Yea, and all the prophets from Samuel and those that follow after, as many as have spoken, have likewise foretold of these days.' So there was this great prophecy that the Son of God, the Saviour of the world, would be a prophet.

But let us go further: our Lord Himself claimed to be a prophet. In Luke 13:33 our Lord, replying to some of His followers who were warning Him not to go to Jerusalem, said, 'Nevertheless I must walk to day and to morrow, and the day following: for it cannot be that a prophet perish out of Jerusalem.' He prophesied there that He was going to die in the neighbourhood of Jerusalem, and this was the case with all the prophets, they were all stoned and died in Jerusalem. In John's Gospel you also find repeated statements by our Lord that everything He taught was given to Him by God. 'The words that I speak unto you I speak not of myself' (John 14:10). Or again in John 8:26 we read, 'But he that sent me is true; and I speak to the world those things which I have heard of him.' These are very explicit. He was speaking there, as a prophet, the message that had been given to Him. We have the same thing in John 12:49–50: 'I have not spoken of myself; but the Father which sent me, he gave me a commandment, what I should say, and what I should speak. And I know that his commandment is life everlasting: whatsoever I speak therefore, even as the Father said unto me, so I speak.' And the people themselves recognised that He was a prophet: 'For he taught them as one having authority, and not as the scribes' (Matt. 7:29). There, then, is the certain evidence that our Lord was indeed the Prophet predicted and prophesied by Moses.

Second: in what ways did our Lord exercise this prophetic function? First, He exercised it even before the incarnation, even before He came into this world. John 1:9 says, 'That was the true Light, which lighteth every man that cometh into the world.' This is tremendously important. It is the doctrine of Christ as the *Logos*, as the

Word of God, giving knowledge and light.

Now there is a light in the world apart from the gospel. Take all human glimmers of moral and intelligent enlightenment, take everything in the world that limits the darkness of Satan, where does it come from? The Bible says that the light in all people, whether unregenerate or regenerate, comes from God, from Christ, any light has come from Him. Now, if we were lecturing on theology we would go on to speak of this doctrine as the doctrine of *common grace*. People like Shakespeare, and the great scientists who are given knowledge and understanding, all receive their ability through Christ who is the Word that lights every man; no light, no knowledge, no understanding whatsoever, comes apart from Him. And as we have seen, He who was described in the Old Testament as the Angel of the Covenant was undoubtedly the Lord Jesus Christ. One of the reasons why He came as the Angel of the Covenant was to teach, instruct and warn. Christ was in a prophetic office even before the incarnation. In Isaiah 9:6 He is called 'Counsellor'; a teacher, an instructor, one who gives wisdom.

Still more specifically, all knowledge, all light and instruction, every ability that was given to the prophets came from Christ. The apostle Peter talks about this when he speaks of the prophets before Christ, 'Searching what, or what manner of time the Spirit of Christ which was in them did signify, when it testified beforehand the sufferings of Christ, and the glory that should follow' (1 Pet. 1:11). Christ was the Spirit enlightening the prophets even about Himself. As they spoke their prophecies and expressed them, He was the Prophet teaching the prophets; He gave them their message.

Then, second, He also exercised the function which was laid on Him as a prophet here on earth after the incarnation. He said, 'I am the light of the world: he that followeth me shall not walk in darkness, but shall have the light of life' (John 8:12). What is the light? He is the light, the Prophet, the one who came to teach. Then again in John we see that, 'No man hath seen God at any time; the only begotten Son, which is in the bosom of the Father, he hath declared him' (John 1:18). He manifested light, He gave out knowledge and instruction concerning Him whom no man has seen. The Son declared Him and revealed Him.

How did He act as Prophet on earth? He did so in all His teaching: His teaching concerning God, the Father; His exposition of the law in the Sermon on the Mount; in all He told us of God's love, of God's gracious purpose, of His nature and His person. All this was a part of the exercise of His prophetic function, and, supremely, He told us about Himself. All this is vital, and I emphasise it because we sometimes forget that a part of our salvation consists in our receiving this knowledge that our Lord has given. That is why we must realise that this gospel applies to us. All He taught applies to us; the gospel is vital for Christian people and for Christian living. Christ is our Prophet as well as our Priest.

And then He taught us by His life and example. 'He that hath seen me hath seen the Father' (John 14:9). 'Look at me,' He said, in effect. 'Have not my works shown you?' (See John 10:37–8.) 'Hast thou not known me, Philip?' (John 14:9). If you only look at Me you will learn about God.

We are to live as He lived, to follow in His steps, as Peter tells us in 1 Peter 2:21–2: 'Christ also suffered for us, leaving us an example, that ye should follow his steps: who did no sin, neither was guile found in his mouth.' He left us an example, showing His love and forbearance and all His other attributes and we are to live as He did. So He exercised His prophetic function while here on earth.

Then let me go on to show you how He has continued to exercise His prophetic function ever since His ascension, after He left earth and returned to heaven. He said that He would speak through the Holy Spirit. The Holy Spirit would not speak of Himself, or about Himself, but the Holy Spirit would be told what to say. He would send the Holy Spirit to instruct. As the Son did not speak of Himself but from the Father, so the Spirit speaks as our Lord instructs Him.

Then we are given direct revelation by the Spirit. Paul, writing to the Corinthians, says, 'Now we have received, not the spirit of the world, but the spirit which is of God; that we might know the things that are freely given to us of God' (1 Cor. 2:12). The Church has received this revelation in the same way; every one of these books in the New Testament was guided by the Spirit and controlled by Him; there is no error. And Christ still exercised His prophetic function as He guided the Church by the Spirit. He guided the Church when the canon of the New Testament was being formed. He guided them as to what was to be put into the canon – He led them into all truth as He had promised. Our Lord exercises His prophetic function even in us. He is still teaching us through the Spirit concerning spiritual things, as Paul writes in 1 Corinthians 2.

Finally, He will continue in this prophetic office until He has ultimately presented us spotless before God. He has given us this final truth that He will continue His prophetic office until we see Him, until we share His glory, the glory which He had with the Father before the foundation of the world (see John 17:24). He will lead us, He will instruct us until we see God, until we have the ultimate beatific vision in glory.

I have gone into this in detail because it seems to me so vitally important. John 3:13 says, 'And this is the condemnation, that light is come into the world, and men loved darkness rather than light . . .' Sin is ignorance and darkness; He says there is no excuse, the light has come. Or again in John 15:22, we read, 'If I had not come and spoken unto them, they had not had sin: but now they have no cloke for their sin.' 'I have come and brought light,' He said in effect, 'before, they were in darkness, but now they have no excuse for their sin.' Then finally in John 12:47–8 we read, 'If any man hear my words, and believe not, I judge him not: for I came not to judge the world, but to save the world. He that rejecteth me, and receiveth not my words, hath one that judgeth him: the word that I have spoken, the same shall judge him in the last day.'

We cannot, and we must not forget that our blessed Lord and Saviour is a prophet. As the Prophet He has brought the light and knowledge into this world which it lacked. He alone can lead us to God and give us the knowledge of God which we desire. It is He who finally brings all knowledge and instruction to those lost in the ignorance and darkness of sin.

27

Christ the Priest

In our consideration of the work of the Lord Jesus Christ, we have found that essentially He is described in the Scriptures as the mediator, the one who stands between God and ourselves. And, further, we have seen that He has three main functions to perform as the mediator: he is Prophet, Priest and King, and we need Him in these three ways. Because of the terrible ignorance that results from sin, we need someone to teach us. Because sin is constantly described in the Scriptures as ignorance – sinners are those who dwell in darkness, their minds are darkened, they need to be enlightened – He came as the light of the world, the teacher, the Prophet, and we considered the ways in which He prophesies.

Now we are going on to consider what the Scriptures tell us about Him as *Priest.* The priest is one who represents us with God, the prophet is one who represented God with us. The prophet is one who came with a message from God to man; the priest is one who goes from man to God, one who approaches God on behalf of man. And, as we have seen, we shall be constantly repeating and emphasising our greatest need of all, which is, of course, the need of a priest. We need not only to be delivered from the darkness of sin and its ignorance, we need still more to be delivered from its guilt and from the poverty that attaches to the guilt of sin.

Now the Bible teaches us everywhere that the Lord Jesus Christ is our great High Priest – what exactly does it mean by that? There is a wonderful account of this in Hebrews 5:1–5. The author's object in writing his epistle, in a sense, was to show the pre-eminence of the Lord Jesus Christ. In particular, he wanted to show His pre-eminence over Aaron, and especially that He is the great High Priest who had done this perfect work. But the author says that he finds himself in difficulties. His difficulty is that he wants to expound the fact that the Lord Jesus Christ is our great High Priest 'after the order of Melchisedec', but, he says, 'We have many things to say, and hard to be uttered, seeing ye are dull of hearing.' Then he goes on to explain that a little, and to say that his difficulty is that these Hebrew Christians are still shaky about the 'first principles' of the doctrine of Christ. They are still 'babes', because they are still living on spiritual and religious milk and are not capable of digesting meat, having never really exercised the faculties and the powers which God Himself has given them in order to discern both good and evil.

And, unfortunately, there are still large numbers of Christians who are in that position and who say, 'I cannot stand doctrine; it is too much for me. I find it difficult and boring. Give me the sort of Bible lecture which will do the whole of Hebrews in one evening and I will be very happy, but this doctrine I find hard to follow.' Now if that is so, the only thing that is true of such people is that they are babes in Christ, and it is because so many of them are babes that they miss so much about the Christian faith, and in addition so often find themselves in trouble and perplexity, not knowing what to do or think.

But at the same time we must not think that this means that these doctrines are simple. It is because they are not simple that they have so frequently been the cause of difficulty in the long history of the Christian Church. I suppose there has been no subject about which there has been such confusion as this doctrine which we are now considering. The devil obviously has been more concerned to attack the faith at this point than at any other. This doctrine is the crucial thing, so he has concentrated his energy on it in an exceptional way, and the result is that throughout the centuries you have had errors and heresies with regard to this matter, and you have them still in this modern world. But that makes it all the more important that we should study it, however difficult it may be, in order that we may know what the truth is, and then we shall be able to refute the false teachings that are around and about us.

So many cults are very active at the present time. False teachers claim that they only have the real Christian faith and that those of us who preach the evangelical faith are not emphasising what they emphasise. Now the thing to do with all those teachings is to examine what they have to say about the atonement, about the way of reconciliation, and if you do that you will find that it is at that point that they are defective. So that really this is of the utmost importance for us. It is always important that we should know what to do and what to believe, but it is of tremendous importance if we want to safeguard both ourselves, and others who may be weaker than us, from being led away by these strong delusions and subtleties of sin which so often masquerade today as angels of light.

So it seems to me that the best way of facing this matter is to start first of all by a consideration of what the Bible teaches about a priest or the priesthood in general. That is a very good way of approaching this doctrine and there is a great deal of teaching in the Scriptures on the subject. In other words, the way to discover what the Bible says about the Lord Himself as the great High Priest is to take it on a lower level to start with, because it is all one piece – the Old Testament points to the New; it is a kind of type of which Christ Himself is the antitype.

What, therefore, do we know about the nature and function of a priest? Well, the best definition which we find anywhere in the Scriptures is in those first five verses of Hebrews 5. Let me give you some headings from what we are there told about a priest.

The first thing we are told is that he must be taken from among men in order to be their representative (v. 1).

Second, we are told that he is chosen and appointed by God – 'No man taketh this honour unto himself, but he that is called of God, as was Aaron' (v. 4).

Third, he is active in the interests of men in things pertaining to God. That is brought out quite clearly: 'For every high priest taken from among men is ordained for men in things pertaining to God' (v. 1).

The fourth characteristic is that he has to offer gifts and sacrifices for sins (v. 1).

Those are the four things which are emphasised in those verses. But it is also taught elsewhere in the Scriptures that a priest must be holy, that he must be morally pure, that he must be consecrated to the Lord. Leviticus 21:6–8 says:

> They shall be holy unto their God, and not profane the name of their God: for the offerings of the Lord made by fire, and the bread of their God, they do offer: therefore they shall be holy. They shall not take a wife that is a whore, or profane; neither shall they take a woman put away from her husband: for he is holy unto his God. Thou shalt sanctify him therefore; for he offereth the bread of thy God: he shall be holy unto thee: for I the Lord, which sanctify you, am holy.

Priests were set apart; they did not have to do certain things that other people did; they were consecrated to the Lord.

The function of a priest, therefore, we can summarise in this way. The priest is essentially a mediator who does two main things. First, he propitiates by sacrifices; second, he intercedes on behalf of the people. So let us consider this word 'propitiation'. It is a word that is used in the third chapter of Romans in that great section starting with verse 24: 'Being justified freely by his grace through the redemption that is in Christ Jesus: whom God hath set forth to be a propitiation through faith in his blood, to declare his righteousness for the remission of sins that are past, through the forbearance of God,' and John used it again in his first epistle: 'And he is the propitiation for our sins: and not for ours only, but also for the sins of the whole world' (1 John 2:2). What, then, is propitiation? It is that which satisfies the demands of violated holiness; it means a satisfaction that is rendered to the violated holiness of God Himself.

Now I have summarised the functions of a priest under those two main headings. It is his first business to propitiate God and then he has to intercede on behalf of the people, and that at once brings us to a very vital aspect of this whole subject. The priest propitiates by making offerings and sacrifices; you cannot read the Old Testament without constantly coming across that. But I find that many Christian people never read those portions of Scripture; they say that they do not understand them. I agree that they are difficult, but they are mentioned in the New Testament, and especially in the epistle to the Hebrews, so let us look at the main teaching of the Scriptures about offerings and sacrifices.

Now these were offered before the time of Moses as well as after him. Offerings and sacrifices were, however, defined in a very special way in the law that God gave to Moses – you will find it in the book of Leviticus. They were tabulated and defined in a more detailed way there, but there had been offerings and sacrifices before that. So what meaning must we attach to them? We need not waste time in dealing at length with the false views, though I am sorely tempted to do so because there are so many today who read books on what is called 'Comparative Religions' where very false ideas are taught about these matters. Not only that, all who know anything about missionary work in different countries will know that pagan people have entirely wrong notions as to the purpose and function of offerings and sacrifices.

So let us, in passing, just hurriedly mention some of these false views. There are those who believe and teach that the main function of these offerings and sacrifices is to serve as a kind of gift which is meant to secure favour. That, they say, is their object. People make offerings in order to get favour from their god. And there are those who teach that that is the meaning of these things in the Bible. They say that you must not believe what the Bible tells you, because it tells you that God made man perfect and that man started in a relationship to God and then went astray. But they teach that men started off as animists who thought that every natural object had its own god. They went up the scale until they eventually arrived at a belief in one God, but they retained, as it were, their primitive ideas of sacrifices, which were incorporated wrongly into Christianity.

Or it is said that a sacrifice is a kind of symbol which represents a communion of life with a god. Men kill an animal and take that animal's blood and put it on the altar. They believe that the spirit of their god is in the animal, so by putting the blood of the animal on the altar, they think that they are having communion with the god through this symbol of the blood.

Then there are others who believe that sacrifices are a sort of sacramental communion. They say that God is actually in the animal, so when they kill the animal and eat it they are feeding on their god and are receiving his life and are built up in him in that way.

Others teach that sacrifices and offerings are just a way of paying homage or tribute to a god.

Those, then, are the false ideas about offerings and sacrifices; but what is taught in the Scriptures? To answer that, I must introduce you to a term. What is taught in the Scriptures is that offerings and sacrifices, especially the sin and trespass offerings – and this was the case before the Mosaic system was introduced – are *piacular*. Now what is the meaning of that? Well, I took the trouble to turn up two volumes of the Oxford Dictionary to see what it would have to say about that word and it said that piacular means expiatory. I thought, 'That is very interesting; how characteristic of a dictionary – it keeps you looking up words! You are in trouble about piacular, so you are introduced to expiatory!' However, let us look at some of these terms together because they are of vital importance, and we must be clear in our minds as to what they mean.

First, propitiation, which means, as we have seen, satisfying the demands of violated holiness.

Second, expiation. To expiate means to extinguish guilt, to pay the penalty, to make reparation for something. When sin is expiated it is put aside, it is blotted out, it is wiped out, it is done away with.

Third, atonement. To atone means to set at one; it really means at-one-ment; it means that two people who were formerly divided are brought together and made as one. So the whole business of reconciliation is the restoration of friendly relations between two parties that formerly were separated; and the great biblical doctrine of reconciliation tells us how God and sinners have been brought together, how an at-one-ment has been produced.

So, to summarise, there are three main things which are the essentials for our Lord to do as our Priest in order to secure this reconciliation of sinful people with God. First, satisfaction must be offered to the offended God (propitiation). Second, there must be a substitution of suffering and death on the part of someone who is innocent for the deserved punishment of the guilty (expiation). And third, a community of life needs to be brought about between the one who has been offended and the offender (atonement). Now the claim of the Scriptures is that the Lord Jesus Christ has done all that.

If you look at all this in terms of the Old Testament sacrifices and what was claimed for them, you will see that they did those three things. For instance, we are told quite definitely and explicitly in Leviticus 1:4: 'And he shall put his hand upon the head of the burnt offering; and it shall be accepted for him to make atonement for him.' And in 4:20: 'And he shall do with the bullock as he did with the bullock for a sin offering, so shall he do with this: and the priest shall make an atonement for them, and it shall be forgiven them.' Then we read in Leviticus again how the people or the priest representing them had to put their hands on the head of the animal that was to be sacrificed – what was the object of doing that? It was the sign of the transference of their sins and their guilt to the animal to be killed on their behalf. So you see the sacrifice was definitely piacular, or expiatory – the guilt was transferred in order that the sin and guilt might be removed.

In the same way we read about the sprinkling of the blood on the altar and on the mercy seat. That drop of blood was another reminder of sin, showing that life is in the blood, and that this life had been taken and put on the mercy seat in order that sinful people might be propitiated with God; the offence that had been committed was thereby dealt with. And further, of course, we are constantly told in the Old Testament that the effect of doing all this was that the sins of the people were thereby forgiven and covered (Lev. 4:26).

That seems to have been the great teaching of the Old Testament sacrifices. They were offered on behalf of God's chosen people, the children of Israel, who, though they were the children of God, still fell into sin and thereby got into a wrong relationship with God. And the purpose of the burnt offerings and sacrifices was that God's people might be restored again to their communion and covenant with Him, to their place and privilege as His people, that they might enjoy His blessings which had been forfeited either by neglect or transgression.

And, of course, another great function was that sacrifices and burnt offerings were types of the Lord Jesus Christ and of God's way of reconciling man to Himself. They were pointing to Him in various ways – but we shall come back to that later.

There, then, is the main Scriptural teaching with regard to the function of a priest. We have seen what would be true of Him. He was a man and we have seen that his work consisted of making sacrifices and sacrifices for these reasons, and at the same time He goes on to intercede for the people.

Now the great claim of the Scriptures everywhere is that our Lord and Saviour Jesus Christ is our great High Priest. Before I give you the Scriptural evidence, let me point out that there is one great difference between Him and everything we read about priests in the Old Testament. In the Old Testament the priest had to find his sacrifices – the lamb, and so on – but in the case of the Lord Jesus Christ, the priest and the sacrifice were one and the same. He is the Priest. What did He offer? He offered Himself, He offered His own life, His body, as the sacrifice. So once more we find that He combines in His person the things that were separated in the Old Testament. We have seen that under the old dispensation the prophet, priest and king were separate people, but Christ is all three.

So what are the evidences for saying that He is God's appointed High Priest? Well, it is interesting to observe that there is only one book in the Bible which describes Him directly and explicitly as Priest, and that is, of course, the epistle to the Hebrews. Hebrews describes Him as such in a number of verses – Hebrews 3:1; 4:14; 5:5; 6:20; 7:26; 8:1. Collect them for yourself, it is a very rewarding study to trace this and to follow it right through.

But, of course, in many other places the teaching is implicit – by implication it is there. For instance, listen to our Lord Himself. He said, 'For even the Son of man came not to be ministered unto, but to minister, and to give his life a ransom for many' (Mark 10:45). This is also something that is constantly taught by the apostle Paul. In Romans 3:24–5 he says: 'Being justified freely by his grace through the redemption that is in Christ Jesus: whom God hath set forth to be a propitiation through faith in his blood, to declare his righteousness for the remission of sins that are past, through the forbearance of God.' He says the same thing in Romans 5:6–8, and in 1 Corinthians 5:7: 'Christ our passover is sacrificed for us.' Then 1 Corinthians 15:3 is a great statement of this doctrine, and I could quote many others. You find the same teaching in the writings of the apostle John. John the Baptist said, 'Behold the Lamb of God, which taketh away the sin of the world' (John 1:29). Or again we read in John 3:14–15: 'And as Moses lifted up the serpent in the wilderness, even so must the Son of man be lifted up: that whosoever believeth in him should not perish, but have eternal life' – it is the same teaching, and also in 1 John 2:2 we read, 'And he is the propitiation for our sins: and not for ours only, but also for the sins of the whole world.' Peter teaches this in his epistle, 'But with the precious blood of Christ, as of a lamb without blemish and without spot' (1 Pet. 1:19); 'Who his own self bare our sins in his own body on the tree, that we, being dead to sins, should live unto righteousness: by whose stripes ye were healed' (1 Pet. 2:24); 'For Christ also hath once suffered for sins, the just for the unjust, that he might bring us to God, being put to death in the flesh, but quickened by the Spirit' (1 Pet. 3:18).

Now the claim is that He is our great High Priest, and if you examine the teaching concerning Him in the light of the desiderata which are laid down in Hebrews 5, you will find that He satisfies them every one: He is taken from among men; He does not take this unto Himself; He is called and appointed of God. Furthermore, He makes representation for the people in the things pertaining to God and He offers gifts and sacrifices. So He fulfils everything perfectly and completely.

And not only that, having thus as the Priest offered the sacrifices, He then intercedes on behalf of His people. We shall just touch on that briefly now because to look at our Lord as the one who intercedes on our behalf is to anticipate later studies, but it is good, perhaps, to consider our Lord's work as Priest as a whole. He prayed for His followers just before His death – you find that in John 17, in His high priestly prayer – and we are told that 'he ever liveth to make intercession for us', in heaven with God (Heb. 7:25). He is our Advocate, and it is quite clear that when He pleads on our behalf, His very presence is an intercession in itself because it is a reminder of the expiation that has been made, the propitiation that has been offered. In John 17 we see Him praying that we may be kept from the evil one, that we may be sanctified by the truth, and that we may be where He is to observe and behold the glory which He had with the Father before the world was made.

His intercession is an endless one, and we, as believers and as children of God walking through this world, should we fall into sin – well, it is a blessed knowledge which we have, that we have an Advocate with the Father, an Advocate who is still the propitiation and who has propitiated once and for ever (1 John 2). This is the one thing that can give us assurance that our sin is forgiven, that we must not lie down in sin. It tells us that we must not listen to the devil when he would have us believe that because of that sin we have lost our relationship with God and that it can never be restored again. We answer all that by saying, 'The Advocate is there and He is the propitiation, and we know that we are forgiven if we confess our sins for he is faithful and just to forgive us our sins, and [again] to cleanse us from all unrighteousness' (1 John 1:9).

So you see that our Lord satisfied all the demands which are laid down. He did it in His person through being born as a man. He could not have been our High Priest if He had not taken human nature unto Himself. He must be one who is 'taken from among men', so the incarnation was essential. He therefore became man, the Word was made flesh. He took unto Himself human nature in order that He might represent us as one taken from among us, and knowing us and understanding our frame. Having Himself experienced the infirmities, though still without sin, having been tempted in all points like as we are, yet without sin, He is the High Priest who can represent us and speak on our behalf. And we have seen that He has an offering to offer, a sacrifice to present that has been accepted of God. So He intercedes and ever lives to make intercession for all who come to God by Him.

28

The Atonement

We have come in our consideration of these biblical doctrines to the point at which we find ourselves face to face with the great doctrine of the atonement. We have seen that there is only one way whereby men and women can be reconciled to God and that is in and through our Lord and Saviour Jesus Christ, and we have started our consideration of His work, having first considered His person. The work is divided, as we have seen, according to the Scriptures themselves – Christ is Prophet, Priest and King. We have considered the teaching concerning Christ as Prophet and we are now considering His work as Priest. We have seen that He satisfies the desiderata which were laid down so clearly in Hebrews 5:1–5; He fulfils all those demands. And we saw that the two main functions of the Priest are to present offerings and sacrifices and to make intercession. I ended that lecture by saying that He has an offering to offer and a sacrifice to present that God has accepted. This brings us inevitably to the consideration of what it is our Lord does offer, and did offer to God, as our great High Priest. And at once we come face to face with the doctrine of the atonement. This concerns primarily, but not only, as I shall be at pains to emphasise, the death of the Lord Jesus Christ, and therefore our main subject now will be a consideration of the biblical teaching with regard to that.

Now the great question is: What exactly did happen when our Lord died upon the cross? Obviously this is a most vital question, indeed, the most vital question we can ever face together. It would be vital even if we were to look at these things merely from the prominence that is given to this truth in the New Testament itself. It is an actual fact that the death of our Lord upon the cross is mentioned directly

175 times in the New Testament and indirectly many more times. That in itself is staggering and arresting, and it shows the importance which is given to it in the New Testament Scriptures.

Or look at it like this: take the four Gospels; we realise that they are but four portraits of our Lord; they do not tell us everything about Him. John, you remember, ended His Gospel by saying, 'And there are also many other things which Jesus did, the which, if they should be written every one, I suppose that even the world itself could not contain the books that should be written' (John 21:25). But these are written; they are samples, if you like, they are books, they are portraits. And, of course, they are short. Each one of the Gospels is a comparatively short book and yet the striking thing is that in each of them practically one third of the space is devoted to the death of our Lord. It is exactly one third of Matthew; it is nearly one quarter of Luke; and in the case of Mark and John it is over one third.

So we can say that on average, of the space that is given to the coming of the Son of God into this world and all that He did and said, one third is devoted to His death and the events immediately leading up to it. So obviously the implication is that the Gospels are thus bringing us to see that while His incarnation and His life and teaching are of vital importance, the event that exceeds all others in importance is His death upon the cross. So there, again, is another reason why we should consider this very, very carefully and especially, let me remind you, when we bear in mind that the people who wrote those Gospels, under the guidance and leading of the Holy Spirit, knew very well that this very thing that they were so emphasising was, as Paul reminds the Corinthians, a 'stumbling block' to the Jews, and 'foolishness' to the Greeks (see 1 Cor. 1:23). Though they knew all that, they put it in the forefront.

Then when you look at the book of Acts, you will find that His death is given the same prominence. The apostle Paul's method, wherever he went, was that he went into the synagogue and he did two things. He proved and established that 'the Christ must needs have suffered', and, second, he said that 'This Jesus, whom I preach unto you, is Christ' (Acts 17:3); and when you go on to the epistles the same thing is made abundantly clear. The apostle says, 'I determined not to know any thing among you, save Jesus Christ, and him crucified' (1 Cor. 2:2); and he goes on repeating it: 'I delivered unto you first of all that which I also received, how that Christ died for our sins according to the scriptures . . .' (1 Cor. 15:3); and there are other similar verses.

Also, as you look at the epistles of the other writers you find the same thing; 'Ye were not redeemed with corruptible things, as silver and gold . . . but with the precious blood of Christ, as of a lamb without blemish and without spot . . .' writes Peter (1 Pet. 1:18–19). 'He is the propitiation for our sins: and not for ours only, but also for the sins of the whole world,' says John (1 John 2:2). And the same is true of Revelation: '[They] have washed their robes, and made them white in the blood of the Lamb' (Rev. 7:14), and so on. And so anybody who reads the New Testament, even superficially, unless he is a victim of serious prejudice, is bound to gather the impression that, according to the writers of this book at any rate, the death of the Lord Jesus Christ is of paramount importance. That is why we are bound to consider this, and the real question that confronts us is: What exactly happened there? What was really taking place when our Lord died upon the cross? What is the meaning, the explanation, of that death?

Now I know that many people are not really concerned to know that. They say, 'No, I am not theological or doctrinal; all I know is that the cross is marvellous and wonderful and that the Lord died there.' And there are many who seem to think that that is the right attitude. They think that this is too sacred for anybody to examine, that you must never come to the cross with your mind but only with your heart, that the doctrine of the cross is something to be felt, not understood. But nothing is more terribly dangerous than that. If I understand the New Testament aright, there is no place where we should be more careful to go with our minds fully operating as to the cross on Calvary's hill. And I will tell you why: it is because this is the central thing; there is no truth concerning which the adversary and the enemy of our souls is so anxious to muddle and confuse us as this particular truth.

The history of the Church, as I shall show you briefly, is something that bears endless record to that fact. Let us put it like this: those people who are not interested in doctrine say that all they need is to fall on their knees before the cross; they say that they are not interested in the meaning. But my reply is that that is impossible. Everybody has *some* view of the cross; and when you say you believe in Christ and look at the cross, you must ask yourself what you believe about it. You have your own interpretation and because of the terrible danger of having the wrong interpretation, we must examine the truth and be certain that we are biblical in our understanding of what happened upon the cross.

I emphasise this because I find that so many people – forgive me for saying it once more, but this is one thing about the evangelical position today that really does alarm me – so many people have this tendency to say that it does not matter very much what people believe, that the doctrinal definitions do not count as long as people talk about the cross. I remember a few years ago a man said to me: 'I hear that so and so – naming a well-known preacher – has changed recently.'

'Oh,' I replied, 'on what grounds?'

'Well,' said the man, 'he has just produced a book of sermons on the cross.' And because this preacher had done that, my friend had assumed that he had become evangelical. But when he read the book, he discovered that the man's view had not changed; it was a view that made the cross of Christ of none effect. He had imposed upon the records his own philosophical ideas and fancies. It is very dangerous to assume that because a man is always talking about the cross – he may even have a cross suspended above the pulpit or somewhere else in his church – that he has the true doctrine of the cross.

No, the question is what do we believe about the cross? It is the apostle Paul who tells us that we can make it of none effect 'through philosophy and vain deceit' (Col. 2:8). The cross of Jesus Christ, the death of Christ, is still an offence to the natural man or woman and I sometimes think that they show that most plainly when they talk about it in a wrong and false way. And so I make no apology for considering with you some of the wrong ideas with regard to what happened when the Son of God died upon the cross.

Some people regard it as a tragedy or as an accident. They say it was just one of those things that should never have happened; it was entirely due to the stupidity of the people. It was partly political, they say. The high priests and Pharisees and scribes believed that the people were being misled and that there was a danger that their authority would be taken from them, so they worked up an opposing party. These people go further and say that it was something that took our Lord completely by surprise, that He never expected it and when He said, 'It is finished,' He was really saying (I am quoting from a book): 'It is all over.' His life had ended in failure; He could, they say, have persuaded the people to follow Him and live a godly life, but they would not listen. He was only thirty-three; what a tragedy it was that this young teacher was put to death so unexpectedly and so surprisingly, especially to Himself.

Well, I am sure it is scarcely necessary for me to refute something which is so far removed from the scriptural representation. Our Lord talked about the cross, and He prepared His own followers for it, especially after Simon Peter's confession at Caesarea Philippi when our Lord at once began to teach the disciples about the cross, about His death and resurrection. Peter objected because he did not understand, but, you see, the Lord was beginning to teach them (Matt. 16:13–23). On another occasion He said, 'The Son of man came not to be ministered unto, but to minister, and to give his life a ransom for many' (Matt. 20:28) – this was an explicit statement of His reason for coming to this earth and dying. Read the Gospel of John especially and keep your eye upon the phrase 'the hour'. Our Lord repeatedly talked about some hour that was to come, the hour for which He had come into the world; it was about to arrive, it was the hour of His death, leading finally to His glorification (John 12:23; 17:1). Then we are told that on the Mount of Transfiguration, Moses and Elijah talked about 'his decease which he should accomplish at Jerusalem' (Luke 9:31). Are we not also told that 'He stedfastly set His face to go to Jerusalem' (Luke 9:51) and when His disciples warned Him against going He said, 'It cannot be that a prophet perish out of Jerusalem' (Luke 13:33). He knew He was going to die.

That other idea is too monstrous because there is all this abundant evidence to show that He came into the world in order to die. As the author of the epistle to the Hebrews puts it, He came 'to taste death for every man' (Heb. 2:9). He tells us later on that, 'As the children are partakers of flesh and blood, he also himself likewise took part of the same; that through death he might destroy him that had the power of death, that is, the devil' (Heb. 2:14). Then we are told that after His resurrection He talked to His disciples, who were somewhat confused, and told them to read through the Scriptures, pointing out that they would see from the Scriptures that everything that had happened to Him had been predicted and that He had come to fulfil the things that God had already promised (Luke 24:13–35).

Then when you come to the explanations of the apostles themselves in their writings, you find they say exactly the same thing. In his sermon on the Day of Pentecost Peter did not say that Christ's death had been an accident. He said, 'Him, being delivered by the determinate counsel and foreknowledge of God, ye have taken, and by wicked hands have crucified and slain' (Acts 2:23), and he repeats that message in his first epistle. He tells us that this thing was planned in eternity; that it had now literally happened and was being preached and declared (1 Pet. 1:20).

But let me point out something which is of fascinating interest in this connection. There is one most important passage in Matthew's Gospel: Matthew 26:1–5, especially verse 5, which settles this matter once and for ever. In verse 5, the word 'day' should not be there; what the rulers said was, 'Not on the feast day' – not during the festival – 'lest there be an uproar among the people.' Now what all that means is this: here was our Lord on the Tuesday of that week, which is now sometimes called Holy Week. He was predicting that He would be betrayed and crucified on the Friday: 'Ye know that after two days is the feast of the passover' – that is the first thing – 'and the Son of man is betrayed to be crucified' – He was fixing the time. You notice that these authorities who were plotting His death said: 'Not on the feast day,' not during the festival. They agreed, in other words, that He was not to be crucified on Good Friday, but He was crucified then, as you know. Now it was the custom that the Jews should not put anybody to death during the festival – if you want confirmation of that, you will find it in Acts 12 where we are told that Peter had been arrested by King Herod, but they were told to keep him in prison because, 'Then were the days of unleavened bread' (Acts 12:3–4). But our Lord not only knew that He was going to die, He knew the exact moment He was going to die and He gave warning of it those three days ahead of time. Yet people tell us glibly that it took Him by surprise, that it was an accident!

Another wrong idea – and the people who hold it feel that they are a bit in advance of the previous people – is that His was the death of a martyr. What they mean is this. Here was this wonderful teacher; people tried to make Him recant but He would not, He was ready to die, so He died a martyr's death. It seems to me that a very simple statement can be made about this, and I say it with reverence. If the death of the Lord Jesus Christ was the death of a martyr and nothing more, then He was inferior to many martyrs who have died in this world. I prove that like this: the whole glory of the martyrs is that they went to the stake, or whatever it was, with triumph and rejoicing. They thanked God that at last they had been found worthy to suffer for His name's sake – indeed, they rejoiced while the flames were licking their very flesh.

That is the martyr's death, but what do you find when you come to our Lord? You find that every time He thought of it He groaned in spirit. When He knew that His hour was come He said, 'What shall I say? Father, save me from this hour: but for this cause came I unto this hour' (John 12:27). But the thought was there: might He be spared from this hour? He shrank from it. What is the meaning of the agony in the Garden of Gethsemane? He pleaded with His Father, 'If it be possible, let this cup pass from me' (Matt. 26:39) – the martyrs never prayed like that. No, the answer is quite simple: it was not the death of a martyr. That is the only explanation: it was in a category of its own, it was bigger in every sense than any martyr's death ever has been, or can be. It was a unique death which can only adequately be explained in one way.

Very well, His death was not an accident; it was not a tragedy; it was not a martyr's death; nor was it something that might or might not have happened and all would have been well. No, the New Testament makes it plain that it was something that was essential to man's salvation. But even when you have said that, you have not said enough. In what way was it essential? Now it is at this point that a variety of explanations have been put forward throughout the long history of the Church, and they are still being put forward. There are people, for instance, who teach that the death of Christ is for our salvation, but is only a part of our salvation. The explanation they give for this view is quite unscriptural. So once more I must ask you to consider some of these false explanations before we can pass on to the true explanation. Let me be quite clear about this. I am not foolish enough to suggest that I can understand the meaning of the death of my Lord upon the cross exhaustively. I cannot. But I can say that an explanation is given in the Scriptures themselves which I must uphold; and I must test any view that anybody may put forward with regard to the death of our Lord by what the Scriptures show me I am to know. As we have seen, it is our business, always, to go as far as revelation leads us. It is our duty never to try to go beyond that, and I think I shall be able to show you that in all I shall put forward I am not going beyond revelation. But I am certainly going, and must go, as far as revelation takes me.

So let us consider some of the false theories that have been put forward throughout the centuries and are still being put forward with regard to the death of our Lord. Here is the first – I am taking them historically. It is the so-called *ransom theory*, not the true ransom teaching, but a false theory. Some of the early Christians themselves taught that when our Lord died upon the cross He was paying homage to the devil; He was paying a ransom price to the devil in order that He might liberate those who were held captive. Now our answer is that there is no scriptural statement about that. The Scriptures do give teaching with respect to the devil and his powers and the cross, and I shall return to that, but they in no way suggest that he has any right or authority. He is a usurper, he has no rights and our Lord did not acknowledge him in any way at all. So we must reject that theory *in toto*.

The next false teaching was put forward towards the end of the eleventh century by an Archbishop of Canterbury called Anselm. It was the first attempt ever made to formulate a false doctrine of the atonement or the death of our Lord. What is Anselm's theory? Sometimes called the *satisfaction* or the *commercial theory*, it says that when man sinned, the honour – not the justice, you notice – of God had been wounded. The sin was an insult to God and, therefore, Anselm said, before men and women could be delivered and forgiven, God's honour must somehow be vindicated. But men and women themselves could not do that, as they had sinned against God. God could respond to them in one of two ways: He could punish them or forgive them; but, Anselm said, God cannot forgive until His honour has been satisfied. So the teaching was that our Lord had come to pay tribute to the honour of God.

Anselm said that by His death Christ had paid this tribute to the honour of God. He was sinless and He had no need to die, but He did die and so brought infinite glory to God. In serving God He went even to the death of the cross and thereby He did something beyond what was necessary. He had kept the law, because He was 'under the law' (Gal. 4:4), and the honour of God was satisfied. So God was pleased and wanted to reward His Son for dying, but the Son needed no reward for Himself and He said, 'Give the reward to the people.' That theory would have us believe that our salvation is a work of supererogation, a kind of extra work that the Lord has done and has given to us as a free reward. Now there are many objections to this theory, which I hope to show you when we come to consider the substitutionary teaching and explanation of Christ's death, but the vital objection to this particular idea of Anselm's is that it does not mention the justice of God, merely a kind of wounded honour. Christ's death is not, therefore, essential, whereas the biblical teaching shows that it is

God's justice that makes Christ's death absolutely essential.

Another theory is commonly called the *moral influence* theory. Now this is the most popular of the theories; let me summarise it in this way. It says that God had no difficulty in forgiving us; as far as God was concerned there was no need to do anything. His love is so great that He always, at every point, is full of forgiveness; but the difficulty was to get mankind to believe that. So, they say, what really happened on the cross was a marvellous display of the love of God. I remember once listening to the sermon of a man who ridiculed the substitutionary atonement. 'You must not say,' he said, 'that God was offering forgiveness because of the cross. God forgives even without the cross, but the cross was the proof of God's love. God is telling us on the cross: "Though you have killed my only begotten Son, I will still forgive you."' Christ's death was a manifestation of the love of God. In the cross we see Him suffering in and with His sinful creatures and taking upon Himself the woes and griefs of human life. So the cross is meant to break us down; as we look at it our hard hearts are to be softened. The death of Christ is to do something to us alone.

Now that theory, again, as I think we shall see when we come to the positive theory, is entirely wrong, because it does not mention the justice of God at all. It says that nothing was necessary on God's side – there was no obstacle there – but the trouble was only with man. So Christ is not a mediator, because He was dealing with man and not at all with God. The theory takes no notice whatsoever of some of the most glorious scriptural statements which we shall be considering together.

Another idea is that the *death of Christ is just an example*. He came into the world to live a perfect life. He kept the law, yes, and He wanted to leave a good example of obedience to God and His will, so He went as far as death. He was ready to do even that in order to do God's will and thereby He provided us with an example. The answer to that is that we still have to save ourselves and we save ourselves by imitating His example. We are not saved by Him, it is not His blood that redeems us. Furthermore, what about those who lived before Christ?

Another theory is given the name of the *governmental theory*. I mention it partly because it was the view of the cross that was advocated by the great preacher of the last century, Dr Dale of Birmingham. Originally propounded by Grotius, a Dutchman in the seventeenth century, it says that the death of our Lord did not take place because the justice of God demanded it since God's law is not something which is absolutely final. If He wished He could change it. So He could have forgiven men and women in another way if He had chosen to do so, but He chose to do it in this way because, in order to preserve moral life in this world, God had to do something drastic about sin. If He had forgiven sin without Christ's death, we would have said that it did not matter very much whether we sinned or not. But if we said that, where would the moral character of the universe be? So, to preserve His own moral government of the universe, and because He takes such a serious view of sin, says this theory, God sent His Son to the cross, and the Son went to the cross in order that mankind might realise that sin is serious and forbidden.

Of course, once again there are fundamental objections. The justice of God is ignored and, still more serious, supporters of His view do not understand that God, because He is God, cannot go back upon His own law. As I want to show you when we come to the positive doctrine, there is a teaching of the death on the cross which is altogether greater than this. It is that Christ died upon the cross for no reason except this; it *had* to happen; it was an absolute necessity; there was no other way whereby man could be forgiven.

I must mention one other theory and that is the *mystical theory*. This was popularised in London early in the nineteenth century by Edward Irving who had come down from Glasgow where he had been assistant to the great Dr Chalmers, one of the most eloquent preachers of that time. Edward Irving captured London; society crowded after him, drawn by his oratory. It was he who introduced the modern idea of speaking in tongues. He founded what is called the Catholic Apostolic Church in Gordon Square and there he developed strange ideas. Alas, he went astray in many respects, not only in his view of the death of Christ upon the cross. But we are interested in his view of Christ's atonement. It was not his own original idea. He said that Christ, the Son of God, came from heaven, and took the form of human nature. But Irving did not believe that Christ's human nature was perfect; he said that the human nature that Christ had was sinful, but He kept it without sin by the power of the Spirit. Not only that, but by dying upon the cross He purged sin out of it, so what really happened was that our Lord, by living and by dying, purged human nature of sin. He removed the original depravity and united human nature to God. Again, there is nothing here about satisfying God's justice, nothing about honouring the law; the very essence of the true idea taught in the Scriptures is not there at all, merely this strange, mystical conception which is never taught anywhere in the Scriptures.

And finally, and this is the most modern of all the ideas, there is what is called the *vicarious repentance* idea of the atonement. This was very popular at the beginning of the twentieth century and there are many who teach it. It is said that what our Lord was really doing on the cross was offering repentance on behalf of mankind. Man has no true conception of sin and therefore he cannot repent truly. God cannot forgive until man does repent, so what our Lord was doing was making a confession on behalf of mankind. He was saying, 'Sin is a terrible thing; I am going to show mankind that it deserves death, and I am offering repentance on their behalf by dying on the cross, submitting to that as an act of repentance.'

There is one vital objection to this theory and it is that our Lord, as we shall see, certainly took our sins upon Him, but there was one thing that our Lord of necessity could not do: He had no experience of what it is to sin; He had no experience of what it is to feel guilty; He had no feeling of remorse. Because He is God and man, because He is perfect, He could not know what you and I know when we have sinned; and surely it is quite impossible for anyone to repent, or to offer penance, without a feeling of guilt, without a sensation of what sin, in a creature, is against God. Without having our sensation and feeling and experience of being in sin, our Lord could not repent on our behalf.

Now we have spent some time in considering these false ideas of what happened when our Lord died upon the cross on Calvary's hill. Having got them out of the way, we shall come next to the positive biblical teaching. I shall give you evidence and arguments; we shall look at it together and we shall see that the substitutionary idea of the atonement, which is the biblical teaching, not only clarifies the whole thing where nothing else can, but it magnifies the cross and the love of God in a way that all these other theories, which have been put forward in order to safeguard the love of God, completely fail to do.

29
Substitution

Having considered some of the false theories with respect to the doctrine of what exactly happened when the Son of God died on the cross, we come now to a positive exposition of what I claim to be the biblical teaching. It is certainly the view of the atonement that was taught by all the Protestant Fathers. It was taught by Martin Luther and John Calvin and by the Reformers in Britain.

So what is it? The biblical teaching emphasises the supremacy of the substitutionary element in the atonement. It asserts that the Lord Jesus Christ suffered the penalty of the broken law vicariously, as the substitute for His people. That is, in a brief compass, a statement of what has been known as the *reformed view of the biblical doctrine of the atonement*. Now you will notice at once that there is a difference between this and those false theories which we have considered. This view has two main characteristics. The first is the emphasis upon the fact that Jesus Christ has done something as our substitute, and the second is the penal aspect – it states that the law pronounced a penalty which He, as our substitute, has borne in our stead.

Notice that neither of those two characteristics was really mentioned in any of the false theories that we previously mentioned. The objection to this view has mainly been with respect to the penal aspect, but I shall not delay over this objection because I am anxious to give you a positive statement of the doctrine. Let us then look at the biblical teaching on which this view is based. There are many different ways in which one could approach this subject but the most satisfactory way, it seems to me, is under the following headings.

The first is this: the New Testament clearly teaches that our Lord's work is entirely in line with the Old Testament teaching on sacrifices.

Our Lord Himself claimed that, you remember, and did so more than once. As we have already seen, He was the Priest who offered the sacrifice. The New Testament teaching about Christ's work parallels everything we are told about the work of the priest who made offerings and the sacrifices under the Old Testament dispensation. Our Lord Himself said, 'Think not that I am come to destroy the law, or the prophets: I am not come to destroy, but to fulfil' (Matt. 5:17) — that was His specific claim, and it has reference to all the Levitical rules about sacrifices. It includes the whole law in all its fulness, not only the moral aspect, but, in a very special way, the ritual aspect which is concerned with the offerings and the sacrifices. And not only did He claim it there, He made the same claim after the resurrection: 'And he said unto them, These are the words which I spake unto you, while I was yet with you, that all things must be fulfilled, which were written in the law of Moses, and in the prophets, and in the psalms, concerning me' (Luke 24:44).

But then, of course, there is a sense in which the whole of the epistle to the Hebrews was written to establish that point. The argument of Hebrews is that the Old Testament was nothing but a kind of shadow, pointing everywhere to the substance; it reveals to us the types pointing to the prototype. 'You must not go back to the shadow,' says the writer in effect, 'now you have the substance.' Since the Old Testament types pointed forward to Him, we are entitled to argue that they were of the same kind and the same essential quality. If you read chapters 7 and 9, particularly, of the epistle to the Hebrews, you will see that argument worked out in considerable detail.

What, then, does the Old Testament teach with regard to the function of the sacrifices that were offered by the priest? The first thing we are told is that the purpose of the burnt offerings and sin offerings was to propitiate God. They were designed to make God look with favour and with pleasure upon the people who had sinned against Him. We have already looked at that term but let us consider it again as we find it in the well-known parable of the Pharisee and the tax-collector who went up to the Temple to pray. In the *Authorised Version*, we are told that the tax-collector 'would not lift up so much as his eyes', but said, 'God be merciful to me a sinner.' Now what he really said was, 'God be propitiated to me a sinner' (Luke 18:13). The object of the sacrifices was that God should look upon sinful people in a benign manner, in a manner that was ready to receive them.

I emphasise that because you remember how many of those false theories would have us believe that the sole purpose of the death of our Lord upon the cross was to do something to *us*. But at the very beginning they are wrong. The object of the burnt offerings and sacrifices was – if I may put it reverently – to do something to God, not to influence man; they were designed to propitiate God. This is a most important point.

The second thing that we see clearly in these Old Testament Scriptures is that this propitiation was secured by the expiation of the guilt, and the definition of expiation, let me remind you, is to wipe out the guilt of sins. These sacrifices were meant to propitiate God, and the result of that was that God expiated the people's sins.

And the third thing the sacrifices and burnt offerings teach is that this expiation was effected by the vicarious punishment of a victim. You remember what happened? A victim was taken, an animal was substituted for the sinner, and this animal then became the one who bore the punishment of the sinner. So we are entitled to teach that those Old Testament sacrifices show, very plainly and clearly, that it is because the animal was substituted for the offender and his sin was dealt with in the animal, that his guilt was expiated, and God was propitiated with respect to him.

So the last thing the sacrifices teach is that the effect of such sin offerings and burnt offerings was the pardon of the offender and his restoration to communion with God.

If you study the book of Leviticus you will find that that was the great function and purpose of those sin offerings, and the burnt offerings in particular. Sin was dealt with in a substitute and the result of that was that the sins of the people were covered and they were restored to a position in which they could be blessed by God. There is a phrase in Hebrews 9:22 which sums all that up: 'without shedding of blood is no remission'. That is the great message of the Old Testament. That is why God, through Moses, commanded the children of Israel to take all those animals and kill them and offer their blood. And all the ceremonial, which people so often omit in their reading of the Bible because, they say, 'It has nothing to do with me,' has everything to do with us! God was teaching the people that 'without shedding of blood is no remission' of sin. The Old Testament sacrifices were pointing forward to the perfect sin offering that was to come; they are types of the Lord Jesus Christ in His death.

That is the first major principle, now let us come to the second. The New Testament teaches specifically that Christ saves us by His death

– that is its essential teaching. There is so much Scripture which could be quoted at this point; let me just give you the most important references. In John 1:29 we read: 'Behold the Lamb of God, which taketh away the sin of the world.' Here John the Baptist describes Him as 'the Lamb of God', going back to those Old Testament lambs that were offered. Take also Paul's words to the Corinthians: 'Christ our passover is sacrificed for us' (1 Cor. 5:7). Or again, Romans 3:25: 'Whom God hath set forth to be a propitiation . . . for the remission of sins that are past, through the forbearance of God.'

Then there is Romans 5:6: 'For when we were yet without strength, in due time Christ died for the ungodly,' and the same thing is repeated in the tenth verse of that fifth chapter: 'For if, when we were enemies, we were reconciled to God by the death of his Son, much more, being reconciled, we shall be saved by his life.' Again, Galatians 1:4 reads, 'Who gave himself for our sins, that he might deliver us from this present evil world, according to the will of God and our Father.' And Paul says in Ephesians 1:7, 'In whom we have redemption through his blood, the forgiveness of sins, according to the riches of his grace.'

Ephesians 2:13 says, 'But now in Christ Jesus ye who sometimes were far off are made nigh by the blood of Christ.' The 'blood of Christ' means life laid down, and in the epistle to the Hebrews you find this stated almost everywhere, especially in Hebrews 9:12: 'Neither by the blood of goats and calves, but by his own blood he entered in once into the holy place, having obtained eternal redemption for us.' He has obtained eternal redemption for us by laying down His life on our behalf. The fourteenth verse in the same chapter is of equal significance: 'How much more shall the blood of Christ, who through the eternal Spirit offered himself without spot to God, purge your conscience from dead works to serve the living God.'

The tenth chapter of the epistle to the Hebrews also has a very important statement here: 'By the which will we are sanctified through the offering of the body of Jesus Christ once for all' (v. 10); then: 'But this man, after he had offered one sacrifice for sins for ever, sat down on the right hand of God' (v. 12); and: 'For by one offering he hath perfected for ever them that are sanctified' (v. 14). (Notice the repetition of the word *one*.) Peter, too, says the same thing: 'Forasmuch as ye know that ye were not redeemed with corruptible things . . . but with the precious blood of Christ, as of a lamb without blemish and without spot' (1 Pet. 1:18–19). You see, we cannot understand these terms unless we are familiar with the Old Testament.

Then take 1 Peter 3:18: 'For Christ also hath once suffered for sins, the just for the unjust, that he might bring us to God, being put to death in the flesh, but quickened by the Spirit,' and 2 Peter 2:1 says: 'But there were false prophets also among the people, even as there shall be false teachers among you, who privily shall bring in damnable heresies, *even denying the Lord that bought them*, and bring upon themselves swift destruction.'

The apostle John writes, 'But if we walk in the light, as he is in the light, we have fellowship with one another, and the blood of Jesus Christ his Son cleanseth us from all sin' (1 John 1:7); and in the book of Revelation we read, 'Unto him that loved us, and washed us from our sins in his own blood' (Rev. 1:5).

Now that is a small selection of the New Testament statements, but what a selection! They are some of the pivotal passages that at once bring before us the idea of the substitute and the penal suffering, the bearing of the guilt and the guilt being punished in the substitute. And you notice the repetition of *the blood*. I have known people who have called themselves Christian who have said that they dislike this thought about the blood. But apart from the blood we have no redemption! 'In whom we have redemption through his blood.' It is by the precious blood of Christ, the laying down of the life, the poured out life, that our redemption is secured.

But let us go on to the third proposition. The New Testament terms that are applied to Him and to His work for us and on our behalf prove the truth of this doctrine. Take first the word *ransom*. You will find that mentioned in Matthew 20:28: 'Even as the Son of man came not to be ministered unto, but to minister, and to give his life a ransom for many'; and in 1 Timothy 2:5–6: 'There is one God, and one mediator between God and men, the man Christ Jesus; who gave himself a ransom for all, to be testified in due time.' And what is a ransom? It is a price paid for liberating either a person or thing that has been taken or possessed by another. And the teaching here is that Christ, by His death, looses our bonds and sets us free, who were prisoners; and that He does so by paying the price; and the price He has paid is His own precious blood. 'Ye are not your own,' says Paul.

'For ye are bought with a price' (1 Cor. 6:19–20). Again, Peter puts it, 'Ye know that ye were not redeemed with corruptible things, as silver and gold . . . but with the precious blood of Christ' (1 Pet.

1:18–19) – ransom money has been paid and the captives are set free.

The word *redemption* has the same idea. You redeem something by paying a price to get it back, and it has come back to you.

The next word is *propitiation*. This is mentioned in Romans 3:25: 'Whom God hath set forth to be a propitiation through faith in his blood, to declare his righteousness for the remission of sins that are past, through the forbearance of God'; and in 1 John 2:2: 'And he is the propitiation for our sins: and not for ours only, but also for the sins of the whole world.' Now a propitiation is an appeasing, or the means of appeasing. The offering was taken by God and it was meant to appease the wrath of God. There are some who say that the meaning of the term is derived from the 'mercy seat', or the lid of the ark of the covenant which was in the Holiest of Holies in the Temple. Once a year, on the Day of Atonement, the high priest sprinkled sacrificial blood upon it to cover the sins of the people. Our Lord's death is that by which God covers, overlooks and pardons, our sins. Indeed, the teaching goes further in the New Testament dispensation: our sins are blotted out, so that a penitent and believing sinner is again reconciled to God.

And that is the next term – *reconciliation*. You will find it in Romans 5:10: 'For if, when we were enemies, we were reconciled to God by the death of his Son, much more, being reconciled, we shall be saved by his life.' And it is also to be found several times in 2 Corinthians 5:18–19. Those, then, are certain terms that we have to reckon with – ransom, redemption, propitiation and reconciliation and each time they refer to His death.

But let us come to the fourth proposition. There are certain crucial New Testament terms which teach substitution and specifically emphasise the vicarious element in His death. He is one who acts for us. First of all, again consider the Old Testament types. Those Old Testament animals that were offered were vicarious and the way we prove that is this: the priest was commanded to place his hands upon the head of the beast. Why was that? It was to transfer the people's guilt on to the beast and the beast was then killed. Yes, but before it was killed, their sins had been transferred to it – it was the substitute.

So our sins have been laid on the Lord Jesus Christ and He has borne them. Isaiah 53 is a crucial passage here. 'The Lord hath laid on him the iniquity of us all' (v. 6); this verse specifically says that our sins have been laid on Him; and it is there again in verse 12: 'Therefore will I divide him a portion with the great, and he shall divide the spoil with the strong; because he hath poured out his soul unto death: and he was numbered with the transgressors; and he bare the sin of many, and made intercession for the transgressors.' Again I would remind you of John 1:29: 'Behold the Lamb of God, which taketh away the sin of the world'; 2 Corinthians 5:21: 'For he hath made him to be sin for us, who knew no sin; that we might be made the righteousness of God in him'; and Galatians 3:13: 'Christ hath redeemed us from the curse of the law, being made a curse for us: for it is written, Cursed is every one that hangeth on a tree.' We are told that we are delivered from the curse of the law because Christ has been made a curse for us. Again, you will find it in Hebrews 9:28: 'So Christ was once offered to bear the sins of many'; and 1 Peter 2:24: 'Who his own self bare our sins in his own body on the tree, that we, being dead to sins, should live unto righteousness: by whose stripes ye were healed.' The teaching is quite clear: the guilt of our sin is now transferred to Him; He becomes liable for the punishment that was due; our sins are imputed to Him.

Then the next evidence under this heading is to be found in particular words which are translated by the word *for*. There are three different words in the Greek which are translated in our English Bible as 'for'. One means 'on account of'. You get that, for instance, in Romans 8:3: '*for* [on account of] sin', and in Galatians 1:4: 'who gave himself *for* our sins'; and again in 1 Peter 3:18 where we are told, 'For Christ also hath once suffered *for* sins, the just for the unjust, that he might bring us to God' – suffering for us, you notice it each time. Then there is the statement in 1 Corinthians 15:3: 'For I delivered unto you first of all that which I also received, how that Christ died *for* our sins according to the scriptures.' He has fulfilled the Old Testament sacrifices, and again we find in 1 John 2:2: 'He is the propitiation *for* our sins: and not for ours only, but also for the sins of the whole world.'

Another word which is translated 'for' means 'on behalf of', or, 'for the benefit of'. In other words, the idea of substitution comes in very strongly here. We see it in 2 Corinthians 5:14: 'For the love of Christ constraineth us; because we thus judge, that if one died *for* all, then were all dead.' Verses 20 and 21 continue: 'Now then we are ambassadors for Christ, as though God did beseech you by us: we pray you in Christ's stead, be ye reconciled to God. For he hath made him to be sin *for* us, who knew no sin; that we might be made the righteousness of God in him.' This is constantly repeated, for example, we see it again in 1 Timothy 2:5–6 and in 1 Peter 3:18.

But the strongest of these words translated 'for' is the one which is found in Matthew 20:28 and Mark 10:45: 'Even as the Son of man came not to be ministered unto, but to minister, and to give his life a ransom *for* many.' In its fullest sense it means, 'as a substitute for' many. So there is the evidence which specifically teaches His substitution and all these passages emphasise the vicarious element.

The fifth evidence is that there are numbers of statements which emphasise our union with the Lord Jesus Christ. The main place you find this, of course, is in the epistle to the Romans, in the great argument in the fifth chapter, beginning at verse 11, and especially in verse 12. The argument is this: that just as we all were responsible for Adam's sin, and died according to the similitude of Adam's transgression, so we are saved by Christ. Take the one sentence: 'For as by one man's disobedience many were made sinners, so by the obedience of one shall many be made righteous' (v. 19). The teaching is that the whole human race is in Adam so, when Adam fell, we all fell. Then the other side is that all who are in Christ have the full benefit of everything He has done; in other words, when He died, they died.

And that is still more clear in Romans 6:3–8:

> Know ye not, that so many of us as were baptized into Jesus Christ were baptized into his death? Therefore we are buried with him by baptism into death: that like as Christ was raised up from the dead by the glory of the Father, even so we also should walk in newness of life. For if we have been planted together in the likeness of his death, we shall be also in the likeness of his resurrection: knowing this, that our old man is crucified with him, that the body of sin might be destroyed, that henceforth we should not serve sin. For he that is dead is freed from sin. Now if we be dead with Christ, we believe that we shall also live with him.

You see the argument? We are in Christ; we are a part of Him; we are one with Him; we are identified with Him; as we were in Adam, so we are in Christ.

That again is the great argument of 1 Corinthians 15, the great passage on the resurrection: 'As in Adam all die, even so in Christ shall all be made alive' (v. 22). He acts on our behalf, we have died with Him, we rise with Him, we are in Him and belong to Him – a most important and vital argument.

But I cannot stay with that because I must hurry to the sixth proposition or argument. All the statements which tell us that His death liberates us from the law are of crucial importance. All the statements that show that He has set us free from the law teach this same substitution and penal idea of the atonement. 'For sin shall not have dominion over you: for ye are not under the law, but under grace' (Rom. 6:14); in other words, He has delivered us from the law. And there are other arguments that show the same thing. Take the one in Romans 7, the first part particularly, where our position, before He saves us, is compared to a married woman. She is bound as long as her husband is alive, but if he dies she is free. So we were bound by the law, but have been set free by Christ's death.

In 2 Corinthians 5:19 we read, 'To wit, that God was in Christ, reconciling the world unto himself, not imputing their trespasses unto them; and hath committed unto us the word of reconciliation.' That, too, is an important statement. We are told that our trespasses had been imputed unto us because they belonged to us, but that is no longer so – why? Because He has been made sin for us. God has imputed our sins to Christ. He has punished them in Christ and now He does not impute our sins to us, but imputes to us the righteousness of His own Son. Again, take Galatians 2:19–20: 'For I through the law,' says Paul, 'am dead to the law, that I might live unto God' – because of what Christ has done, he has died with Christ – 'I am crucified with Christ: nevertheless I live; yet not I, but Christ liveth in me.' He has set me free from the law. 'Christ hath redeemed us from the curse of the law, being made a curse for us: for it is written, Cursed is every one that hangeth on a tree' (Gal. 3:13). What can be stronger than that?

Now all these passages show that He has delivered us from the law, the penalty of the law, the penalty of our guilt, the curse. It cannot be more specific, but still I want to go on to a final statement or proposition and, in many ways I think that this is the most important of all. There are a number of statements which emphasise the Godward aspect and God's activity in the death of our Lord. You see the importance of that? All those false theories kept looking at us, and if they did not look at us, they started looking at the Lord Himself. But I shall give you statements which show that God the Father was in this.

First of all, certain Scriptures teach us that it was in God's mind and plan before the foundation of the world – there is an eternal aspect to what happened on the cross on Calvary's hill. Take Acts 2:23: 'Him, being delivered by the determinate counsel and foreknowledge of God, ye have taken, and by wicked hands have crucified and slain.' It was the determinate counsel and foreknowledge of God that sent Him to the cross. Or 1 Peter 1:20 says: 'Who verily was foreordained before the foundation of the world, but was manifest in these last times for you' – it was planned before the foundation of the world. And again we read in Revelation 13:8, 'And all that dwell upon the earth shall worship him, whose names are not written in the book of life of the Lamb slain from the foundation of the world.' There are some who say that that should have been rendered, '. . . whose names are not written from the foundation of the world in the book of life of the Lamb slain'. It does not matter which, the fact is that names were written in the book of life before the foundation of the world and when He did that, He did it because He knew that that person was to be covered by the death of His only begotten Son.

But let me end by giving you this specific statement which literally tells us that it was God who was doing this thing on Calvary: Isaiah 53:6: 'All we like sheep have gone astray; we have turned every one to his own way; and the Lord hath laid on him the iniquity of us all.' But have you ever realised that John 3:16 says this? 'For God so loved the world, that he gave his only begotten Son' – to the death of the cross – it is God who gave Him. Take again Romans 3:25: 'Whom God hath set forth to be a propitiation through faith in his blood, to declare his righteousness for the remission of sins that are past, through the forbearance of God' – there it is again. Or Romans 8:32: 'He that spared not his own Son, but delivered him up for us all, how shall he not with him also freely give us all things?' He, God, He 'spared not His own Son but delivered Him' – it was God who did it.

Then there is that great statement in 2 Corinthians 5:18–19, 'And all things are of God, who hath reconciled us to himself by Jesus Christ, and hath given to us the ministry of reconciliation. To wit, that God was in Christ, reconciling the world unto himself . . .' It was God who was doing it, God the eternal Father. God was doing this by means of the cross, through Christ.

And then, above them all there is the last verse of 2 Corinthians 5, 'For he hath made him to be sin for us, who knew no sin; that we might be made the righteousness of God in him' (v. 21). You will never find anything stronger than that and any view you might hold of the atonement must cater for that. Indeed, I feel that that one verse is enough. There it is, a specific statement of the eternal Father: *He* made Him sin, *He* imputed the guilt of our sins to Him; *He* put them upon Him; and then *He* tells us that *He* punished them in Him. Any idea or theory of the atonement must always give full weight and significance to the activity of God the Father.

In my next lecture I will go on to one final piece of scriptural evidence which I think will clinch this debate for you.

30
The Necessity of the Atonement

We are now considering, let me remind you, what has always been regarded as the essential Protestant doctrine concerning the atonement. Not that it is confined by any means to the period in the Church subsequent to the Protestant Reformation, because it can be clearly shown that it has, in a sense, always been the main exposition of the doctrine of the atonement from the very beginning, but it is often called the Protestant emphasis. A better name is, of course, the *substitutionary* teaching of the atonement because it is the doctrine which emphasises the substitutionary penal elements in the atonement, and we summarised it under seven main headings.

I ended the last lecture by saying that I had another, a final argument and, speaking for myself, this is one of the most cogent if not, indeed, the most cogent of the arguments. I would put this eighth point like this: we are going to consider statements in the Scriptures which emphasise the fact that the death of our Lord upon the cross was an absolute necessity. Obviously these are very crucial matters so I would subdivide those statements in this way: first of all, statements which describe our Lord's own conduct; second, statements which He made Himself about His death; and third, statements which others made about it. All these, it seems to me, prove quite conclusively that His death was an absolute necessity.

The first, of course, is what we are told about the events in the Garden of Gethsemane. Why did our Lord endure that agony? Why did He sweat those great drops of blood? What is the meaning of it? The view that our Lord's death was a martyr's death, is, as we have seen, a totally inadequate explanation – the martyrs did not behave as Christ did face to face with death. Our Lord in the Garden was facing the fact that there was an element in His death which was utterly abhorrent to Him, something that caused Him such agony as to lead to this bloodstained sweat. We have to explain that, it must be accounted for, and I suggest to you that all those other ideas and theories about the atonement completely fail to do so.

But, you remember, we are left, not only with the need of explaining what took place in the Garden, but also what our Lord said. Do you remember His prayer, 'O my Father, *if it be possible* let this cup pass from me' (Matt. 26:39)? He went on to say, 'Nevertheless not as I will, but as thou wilt.' But the request was there. Now that cannot refer merely to the fact of physical death, because, again, this would make Him inferior to the martyrs, His own followers. No, something, which He foresaw, was going to happen in His death which He was anxious to avoid if it was possible.

Now, we must emphasise this. It was the only time during His earthly life that our Lord ever made a request like this to His Father and obviously, therefore, it was something very exceptional. It points to this, that there was something in His death that was absolutely necessary. The question He asked was: Is it an absolute necessity? Is it possible for me to do this work in any other way? Let not this happen if it is possible. But, He said, if it is not possible, I submit to it. Now there, surely, is a final and conclusive argument that the death of our Lord upon the cross, in the way in which it happened, was an utter necessity.

Nothing can be stronger that that, but then we can add something that confirms it and, in a sense, repeats it. It is the cry of dereliction upon the cross: 'My God, my God, why hast thou forsaken me?' (Mark 15:34). Now, no doctrine of the atonement is adequate which does not explain that. And again, it is obviously inadequate to suggest that mere physical suffering produced that cry, because the whole argument about the martyrs again applies. No, no, something was happening there which was in a category on its own. Our Lord was conscious of being forsaken of God. His communion with the eternal Father was temporarily broken. He, who had come from the eternal bosom and had been with God from the beginning, for the one and only time in all eternity was not able to see the face of God. Surely again, here is another of those all-important and conclusive arguments which demonstrate, beyond any cavil whatsoever, that when a thing like that happened there could be only one reason for it – it *had* to happen. None of the other theories can account for that cry of dereliction.

Then the second group of statements I would describe as statements which directly affirm the absolute necessity of His death on the cross. Those others have been stating it more or less indirectly but here now is something direct. It is the specific statement which is to be found in Romans 3:25–6 and which is undoubtedly the *locus classicus* in connection with this whole subject: 'Whom God hath set forth to be a propitiation through faith in his blood, to declare his righteousness for the remission of sins that are past, through the forbearance of God; to declare, I say, at this time his righteousness:' – God's righteousness – 'that he' – God – 'might be just, and the justifier of him which believeth in Jesus.'

Now that is a tremendous statement. You see, Paul is saying that the problem which arises is this: How could God overlook or cover the sins of the children of Israel under the old dispensation? How can we account for the remission of sins that are past through the forbearance of God? And Paul's answer is that the death of our Lord upon the cross does that; that is one of the things it is meant to do. But, Paul says, it goes beyond that. His death not only explains how God could cover the sins that are past, it explains how God can forgive sin at any time, and it is the only explanation. Here is the problem: How can God, at one and the same time, be just and yet the justifier of him that believeth in Jesus? How can this eternal, holy God who is just and righteous and unchangeable, 'the Father of lights, with whom is no variableness, neither shadow of turning' (Jas. 1:17), the God who 'is light, and in him is no darkness at all' (1 John 1:5), the God who is of such a pure countenance that He cannot even behold evil and sin, how can He forgive sin and still remain what He eternally is?

And the answer that the apostle gives is this: The only way in which God can do that is what He did to His Son upon the cross – He has set Him forth as a propitiation of sins, and He has done it in that way, 'to declare . . . at this time his righteousness: that he might be just, and the justifier of him which believeth in Jesus.' And, you see, there is only one explanation of that. God, who is just, can forgive sin because He has punished sin in the person of His only begotten Son. So He remains righteous; He remains just. He has done to sin what He said He would do, and yet, because He has done it in the substitute, He can forgive us, He can justify us 'who believe in Jesus'.

Now the argument of the apostle is that that was the only way in which God could forgive sins. And indeed, I say again, that for myself, if I had no other text, that would be enough. None of the other theories can explain that text, and they do not. The only explanation for Christ's death is that it was an absolute necessity. It was the only way in which, if I may so term it, the eternal character of God could be reconciled with itself and could be vindicated, not only before the whole world of men, but before the principalities and powers in heavenly places, indeed, even before the devil and all the citizens of hell. God proclaims His eternal justice and yet can forgive the sins of those who believe in Jesus – a most amazing, a most profound statement.

And then my third and last group of references under this heading I put like this: there are certain other statements in the Scriptures which suggest that this was an absolute necessity. Take, for instance, Hebrews 2:9 where the author says, 'But we see Jesus, who was made a little lower than the angels for the suffering of death, crowned with glory and honour; that he by the grace of God should taste death for every man.' He had to suffer death; He had to 'taste death'. Now take that word 'taste'. What a word it is – what a strong word. Do we realise the full content of that tasting? There is a sense in which it can be said that the Lord Jesus Christ is the only one who has ever tasted death in all its bitterness and horror. That is why we see Him there sweating blood in the Garden. That is why we hear Him crying out upon the cross. That is why He died so soon and the authorities were surprised that He was already dead. That is why His heart literally broke, it actually ruptured. It was because he *tasted*. And my argument is this: Would God the eternal Father ever allow His only begotten, beloved Son to endure that if it were not absolutely essential?

But take another statement which says the same thing – Romans 8:32: 'He that spared not his own Son, but delivered him up for us all, how shall he not with him also freely give us all things?' Notice especially the first part: 'He that *spared* not'. What does that mean? Spared Him from what? Spared Him from that agony, that shame. He delivered Him up. He, God the Father, delivered Him to that; it was the only way. The Son volunteered, the Son went voluntarily, but it was the Father who sent Him. He did not spare Him. And when the Son bore our sins the Father spared Him nothing. The full wrath of God against sin, the full blast of it, descended upon Him. 'He that spared not His own Son, but delivered Him up for us all.' Indeed John 3:16 says exactly the same thing: 'For God so loved the world, that he gave . . .', and that giving includes the shame and the suffering and the agony of the death upon the cross. And my argument again is this: is it conceivable that God would have delivered up His own Son to that, even to the point of that break in the eternal communion that was between them? Is it conceivable, I ask, that God would have done that unless it was an absolute necessity? Well, this doctrine, this substitutionary penal view of the doctrine of the atonement asserts all that and that is why I say again that it is the only adequate and satisfactory explanation of the biblical teaching.

But if you require certain subsidiary arguments, take these: first, the doctrine of the wrath of God. If you believe at all in the doctrine of the wrath of God against sin, then obviously sin must be punished. The penal element comes in and that leads to the necessity of substitution. Or take this argument – the majesty and the immutability of the divine law. 'Till heaven and earth pass, one jot or one tittle shall in no wise pass from the law, till all be fulfilled' (Matt. 5:18). 'Heaven and earth shall pass away, but my words shall not pass away,' said Jesus (Matt. 24:35).

Then another argument is that if we do agree that sin is guilt and not merely something negative, not merely some weakness, not merely some theory to develop, if we agreed, when we were considering the doctrine of sin, that sin is transgression and lawlessness, that sin, therefore, involves guilt, then, obviously, we will have to agree that guilt has got to be dealt with, and that somehow or another it must be punished. And this is the only view of the atonement that really does that.

Then, lastly, there is no other theory which shows us why it is essential to believe in Christ and why it is believing in Him and on Him that saves us. Take any one of those other views. The moral influence view, which tells us that the love of God is displayed by the death of Christ upon the cross, says that the cross is supposed to melt our hard hearts and do away with our enmity against God. Well, I say, if that is its function, what it does is make me believe in God. I do not have to believe in Christ. He has merely shown me God. I must believe in the God whom Christ has shown me, not in Christ. And if He is an example, it is the same thing, and so with all the other theories. This is the only view of the atonement that shows us why we must believe in Christ; that we do not know God without believing in Christ, and that belief in Christ is the thing that saves us.

Very well, that, then, allows us to consider, very hurriedly, some of the objections that are brought forward to this particular teaching. Of course, all people who deny that sin is something which renders us guilty disagree with this doctrine. I cannot stay to argue that. We have already demonstrated that sin is guilt, and so if you believe that, you must immediately accept this doctrine.

Then there is the argument which says that surely God's love is enough. The argument is put like this. It says, 'We forgive one another without any substitution and without any punishment, and if we, in our love for one another, can do that, surely God, whose love is still greater, should be able to do it with still greater ease.' To which, of course, the reply is this: If God were only love there might be some force in that argument, but God is light, and God is holy, and God is just, and God is righteous. Not only that; there is no greater fallacy than the argument that goes from men to God. It is a very common error today. People are constantly arguing like that – if this is true of us, they say, how much more so of God? As if God were in series with us! The truth is, of course, that we are in sin and all our ideas are wrong; our conception of love is more wrong than anything else and if we begin to think of God's love in terms of what *we* do and what *we* think, then – I say it with reverence – God help us! If we are going to attribute our sentimental, loose, unjust and unrighteous notions of love to the everlasting Godhead, then we place ourselves in the most precarious position.

Another form of that last objection is that this substitutionary view of the atonement detracts from God's character, from His justice. People say that it would be unjust in God to punish someone who is innocent, to which the reply is that when the innocent person volunteers and takes upon Himself the sins of others and asks God to put them on Him, and punish them in Him, there is obviously no injustice at all. This was the great decision of the eternal Council, between Father, Son and Holy Spirit. The Son said, 'Here I am, send me,' and God provided Him a body. There was perfect agreement and therefore no injustice.

I have just dealt with the argument that says that the substitutionary view of the atonement detracts from God's love. People say, 'Fancy God demanding blood as an appeasement before He can forgive!' And the reply to that is what I have just been saying. Then there are those who feel that we derogate from the pardoning grace of God when we insist that God demands a payment before forgiving. But, again, the answer is still the same – that God is one. He is a God of holiness and justice. We cannot separate all the great and eternal attributes of God. Therefore this argument collapses.

Then there is another argument which used to be very popular. It is not as popular today but still one finds it. People say that the substitutionary penal view of the atonement was the invention of the apostle Paul. They say that if it were true, of course our Lord would have taught it, but you do not find it in the Gospels, you only find it in the epistles. But that is not correct. We saw in the last lecture that our Lord *did* say this. He said, 'The Son of man came not to be ministered unto, but to minister, and to give his life a ransom for many' (Matt. 20:28). It is all there in that word 'ransom', as we saw, but that is not the end of the argument. There were very good reasons why our Lord could not give a full exposition of the doctrine of the atonement before He accomplished it upon the cross.

Do you remember what happened? Let me suggest this as a bit of research for you. Read your Gospels and observe what happened every time our Lord spoke about His death. You will find that each time the disciples misunderstood it; they did not grasp it; they were cast down by it and objected to it; and our Lord Himself explained why this was so. He turned to them just at the end – you will find this in John 16:12 – and He said, 'I have yet many things to say unto you, but ye cannot bear them now,' and they could not bear them. Their minds were darkened, their hearts seemed to be held. It is most interesting to watch that in the Gospels and it is not difficult to understand.

Indeed, their whole idea of Him was still not clear. Peter had made his confession at Caesarea Philippi but he had not understood it all. It was the resurrection that convinced them of the ultimate truth concerning the fact that He was the only begotten Son of God, and in the light of that they began to understand the atonement. After His resurrection, you remember, we saw that He took them through it all, right through the Old Testament, and then they were able to receive it. So that argument which people put forward about our Lord not teaching the substitutionary view likewise has no real substance and no foundation.

Let me sum it up like this: the real difficulty people have with this doctrine is generally due to the fact that their whole view of God is inadequate. They forget some aspect of His character. They emphasise one side only, to the exclusion of others. If they were to take God as He is and to realise the truth about Him, their difficulties would vanish.

There is one argument that I am particularly anxious to demolish and it is this: there are those who say, 'I don't like that substitutionary penal view because what it says is that God was reluctant to forgive us, and that our Lord had to die and go to God and plead His death and plead the merit of His blood before God would forgive.' Unfortunately, sometimes evangelical preachers have put the doctrine like that, and there are hymns which do the same, as if our Lord had to plead with God in order to persuade God to forgive! It is a terrible travesty of biblical truth!

I have already answered this argument. I dealt with it when I showed that it is God Himself who has done all this. Why did the Son ever come to earth? Why did the Son die? And the answer is, 'God so loved the world.' It was the love of God that thought out this way of salvation so that God might be 'just and the justifier of him that believeth in Jesus.' It was His love that carried it out. The cross is not something that influences the love of God; no, the love of God produced it. That is the order. Were it not for His love, God would have punished sin in us, and we should all suffer eternal death. Indeed, I do not hesitate to go so far as to say this: nothing anywhere in the Scripture in any way approaches the substitutionary and penal doctrine of the atonement as an exposition and an explanation of the love of God. Is there anything greater than this, that God should take your sins and mine and put them on His own Son and punish His own Son, not sparing Him anything, causing Him to suffer all that, that you and I might be forgiven? Can you tell me any greater exhibition of the love of God than that? The moral influence theory and all these other theories which people put forward because, they claim, they believe in the love of God, actually fail to comprehend it. It is *there* you see the love of God, when His own Son suffered, as our substitute, the penalty of the law that you and I have incurred and so richly deserve.

As we have seen, we must be forgiven and reconciled to God fully before we can be justified. The law must be honoured, it must be satisfied, and that is something that must take place in two respects. First and foremost the law comes to us and tells us that unless we keep it and honour it, unless we live it, we are condemned. 'Moses describeth the righteousness which is of the law,' says Paul, like this: 'That the man which doeth those things shall live by them' (Rom. 10:5). We failed to keep God's law, but our Lord dealt with that guilt, as we have seen, upon the cross. He was there; He offered Himself. He presented Himself, His body, His life. And God put our sins upon Him. He was passive; God was doing it. It was God's action; Christ's passive obedience.

Ah yes, but in His life He gave an active obedience. Paul says, 'When the fulness of the time was come, God sent forth his Son, made of a woman, made under the law, to redeem them that were under the law' (Gal. 4:4–5). And this is how He did it: He rendered a perfect obedience to the law. He kept it fully. He carried it out in every jot and tittle. He said He was going to do it: 'Think not that I am come to destroy the law, or the prophets: I am not come to destroy, but to fulfil' (Matt. 5:17). And as we have seen, 'One jot or one tittle shall in no wise pass from the law, till all be fulfilled' (Matt. 5:18). And He did so. He kept the law perfectly.

This, then, is how He saves us. We are in Him, as Paul says in Romans 5. We were all in Adam. Adam was our representative, our federal head. When he fell we all fell with Him. We, who are saved, Paul argues, are in Christ. As we were in Adam, so we are in Christ. All that was true of Adam is true of us. All that Adam did became true of us. And all that is true of Christ is true of us. All that Christ did becomes true of us. When Christ honoured and kept the law by His act of obedience He was not only doing it for Himself, He was doing it for me, and therefore I can say with the apostle Paul, 'Ye are not under the law, but under grace' (Rom. 6:14). Christians are no longer under the law in the sense that it is the keeping of the law that will save them. As far as they are concerned, the law has been kept, it has been honoured, it is imputed to them for righteousness. God 'hath made him to be sin for us, who knew no sin; that we might be made the righteousness of God in him' (2 Cor. 5:21). Or take the mighty statement in Romans 8: 'For what the law could not do, in that it was weak through the flesh, God sending his own Son in the likeness of sinful flesh, and for sin, condemned sin in the flesh' (Rom. 8:3). Why? 'That the righteousness of the law might be fulfilled in us' (v. 4).

In other words, it is this great doctrine of our being one with Christ, in Christ. The atonement works in that way. What He did actively is imputed to us. What He did passively is imputed to us. So in Christ, believing in Christ, incorporated in Him, we can face the law without any fear, without any tremor or quiver. Indeed, I would go so far as to say that unless we are able to say that, there is something wrong with our faith. We are no longer under the law, we are under grace and we all ought to be ready to say with Augustus Toplady,

> The terrors of law and of God
> With me can have nothing to do,

> My Saviour's obedience and blood
> Hide all my transgressions from view.

What a glorious statement! But how very inadequate so many of our hymns on the death of Christ are. How few of them state these magnificent doctrines as they are stated in the Scriptures. Toplady has stated it there – it is the hymn which begins,

> A debtor to mercy alone,
> Of covenant mercy I sing,
> Nor fear with thy righteousness on,
> My person and offering to bring.

'The terrors of law and of God,' says a man who is a sinner, but he must say it, and so must we, 'with me can have nothing to do.' Why? 'My Saviour's obedience' – active – 'and blood' – passive; 'My Saviour's obedience and blood hide all my transgressions from view.'

So then, when we come eventually to consider the doctrine of justification, we shall have to return to this and we shall see more fully what it means. But with regard to the atonement, it means that I am fully atoned for, and thus covered, because my sins are blotted out and because I have the righteousness of Christ. We shall go on to consider some of the results and consequences of this perfect work of our Lord on our behalf, and it is a greater subject than we sometimes think.

31

Christ the Victor

We have been giving an exposition of what has always been the traditional Protestant interpretation of the doctrine of the atonement, namely, that it is substitutionary and penal and that our sins were actually punished in our Lord, in His body upon the cross. We also considered certain objections to that view of the atonement and the replies to those objections. And now, at this point, we must turn to a consideration of certain results of this work of our Lord.

It is rather difficult to know how to put this matter of the results and it seems to me, after much consideration, that perhaps the best way of putting it is this: there are certain results of the work of our Lord which might, perhaps, be more conveniently considered as a part of His work. In other words, there are those who would say that as a part of our doctrine of the atonement we should consider certain additional matters over and above the ones that we have already emphasised. The main work of our Lord in His death upon the cross was, beyond any question at all in the light of scriptural teaching, the work that was essential to propitiate God – the substitutionary, penal part of the work. But there are many statements in Scripture which show very clearly that at the same time as He was doing that, our Lord was also doing certain other things. And I, personally, would not disagree with those who would argue that these other things are, in a sense therefore, a part of the atonement.

There is, then, this further addition to be made. Our Lord, upon the cross, as we have seen, was rendering passive obedience. God was putting our sins upon Him and dealing with them. We did indicate that, in His life prior to that, He had rendered active obedience which is also part of the atonement, but, in addition to that, there was a further activity and this emphasises the active element in our Lord's work on our behalf. This is a view that has often been taught in the Church. Some of the early Church fathers in the first centuries were very concerned indeed to emphasise this aspect. You will remember that in considering some of the false theories of the atonement, we mentioned, among others, the view which taught that our Lord had paid a ransom to the devil. Now we rejected that, but there is something in it which is perfectly true. Our Lord, in doing this work, did deal with the devil, and it is that aspect of His positive work that I am anxious to emphasise here.

Now this view of the atonement has sometimes been called the *classical view*, classical, because it was taught in the early centuries and has been repeated very often since. A man who repeated it in his usual forceful manner was Martin Luther. He generally put it in this way: he said that man, in this life and born in sin, has five main enemies: Satan, sin, death, the law and the wrath of God, and, according to Luther, before a man can be saved those five enemies have to be dealt with. Now, without committing ourselves to this entirely, let us look at it like this. There is no question at all, as I shall show you, that the Scriptures do teach very definitely and clearly that our Lord in His work did deal with these five factors. We have already dealt with the law in expounding the substitutionary interpretation of the atonement, and in the same way, of course, we have dealt with the doctrine of the wrath of God; but it remains for us to deal with the other three – Satan, sin and death.

Now I call your attention to this, not only because it is taught in the Scripture but because this aspect of the atonement tends to receive a great deal of attention at the present time. There has been a modern revival of this view. It is being taught in a striking way by certain Lutheran teachers in Sweden and they, in turn, are influencing thought in Britain. A book was published in 1931 which has made this view very popular. It is called *Christus Victor*, and is by a Swedish writer called Gustav Aulen; those who are interested in this would greatly enjoy reading that small book.

Let me make this quite clear. I do not say that I agree, ultimately, with the views put forward by Aulen, but I do think that his description of this view is well worth reading. Unfortunately, like many others, he tends to minimise the importance of the substitutionary and the penal view and emphasises the other active view. My own position would be, primarily and most essentially, as we have seen, that our Lord came into this world in order to bear the punishment of our sins in His own body on the tree, to be a substitute for us; that is the first thing.

So as we go on now to these other things, we are doing so not to subtract from what we have said but to add to it. And, to me, one of the great pities about this present tendency is that they are putting forward this active element to detract from the other view, instead of adding to it. So, having issued that warning, let me put it like this: there is no doubt at all but that our Lord in doing His work was waging a battle. Look at your hymn books and you will find that many of the hymns refer to Him as 'the mighty Victor'. Not only has He come to bear the punishment of our sins at the behest of His Father, not only was something happening between the Father and the Son upon the cross, but at the same time the Son was waging a mighty battle.

So as you look at the resurrection you are looking at a victor. The mighty Victor has arisen. That is why we should always be filled with a sense of triumph as we think of His resurrection. And one of the enemies that He dealt with was, of course, Satan himself, Satan and all his forces. Now first let me give you the Scriptures which state this. In 1 John 3:8 we read this: 'For this purpose the Son of God was manifested, that he might destroy the works of the devil.' There it is, a general statement of one of the purposes of His coming into this world. Then take John 12:31. Our Lord says, 'Now is the judgment of this world: now shall the prince of this world be cast out.' There He says it Himself. Then listen to the apostle Paul in Colossians 2:15: 'And having spoiled principalities and powers, he made a shew of them openly, triumphing over them in it.' This is a reference to the cross – a most important statement. And then another important passage is Hebrews 2:14–15 where we are told that He took on Him flesh and blood for this reason: 'That through death he might destroy him that had the power of death, that is, the devil; and deliver them who through fear of death were all their lifetime subject to bondage.' Now, obviously, we must reckon at once with those Scriptures, and you see why it is that there are those who very rightly say that when we are considering our Lord's work and what our Lord has done to reconcile us to God and to put us right with the Father, we must, in addition to talking about His substitutionary work, mention this active work which He did against the devil. So the question is: How do we interpret these verses?

Our Lord, we are told, came to destroy the works of the devil, to cast out the devil. We are told that He put Satan and his forces to an open show especially by dying upon the cross. But how do we interpret this? Well, surely, in this way. By his life of perfect obedience to the law of God and by His honouring God in everything that He did, He was, incidentally, attacking and ultimately defeating the devil. He did so very specifically in conquering temptation. The devil tempted Him. He tried to kill Him through Herod and others at the beginning, and, as the record shows, he attacked Him and tempted Him in the wilderness. And when our Lord defeated him there, we are told that the devil only left Him for a season. He came back and attacked our Lord in the Garden of Gethsemane. He attacked Him upon the cross. He was attacking Him everywhere. But our Lord defeated him and thereby destroyed his works.

Now this was particularly true, of course, upon the cross. Our authority for saying this is the apostle Paul, again, in that statement in Colossians 2. How exactly did our Lord put to an open show the devil and his powers upon the cross? Well it is clear that it is something like this: the devil undoubtedly thought that our Lord would shrink from death because of the physical suffering involved. His hope was that when it came to the point, our Lord would suddenly fail on physical grounds. In addition to that, he probably also thought that our Lord's obedience would fail. His argument was that it was all right for our Lord to obey His Father while it was a question of living and not committing sin and honouring the law. But when it became a matter of death, His obedience might fail.

Furthermore, he probably thought also that our Lord's faith might fail. There were some grounds for this. It was a tremendous thing, as we have seen, and our Lord Himself, you remember, in the high priestly prayer, prayed to His Father saying, 'Glorify thy Son, that thy Son also may glorify thee' (John 17:1). Undoubtedly He was appealing to God to strengthen Him that He might fully glorify His name. The author of the epistle to the Hebrews tells us that 'when he had offered up prayers and supplications with strong crying and tears', he was heard because of His piety, because of His godly fear (Heb. 5:7). The test was very severe and the devil thought that our Lord's faith in His Father might fail at that point; and especially, of course, did he assume that this would happen when it came to that ultimate point, when, our sins being laid upon Him, that separation took place between our Lord and the Father.

So there is very little doubt but that the devil and his forces thought that at the cross their supreme moment of victory was going to arrive, that our Lord would fail for one of these reasons or perhaps all of them together. But what actually happened was that our Lord triumphed. He triumphed in that He proved that He is indeed the Son of God. He did that in the whole of His life but He did it especially upon the cross. To the thief who said to Him, 'Lord, remember me when thou comest into thy kingdom,' His reply was, 'To day shalt thou be with me in paradise' (Luke 23:42–3). His very statement, 'It is finished' (John 19:30) proves that He had finished the work which the Father had given Him to do. He had already prayed about that in John 17, but there upon the cross He said, 'It is finished.' In other words He said, 'I have finished it; I have gone right through, right through to the end,' and then, having done so, He committed His spirit to the Father.

And, then, of course, finally, this was all proved by the fact of the resurrection: 'Declared to be the Son of God with power, according to the spirit of holiness, by the resurrection from the dead' (Rom. 1:4). By His implicit obedience, and by His faith, and by going right through with it, our Lord finally demolished the whole case of the enemy, the lie of the enemy. The devil, we are told, is a liar. He has misrepresented God to men; he did it in the Garden of Eden: 'Hath God said?' (Gen. 3:1). By which he meant, 'Is it fair for God to say?' 'God is against you,' he said to Adam and Eve. He has been a liar from the beginning and his supreme lie is against God and against the love of God in particular. But as we have seen, more clearly than any-where else, the love of God was displayed upon the cross. There we know that the love of God is as great as this, that He did not spare 'his own Son, but delivered him up for us all' (Rom. 8:32). He gave His only Son, even unto the cruel death of the cross. He 'made him to be sin for us, who knew no sin' (2 Cor. 5:21), and He did it all for rebels, for sinners, for those who deserve nothing but hell. It is the supreme manifestation of the love of God, and therefore it is the point above all others where the life of the enemy was destroyed, where the works of the devil were put to nothing, and where he was finally put to an open shame and utterly and completely routed.

So, then, we must emphasise that upon the cross our Lord was doing all that. But still, you notice, I have not mentioned what we are told in Hebrews 2:14, and I have not mentioned it under that heading because I choose to take it under my next heading, which is this: our

Lord has not only vanquished the devil, He has also vanquished death. Now death is one of the enemies that sinful men and women always have to meet. That is the statement, of course, which is made in Hebrews 2:14–15: 'Forasmuch then as the children are partakers of flesh and blood, he also himself likewise took part of the same; that through death he might destroy him that had the power of death, that is, the devil; and deliver them who through fear of death were all their lifetime subject to bondage.'

Now obviously this is a very important statement and it has often caused people a good deal of perplexity. They ask, 'What does it mean when it says that the devil has the power of death? We thought the devil was a usurper and has no power at all. So what right have you to say that he is the one who controls the power of death?' Incidentally, you see where the idea gained currency that it was to the devil that the ransom was paid. It was because they faced this verse in Hebrews 2:14 that some of the early Church fathers said that our Lord had paid the ransom price in order to liberate us from the power of death. They based it on that verse, but clearly it was a false interpretation.

So what does it mean? Well, surely, it must mean this: the devil, as we see clearly, not only in the book of Job but everywhere else in Scripture, only has power as God allows him to have it. He has no absolute power. He has no authority in and of himself, but God allows him to exercise certain powers, and undoubtedly one of them is this power over the realm of death. That is why in other places the devil is described as 'the god of this world' (2 Cor. 4:4); and 'the prince of the power of the air, the spirit that now worketh in the children of disobedience' (Eph 2:2).

You can look at it like this. Man, when he sinned, when he listened to the suggestion of the devil, fell from God, fell from his true relationship with God and from that life which he had with God, and he fell into the dominion of the devil, the realm in which the devil already lived. The devil himself, by falling, had fallen into a state of death. There is a reference in 2 Peter 2:4 to the fallen spirits that are held captive in chains. That is the same suggestion. The devil, by falling, became the head of that realm which is outside the life of God, and so you can describe it as the realm of death. Therefore it follows that when Adam fell he went into the realm of death; he entered under the dominion of Satan which is the dominion of death. Satan is the one who reigns in everything that is covered by this final death, and that, I suggest, is what is meant here by saying that the devil has the power of death.

Let me put it still more explicitly. Christ delivers us from that power of death in this way. Paul says in 1 Corinthians 15:56–7, 'The sting of death is sin; and the strength of sin is the law. But thanks be to God, which giveth us the victory through our Lord Jesus Christ.' Now that means that the thing which really makes death terrible and which makes the sting so powerful is sin. It is not death itself but the fact that it is the consequence of sin.

In other words, you and I are guilty under the law and it is that fact which makes death terrible, because, to the unregenerate, death just means that they go on to that endless condition of spiritual death, outside the life of God. And that is why men and women apart from Christ are all their lifetime subject to bondage through this fear of death. People who do not believe in God, and who do not believe in sin or in the devil, nevertheless hate the thought of death. Why? Well, in spite of their minds, they have the fear in them; it has come down through the whole human race from the beginning. They think, and they are right, that death is an enemy, that death is something horrible, that it is a realm which holds us enchained in misery and wretchedness. And it is the devil who asserts that right. Because we are born in sin, and because of our own sin, we are under his authority and under his power.

And what our Lord did was this – He satisfied the law; the law no longer condemns us, so we are no longer condemned to death, and therefore we come out of the territory of death and out of the territory of Satan and sin. We are liberated from this other enemy which is called death. The author of the epistle to the Hebrews teaches quite clearly that by dying upon the cross, our Lord was not only conquering Satan, he was conquering death. Thanks be unto God, Paul says, we have the victory in Christ. Death has lost its terror. 'O death, where is thy sting? O grave, where is thy victory?' (1 Cor. 15:55). That is the Christian's view of death. We can face it and speak like that because of what Christ has done. Death should have lost its terror for us. The devil can no longer terrorise us with it; because we are out of the realm of death we are out of the realm of Satan also. So there you see that in addition to the devil, the second enemy, which is death, is likewise conquered.

The third enemy – sin – is conquered in exactly the same way. Paul says in Romans 6:2: 'How shall we, that are dead to sin, live any longer therein?' Now that is a very strong statement. We who are

Christians, he says, are dead to sin, and in the eleventh verse he puts it like this: 'Likewise reckon ye also yourselves to be dead indeed unto sin, but alive unto God through Jesus Christ our Lord.' In the twelfth verse he says, 'Let not sin therefore reign in your mortal body, that ye should obey it in the lusts thereof.' 'For sin' – in verse 14 – 'shall not have dominion over you: for ye are not under the law, but under grace.'

So again we can put it like this: man, as the result of his fall, his disobedience of God, not only fell under the dominion of the devil, he also fell, as we saw when we were dealing with the doctrine of the fall, under the dominion of sin; and we all know that by experience. Sin reigns in the natural person, in lust, in desire, in the bias towards evil. In addition to what the devil does to him from the outside, as it were, sin is reigning within, in man himself, he is under its dominion. But, says the apostle Paul, there in those words in Romans 6, by the death of our Lord upon the cross we are delivered from the dominion of sin; we have 'died unto sin' (v. 10); 'sin shall not have dominion' over us (v. 14).

Or, to take the words of the apostle John, 'Whosoever is born of God doth not commit sin' (1 John 3:9). By this John means that he does not abide in sin; he does not continue in a state of sin. There are still remnants of sin, in his old nature, but he is no longer under the dominion of sin. He may fall, but he does not belong to sin's territory. He may be foolish enough to listen to the enemy, but that does not mean that he belongs to the dominion of the enemy.

So you see that our Lord by His work, and especially His work upon the cross, in addition to bearing the penalty and punishment of our sins as our substitute, was also destroying the works of the devil. He was delivering us from the bondage and the dominion of the devil, and was also delivering us from the territory of death. We are no longer dead in trespasses and sins; we do not belong to the realm of death, we are alive unto God. And likewise He has delivered us from the tyranny and thraldom and power of sin.

Having, then, put it like that, I can go on to what I would call the results proper, because, as I have explained, though we might have regarded all those things as results, I think it is better to put them as a part of the work. Now here again the classification is important but a little difficult, and I suggest to you that the following is the best classification. The first result of our Lord's work that we must of necessity consider is that with regard to God Himself. It is clear that as the result of our Lord's work God is propitiated, He is satisfied, He is 'just and the justifier of him which believeth in Jesus' (Rom. 3:26). As the result of our Lord's work it is God Himself that justifies. Do you remember Paul's famous question in the eighth chapter of Romans? 'Who is he that condemneth?' he asks. 'Who shall lay anything to the charge of God's elect?' And the answer is, 'It is God [Himself] that justifieth' (Rom. 8:34, 33). And He does so because of the work of Christ. What a tremendous statement.

May I again just warn you in passing that we must be careful how we say all this lest somebody think that we are teaching that there is some essential change in the inner being of God as the result of our Lord's work. That is quite wrong. The only change that is effected by our Lord's work is God's relationship to us. It does not change God's character. It does not affect His love because, as we saw, it was His love that sent Christ. There is no change in the inner nature and being of God. But there is a very definite change, and thank God for it, in His relationship to us, because now He looks upon us as children, whereas formerly we were under His wrath.

The second result is this – and it is an extraordinary statement – I wonder whether you have ever realised that our Lord, by doing His work upon the cross, has even effected a change in heaven? Let me give you my authority. We read in Hebrews 9:23, 'It was therefore necessary that the patterns of things in the heavens should be purified with these; but the heavenly things themselves with better sacrifices than these.' God called Moses up to the Mount and there He gave him instructions about the building of the tabernacle, about the measurements, and how he was to furnish it and exactly what he was to do. And, as the author of Hebrews reminds us, when God had shown Moses everything, He gave him these words of instruction: 'See . . . that thou make all things according to the pattern shewed to thee in the mount' (Heb. 8:5). So Moses went down and carried out the instructions. And, as the epistle to the Hebrews reminds us, everything that Moses made had to be purified and it was purified by taking the blood of calves and of goats and water and scarlet wool and hyssop, by sprinkling the book of the law and the people and the various vessels of the ministry and everything in connection with the tabernacle.

Now this is the author's argument: 'It was therefore necessary,' he says, 'that the *patterns*' – in other words, these earthly things; the tabernacle in the wilderness was not 'the things in the heavens', it was only something made on the pattern of those things – 'the patterns of things in the heavens should be purified with these' – the blood of bulls and of goats, water, and so on – 'but the heavenly things themselves [must be purified] with better sacrifices than these.' And then he goes on, 'For Christ is not entered into the holy places made with hands, which are the figures of the true; but into heaven itself, now to appear in the presence of God for us' (Heb. 9:23–4).

So his argument can be put like this: the patterns were purified by blood of bulls and goats but that is not good enough to purify the thing itself, the heavenly tabernacle; this must be purified by something better. And it has been purified by something better. It has been purified by the blood of the Son of God Himself. He offered His own blood. I do beg of you to read again this ninth chapter of Hebrews, indeed, read chapter 8 as well! Go further and read the entire epistle in order that you may grasp this argument. It is a most glorious statement and one of the most mysterious statements in the whole of the Bible. We are taught here quite clearly that it was necessary that the heavenly place itself should be purified and that it has been purified by the blood of Jesus Christ Himself.

Now the question is: What does this mean? Let me be quite frank and answer that there is a sense in which no one can be too dogmatic about the answer to that question. But it seems to me we must say this: in some mysterious way there is a tabernacle in the heavenly places. There are statements about our Lord entering into that heavenly tabernacle, that holiest of all. I do not pretend to understand it but the statements are made and therefore we must believe that what was made on earth was made on the pattern of that which is in heaven.

And, further, we can say this: Satan fell from heaven. Our Lord says, 'I beheld Satan as lightning fall from heaven' (Luke 10:18). Satan, as we saw when we were considering the biblical teaching concerning him, was undoubtedly the brightest of the angels in the presence of God, and when he fell, when he rose up with pride and rebelled against God, he did so in the heavens itself. And thus, it seems to me, we arrive at a kind of understanding of what is meant here by the necessity to purify even the heavenly tabernacle itself. In a way that we cannot understand, and that seems to be inscrutable, evil has affected heaven itself. This vile, this foul thing that first caused the fall of Satan, and then caused the fall of man has, if one may use such language, introduced a kind of impurity even into heaven – into the heavenly tabernacle, at any rate. And according to this teaching, as I understand it, it was necessary for our Lord to purify and to purge the heavenly tabernacle of that taint, and the statement here is to the effect that He has done so.

This, I think, helps us to understand various statements which we find in Scripture, such as Colossians 1:20 where we read, 'And having made peace through the blood of his cross, by him to reconcile all things unto himself; by him, I say, whether they be things in earth or things in heaven.' Through Christ God is going to reconcile all things unto Himself in heaven as well as on earth. I am not suggesting that that is the only explanation but I am suggesting that that is a part of the explanation. And so we are confronted by this truly amazing and remarkable statement, that our Lord, as it were, had to take His own blood, even into heaven itself to get rid of this taint, this foul smear that was left by the fall of Satan. And so, ultimately, heaven, to use the language of the author of Hebrews, is purified entirely; and all evil and all its effects everywhere in heaven as well as upon earth have been removed.

I would again impress upon you the importance of bearing in mind this further element in our Lord's work. We must not confine our doctrine and our teaching concerning the work of Christ solely to His acting as our substitute and sin bearer. Let us remember that at the same time He has done what we have been considering with regard to the devil and sin and death. And if you agree with Luther that the law and the wrath of God must be regarded as enemies against us, He has also dealt with them, and thus everything that stands between us and God has been dealt with and has been removed.

Personally, I always like to think that our Lord had all that in His mind when He uttered those beautiful and comforting words which are to be found at the beginning of John 14: 'Let not your heart be troubled.' He had just been telling His disciples about His going, then: 'Let not your heart be troubled,' He said, 'ye believe in God, believe also in me. In my Father's house are many mansions: if it were not so, I would have told you.' Then, He said, 'I go to prepare a place for you' (John 14:1–2), and I think that He meant that He was going to remove every obstacle that stood between us and heaven and being with God and enjoying His glorious presence. He cannot prepare a mansion for us in heaven without first of all destroying the works of the devil, destroying sin and its dominion, destroying death and the grave. In addition to satisfying God's justice and God's holy law and offering this propitiation that removed the wrath of God, He had to do all that before He could prepare a place for us in heaven and then come back and receive us unto Himself, that where He is we may be also.

32

The Blessings of the New Covenant

We have reached the stage in our consideration of the biblical doctrine of the atonement in which we are looking at the results of the work of our Lord upon the cross. We have considered two of the immediate consequences. The first was the effect upon God's relationship with sinful mankind, and the second was the effect upon heaven itself. Now we must consider other consequences and sequels of this great work.

Another thing, according to the teaching of the Scriptures, that happened when our Lord died was that the new covenant was ratified. God made a new covenant with man and that covenant was ratified by the blood of Jesus Christ shed upon the cross. Now there are a number of verses, especially in the epistle to the Hebrews, that state that quite clearly. Let me remind you of some of them. In Hebrews 7:22 we read this: 'By so much was Jesus made a surety of a better covenant' – it is 'testament' in the *Authorised Version*, but it is better to translate it by the word 'covenant', that is, the new covenant. And then in Hebrews 8:6 we read, 'But now hath he [Christ] obtained a more excellent ministry, by how much also he is the mediator of a better covenant, which was established upon better promises.'

Then still more important are those statements made in the ninth chapter which we have already considered, especially verses 15–22, which, as you will recall, start like this: 'And for this cause he is the mediator of the new testament [covenant], that by means of death, for the redemption of the transgressions that were under the first testament, they which are called might receive the promise of eternal inheritance. For where a testament [covenant] is, there must also of necessity be the death of the testator [or the covenantor].' And the writer goes on to say that death is essential in this ratification of the covenant. Then you get the same teaching in the tenth chapter, particularly verses 15–18, and there is also a notable statement in verse 29: 'Of how much sorer punishment, suppose ye, shall he be thought worthy, who hath trodden under foot the Son of God, and hath counted the blood of the covenant, wherewith he was sanctified, an unholy thing, and hath done despite unto the Spirit of grace?' That is one of the terrible warnings that are found in the epistle to the Hebrews. And then it is also stated in chapter 13, in those beautiful words in verses 20–1: 'Now the God of peace, that brought again from the dead our Lord Jesus, that great shepherd of the sheep, through the blood of the everlasting covenant, make you perfect in every good work to do His will, working in you that which is well-pleasing in His sight, through Jesus Christ.'

Now there are a number of statements which are indicative of the fact that this new covenant between God and man was ratified by the shedding of the blood of Jesus Christ. Our Lord Himself had foretold this. In Luke 22:20 we read, 'Likewise also [he took] the cup after supper, saying, This cup is the new testament [the new covenant] in my blood, which is shed for you,' and the same is to be found in the corresponding passages in Matthew and Mark. Furthermore, the apostle Paul quotes it in his statement about the communion service in 1 Corinthians 11:23–5: 'The Lord Jesus the same night in which he was betrayed took bread: and . . . After the same manner also he took the cup, when he had supped, saying, This cup is the new testament in my blood.' So that is a specific statement by our Lord Himself in which He said that the new covenant was ratified by the shedding of His blood.

Now, obviously, this is a most important subject and it is because of its importance that I would remind you of how this teaching is given us first of all in the Old Testament. All God's covenants with mankind were ratified by blood. The first account of this, and in many ways one of the fullest, is found in Genesis 15 where we are told about God making a covenant with Abraham. We read in verses 9–10 that God said to Abraham, 'Take me an heifer of three years old, and a she goat of three years old, and a ram of three years old, and a turtledove, and a young pigeon. And he took unto him all these, and divided them in the midst, and laid each piece one against another: but the birds divided he not.' Then in verses 17–18 we read, 'And it came to pass, that, when the sun went down, and it was dark, behold a smoking furnace, and a burning lamp that passed between those pieces. In the same day the Lord made a covenant with Abraham saying, Unto thy seed have I given this land, from the river of Egypt unto the great river, the river Euphrates.'

Also, if you read the other verses that come between those two groups of verses, you will find that God made further promises, some of the most gracious and wonderful promises that He ever made to Abraham. But the point I am emphasising is that the covenant was ratified by the shedding of the blood of these animals and by this remarkable sign that God gave there to Abraham.

But exactly the same thing happened when God renewed that covenant with Moses and added certain sub-covenants. You may remember that when we were dealing with the biblical doctrine of the covenant, we pointed out that the fundamental covenant was made with Abraham. It was hinted at even in the Garden of Eden but it was made specifically with Abraham and then there was an addition, for the time being, made with Moses. It is described in Exodus 24:5−8, but I would especially emphasise verse 8: 'Behold the blood of the covenant, which the Lord hath made with you concerning all these words'; and you will find that a description is given of how the blood was sprinkled, even upon the book of the covenant itself and upon the altar and upon certain other utensils (cf. Heb. 9:19−21).

We see, then, that this is a great principle in the Bible. God never makes a covenant with man without ratifying it by the shedding of blood. And the thing we are concerned about now is that when our Lord died upon the cross His blood was shed. In addition to all that we have already considered, this new covenant between God and man was thereby ratified and truly introduced. And it is, therefore, something which we should always bear in mind when we are considering the covenant. God had promised this new covenant, you remember, through Abraham. Through Jeremiah He had promised that He would make a new covenant with the people (Jer. 31:31), not like the covenant He had made with them when He took them out of Egypt, and you will find that that new covenant is described in the eighth chapter of Hebrews: 'For finding fault with them, he saith, Behold, the days come, saith the Lord, when I will make a new covenant with the house of Israel and with the house of Judah: not according to the covenant that I made with their fathers in the day when I took them by the hand to lead them out of the land of Egypt; because they continued not in my covenant, and I regarded them not, saith the Lord.

For this is the covenant that I will make with the house of Israel . . .'
(vv. 8–10). And then He goes on to describe that new covenant.

There, then, is a very great principle and a wonderful truth. And it
leads us on to the next result, which is, from our standpoint, one of
the most glorious of all because we are now going to consider the
results that accrue to us who are believers, what the cross of Jesus
Christ has done for us. We shall consider this in detail when we come
to consider the application to mankind of the salvation worked out
upon the cross. But at this point we must, at any rate, give a summary,
and we can put it like this: *all* the blessings we enjoy as Christian
people come to us because of what happened on the cross. The cross
is the most crucial event in history. It is from the cross that every
benefit ultimately comes. What, then, are these benefits which we can
describe as the blessings of the new covenant? Well, let us continue to
read this eighth chapter of Hebrews, starting at verse 10:

> For this is the covenant that I will make with the house of Israel after those
> days, saith the Lord; I will put my laws into their mind, and write them in
> their hearts: and I will be to them a God, and they shall be to me a people:
> and they shall not teach every man his neighbour, and every man his
> brother, saying, Know the Lord: for all shall know me, from the least to
> the greatest. For I will be merciful to their unrighteousness, and their sins
> and their iniquities will I remember no more.
>
> Hebrews 8:10–12

That is the new covenant. Then the author of the epistle to the Hebrews winds it up by saying, 'In that he saith, A new covenant, he hath
made the first old' (v. 13).

But we are concerned now with the blessings of this new covenant.
What are they? Well, we must put first and foremost *the forgiveness
of our sins*. And we must emphasise that our sins are forgiven once
and for all. This is what the writer to the Hebrews wants to emphasise
in chapter 10. He starts off by saying, 'For the law having a shadow of
good things to come, and not the very image of the things, can never
with those sacrifices which they offered year by year continually make
the comers thereunto perfect. For then would they not have ceased to
be offered? because that the worshippers once purged should have
had no more conscience of sins' (vv. 1–2). But, he says, that was not
the case. In those sacrifices there was a remembrance made of sins
every year. They were simply covered, they were not dealt with, they
were not blotted out. But the glory of our position is that what our

Lord did, and what was done in Him, upon the cross, was once and for all. If you read that great tenth chapter of Hebrews again, keeping your eye on that, you will find that it is the thing that the writer emphasises and it is one of the most glorious truths that you and I can ever grasp. 'For by one offering he hath perfected for ever them that are sanctified' (v. 14) – you and me. In that one act God has dealt with sin and has forgiven it once and for ever.

Do you regard this as an overstatement, as too bold a statement? But as I understand the Scripture, this is the teaching. As Christian people, as children of God, we must say that all our sins – past, present and future – were dealt with once and for all, perfectly, upon the cross. There is no need for any fresh action on the part of God to deal with any sin that any believer may ever commit. It *has* been dealt with. 'The blood of Jesus Christ, his Son,' says John in 1 John 1, meaning the same thing, 'cleanseth us' – still cleanses, ever will cleanse – 'from all sin' (v. 7).

I am tempted to stay with that, but we must go on. If you are a believer, if you are a Christian, then God, I say it with reverence, remembers your sins no more. God can do something that you and I cannot do. *We* cannot forget our sins, we find it very difficult to forget the sins of other people, but God can cast sins into the sea of His forgetfulness. There is no more remembrance of sins. He has dealt with them, finally and absolutely, perfectly and completely, in the work done upon the cross.

Then the next thing that we emphasise is that in the light of that, we have a new way of approaching God, a new access to Him. Our consciences are now cleansed. 'Let us draw near,' we read in verse 22 of this same tenth chapter, 'Let us draw near with a true heart in full assurance of faith, having our hearts sprinkled from an evil conscience, and our bodies washed with pure water.' In other words, as we saw in that summary of this new covenant in chapter 8, there is nothing more wonderful about it than this, that it enables us to come into the presence of God with a holy boldness. Under the old dispensation the high priest alone went into the holiest of all, once a year only and in fear and trembling, and the people were always apprehensive as to whether he would come out. And when they heard the movement, the ringing of the little bells on the hem of his garment, how delighted they were that he could have gone into the presence of God and still come out. But you and I by the blood of Jesus . . . !

Is there anything, I wonder, in the whole of Scripture which is more glorious than this nineteenth verse, 'Having therefore, brethren, bold-ness to enter into the holiest' – the holiest of all – 'by the blood of Jesus.' That is how we should approach God. That is the new coven-ant. He has opened the way. He Himself has prepared it, and where the high priest went only once a year, we can go whenever we desire to go, 'by the blood of Jesus'. Oh yes, it is a *holy* boldness, but it is a boldness, remember. Emphasise both words. It must be holy for our God is a consuming fire. We approach Him with reverence and with godly fear (Heb. 12:28) – yes; but we approach Him with a holy boldness; with assurance and confidence in the blood of Jesus; with full assurance of faith.

So let us be clear about this. It is no sign of humility, no mark of saintliness, to go into the presence of God doubting whether God is forgiving you. That is unbelief, lack of faith. That is a failure to understand the truth. So, my friend, never again try to give the impression that you are such a sensitive Christian that you do not like to be certain that your sins are forgiven. It is our business to *know* that our sins are forgiven! We derogate from the grace and the glory of God and the wonder of this gospel if we are uncertain about it: 'Having therefore, brethren, *boldness* to enter into the holiest of all.' Not in my merit, not in my righteousness, not in terms of my under-standing, but by the blood of Jesus. He has opened the way. And, therefore, we go knowing that God has said in this new covenant, 'I will be to them a God, and they shall be to me a people' (Heb. 8:10). It is the most glorious thing ever said to men and women; we are God's people. And there you can put, if you like, the great doctrine of adoption, which we shall consider later. Not only are we given new birth, we are also adopted into the family of God. All these blessings are included in that one great statement. Regeneration, adoption are there, and, of course, justification and sanctification, and all the other doctrines.

But I am anxious to emphasise this aspect: that as the result of this new covenant we are no longer under law but under grace. Now we go, of course, to Paul for that, to Romans 6 where he has given his greatest exposition of it. 'For sin,' says Paul in verse 14, 'shall not have dominion over you.' Why? Well, here is the answer. 'For ye are not under the law, but under grace.' They had been under law – the subsection of the old covenant had been the introduction of the law. That is why our Lord had to be 'made of a woman, made under the law, to redeem them that were under the law' (Gal. 4:4–5). But, as

Christians, we are not under the law but under grace. Paul says the same thing in Romans 7:4, 'Wherefore, my brethren,' he says, 'ye also are become dead to the law by the body of Christ; that ye should be married to another, even to him who is raised from the dead, that we should bring forth fruit unto God.' When Christ died to the law, you and I, in Christ, died to the law also. You will find it again in those words that I have already quoted from Galatians 4:4–5.

I trust we are all clear about this. We shall, of course, have to repeat it as we go on to other aspects of the doctrines. It does not mean we do not have to keep the Ten Commandments. They still apply to us. But we are not under the law in this sense: when God gave that law through Moses, He said to the people, If you keep this law, you will save yourselves, and I will forgive you. *If.* It was left to them to carry it out. They were under the law in the sense that that was the way in which they faced the question of salvation. And it was impossible. But we are not under the law in that sense. Christ has kept the law for us; He has honoured it, as we have already seen. So we are now in this new relationship. He has delivered us from the law and the curse of the law in order that we may live the law and keep it. Paul puts it perfectly in Romans 8: 'For what the law could not do, in that it was weak through the flesh, God sending his own Son in the likeness of sinful flesh, and for sin, condemned sin in the flesh: that' – in order that – 'the righteousness of the law might be fulfilled in us, who walk not after the flesh, but after the Spirit' (Rom. 8:3–4). So, in a judicial, forensic sense, we are not under the law; but God have mercy upon the man who says, 'Because I am not under the law I can do what I like.' What Paul says to him is this: 'What shall we say then? Shall we continue in sin, that grace may abound?' (Rom. 6:1). Because we are not under the law, can we do what we like? Be not deceived, says the apostle: 'God forbid.' Our Lord died for us in order to enable us to live the law and to keep it, not to give us licence to sin. That is the terrible sin of antinomianism, one of the most dangerous heresies that can ever afflict the people of God. It is the idea that as long as you believe the right things and say them, it does not matter what you do. 'Faith without works is dead,' said James (James 2:20). There is no value in a profession unless it leads to results in our lives.

Now I can prove that still more conclusively in this way: you will notice that in the new covenant God now does something with this law which he did not do before. Before, He had written it on tablets of stone, it was outside us, but now this is what He is going to do: 'I will put my laws into their mind, and write them in their hearts' (Heb. 8:10). That is why I denounce the terrible sin of antinomianism. The man who says, 'I'm no longer under law, I'm under grace,' and who regards that as licence to sin is showing his ignorance of the new covenant. What the new covenant does is this: instead of giving me a law which is external and asking me to keep it, God puts that very law into my mind; He writes it in my heart; He puts it within me so that I want to obey it. 'His commandments are not grievous' to the Christian (1 John 5:3) because they have been imprinted upon the very tablets of our mind and of our heart.

But we can go even further, and this is the final nail which should put out once and for ever that false antinomian idea, consider what is actually said in those noble verses in Hebrews 13:20-1: 'Now the God of peace, that brought again from the dead our Lord Jesus, that great shepherd of the sheep, through the blood of the everlasting covenant, make you perfect in every good work to do his will' – notice – 'working in you that which is well-pleasing in his sight, through Jesus Christ.' Here is the most glorious thing of all. In the new covenant God, in Christ, through the Holy Spirit, has not only put the law in our minds and our hearts, He is even working in us a predisposition in favour of it, a desire to keep it, and He gives us power to do so.

I wonder whether you have ever realised before that there in those two verses you have exactly the same statement which the apostle Paul makes in Philippians 2:12-13? These words are more familiar, are they not? 'Work out your own salvation with fear and trembling. For it is God which worketh in you both to will and to do' – He puts in the desires – 'both to will and to do' – both the power and the ability to do it. God is working all that in us. That is an essential part of this amazing new covenant that was ratified by the shed blood of the Son of God upon the cross on Calvary's hill.

But there is still something else. This new covenant also guarantees our continuance in this life. A wonderful statement of this is made in Hebrews 7:25. The author is contrasting the old priests with this perfect High Priest, this unique Priest 'after the order of Melchisedec', and there is nothing more wonderful about Him than this: 'They truly were many priests, because they were not suffered to continue by reason of death: but this man, because he continueth ever, hath an unchangeable priesthood' (v. 23). Oh yes, but how does it affect me? Like this: 'Wherefore' – because of His unchangeable priesthood – 'he is able also to save them to the uttermost that come unto God by him, seeing he ever liveth to make intercession for them.' He is always there; He will never fail.

And that is the kind of High Priest we need. For we fall into sin and we need to go back; we need to confess and we need further cleansing and we have this blessed assurance that He will never fail. He has sat down for ever and He will never move. He is ever making intercession. He saves us, therefore, to the uttermost, to the very end. I remember once hearing a man preach on that verse and he said it could be paraphrased: 'Wherefore He saveth to the guttermost,' as if it were a description of the scope, or the ambit of this power of salvation. It is not that. He does save to the guttermost, thank God, because He saves from all sin and from all forms of sin, but that is not what is being emphasised here.

It is, rather, that He does not merely start the process and then forsake it. You see, these other priests were men who were priests, yes, but they became old and infirm and died, so others had to be appointed. And there was a danger, perhaps, that a gap might occur and the people might not be covered, but there is no danger of that with the Lord Jesus Christ. He ever liveth and therefore He is able to 'save to the uttermost'. He not only starts our salvation, He goes on with it. He will continue until He presents us faultless and blameless and without spot in the presence of His holy Father. He guarantees the perpetuity, the continuance, of the work.

And the result of all this is that you and I enjoy the blessings of assurance of salvation. Our salvation is certain. Let me give you one verse to establish this, again out of the tenth chapter of Hebrews: 'For by one offering he hath perfected for ever them that are sanctified' (v. 14). Now there is nothing stronger than that, and you will never find anything that can give you a greater assurance. That is why the writer keeps making that appeal: 'Having therefore, brethren, boldness to enter . . . and having an high priest over the house of God; let us draw near with a true heart in full assurance of faith' (vv. 19, 21–2) and so on. The writer continually repeats it, and he does so, of course, because we can be sure of this: our Lord is seated there at the right hand of God; He has completed the work that was necessary and will sit there until the final consummation.

A little earlier on, the writer says, 'Every priest standeth daily ministering and offering oftentimes the same sacrifices, which can never take away sins: but this man, after he had offered one sacrifice for sins for ever, sat down on the right hand of God' – notice – 'from henceforth expecting till his enemies be made his footstool' (Heb. 10:11–13). Now that means this: He is the Deliverer, the Messiah. He has conquered all; He is waiting; He is sitting, until all His enemies shall be made His footstool and then He will finally usher in His kingdom. And because that is certain about Him, it is certain about me. I am in Him. I belong to Him. And, therefore, as I think of Him seated there, waiting until all His enemies are made His footstool, I know that my future is certain. In Him that glory is absolutely certain. His being seated is the proof of that. He has sat down. Why? Because He has finished the work. He is simply expecting now – sitting is an attitude of expectation – until His enemies shall be made His footstool. And because of our relationship to Him, it means that our eternal future and glory are guaranteed. Nothing and no one shall be able to separate us from Him. He has said, 'No man is able to pluck them out of my Father's hand' (John 10:29). We belong to this Shepherd, and no thief and no enemy can ever take us from Him.

So there we have a kind of summary of the blessings that accrue to us who are believers from the work that was done upon the cross. Once more I find myself in the position of falling very far short of what I had intended to do. I make no apologies. I cannot stand in this pulpit, passively, and talk about such things without being moved. And I have been preaching to you. These are announced as lectures and as discourses but I thank God that I cannot lecture on such a theme. When I realise what it means, and means to me, and means for me, my passions are aroused, my feelings are disturbed, my whole self is engaged, though I had intended perhaps just to read out a list of the results and the benefits and the blessings that accrue to us from what happened upon the cross. Oh, as we have looked at them together, have we not all felt our hearts moved and warmed? Do you realise, my friend, that this is true of you? Do you realise that you are in this new covenant, that it has been ratified by the blood of the Son of God? It is sealed, signed and settled. Do you know your title deeds? Have you got them? Are you certain that your sins are forgiven? Do you go to God with this holy boldness, knowing that you are accepted; knowing that He is your God and that you are His child? You should, and if you have not known it until now, go and confess it to God with shame. Confess your unbelief, confess your ignorance, but, believing and accepting the truth, act upon it, go in faith to Him. Do not wait for any feeling. Believe the word and act on it and you will get the feeling. Do not let the devil rob you of joy and assurance. Stand in the position that is given you by this faith. Go to God and thank Him for it all and your heart will begin to warm. Your feelings will begin to move. The more you thank God for it in faith, the more you will enjoy it and rejoice in it and the more you will feel the love of it all.

33
Christ the King

We are considering the results and the consequences of the work of our Lord and Saviour Jesus Christ, and especially His work upon the cross, the results and the consequences of the atonement. And perhaps, in order that we may carry the sequence – the logical sequence – in our minds, I will hurriedly remind you of what we have already considered.

First of all, we saw that there were certain consequences in the relationship of God to man. There was no change in God's character, in God's being, but clearly there was a change in God's relationship to mankind.

Then, second, we saw that there was a change in heaven itself; as the epistle to the Hebrews teaches us, the heavenly sanctuary had to be purified – and was purified – by the blood of Jesus Christ. In other words, all effects of sin and of the fall of Satan – including in heaven itself – have been dealt with.

Third, by dying upon the cross, and in the shedding of His blood, the new covenant between God and man was ratified. We also considered some of the results that accrue to those of us who are believers in the Lord Jesus Christ. We become inheritors of this new covenant, and we saw some of the glorious privileges which we enjoy as the result of that.

The next consequence, which we must now go on to consider, is that in addition to these special and particular blessings that are received and experienced by His people, there are certain common blessings which result from the work of our Lord upon the cross. Now this is something which is oftentimes forgotten, ignored or not realised as it should be, but there can be very little doubt that were it not for the work of our Lord and Saviour Jesus Christ, the world would probably have come to an end and would have been destroyed the moment Adam sinned and fell. It is surely in the light of the cross and the work that His Son was going to do, that God spared the world.

We have seen already that there is very plain teaching to this effect. We have seen that all the sins committed by people during the Old Testament dispensation were only covered because of what was going to happen on the cross. God could forgive the sins of His own people under the old dispensation only because this work was going to be done. That is the argument of Romans 3:25–6, is it not? It was there, Paul tells us, that God justified the passing over of the sins of the old dispensation. Well, in the same way it can surely be said that the only thing that made it possible for God to continue to have any dealings or any relationship with this world at all was the work that our Lord was going to do. So it was the cross, as it were, that spared the world and allowed it to continue.

And in the same way, it is the cross and the cross alone that spares the life of anybody who ever sins at any time. It is only because of the work of the cross that God can even tolerate sin in any shape or in any sense. Now that, therefore, I put under the heading of common blessing. And let us be careful to emphasise that even the unbeliever derives that blessing from the cross. The fact that he is not cut off immediately is entirely due to that. It is in the light of the cross that God can exercise His patience towards those who are opposed to Him and remain finally impenitent.

And in the same way the blessings of what is generally called common grace are likewise to be derived from the cross. We have already considered common grace in an earlier lecture. It is differentiated from special grace, which is the grace of redemption, the grace of God towards those of us who are saved in the Lord Jesus Christ. But there is such a thing as common grace. It means any type of blessing that is derived by anybody in this world. For instance, you will remember how our Lord said in the Sermon on the Mount that God 'maketh his sun to rise on the evil and on the good, and sendeth rain on the just and on the unjust' (Matt. 5:45). Now that is common grace. The unjust and the ungodly derive the benefits that come from the sun and rain.

Not only that, they derive many other benefits. There are many general benefits of Christian salvation which are enjoyed by people who are not saved themselves. Take, for instance, any great revival which has ever taken place. Now a revival not only means the salvation of a number of individuals, there are certain general common blessings that always accompany it. There is no doubt at all but that the great evangelical awakening of two hundred years ago was the means of bringing untold blessings to millions of people who died impenitent and unbelieving. As the result of that awakening in the eighteenth century, not only were thousands of people converted, but the whole level of life in this country was raised. As the result of that revival, the Factory Acts were passed and many other beneficial things came about.

Now those are instances of common grace, and it is important that we should impress this upon the minds of those who are unbelievers. Though they do not believe in the Lord Jesus Christ and His atoning work upon the cross, they have derived benefits from that work, certain common, general benefits. And thus, you see, when you come to think of it, this world in which we live has derived a great deal from the work of the Son of God.

The next heading is this: it is clear from the teaching of Scripture that even the angels have benefited from this work. Now there are two key passages which teach this. Ephesians 1:10 is the first where we read, 'That in the dispensation of the fulness of times he might gather together in one all things in Christ, both which are in heaven, and which are on earth; even in him.' The parallel statement is in Colossians 1:20: 'And having made peace through the blood of his cross, by him to reconcile all things unto himself; by him, I say, whether they be things in earth, or things in heaven.'

Now these are both very great and very mysterious statements. There is certainly no unanimity of opinion as to what exactly they mean. But it is generally agreed by most commentators that they do not merely refer to blessings in the physical heavens but to more than that, and there can be no doubt but that it does mean that the angels in some extraordinary way derive a benefit. They do not derive the benefit of salvation, as we do, but there have been those who have suggested – and I must say the suggestion commends itself to me – that when Satan fell, the angels lost their leader, their head. I mean even the good angels. It seems clear that the devil – the one who became the devil – was the leader of all the host of angels. You remember that a number of angels fell with him, the evil angels, who belonged to Satan. Yes, but it seems, therefore, that the good angels which did not fall with him were left, as it were, without a head. And the suggestion is (it has been put forward many times in the history of the Church) that our Lord, when He returned to heaven and in the fulness of this redemption, made Himself the head of all the angelic host. He is the head of all creation, not merely that which we see here on earth, but of all created beings in heaven as well as upon earth. And so we see that even the angels have derived this benefit as the result of His work during His life in this world. And that is something which surely should cause us to be filled with a sense of wonder and amazement.

Now with that I would couple this: certain cosmic results follow from what our Lord has done. The whole universe benefits by the work of our Lord upon the cross. That is undoubtedly a meaning which simply cannot be excluded from Ephesians 1:10 and Colossians 1:20 which we have just looked at. You remember how Paul argues in Romans 8: 'For the creature was made subject to vanity, not willingly, but by reason of him who hath subjected the same in hope' (v. 20). The whole creation, he says, groans and is in travail waiting for 'the manifestation of the sons of God' (v. 19). You see, when man fell, even creation suffered. We considered that when we dealt with the doctrine of the fall. The ground was cursed, briars grew, thorns began to appear and illness came in – all those consequences in nature. Well, our Lord's death upon the cross has dealt with all that as well. It is not merely that you and I as individuals are reconciled to God, but ultimately the whole cosmos will be reconciled to Him. Eventually, we are told, there will be 'new heavens and a new earth' wherein dwelleth righteousness (2 Pet. 3:13). That is the ultimate result, in a cosmic sense, of the work of the Lord upon the cross, and it could not have been produced without that work. He is the one who mediates in every respect, not only between men and God but between the whole cosmos and God. It is very wonderful to think that eventually, as Paul argues, all things – 'whether they be things in earth or things in heaven' – all things will finally be reconciled back to God. You notice Paul does put it like that: 'And having made peace through the blood of his cross, by him to reconcile all things unto himself' (Col. 1:20).

So, then, we have been looking at the results of our Lord's work as it is to be seen in its effects upon all those who have suffered and upon all things that have suffered as a result of sin. Now then we come to something which, in a sense, is still more amazing. We must now go on to consider the results as regards the Lord Jesus Christ Himself, because there is very plain and explicit teaching in the Scripture to the effect that our Lord Himself has been affected by His own work upon the cross. Now the crucial passage here, of course, is in Philippians 2:5–11 and we must read it all because it is such a great statement.

Let this mind be in you, which was also in Christ Jesus: who, being in the form of God, thought it not robbery to be equal with God: but made himself of no reputation, and took upon him the form of a servant, and was made in the likeness of men: and being found in fashion as a man, he humbled himself, and became obedient unto death, even the death of the cross. *Wherefore* [because of that, as the result of that] *God also hath highly exalted him, and given him a name which is above every name*: that at the name of Jesus every knee should bow, of things in heaven and things in earth, and things under the earth; and that every tongue should confess that Jesus Christ is Lord, to the glory of God the Father.

Now there are other statements which say the same thing. Our Lord Himself has said it: 'The hour is come, that the Son of man should be glorified' (John 12:23). And then you remember in the high priestly prayer in John 17 we get this: 'Glorify thy Son, that thy Son also may glorify thee' (v. 1). He realised that as the result of His death upon the cross He was going to be glorified and that God was going to glorify Him in it and through it and as the result of it. There are many who have stumbled at this because they say that surely He had always shared the eternal glory of the Father and had never ceased to do so. That, of course, is perfectly true. So this glory to which He refers here and to which Paul refers in the second chapter of Philippians, must be some special and, in a sense, a new glory.

And surely it must be this: there is a special glory which attaches to the Lord Jesus Christ as the glorified God-man. This is a different glory. He had the glory of the Father before the foundation of the world, before His incarnation. Yes, but at the incarnation something unique happened. He took human nature unto Himself. He was then God-man. And it was the God-man who was going to be glorified. No longer would He be in the state of humiliation, He was going to the state of exaltation. This is a very important and vital distinction. And He was given this special, this messianic glory, as the God-man because of, as the result of, His humbling Himself to the obedience of death, even of the cross. And this is important for us in that we know at this moment that there, sharing the glory of the eternal Father in this unique sense, is one who represents us. Human nature has been taken up by Him and with Him and is now glorified in Him. This is something that was not true before the incarnation. Human nature had not been there in the glory before; it is there now. There is a new glory, a special glory, His messianic glory.

But also we read something further. We read that as the result of His work upon the cross, the fulness of the Holy Spirit was given to Him for the formation of the Church, of which He is the Head. Now this is, of course, of obvious, vital importance. Let me give you two pieces of evidence. Take the statement in John 7:39: 'For the Holy Ghost was not yet given; because that Jesus was not yet glorified.' This is a prophecy, a prediction, about the day that was going to arrive when those who came to Him should receive the Holy Spirit and out of their inward parts should flow rivers of living water – a great picture of the work of the Church and of the members of the Church throughout the centuries. But, says John, this is future.

Then take Peter's sermon to the crowds at Jerusalem on the Day of Pentecost. He was giving them an explanation of the descent of the Holy Spirit and this is what he said: 'Therefore being by the right hand of God exalted' – he was referring to our Lord – 'and having received of the Father the promise of the Holy Ghost, he hath shed forth this, which ye now see and hear' (Acts 2:33). Now the explanation of all this, said Peter, is that this Jesus, who is the Son of God, who had been delivered to death by the determinate counsel and foreknowledge of God, has been raised again from the dead by God. And now God has exalted Him and given Him this gift which He had promised before, this gift of the Spirit, which He had now shed forth, and so constituted the Church. This is a direct consequence of His atoning work: God the Father gave to the Son this fulness of the gift of the Spirit, so that with it and by means of it and through it He might form this body of His which He called the Church, of which He Himself is the Head.

The same thing is stated towards the end of Ephesians 1 where Paul prays:

That ye may know . . . what is the exceeding greatness of his power to us-ward who believe, according to the working of his mighty power, which he wrought in Christ, when he raised him from the dead, and set him at his own right hand in the heavenly places, far above all principality, and power, and might, and dominion, and every name that is named, not only in this world, but also in that which is to come: and hath put all things under his feet, and gave him to be the head over all things to the church, which is his body, the fulness of him that filleth all in all.

Ephesians 1:18−23

There are also other passages which teach precisely the same thing. But we cannot stay with that, we just note that it is a direct consequence of the atoning work.

Then let us go on to another consequence which is also dealt with in the epistle to the Ephesians: 'Wherefore he saith, When he ascended up on high, he led captivity captive, and gave gifts unto men' (Eph. 4:8). In other words, this is once more a consequence of His humiliation and His work upon the cross. Our Lord ascended, He is given these gifts for men by God and He gives these various gifts to those members of His body who constitute the Church. There is a list of the gifts in 1 Corinthians 12 and a shorter list in Ephesians 4. But the point is that He is only able to give us these gifts because of His work and His exaltation. Now we did not consider the gifts in the last lecture because I deliberately held them back until this point. We looked there at the general blessings of salvation and our relationship to God, but every faculty, every special spiritual gift which we have — and everyone of us is given some gift — every gift that we use is given to us as the result of the atoning work of Christ.

Then let us come to something which again is transcendent in its glory. I want to consider with you now the results of the work of our Lord while here on earth, and especially upon the cross, upon His kingship. Now let me again try and link up the sequence of thought. We have seen that our Lord and Saviour Jesus Christ is Prophet, Priest and King. Now here we are making the transition from His work as Priest to His work as King and this work of His as King is — according to this teaching — a direct outcome of His work upon the cross. So the one leads to the other. We said that we divided the work into the three departments, not because they are absolute divisions, nor in order to separate them, because He is the same person always, but for the sake of clarity of thought.

So now we can look at His kingship in the light of His work upon the cross. As the second Person in the blessed Trinity, our Lord has always shared in God's dominion over all from the commencement of creation. But, as God-man, He has a special kingship which is generally referred to and described as as His *mediatorial* kingship — His kingship as mediator. Now let me give you a definition of that: His mediatorial kingship is His official power to rule all things in heaven and earth for the glory of God and for the execution of God's purpose of salvation.

This is a great theme in Scripture. Now there can be no question at all but that our Lord was appointed to this mediatorial kingship in eternity, before time. There are many references in the Bible to events which happened before time, 'before the foundation of the world' (Eph. 1:4): our names were 'written in the Lamb's book of life' (Rev. 21:27) and so on. As we have seen, there was an eternal council in heaven between the Father, the Son and the Holy Spirit when this whole plan of salvation was fully discussed and worked out and there is no question but that this particular work was handed over to the Son. The whole work of salvation was placed in His hands. He was the one who was going to come and do it. When He took upon Himself the responsibility of saving the world from the consequences of the fall and of sin – all before man was ever created – from that moment this aspect of the work was handed over to Him. The kingdom was handed over to Him, He became the mediatorial King.

That is when the appointment was *made*. But when did He begin to *function* as this King? And here the answer must be that He began to rule in that respect immediately after the fall. Oh no, not after He was born, but immediately after the fall of Adam because, as we have already seen, it is quite clear that, were this not the case, Adam would have been destroyed there and then. God, you remember, gave the promise about the seed of the woman. That is an indication that He had already been appointed as the mediatorial King. The fall was known beforehand and He was appointed beforehand. The announcement was made in Eden, but the fact was already established, and already our Lord came in, as it were. If I may use a picture, He even there stood between Adam and God and saved Adam from destruction at that point.

You will remember what we saw when we were considering the angel of Jehovah, how we agreed that He was none other than the Lord Jesus Christ Himself. Whenever He appeared, it was always a part of this work of salvation and of redemption. Indeed, there is very little doubt that He was working in this way through the judges and the kings. The whole of the history of the children of Israel is a part of the plan of salvation. Let us never forget that. So the judges and the kings were a part of the process. God was preparing the people out of whom the Messiah was to come according to the flesh. So He was already functioning as the mediatorial King, even there.

But, of course, He was clearly publicly and formally declared to be the mediatorial King at the time of His ascension. He was the King when He was here on earth among men but He had not then assumed the throne; He had not been publicly declared or formally placed upon it. That clearly happened at the time of His elevation and exaltation.

Now there are, again, a number of statements which indicate this very clearly. For instance, in Acts 2:29–30 we read, 'Men and brethren, let me freely speak unto you,' said Peter, 'of the patriarch David, that he is both dead and buried, and his sepulchre is with us unto this day. Therefore being a prophet, and knowing that God had sworn with an oath to him, that of the fruit of his loins, according to the flesh, he would raise up Christ to sit on his throne.' He would raise Him up. And He has done so, at the ascension and the exaltation. And again in verse 36, 'Therefore let all the house of Israel know assuredly, that God hath made that same Jesus, whom ye have crucified, both Lord and Christ.' He has made Him that; it is the official declaration. He has assumed the mediatorial throne in a formal sense. And again I would refer you to that great passage in the second chapter of Philippians.

What, then, are the aspects of this kingship? How does He exercise it? First of all, we had perhaps better be agreed as to what kingship means and as to what His kingdom is. What is the kingdom of God, the kingdom of Christ? Well, it means His reign, His rule. Wherever the rule of Christ is acknowledged and delighted in, there is Christ's kingdom, and there Christ is King. So, then, if you accept that definition, we can look at His kingdom in this way.

First of all, the spiritual aspect of the kingdom. Christ reigns as King over His people, over the Church, He is the Head of the Church, He is the King of the Church. He reigns in the hearts of all of us who are believers in Him. He administers His kingdom by means of His Word and by means of the Holy Spirit. Every statement about His headship of the Church is an indication of His kingship. And it is exercised in a spiritual manner. Now some people are sometimes confused as to the relationship between the kingdom of God and the Church. The way to look at it is this: the kingdom of God and the Church are not co-equal; they are not co-extensive; they are not the same thing (though the kingdom of God and the kingdom of heaven are). The kingdom of

God is the rule of God, wherever He reigns there is His kingdom, and the Church is one of the external manifestations of it. He rules, He reigns in the Church in the hearts of His people in this spiritual sense. So we must differentiate between the kingdom and the Church. At the moment, His reign in the Church is invisible, but one day it will be visible.

Second, there is the general aspect of the kingship. We read in Psalm 2, 'Ask of me, and I shall give thee the heathen for thine inheritance, and the uttermost parts of the earth for thy possession' (v. 8). Our Lord Himself said, 'All power is given unto me in heaven and in earth' (Matt. 28:18), and 'Thou hast given him power over all flesh' (John 17:2). Hebrews 2:8–9 and Ephesians 1:20–3 tell us the same thing and, of course, there is the great passage in Philippians 2 where we read, 'Wherefore God also hath highly exalted him, and given him a name which is above every name: that at the name of Jesus every knee should bow, of things in heaven, and things in earth, and things under the earth; and that every tongue should confess that Jesus Christ is Lord, to the glory of God the Father.'

He has all power. He is crowned because He suffered and conquered, and He has control over everything for the sake of His people, for their protection and for their ultimate salvation. That is why we read in Romans 8:28, 'And we know that all things work together for good to them that love God, to them who are the called according to his purpose.'

This mediatorial kingship will last until the new heavens and the new earth have been brought into being – until 'the creature itself also shall be delivered from the bondage of corruption into the glorious liberty of the children of God' (Rom. 8:21). It will last until the great passage in 1 Corinthians 15 is fulfilled:

Then cometh the end, when he shall have delivered up the kingdom to God, even the Father; when he shall have put down all rule and all authority and power. For he must reign, till he hath put all enemies under his feet. The last enemy that shall be destroyed is death. For he hath put all things under his feet. But when he saith, all things are put under him, it is manifest that he is excepted, which did put all things under him. And when all things shall be subdued unto him, then shall the Son also himself be subject unto him that put all things under him, that God may be all in all.

1 Cor. 15:24–8